WEBSTER'S
FAMILY
ENCYCLOPEDIA

WEBSTER'S FAMILY ENCYCLOPEDIA

VOLUME 8

1995 Edition

Exclusively distributed by
Archer Worldwide, Inc.
Great Neck, New York, USA

Copyright © 1981, 1983, 1986, 1987, 1988, 1989, 1990, 1991, 1992
1993, 1994 Market House Books Aylesbury

Worldwide distribution rights assigned to Archer Worldwide, Inc.
Great Neck, New York 11021

All rights reserved. No part of this publication may be reproduced
or transmitted, in any form or by any means, without permission.

Printed in the United States of America.

Abbreviations Used in Webster's Family Encyclopedia

AD	After Christ	ht	height	N.M.	New Mexico
Adm.	Admiral	i.e.	that is	NNE	north-northeast
Ala.	Alabama	in	inches	NNW	north-northwest
Apr	April	Ind.	Indiana	Nov	November
AR	Autonomous	Ill.	Illinois	NW	northwest
	Republic	Jan	January	N.Y.	New York
at no	atomic number	K	Kelvin	OAS	Organization of
at wt	atomic weight	Kans.	Kansas		American States
Aug	August	kg	kilograms	Oct	October
b.	born	km	kilometers	Okla.	Oklahoma
BC	Before Christ	kph	kilometers per	OPEC	Organization of
bp	boiling point		hour		Petroleum Ex-
C	Celsius, Centi-	kW	kilowatts		porting Countries
	grade	lb	pounds	Pa.	Pennsylvania
c.	circa	Lt.	Lieutenant	PLO	Palestine Libera-
Calif.	California	Lt. Gen.	Lieutenant		tion Organization
Capt.	Captain		General	Pres.	President
CIS	Commonwealth	m	meters	R.I.	Rhode Island
	of Independent	M. Sgt.	Master Sergeant	S	south, southern
	States	Mar	March	S.C.	South Carolina
cm	centimeters	Mass.	Massachusetts	SE	southeast
Co.	Company	Md.	Maryland	Sen.	Senator
Col.	Colonel	mi	miles	Sept	September
Conn.	Connecticut	Mich.	Michigan	Sgt.	Sergeant
d.	died	Minn.	Minnesota	sq mi	square miles
Dec	December	Miss.	Mississippi	SSE	south-southeast
Del.	Delaware	mm	millimeters	SSW	south-southwest
E	east, eastern	Mo.	Missouri	SW	southwest
EC	European Com-	MP	Member of	Tenn.	Tennessee
	munity		Parliament	Tex.	Texas
e.g.	for example	mp	melting point	UN	United Nations
est	estimated	mph	miles per hour	US	United States
F	Fahrenheit	N	north, northern	USSR	Union of Soviet
Feb	February	NATO	North Atlantic		Socialist
Fl. Lt.	Flight Lieutenant		Treaty		Republics
Fla.	Florida		Organization	Va.	Virginia
ft	feet	NE	northeast	Vt.	Vermont
Ga.	Georgia	Neb.	Nebraska	W	west, western
Gen.	General	N.H.	New Hampshire	wt	weight
Gov.	Governor	N.J.	New Jersey		

phalarope A lightly built migratory shorebird belonging to a family (*Phalaropodidae*; 3 species) in which the female fights for a territory and courts the male, which rears the young; 8–10 in (20–25 cm) long, phalaropes have a slim neck, lobed toes, and a gray and red-brown plumage. Two species breed in the Arctic and one inland in North America.

phanerogam Any plant that reproduces by means of flowers and seeds. Phanerogams comprise the angiosperms (flowering plants) and the gymnosperms (conifers, etc.). *Compare* cryptogam.

Phanerozoic time Geological time from the end of the Precambrian to the present day, about 590 million years. It refers to the eon of "evident life," when abundant and clearly recognizable fossils were laid down. *Compare* Cryptozoic time.

pharaoh The title of ancient Egyptian rulers. The word derives via Hebrew from the Egyptian for great house. There were various symbols of kingship: the crook and flail and the white, red, or blue crown. The royal cobra, the sun god Ra's symbol, bound around the brow, signified divinity; pharaoh represented Ra reigning on earth. The first dynasty, or line of pharaohs, was founded about 3200 BC.

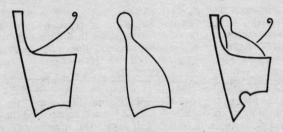

PHARAOH *The pharaoh's double crown, combining the red crown of Lower Egypt with the white crown of Upper Egypt, symbolized the unification of the two lands (c. 3100 BC).*

Pharaoh hound A breed of hunting dog whose ancestors are depicted in sculpture and friezes found in the tombs of the Egyptian pharaohs. The Pharaoh is a slender long-legged hound with a long muzzle and large ears. The short glossy coat is tan, with or without white markings. Height: 22–25 in (56–63 cm) (dogs); 21–24 in (53–61 cm) (bitches).

Pharisees An ancient Jewish religious and political party. They stressed ritual purity and acknowledged a body of traditional laws not contained in the written *Torah. The party originated in the 2nd century BC and vied for political influence with the *Sadducees. In the *Gospels they are frequently criticized by Jesus, although his own teachings are very close to theirs. After the destruction of the *Temple of Jerusalem they ceased to exist, but many of their teachings were taken over into rabbinic Judaism.

pharmacology The study of the action of drugs on living organisms. Pharmacologists examine the uptake of drugs after administration, the routes by which they reach their site of action, their subsequent effects, how drugs are destroyed by the body, their unwanted side effects, and the interaction between different drugs. Clinical ʀarmacology (*or* therapeutics) studies the effects of drugs in treating disease. **Pharmacy** is the science concerned with the preparation, manufacture, packaging, quality, and supply of medicinal drugs. The practice of pharmacy should conform to the standards laid down in the official **pharma-**

copoeia of the country. This is a government-approved list giving details of the manufacture, dosage, uses, and characteristics of drugs. It is compiled by experts in pharmacy and pharmacology. The World Health Organization has issued the *Pharmacopoeia Internationalis* in an attempt to standardize drug preparations throughout the world.

Pharos of Alexandria An ancient lighthouse, one of the *Seven Wonders of the World. Built in about 280 BC by Sostratus of Cnidos for Ptolemy II of Egypt, it was over 440 ft (135 m) high. It was demolished in the 13th century AD.

Pharsalus, Battle of (48 BC) The decisive encounter near present-day Fársala (Greece) in the Roman civil war, in which Julius Caesar defeated Pompey. Pompey's defeat opened the way to Caesar's dictatorship.

pharynx The muscular tract, lined with mucous membrane, between the back of the mouth and esophagus (gullet) and larynx. It acts as a passageway for food between the mouth and gullet and it also conducts air from the nasal cavity (which opens into it) to the larynx and windpipe. The Eustachian tubes from the middle *ear also open into the pharynx. Inflammation of the pharynx (pharyngitis) is a common cause of a sore throat.

phase (astronomy) The appearance of the illuminated face of the moon or a planet at a particular time in its orbit. Lunar phases vary from new moon (unilluminated) through a waxing crescent, first quarter (half/illuminated), a waxing gibbous moon, to full moon (fully illuminated) followed by a waning gibbous moon, last quarter, a waning crescent, and the next new moon.

phase (physics) **1.** The fraction of its whole cycle that a periodically varying system has completed. For example, two *alternating currents of the same frequency are **in phase** if they reach their maximum values at the same instant. If they are out of phase the angle between the *vectors representing the quantities is called the **phase angle**. In an electricity-supply system there are usually three phases, i.e. three separate alternating voltages having the same frequency but being displaced in phase relative to each other by one third of a cycle. **2.** Any portion of a system that is physically distinct is homogeneous throughout, and can be mechanically separated from other phases. For example, a salt solution is a one-phase system, whereas a mixture of ice and water is a two-phase system. *See also* phase rule.

phase rule A rule stating the conditions of equilibrium for a heterogeneous system. It relates the number of degrees of freedom of a system f, the number of *phases p, and the number of components c, by the rule $f = c - p + 2$. It was proposed by J. W. *Gibbs in 1877 and is important in the study of metallurgy, mineralogy, and ceramics.

Phasmida An order of generally flightless insects (2000 species), occurring mostly in tropical and oriental regions. They comprise the *leaf insects and *stick insects, both of which show a striking resemblance to the vegetation on which they live and feed.

pheasant A long-tailed game bird belonging to an Old World subfamily (*Phasianinae*; 50 species) occurring in open or woodland regions; 20–80 in (50–200 cm) long, pheasants are heavily built and have short rounded wings, a short bill, and strong claws for scratching up grain, roots, and grubs. Males are larger than females and brightly colored, with bright fleshy wattles, large leg spurs, and long tail feathers. They have been introduced to many regions for sport or ornament. Family: *Phasianidae* (pheasants, quail, partridges); order: *Galliformes* (pheasants, turkeys, etc.). *See also* golden pheasant; tragopan.

phenobarbital. *See* barbiturates.

phenols A class of organic compounds with the general formula ROH, in which the –OH group is linked directly to a carbon atom in an *aromatic ring. Although formally similar to alcohols, the phenols have widely different properties; in particular, the aromatic ring confers acidic behavior on the –OH group. The simplest example, phenol itself (or **carbolic acid**), C_6H_5OH, is a white deliquescent solid used as a disinfectant and in the production of drugs, weedkillers, and synthetic resins.

phenomenology A philosophical inquiry into intellectual processes, which is characterized by the vigorous exclusion of any preconceptions about existence or causes. It is thus distinct from *psychology, the aim of which is causal explanations rather than pure description. *Husserl was the first to elevate this method into an independent philosophy.

phenothiazines A group of powerful tranquilizing drugs, including chloropromazine and fluphenazine. Used in the treatment of *schizophrenia and *manic-depressive psychosis, they are thought to act by inhibiting the action of a chemical (dopamine) in the brain. *See also* tranquilizers.

phenotype The characteristics of an individual, representing the sum total of the effects of the interaction of its inherited characteristics with its environment. A striking example of this occurs in the Himalayan rabbit, which grows either black or white fur according to the temperature. *Compare* genotype.

phenylketonuria A genetic disease that leads to mental deficiency if untreated. Patients are unable to metabolize the amino acid phenylalanine, which is a normal constituent of diet; the amino acid and its derivatives accumulate in the body and prevent proper mental development. Phenylketonuria can now be easily detected at birth by a routine test. Babies with the disease need a special diet that contains little phenylalanine, which should be maintained until adolescence.

pheromone A chemical substance produced by animals to communicate with others of the same species. The best-known pheromones are the sex attractants secreted by moths to attract mates. Pheromones are also used by ants to lay trails and by mammals to mark out territories.

Phidias (c. 490–c. 417 BC) Athenian sculptor, one of the most influential artists of his time. Phidias designed and supervised the sculptures of the *Parthenon (*see* Elgin Marbles). His works included a bronze statue of *Athena on the Athenian *Acropolis and two famous chryzelephantine statues: Athena in the Parthenon and *Zeus at Olympia (where his workshop has been found).

Phidippides (5th century BC) Greek runner who ran 150 mi (241 km) from Athens to Sparta in two days to ask for help against the Persians before the battle of Marathon in 490 BC. The modern *marathon race derives from this feat.

Philadelphia 40 00N 75 10W A city in Pennsylvania, situated on the Delaware River at the junction of the Schuylkill River. Founded in 1681 by the Quaker William Penn, its religious tolerance attracted a large number of immigrants. It has many historic buildings, including Independence Hall (1732–59), where the Declaration of Independence was adopted and the Liberty Bell is kept. Benjamin Franklin is buried here. A cultural center, it is the site of the University of Pennsylvania (1779) and the Franklin Institute (1824) and has a famous symphony orchestra. It is the fourth-largest US city and has the world's largest freshwater port. Its output of manufactured goods is exceeded only by four other US cities. Industries include oil refining, textiles, and shipbuilding. Population (1990): 1,585,577.

Philadelphus. *See* mock orange.

Philae 24 02N 32 59E A submerged islet in the Nile River, in SE Egypt just above Aswan. Flooding caused by the first Aswan Dam from 1902 onward damaged the many ancient temples on the island. These were moved to a higher island before Philae was totally submerged by Lake Nasser after the construction of the *Aswan High Dam.

PHILAE *The rising waters of Lake Nasser partially submerging the Kiosk of Trajan.*

philately (*or* stamp collecting) Collecting and studying postage stamps as a hobby, which began immediately following their introduction in England (1840). Catalogues were first issued in the early 1860s as collecting became increasingly concerned with such details as watermarks, perforations, and numberings. Collectors usually specialize in a particular theme, country, or type of issue. Rare stamps in good condition, which fetch extremely high auction prices, are a form of investment, while the market among collectors for commemorative stamps or first-day covers is an important source of revenue for post offices.

Philby, H(arry) St John (Bridge) (1885–1960) British explorer and Arabist. He joined the Indian civil service in 1907 and in World War I undertook a political mission to central Arabia. He became a Muslim in 1930 and friend and adviser of Ibn Saud of Saudi Arabia. His son **Harold Adrian Russell Philby** (1912–) was an intelligence officer and Soviet secret agent, known as Kim Philby. He became a Soviet agent in 1933 and entered the British intelligence service in 1940. He defected to Russia in 1963.

Philemon (c. 368–c. 264 BC) Greek dramatist. Born in Sicily, he became a citizen of Athens and also worked in Alexandria. His plays, of which only fragments survive, were frequently acclaimed by his contemporaries as superior to those of his rival, *Menander.

Philemon, Epistle of Paul to A New Testament book written in about 60 AD that is the only strictly private letter of Paul to be preserved. In it he requests Philemon, a Christian friend in Colossae, to welcome and forgive Onesimus, his runaway slave, who had become a Christian after meeting Paul. Onesimus delivered the letter.

Philemon and Baucis In Greek mythology, an old peasant couple who offered hospitality to Zeus and Hermes, who were disguised as mortals. They were subsequently spared from a flood that destroyed the land and their cottage was transformed into a temple. They were granted their wishes to serve as priest and priestess in the temple and finally to die together.

Philidor, André Danican (d. 1730) French musician. As assistant librarian of the Royal Music Library at Versailles he made a large collection of instrumental court music. His youngest son **François André Danican Philidor** (1726–95) wrote several operas and was also a considerable chess player.

Philip (I) the Handsome (1478–1506) King of Castile (1506). Son of Emperor Maximilian I and Mary of Burgundy he succeeded to his mother's possessions in 1482. In 1496 he married Joanna the Mad, who inherited the Castilian throne in 1504. Her insanity led Philip to assume sole control in 1506. Their son became Emperor *Charles V.

Philip (II) of Macedon (382–336 BC) King of Macedon (359–336), who founded the Macedonian empire. Philip unified Macedonia, expanded the economy, and trained a professional army with which he gradually bore down on the Greek city-states. Despite the resolute opposition of *Demosthenes at Athens, the Greeks were defeated at the battle of *Chaeronea (338). Philip planned to lead a combined force against Persia but he was assassinated and the plan was carried out by his son *Alexander (III) the Great.

Philip II Augustus (1165–1223) King of France (1179–1223), who destroyed the *Angevin empire of the English kings. He waged war with Henry II (1187–89), Richard Lionheart (1194–99), and John; he took Normandy in 1204, followed by Maine, Touraine, and Anjou (1204–05), and in 1214 defeated an English-imperial alliance at *Bouvines. He participated in the Third Crusade.

Philip II (1527–98) King of Spain (1556–98). He inherited a vast empire from his father *Charles V, including Naples and Sicily, the Netherlands, and Spanish possessions in America; in 1580 he annexed Portugal. He married Mary I of England in 1554. Philip faced the *Revolt of the Netherlands and the Turkish threat in the Mediterranean, suppressed the *Moriscos, launched the *Spanish Armada against Protestant England (1588), and intervened in the French *Wars of Religion against the Huguenots. On his death Spain was bankrupt and its economy destroyed, largely as a result of the cost of these wars.

Philip (IV) the Fair (1268–1314) King of France (1285–1314). Hostilities with England (1294–1303) were ended by the betrothal of Philip's daughter Isabella of France to Edward II. Conflict with Pope Boniface VIII over the right of lay rulers to tax clergy ended only with Boniface's death (1303) but his successor Clement V was more easily handled and in 1309 moved the papacy to Avignon. In 1306 Philip expelled the Jews from France and his reign also witnessed the suppression of the *Templars (1307–13).

Philip V (1683–1746) The first Bourbon king of Spain (1700–24, 1724–46). The grandson of Louis XIV of France, his accession instigated the War of the *Spanish Succession. He abolished the self-governing privileges of Aragon and centralized the administration. He abdicated in 1724 in favor of his son Luis (1707–24) but returned to the throne when Luis died.

Philip VI (1293–1350) The first Valois king of France (1328–50), succeeding his cousin Charles IV. The failure of the rival claim of Edward III of England to the French throne contributed to the outbreak in 1337 of the *Hundred Years' War, in which Philip suffered severe defeats at Sluis (1340) and Crécy (1346).

Philip, Prince, Duke of Edinburgh (1921–   ) The husband (from 1947) of Elizabeth II of the United Kingdom. A descendant of Queen Victoria and the son of Prince Andrew of Greece, he assumed the name Mountbatten in 1947, when he took British citizenship. He served in the Royal Navy during World War II.

Philip, St In the New Testament, one of the 12 Apostles. He was a native of Bethsaida and was responsible for bringing Nathanael (probably Bartholomew) to Jesus. In medieval art he is symbolized by loaves because of his participation in the miracle of the loaves and fishes. He may have been martyred. Feast day: May 11.

Philippi, Battle of (42 BC) The battle in which Mark Antony and Octavian (later Emperor *Augustus) defeated *Brutus and *Cassius Longinus in the Roman civil war.

Philippians , Epistle of Paul to the A New Testament book written by Paul in about 60 AD to the church at Philippi in Macedonia, the first church that he founded in Europe. He thanks the Philippians for the gifts they have sent to him in prison in Rome and tells how he has continued to spread Christianity while imprisoned. The epistle contains an important doctrinal passage on the nature of Christ and the Incarnation.

Philippine eagle A rare *eagle, *Pithecophaga jefferyi*, occurring in tropical forests of the Philippines, formerly called monkey-eating eagle because it feeds mainly on macaque monkeys. It is 33–40 in (85–100 cm) long and has a brown plumage with pale underparts, a shaggy crest, a huge bill, and very powerful talons.

Philippines, Republic of the A country in SE Asia, consisting of an archipelago of over 7000 islands, of which some 880 are inhabited, between the Pacific Ocean and the South China Sea. Except for the central plain of Luzon (where most of the population is concentrated) there are few extensive lowlands, most of the larger islands, including Mindanao, being mountainous and volcanic and reaching heights of almost 10,000 ft (3000 m). Most of the inhabitants are Filipinos with small minorities of Chinese and others. *Economy*: based principally on agriculture, forestry, and fishing. The production of the staple crops of rice and maize and the main cash crops (sugar, coconuts, bananas, and pineapples) is concentrated around the central plain of Luzon although attempts are being made to develop economic activities elsewhere. The fastest-growing productive sector in recent years has been mining, based on the country's wide range of metallic minerals, which include copper, gold, iron ore, manganese, molybdenum, zinc, lead, and silver. Forests cover over half the land, providing gums and resins, bamboo, and dyes in addition to good-quality hardwoods. The main industries are food processing, textiles, wood processing, and oil refining. Tourism is an expanding industry. *History*: colonized by Spain in 1565, the islands were ceded to the US in 1898 following the Spanish-American War. Occupied (1942–45) by the Japanese during World War II, they became an independent republic in 1946. During the initial years of independence, a succession of presidents, US economic interests, and the Filipino landowning class did little to improve the standard of living of the peasant majority, but following the election of Pres. Ferdinand Marcos in 1965 rapid economic development and a greatly improved infrastructure brought increased prosperity to the Philippines. During the early 1970s growing communist guerrilla activity in the N and a Muslim separatist movement in the S led to the declaration of martial law. A new constitution was adopted in 1973 under which Marcos became president and prime minister in 1978 and a National Assembly was elected. Martial rule was lifted in 1981, and Marcos was reelected for a six-year term. Exiled opposition leader Benigno S. Aquino, returning to contest Marcos' leadership, was assassinated in Manila in 1983. Opposed by Aquino's widow Corazon in a 1986 presidential election, Marcos fled, after popular demonstrations against voting fraud, to exile in Hawaii and was succeeded by her. Aquino's administration faced enormous economic problems and opposition from Marcos supporters, including attempted coups in 1987 and 1989. A devastating earthquake in 1990 killed about 1600 and a 1991 hurricane killed almost 3500. The eruption of Mount Pinatubo forced the evacuation of the US's Clark Air Force Base, and when the Philippine senate would not renew the base's lease, a pullout was set. Marcos died in 1989, and his widow, Imelda, returned to the Philippines in 1992. She was indicted on fraud and corruption charges but still ran for the presidency in May elections that were won by Fidel V. Ramos. President: Fidel Ramos. Official languages: Pilipino (a language based on Tagalog) and English. Official currency: Philippine peso of 100 centavos. Area: 115,830 sq mi (300,000 sq km). Population (1990): 66,647,000. Capital: Manila. Main port: Manila.

Philippine Sea A section of the W Pacific Ocean, N and E of the Philippines. It contains deep trenches, volcanic submarine mountains, and coral reefs and is particularly prone to hurricanes. Its warm currents provide important fishing grounds. Maximum depth: 34,580 ft (10,540 m).

Philip the Bold (1342–1404) Duke of Burgundy (1363–1404), so called because of his military courage, particularly at the battle of Poitiers (1356) in the Hundred Years' War. The youngest son of John the Good of France, during the minority of his nephew Charles the Well-Beloved he was one of the regents of France and later, when Charles became insane, virtual ruler. He was also a noted art patron.

Philip the Good (1396–1467) Duke of Burgundy (1419–67). He recognized Henry V of England as heir to the French throne in 1420 but acknowledged Charles VII as king of France in 1435. In 1430 he founded the Order of the *Golden Fleece. He was a notable patron of artists.

Philip the Magnanimous (1504–67) Landgrave of Hesse, an ally of *Luther. Converted to Protestantism in 1524, Philip led the suppression of the *Peasants' War in 1525. He attempted to reconcile Luther and *Zwingli, who became theologically divided over the Eucharist. In 1531 he helped establish the Schmalkaldic League of Protestant princes. However, in 1540 his bigamous marriage, approved by Luther, was used by Emperor Charles V to split the Protestants and in 1547 the League was defeated by Charles at the battle of Mühlberg.

Philistines A non-Semitic people, who were driven from Egypt about 1200 BC and settled in Canaan, resisting Israelite attacks so vigorously that the region took the name Palestine from its new settlers. Tradition holds that they were originally one of the *Sea Peoples who left Crete as the Mycenaean world collapsed. A warlike seafaring people, without cultural pretensions (hence the derogatory word philistine), they were largely absorbed into the kingdom of Israel under King David about 1000 BC.

Phillips' curve A relationship between the rate of wage increase and unemployment, plotted by the British economist A. W. Phillips in 1958. The Phillips' curve suggested that there was an option between unemployment and inflation, i.e. a little less of one could be achieved if a little more of the other could be accepted. The monetarists (*see* monetarism) hold that the relationship is theoretically unsound and it has indeed broken down in practice.

Philoctetes A legendary Greek hero, who had inherited from his father the bow and arrows of Heracles. On the way to Troy with the Greek expedition he was bitten by a snake. His cries and the stench of his wound forced the Greeks to leave him on Lesbos. Odysseus and Diomedes later returned to fetch him, needing the help of his bow and arrows. He then killed Paris and helped to bring about the fall of Troy.

Philodendron A genus of woody, usually climbing, plants (275 species), native to tropical America. They have oval, oblong, arrow-shaped, or heart-shaped leaves, either deeply cut or colored along the veins, and they cling to trees or other supports by means of aerial roots growing from their stems. Cultivated as ornamental house plants for their foliage, *P. andreanum* and *P. erubescens* are among the most popular species. Family: *Araceae*.

Philo Judaeus (c. 30 BC–45 AD) Jewish philosopher from the *Diaspora community in Alexandria, then the Greek capital of Roman Egypt. Philo's voluminous treatises, written in Greek, reinterpret Jewish religion in terms of Greek philosophy. Some were designed for sophisticated Jews; others defend Judaism against Greek scorn of Jewish culture. In old age Philo represented the Jews on a deputation to the Roman emperor following anti-Semitism in Alexandria. Most of his works have survived owing to their popularity with later Christian writers.

philology The study of language in general, before the growth of modern *linguistics. It originally applied to the study of classical languages and literatures but came to be applied to what is now called comparative linguistics. Comparative studies were undertaken in the 19th century by many philologists, including Jacob *Grimm, who helped to identify and trace the relationships of the *Indo-European languages.

Philomela and Procne In Greek legend, the daughters of an Athenian king. Procne married Tereus, king of Thrace. He fell in love with Philomela, raped her, and cut out her tongue to prevent her telling his secret. By means of an embroidery Philomela told Procne of the outrage and in revenge Procne killed her own son, Itys, and fed his flesh to Tereus. He then attempted to kill the sisters but was turned into a hoopoe and the sisters into a swallow and a nightingale.

philosopher's stone A hypothetical substance sought by alchemists for its ability to turn less valuable minerals into gold. In alchemical literature it is also called the elixir, the tincture, and hundreds of other fanciful names. It was sometimes credited with the power of curing all diseases and of making its possessors immortal. *See* alchemy.

Philosophes A group of French philosophers and writers of the 18th century whose faith in the ultimate authority of reason was expressed in their active concern with social and political reform. They included *Montesquieu, *Voltaire, J.-J. *Rousseau, and *Diderot, the chief editor of their literary monument, the *Encyclopédie* (1751–72; *see* Encyclopedists).

philosophy (Greek: love of wisdom) The field generally concerned with the study of ultimate reality and the first principles of thinking, knowledge, and truth. The main theoretical branches of modern Western philosophy are *epistemology, *ethics, and *metaphysics; *logic (now closely associated with mathematics) and *aesthetics are also traditionally included. Historically, philosophical as opposed to religious or magical speculation arose in Greece in the 6th century BC in the attempts of the school of Miletus (*see* Thales; Anaximander; Anaximenes) to discover the single element underlying all things. The most important phase of ancient philosophy occurred with the teaching of Socrates, who developed the dialectical method and applied it to political and other problems. The works of his successors, Plato and Aristotle, not only shaped the future of European philosophy in most fundamental respects, but also deeply influenced Christian theology. Aristotelianism was preserved in the works of medieval Islamic philosophers, such as Avicenna and Averroes, and reentered Christian Europe in the *scholasticism of Anselm, Abelard, and Aquinas. Although influenced by scholasticism, the work of Descartes, with its systematic doubt and emphasis on reason, signaled the end of the medieval synthesis and the beginning of the modern period and the dominance of science. Spinoza and Leibniz attempted to deal with problems raised by Descartes; their rationalist systems are usually contrasted with the empiricism of the English philosophers, especially Locke, Berkeley, and Hume. Kant, whose aim was to reconcile these approaches and relate the sensible and the intelligible, was one of the most significant thinkers of the 18th century and stimulated the development of German idealism in the works of Fichte, Schelling, and Hegel. Idealism was also stimulated by the writings of Rousseau, whose ideas were the major source of 19th-century romanticism and influenced the work of Schopenhauer and Nietzsche. In England utilitarianism was developed by Bentham and J. S. Mill, dialectical materialism by Marx and Engels, and Hegelian idealism by F. H. Bradley. Pragmatism is particularly associated with the Americans William James and, later, John Dewey. The writings of Bergson and Croce had an influence on a number of writers early in the 20th century. The phenomenology of Husserl (and the works of Kierkegaard) led to the existentialism of Heidegger and Sartre. In contrast to their speculative approach to many of the large issues of traditional philosophy, the principal concern of English-speaking thinkers has been a critical approach that concentrates on logical analysis and the role of language—a development that may be traced in the works of Bertrand Russell, A. N. Whitehead, G. E. Moore, Wittgenstein, the logical positivists (the *Vienna circle), and in the current school of "ordinary language" philosophy centered at Oxford University. Indian and other Eastern types of philosophical thought are closely bound to the religious or cultural framework in which they developed (e.g. *Taoism, *Vedanta, Zen Buddhism).

Phiz. *See* Browne, Hablot.

phlebitis Inflammation of a vein, which is always accompanied by some *thrombosis in the vein.

phloem Plant tissue specialized to transport synthesized foods, mainly sugars, around the plant.

phlogiston theory An 18th-century theory of combustion based on the belief that all combustible substances contain phlogiston, which is liberated when the substance is heated, leaving calx or ash. The more combustible the substance, the more phlogiston it contains. The theory was finally overthrown in the late 18th century by A. *Lavoisier, who correctly explained combustion in terms of oxidation.

phlogopite A *mica mineral, $K_2(Mg, Fe^{2+})_6 (Si_6Al_2O_{20}) (OH,F)_4$. It is brown or bronze colored and occurs in some peridotites and metamorphosed limestones. It is used principally for making commutators.

Phlox A genus of ornamental herbs (about 65 species), mostly native to North America. Growing to about 40 in (1 m) high, they have terminal clusters of tubular flowers with five white, pink, red, or purple spreading petals. The creeping phlox, or moss pink (*P. subulata*), forms carpets of flowers in rock gardens. *P. drummondii* is the source of most garden varieties. Family: *Polemoniaceae*.

Phnom Penh (*also* Pnom Penh, Phnum Pénh) 11 35N 104 55E The capital of Cambodia, a port at the head of the Mekong delta. The capital since about 1432, it is now the site of the royal palace and of many museums and pagodas. A cultural center, it has several universities, including a Buddhist university (1954) and the University of Phnom Penh (1960). The country's commercial center, its industries include textiles and food processing. Population (1988 est): 750,000.

phobia A pathologically strong fear of a particular situation or thing. The main kinds are agoraphobia, which is fear of public places and open spaces; claustrophobia (fear of enclosed places); specific phobias of individual things, such as sharp knives; social phobias of encountering people; and animal phobias, as of spiders, rats, or snakes. Phobias are sometimes learned after a frightening incident, sometimes acquired in childhood from other people, and sometimes result from *depression. They are treated with *behavior therapy; *psychotherapy and drug treatment may also be used.

Phocis A region of ancient central Greece, N of the Gulf of Corinth. The Phocians were intermittently engaged in a struggle to retain control of Apollo's shrine at *Delphi (in Phocis). In the first so-called Sacred War (c. 590 BC) the Phocians lost Delphi. The second, precipitated by their seizure of the city, confirmed their possession. Early in the 4th century they again lost it, retaking it in 356. In the ensuing third Sacred War (355–346) the Phocians were defeated by Philip of Macedon, who proceeded to conquer all of Greece.

Phoenicia A group of city-states on the coastal plain of Syria N of ancient *Canaan. Semitic peoples settled here sometime before 1800 BC and after about 1000 BC they became outstanding navigators and merchants, establishing trading posts all over the E Mediterranean and beyond. Their major cities—*Tyre, *Sidon, and *Byblos—were ports. The Phoenician alphabet, the ancestor of all Western alphabets and perhaps the original one, was the chief Phoenician contribution to cultural progress. Phoenicia fell successively under Egyptian, Babylonian, and Persian influence. It was attacked by *Alexander the Great (332 BC), becoming part of the Hellenistic and later the Roman Empires. Phoenicia's major colony in N Africa was *Carthage.

phoenix A fabulous bird associated with sun worship, especially in Egypt, and representing resurrection and immortality. According to Herodotus, it resembled an eagle in size and shape, had red and golden plumage, and lived for 500 years. Only one bird existed at a time. The dying phoenix was consumed by fire in a nest of aromatic materials and from its ashes a new bird arose.

Phoenix 33 30N 112 03W The capital city of Arizona, on the Salt River. The state's largest city, the commercial center for a cotton and farming region, its industries include the manufacture of aircraft and textiles. Its warm dry climate makes it a popular health resort. Population (1990): 983,403.

Phoenix Islands An uninhabited group of coral atolls in the S Pacific Ocean. They comprise *Canton and Enderbury under joint US-British control and the Birnie, McKean, Phoenix, Hull, Sydney, and Gardner islands in Kiribati. Area: about 11 sq mi (28 sq km).

Phoenix Park Murders (1882) The assassination in Phoenix Park, Dublin, Ireland of the new chief secretary for Ireland, Lord Frederick Cavendish, and the permanent undersecretary, Thomas Burke, by extreme Irish nationalists calling themselves the Invincibles.

phon A unit for measuring the loudness of sound equal to the intensity in *decibels of a sound of frequency 1000 hertz, which appears to the ear to be as loud as the sound to be measured.

phonetics The study of the production and perception of sounds in languages. Sounds are classified in terms of the way in which they are produced by the speech organs. There is a wide range of possible speech sounds but each language uses only a selection of them. The study of the system of sounds within any given language is called **phonology** and the selected individual sounds are called phonemes. Phonetics also includes the study of stress and intonation.

PHOENICIA

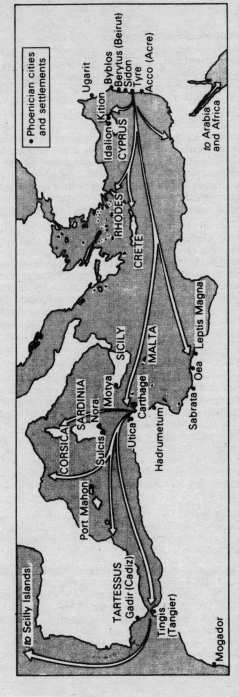

PHOENICIA *From their homeland along the E Mediterranean shore (modern Lebanon and Syria) the Phoenicians traded throughout the Mediterranean and beyond and established many settlements.*

Map labels:
- Phoenician cities and settlements
- Ugarit
- Byblos
- Berytus (Beirut)
- Sidon
- Tyre
- Acco (Acre)
- Kition
- Idalion
- CYPRUS
- RHODES
- CRETE
- to Arabia and Africa
- Leptis Magna
- SICILY
- MALTA
- Oea
- Motya
- SARDINIA
- Nora
- Carthage
- Sabrata
- CORSICA
- Sulcis
- Utica
- Hadrumetum
- Port Mahon
- TARTESSUS
- Gadir (Cadiz)
- Tingis (Tangier)
- Mogador
- to Scilly Islands

phosphorescence. *See* luminescence.

phosphorus (P) A nonmetallic solid element discovered by H. Brand (died c. 1692) in 1669. It exists in at least four forms: white (α and β), red, and black. White phosphorus is a waxy solid, which ignites spontaneously in air to form the pentoxide (P_2O_5). Red phosphorus, a more stable allotrope, is formed when white phosphorus is heated to 753°F (400°C); it is used in matches. Black phosphorus is also stable and forms when white phosphorus is heated to 392–572°F (200–300°C). Phosphorus exists in nature chiefly as the mineral *apatite ($Ca_3(PO_4)_2$), from which the element is obtained, either by reduction with carbon or reaction with silica at high temperatures. Phosphates are used extensively as fertilizers (mainly as "superphosphate"—calcium hydrogen phosphate) but find other uses in detergents, water softeners, and specialist glasses. A wide range of compounds is formed including the hydride (phosphine; PH_3), numerous phosphates (for example Na_3PO_4), and phosphides (for example Na_3P). Phosphorus occurs in DNA and RNA molecules and is therefore essential to life; bones also contain phosphates (*see* apatite) but some organo-phosphorus compounds are extremely toxic and are used as nerve gases. At no 15; at wt 30.9738; mp (white) 111°F (44.1°C); bp (white) 536°F (280°C).

Photius (c. 810–c. 895 AD) Patriarch of Constantinople, whose condemnation of certain practices and doctrines of the Western Church contributed to the rift with the Eastern Church. A leading statesman at the Byzantine court, he was elected patriarch in 858 amid much controversy and before he had been ordained. In 867 he convened a council at Constantinople at which he excommunicated Pope *Nicholas I, who had earlier deposed him, and denounced the *Filioque clause in the creed. Several depositions and reinstatements followed until he was finally exiled to Armenia in 886. He is also famous for his scholarship and is a saint in the Orthodox Church.

photocell (*or* photoelectric cell) A device that makes use of a *photoelectric effect to measure or detect light or other electromagnetic radiation. In the photoemissive cell, a photosensitive cathode emits electrons when it is illuminated; these photoelectrons constitute a current when they flow to the positive anode of the cell. In solid-state devices the light changes the behavior of a p–n junction (as in the photodiode), creating a potential difference by the *photovoltaic effect. In the conductivity cell, the resistance of a substance, such as selenium, changes when light falls on it as a result of *photoconductivity. Photocells are widely used in light-operated controls, such as automatic doors, fire alarms, and burglar alarms; they are also used in solar cells (*see* solar power) and photographic light meters. *See also* selenium cell.

photoconductivity The increase in the conductivity of certain semiconductors, such as selenium, when exposed to light. It occurs when photons excite electrons in the material from the valence band into the conduction band. *See* energy bands; photocell.

photocopying machine A device that prints copies of documents, drawings, etc., from an optical image. The most common technique is a dry electrostatic process known as xerography. A pattern of electric charge is induced by light falling on a layer of *semiconductor material on a conducting surface. Toner powder is sprayed or rolled onto this material, so that it sticks to the highly charged areas. The image so formed is printed onto charged paper, where it is fixed by heating to produce the final copy. Most produce only black-and-white copies; some can print in colors. Xerography is also used for high-speed printing of computer output, with printing heads instead of a light image.

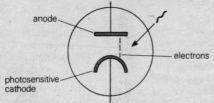

photoemissive cell *Illumination releases electrons from the cathode.*

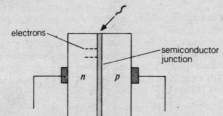

photovoltaic cell *Illumination creates a potential difference at a p–n semiconductor junction.*

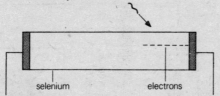

photoconductivity cell *Illumination increases the conductivity of a semiconductor, such as selenium.*

PHOTOCELL

photoelectric effects A number of effects in which electromagnetic radiation interacts with matter, frequently with the emission of electrons. These effects include *photoconductivity, the *photovoltaic effect, and the *Compton effect and the *Auger effect. The frequency of the radiation (f) has to be such that the energy of the photon (hf, where h is Planck's constant) is sufficient to liberate the electron. For solids, the minimum energy required is called the work function; for free atoms or molecules it is equal to the first *ionization potential, the effect then being known as *photoionization. For most substances, an ultraviolet frequency is needed to eject an electron, but for some metals, such as cesium, visible light is sufficient. *See* photocell.

photography The recording of images on sensitized material, by means of visible light, X-rays, or other radiation, and the subsequent chemical processing. The first photograph was taken in 1826 by Joseph Nicéphore Niépce (d. 1833) using the action of light on asphalt solution. In 1839, *Daguerre introduced the daguerrotype, a positive image of milky white on a silver background, produced directly from silver iodide emulsion on plates exposed inside a simple *camera. Modern photography involved a negative made by the development of *film coated with silver salts. The positive picture is obtained by shining light through the negative onto light-sensitive paper with a coating similar to that on the origi-

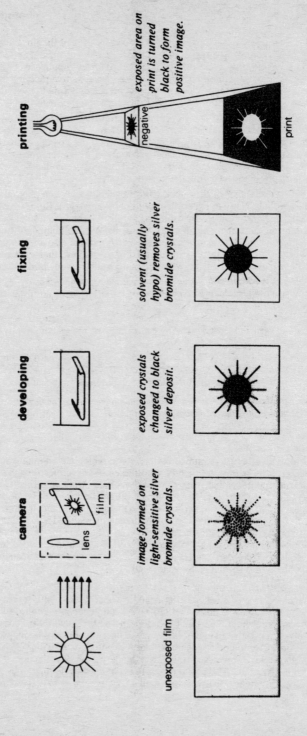

PHOTOGRAPHY *The stages in making a black-and-white photographic print.*

nal film. Lenses can be used to enlarge or reduce the size of the final image on the print. Transparencies, for use with a slide *projector, may also be made. Film is usually developed and printed in a darkroom by dipping it in baths of chemicals. Polaroid photography, however, produces positive pictures directly from the camera in one stage. This system was invented by Edwin Land in 1947 and is used for instant pictures for security passes, laboratory records, etc.

Photography as an art dates back almost to the origins of the technique. Portraiture was already established in the 1850s. The Crimean War in the 1850s and more importantly the Civil War in the 1860s provided the first opportunities for the true miseries of war to be realistically portrayed. However, during the last half of the 19th century photographic interest centered on the landscape, especially as horizons broadened with the growth of travel.

In the 1920s the collages of the cubist painters encouraged such photographers as László *Moholy-Nagy to experiment with photomontages. But by the 1930s the Frenchman Henri *Cartier-Bresson had led fashion back to a more realistic technique: using the camera as an extension of the eye, he composed transient scenes in great detail. Picture magazines, such as *Life,* were also a feature of this period. Postwar photography has developed many of these themes, using the new precision cameras and techniques, and many galleries now have permanent exhibitions of photography.

Photography has also had a profound effect on painting. Some art historians believe that the 20th-century trend toward abstract painting has been primarily a reaction to the camera's ability to do superbly what representationalist painters have often only been able to do indifferently. *See also* color photography; cinematography.

photoionization The *ionization of an atom when it is bombarded with electromagnetic radiation. The frequency of the radiation has to be such that the energy of its *photons exceeds the first *ionization potential of the atom.

photoluminescence. *See* luminescence.

photolysis The breaking of a chemical bond by absorbed electromagnetic radiation. The photon energy of the radiation must exceed the bond energy, and photolytic reactions can be produced by light, ultraviolet radiation, and X-rays. Examples occur in *photosynthesis, suntan, and photography. **Flash photolysis** is a technique for identifying and studying unstable reaction intermediates. The intermediates are produced in a gas by an intense brief flash of light, and their reactions are followed by spectroscopy.

photometry The branch of physics concerned with measuring quantities related to the intensity of light. These quantities are measured in two ways. If the intensity is measured in terms of the energy of the light, they are known as radiant quantities. They may also be measured in terms of their visual effect, since the sensitivity of the eye varies with the wavelength of the light. They are then known as luminous quantities.

photomicrograph. *See* microscope.

photomultiplier An instrument that produces an amplified current when exposed to electromagnetic radiation. Photons striking a photocathode cause the emission of electrons by the *photoelectric effect. These electrons then strike another surface causing a greater number of electrons to be emitted, the process being repeated several times to produce a greatly amplified current. Photomultipliers are used in certain *scintillation counters.

photon The quantum of *electromagnetic radiation, having an energy hf, where h is the *Planck constant and f is the frequency of the radiation. It may also be regarded as an elementary particle with *spin one and zero mass that travels at the speed of *light.

photoperiodism The response of an organism to the relative lengths of day and night, based either on a daily, seasonal, or yearly cycle. Flowering in plants, breeding in animals, and bird migration are examples of photoperiodic responses, which may be modified by such factors as temperature and availability of food. In general the response is a reaction to day length, but the flowering of plants actually depends on the length of the dark period. Thus, short-day plants (e.g. chrysanthemums) flower in response to a long night and long-day plants (e.g. certain cereals) flower when nights are short.

photosphere The visible surface of the *sun, acting as a boundary of several hundred kilometers between the opaque outer (convective) zone of the sun's interior and its transparent atmosphere. Almost all the energy emitted by the sun is radiated from the photosphere. Its temperature falls from about 10,850°F (6000°C) at the convective zone to about 7240°F (4000°C) where the photosphere merges with the *chromosphere. *See also* sunspots.

photosynthesis The means by which plants and certain bacteria produce carbohydrates from carbon dioxide and a hydrogen source. The energy for the process is provided by light absorbed by the green pigment chlorophyll, which is contained in the *chloroplasts. Plants use water (H_2O) as the hydrogen source and release its oxygen as a by-product. Thus the atmospheric oxygen that is continually used in respiration by all living organisms is replenished by photosynthesizing plants. Photosynthesis occurs in the chloroplasts and comprises two sets of reactions. One set, which requires light, produces energy-storing and reducing compounds; the other reactions, which may proceed in the light or dark, use these compounds to add hydrogen atoms to carbon dioxide and make carbohydrates. The overall reactions, which are very complex in detail, can be summarized by the equation $6CO_2 + 6H_2O \rightarrow C_6H_{12}O_6 + 6O_2$.

photovoltaic effect The production of a voltage when light falls on certain materials coated with another substance. The effect can be detected by connecting the two materials through an external circuit to generate a current. It occurs in copper (I) oxide on copper and in selenium on iron. *See also* photocell.

phrenology An obsolete approach to the study of the nervous system, first proposed by a Viennese doctor, F. J. Gall (1758–1828). The degree of mental development was supposed to be indicated by the shape of the skull, reflecting the development of the underlying parts of the brain in which the various mental processes were assumed to take place. Although discredited, it was important in developing ideas about the localization of brain function.

Phrygia The central and W areas of Asia Minor inhabited after the Hittite empire collapsed (12th century BC) by Thracian migrants. The short-lived Phrygian kingdom, centered on its capital Gordium, reached its peak in the late 8th century. The legendary *Midas was king of Phrygia. In about 700 BC Phrygia was conquered by Lydia. Phrygia was a center for the cult of *Cybele, which it passed on to Greece; it also influenced early Greek music. The Phrygians are reputed to have invented embroidery.

Phryne (4th century BC) Greek courtesan. She was the lover of *Praxiteles and probably the model for his most famous statue, the Aphrodite of Cnidos, as well as for the painting of Aphrodite Anadyomene by Apelles.

Phyfe, Duncan (*or* Fife; 1768–1854) US cabinetmaker and furniture designer, born in Scotland. His highly successful firm in New York City produced furniture in the Sheraton, Regency, and French Empire styles.

phyle A tribal subdivision or clan in ancient Greek city-states, its members being tied by descent from a common ancestor. The phyle upheld clan traditions, cults, and loyalties and encouraged aristocratic rule. By the 5th century BC Athens and Sparta had replaced the phylae with artificial district divisions for administrative and military purposes, engendering allegiance to the city rather than the clan.

Phyllanthus A mostly tropical genus of trees, shrubs, herbs, and aquatic plants (600 species), including a few ornamental greenhouse plants. Many have flattened green stems resembling leaves, with yellow, red, or white flowers along their margins. *P. acidus* (Indian gooseberry) has round fleshy ribbed fruits used in pickles and preserves. Family: *Euphorbiaceae.*

phylloxera A plant-eating insect belonging to the family *Phylloxeridae,* closely related to the *aphids. The grape, or vine, phylloxera (*Phylloxera vitifoliae* or *Viteus vitifolii*) is a notorious pest of grapevines. During a complex life cycle, the insect forms galls on the leaves and roots, which damage the plant. The grape phylloxera spread to Europe from North America in the 19th century and almost destroyed the wine industry in France.

phylogeny The history of the *evolution of a species or other group of organisms. By studying the fossil record, comparative anatomy, embryology, biochemistry, and geographical distribution of the groups involved, one can establish the probable lines of descent and degrees of relationship between broad groups of plants or animals to produce a phylogenetic tree. For example, it is believed that whales and carnivorous land mammals developed from insectivorous mammals living more than 65 million years ago. Phylogeny forms the basis for the classification of organisms (*see* taxonomy). It should be distinguished from **ontogeny**, which is the succession of developmental stages through which an individual organism passes during its lifetime. *See also* biogenetic law.

phylum A major unit of classification for animals (*see* taxonomy). Organisms belonging to the same phylum share basic features but are divided into classes, orders, genera, and species according to their supposed degrees of relationship. For example, the phylum *Arthropoda* is a very diverse group including the insects, spiders, scorpions, crustaceans, etc., which all share the features of a tough segmented external skeleton and jointed limbs. In most plant-classification systems the equivalent term is division.

physical medicine The medical specialty concerned with the treatment of physical disabilities. Originally this was restricted to the diagnosis and management of rheumatic diseases, but it has now been extended to the treatment and rehabilitation of patients disabled by back injuries, polio, asthma, and many other disorders.

physics The study of the interrelationship between matter and energy, without reference to chemical change. Traditionally the subject was divided into the study of mechanics, electricity and magnetism, heat and thermodynamics, optics, and acoustics. More modern aspects of the subject include quantum mechanics, relativity, nuclear physics, particle physics, solid-state physics, and astrophysics.

Physiocrats A group of French 18th-century economists, led by François *Quesnay. The Physiocrats believed that the only real productive sector in the economy was agriculture: industry and merchants were seen as mere processors. As mercantile (*see* mercantilism) interests were no longer identified with the wealth of the nation, *laissez-faire and *free trade were advocated.

physiology The study of the functioning of living organisms and their constituent parts. Physiology is closely linked with both *anatomy (the study of structure) and *biochemistry (the chemical reactions that play a vital role in many physiological processes).

physiotherapy The treatment of injuries or disabilities using physical methods, such as massage, manipulation, exercise, and heat. Physiotherapists play an important role in restoring mobility to patients confined for a long period to bed or a wheelchair; they also enable the rehabilitation of those handicapped by strokes, cerebral palsy, polio, etc., or immobilized by fractures. Physiotherapy is also useful in reducing the pain and stiffness of arthritis.

phytochrome A pigment of green plants that exists in two interchangeable forms, one absorbing red light and the other, far-red light. Day-length responses (*see* photoperiodism), greening of young leaves, and the breaking of dormancy in some seeds are among the processes controlled by phytochrome.

phytosaur An extinct amphibious reptile, resembling a modern crocodile, having long pointed jaws with sharp teeth and protective bony plates beneath the skin. Phytosaurs lived during the late Triassic and Jurassic periods (210–135 million years ago) and probably fed on fish. The nostrils were set on a mound near the eyes and not at the end of the snout (as in crocodiles).

pi In mathematics, the ratio of the circumference of a circle to its diameter, denoted by the Greek letter π. It was proved to be an irrational number by J. H. *Lambert and transcendental by F. Lindemann (1852–1939). Its value is 3.14159. . . . *See also* numbers.

Piacenza 45 03N 09 41E A city in N Italy, in Emilia-Romagna on the Po River. Dating from Roman times, it has several notable buildings, including a 12th-century cathedral and a 13th-century town hall. Piacenza is primarily an agricultural trading center. Population (1991 est): 103,536.

Piaf, Edith (Edith Giovanna Gassion; 1915–63) French cabaret and music-hall singer. Originally a street singer, her small size earned her the nickname "piaf" (French slang: sparrow). Many of her songs, which include "Je m'en fou pas mal," "Je ne regrette rien," and "La Vie en rose," reflected the defiance and despair of her own tragic life, which was ended prematurely by her addiction to alcohol and drugs.

Piaget, Jean (1896–1980) Swiss psychologist, noted for his studies of thought processes, especially in children. He described the development of perception, judgment, reasoning, and logic during childhood, which had important consequences for children's education. Among his many books are *The Origin of Intelligence in Children* (1954) and *The Early Growth of Logic in the Child* (1964).

piano A ☐musical instrument consisting of a number of wire strings stretched over a metal frame, which are hit by felt-covered wooden hammers operated by a keyboard. The piano was invented by *Cristofori in the early 18th century; the name derives from the Italian *pianoforte,* soft-loud, referring to the variation in volume obtainable on the piano in contrast to the earlier *clavichord and *harpsichord. In the modern instrument the frame is either horizontal, as in the **grand piano**, or vertical, as in the **upright piano**. Groups of two or three strings are tuned to each note. When a key is struck the escapement mechanism allows the hammer to fall away from the strings after they have been struck; when the key is released a felt damper stops the vibration of the strings. Two pedals allow a wide variation in volume. The right-hand pedal prevents the dampers from cutting off the sound; the left-hand pedal moves the hammers so that they are either closer to the strings (in the upright piano) or only able to strike one or two strings of each group (in the grand piano). The piano has a compass of seven and a quarter octaves; it has the largest repertory of any single instrument. Famous makers of pianos include J. B. Broadwood (1732–1812) and the firms of Bechstein, *Steinway, and Bösendorfer.

EDITH PIAF

pianola. *See* player piano.

Piave River A river in NE Italy. It flows generally S from the Carnic Alps to the Adriatic Sea 20 mi (32 km) NE of Venice. It formed the main Italian line of defense in World War I, following the Austro-German offensive in 1917. Length: 137 mi (220 km).

Picabia, Francis (1879–1953) French painter and writer. Working chiefly in Paris but also in New York (1913–17), Barcelona, and Zürich, he was associated successively with *cubism, *dada, and *surrealism. He is known mainly for his periodical *391* (1917–24), containing his poems, essays, and satirical drawings of machinery.

Picardy (French name: Picardie) A planning region and former province in N France. It was incorporated into France in 1477 by Louis XI of France. During World War I it was the scene of heavy fighting. Area: 7493 sq mi (19,411 sq km). Population (1991 est): 1,819,100.

picaresque novel A type of narrative that recounts the adventures of a single protagonist in a loose episodic form. The term derives from the Spanish *pícaro,* a rogue. Early examples of the form include the Spanish *Lazarillo de Tormes* (1554) and the French *Gil Blas* (1715–35) by *Lesage. English examples include *Moll Flanders* (1722) by *Defoe, *Jonathan Wild* (1743) by *Fielding, and *Peregrine Pickle* (1751) by *Smollett. The form is usually characterized by comedy and social satire rather than by the development of ideas or characters; it was continued in the 19th century by *Thackeray in *Barry Lyndon* (1844) and in the 20th century by Thomas *Mann in *The Confessions of Felix Krull, Confidence Man* (1954).

PICASSO *A photograph of the artist, aged 84, when he lived in southern France.*

Picasso, Pablo (1881–1973) Spanish artist, born in Malaga. The most inventive and versatile of 20th-century painters and a precocious draftsman, Picasso trained in Barcelona but worked chiefly in Paris after 1900. Although his most popular paintings are those of the beggars, acrobats, and harlequins of his blue (1901–04) and rose (1905–08) periods, his most original work began with *Les Demoiselles d'Avignon* (1907), influenced by Cézanne and African sculpture, and resulted in his development of *cubism with *Braque. In 1912 he made the first collage. He later began a series of classical paintings of colossal figures, followed by nightmarish distorted figure studies in the 1920s and 1930s, when he was loosely associated with *surrealism. One of his major works, *Guernica* (1937), is a horrific depiction of the destruction of the Basque capital during the Spanish Civil War. He was also a sculptor, lithographer, ceramicist, and stage designer.

Piccard A family of Swiss scientists and explorers. **Auguste Piccard** (1884–1962) and his twin **Jean-Félix Piccard** (1884–1963) pioneered the scientific study of the stratosphere in balloons, reaching a height of 16,940 meters in 1932. In 1948 Auguste designed a bathyscaphe, using it to explore the sea depths, descending to over 3000 meters in 1953. His son **Jacques Piccard** (1927–   ) collaborated with his father in designing bathyscaphes and reached a depth of 10,917 meters in the vessel *Trieste* in 1960.

piccolo A woodwind instrument, the smallest and shrillest member of the *flute family. It is pitched an octave higher than the flute and its music is written an octave lower than it sounds. It is used in the orchestra and in the military band.

Pickering, Timothy (1745–1829) US soldier and statesman. During the American Revolution he served on the Board of War and Ordnance (1777–80) and was George Washington's quartermaster general (1780–83). He was Indian Commissioner (1790–95). He held cabinet posts under presidents George Washington and John Adams: postmaster general (1791–95), secretary of war (1795–96), and secretary of state (1795–80). He was a US senator (1803–11) and US representative (1813–17).

picketing The act of guarding the entrance to a workplace by strikers to dissuade nonstrikers from working or to obstruct deliveries.

Pickett, George Edward (1825–75) US Confederate general. A graduate of the US Military Academy, he distinguished himself in the *Mexican War and then served on the frontier (1849–61). He joined the Confederate Army at the start of the Civil War, fighting in his native Virginia. He was part of the Battle of *Gettysburg where his troops attacked at Cemetery Ridge; thereafter, "Pickett's Charge" was synonomous with bravery.

Pickford, Mary (Gladys Mary Smith; 1893–1979) Canadian-born US film actress. She played the roles of innocent young heroines in early silent films, such as *The Little American* (1917) and *Pollyanna* (1919). In 1919 she cofounded United Artists with Charlie *Chaplin, D. W. *Griffith, and Douglas *Fairbanks, whom she married.

pick-up A device that converts information stored in a phonograph record into an electrical signal. In a record player, the pick-up cartridge, usually a removable assembly, consists of a stylus and a *transducer. The stylus is forced to vibrate by the undulations in the record groove. The transducer responds electrically to these vibrations. The most common types of transducer use the *piezoelectric effect or *electromagnetic induction, but *capacitor, variable-resistance, and variable-reluctance pick-ups are also used. A stereo pick-up has one stylus that picks up vibrations from both sides of the V-shaped groove. The components of the resulting two-dimensional vibration contributed by each side are at right angles and are separated by two suitably oriented transducers.

Pico della Mirandola, Giovanni, Conte (1463–94) Italian Renaissance philosopher. He was converted by *Ficino to *Neoplatonism and became interested in the Hermetic and Zoroastrian writings. Although Pico was concerned to prove the truth of Christianity through these literatures, he was inevitably regarded with suspicion by the Church, which banned a proposed discussion (1486) by him of philosophical and theological topics. He wrote an important study of the *Kaballah.

pictographic writing systems (*or* pictography) Writing systems in which each symbol represents a concept or word in the form of a sketch or diagram of the object it represents (the referent). Prehistoric pictographic records have been found throughout the world. It is a characteristic of primitive (nontechnological) societies that a careful distinction is not maintained between an object, a word denoting the object, and a pictorial representation of it. Pictography is therefore often associated with magic or ritual rather than the straightforward recording of information. Disadvantages of pictography include the difficulty of representing any word except nouns having concrete referents. Pictographic systems that did not die out therefore generally developed into *ideographic writing systems.

Picts (painted people) The Roman name (referring to their tattoos) for all Scottish tribes living N of the *Antonine Wall. Perpetually hostile to the Romans, the

Picts had forced them to withdraw behind *Hadrian's Wall by 200 AD, and remained independent until Kenneth I MacAlpine unified S Scotland in the 9th century.

piddock A burrowing *bivalve mollusk belonging to the family *Pholadidae,* of cold and temperate seas. Piddocks are adapted for boring into rock, having shells with serrated cutting edges, the largest being 4 in (10 cm) long. They can damage concrete breakwaters, sea walls, and wharves.

pidgin English A form of English, used to facilitate communication between Chinese and Europeans, having a greatly reduced vocabulary, simplified grammar, and modified sound system. The term may also be applied to *Neo-Melanesian and the Beach-la-Mer of the South Seas. *Compare* creole.

Pieck, Wilhelm (1876–1960) German communist politician. He opposed both the Weimar Republic and Nazism and advocated their overthrow by violent revolution with the aid of Soviet troops. In 1946 he was elected joint chairman, with Otto Grotewohl, of the Socialist Unity party in the postwar Soviet zone of Germany and was the first president of the German Democratic Republic (1949–60).

Piedmont (Italian name: Piemonte) A region in NW Italy. Associated with the House of Savoy since the early 11th century, it became the nucleus of Italian unification in the mid-19th century. It consists of the upper Po Valley, bordered by the Alps in the N and W and the Apennines in the S. Manufacturing is important, with engineering and steel centered on Turin; other industries include textiles, chemicals, rubber, and food products. Agriculture is also important, producing rice, cereals, wine, and dairy products. Area: 9807 sq mi (25,400 sq km). Population (1991): 4,438,262. Capital: Turin.

Pierce, Franklin (1804–69) US statesman; 14th president of the US (1853–57). A Democrat, he served in New Hampshire's legislature before becoming a US representative (1833–37) and US senator (1837–42). After a time as US attorney for New Hampshire and a brief stint as an officer in the *Mexican War, he became the Democrats' compromise presidential candidate in 1852 and won the election. As president he worked hard at patching up differences, the largest being the question of slavery, among the various sections of the country. During his administration the *Gadsden Purchase was completed, the *Kansas-Nebraska Act was passed, and the *Ostend Manifesto proved an embarrassment. He failed to win renomination in 1856.

Piero della Francesca (c. 1420–92) Italian Renaissance painter, born in Sansepolcro. He probably trained in Florence, where he worked on frescoes in Sant' Egidio in 1439. *The Baptism of Christ* (National Gallery, London) shows his monumental figure style and the influence of Florentine artists, particularly *Masaccio. He frequently worked at the court of Urbino, where he painted the double portrait of the duke and his wife in profile (Uffizi). His lifelong interest in perspective is reflected in his fresco cycle *The Legend of the True Cross,* painted for the church of S Francesco, Arezzo, and in his treatise *On Perspective in Painting.* After his death his work was neglected until it was reappraised in the 20th century.

Piero di Cosimo (P. di Lorenzo; 1462–1521) Florentine Renaissance painter. He trained under the painter Cosimo Rosselli (1439–1507) but was chiefly influenced by *Leonardo da Vinci and *Signorelli. His mythological paintings and fantasies on the primitive life of mankind are highly original, one of the best examples being *The Death of Procris.*

Pierre 44 23N 100 20W The capital city of South Dakota, on the Missouri River. Founded in 1880, it is a trade center for a grain and dairy-farming region. Population (1990): 12,906.

Pietermaritzburg 29 36S 30 24E A city in South Africa, the capital of Natal. It was founded by Boers (1838) and named for their leaders, Piet Retief and Gert Maritz, massacred by the Zulus. The Church of the Vow (1839), built to commemorate the subsequent Boer victory over the Zulus, now houses the Voortrekker Museum. Part of the University of Natal (1910) stands there. It is the center of a rich farming area. Population (1985): 192,400.

Pietism A movement for spiritual regeneration among Lutherans in 17th-century Germany. It was started by P. J. Spener (1635–1705), whose *Pia Desideria* (1675) proposed instilling new life into official Lutheranism by concentrating upon devotional worship instead of dogmatic theology. Pietism survived in different guises for over 200 years and influenced many subsequent Christian organizations.

piezoelectric effect The production of electric charges on the opposite faces of certain asymmetric crystals when they are compressed or expanded. The charges are of equal magnitude but opposite in sign on the two faces, the sign on each face depending on whether the crystal is expanded or compressed. Such crystals, known as piezoelectric crystals, include quartz and Rochelle salt. The converse effect also occurs: when a voltage is applied across a piezoelectric crystal, it expands or contracts. The effect is used in the piezoelectric oscillator, the crystal microphone, and the piezoelectric loudspeaker.

pig A hoofed mammal belonging to the Old World family *Suidae* (8 species). Also called hogs or swine, pigs have a stocky body with short legs, a short neck, and a large head with a long cylindrical snout used for digging up roots, seeds, small animals, etc., from soil. Wild *boars were originally domesticated about 5000 years ago, probably in Asia, and used for meat and clearing vegetation. Modern breeds include the *Landrace and *Large White and are reared for pork and bacon (*see* livestock farming). Other members of the pig family include the *barirusa and *wart hog. *See also* peccary.

pigeon A bird belonging to a family (*Columbidae;* 300 species) occurring worldwide except in the coldest regions; the smaller long-tailed forms are called doves; 7–30 in (17–75 cm) long, pigeons have soft plumage, a plump body, a small head, short bill and legs, and a characteristic cooing call. Pigeons feed mainly on seeds and other plant material and feed the young on "pigeons' milk"—the sloughed-off lining of the crop. They are often fast fliers and some are highly migratory, domesticated breeds being used as messengers and for racing. Order: *Columbiformes* (pigeons and sandgrouse). *See also* mourning dove; passenger pigeon; wood pigeon.

pigeon racing The sport of racing homing pigeons back to their home lofts (which they must enter). Pigeons were first, and still are, used for carrying messages; Genghis Khan had a system of pigeon post. The first race of over a hundred miles was held in Belgium (1818), where the sport is still very popular. Birds are banded for racing; their times of departure and arrival are then recorded. Pigeons can cover several thousand miles at speeds of more than 90 mph (145 km per hour).

pigeon wheat. *See* Polytrichum.

pig iron The type of iron produced by *blast furnaces, and used as the first stage in *steelmaking. It has a high carbon content (about 4% by weight) and contains impurities, including some slag, which make it brittle. *See also* cast iron.

pigments Insoluble substances, in the form of fine particles, that give color and opacity to *paints, *plastics, and *rubber. They can be broadly divided into naturally occurring pigments (such as red iron oxide), inorganic pigments manufactured from minerals, organic pigments, and *lakes.

pigmies. *See* Pygmies.

pigweed 1. A stout leafy annual herb of the genus *Amaranthus* (about 50 species), found in tropical and temperate regions, often as a weed. Pigweeds have furrowed stems, up to 40 in (1 m) high, with simple pale-green hairy leaves and long branching greenish-white flower spikes. Family: *Amaranthaceae.* **2.** *See* goosefoot.

pika A small mammal belonging to the genus *Ochotona* (14 species), of Asia and North America, also called mouse hare, cony, and rock rabbit; 5–12 in (12.5–30 cm) long and resembling large short-tailed mice, pikas live in cold rocky areas above the tree line. They build stacks of sun-dried vegetation under sheltering ledges to feed on during the winter. Family: *Ochotonidae*; order: *Lagomorpha.*

Pike, Zebulon Montgomery (1779–1813) US soldier and explorer. An army officer on the frontier, he was sent (1805) to find the sources of the Mississippi River. Unsuccessful, he explored most of the Southwest (New Mexico and Colorado), discovered *Pikes Peak (1806), and gathered information about the Spanish. He was killed in battle in Canada during the War of 1812. His *Account of the Expeditions to the Sources of the Mississippi and Through the Western Parts of Louisiana* (1810) greatly aided US expansion.

pike (fish) A freshwater fish of the genus *Esox* found in temperate regions of Eurasia and America. It has an elongated body, up to about 4.5 ft (1.4 m) long, a broad flat snout, and a large mouth with strong teeth. It feeds voraciously on fish and other animals. The common pike (*E. lucius*) is olive-gray above with silvery underparts and pale spots. Family: *Esocidae*; order: *Salmoniformes.*

pike (weapon) A pre-1800 infantry weapon with a wooden shaft 12–21 ft (4–6 m) long, a steel head on an iron sleeve, and an iron butt. It was useless in the face of missile weapons (arrows, musketry) and was replaced by the *bayonet.

pikeperch One of several food and game fish related to perch, especially members of the genera *Lucioperca* and *Stizostedion* found in Europe and North America. The American pikeperches include the species *S. vitreum,* 35 in (90 cm) long, and *S. canadense,* 12 in (30 cm) long. Slender, elongated, and darkly mottled, they are carnivorous, feeding mainly on other fish.

Pikes Peak A mountain in central Colorado, in the Rocky Mountains. It is a popular tourist attraction noted for its spectacular views from the summit, which is ascended by a cog railroad and a road. Height: 14,109 ft (4300 m).

pilaster. *See* orders of architecture.

Pilate, Pontius (1st century AD) Roman governor. As procurator of Judea and Samaria (26–36) he condemned Christ to death but, according to the New Testament Gospels, did so reluctantly, fearing the outcome of any other course. He came into frequent conflict with the Jews and was finally dismissed for his cruel suppression of a Samaritan rebellion. In one tradition he committed suicide, but in the Ethiopian Church he is regarded as a saint and martyr.

pilchard An important food fish, *Sardina pilchardus,* related to the herring and sprat, that occurs in abundance in the Mediterranean, E Atlantic, and English Channel. Its slender body, 10–19 in (25–35 cm) long, is bluish green above and whitish below and it swims in large shoals feeding on crustaceans and fish eggs. Pilchards up to one year old are called *sardines and are fished extensively off the coast of Spain and Portugal. Pilchards are eaten fresh and canned.

Pilcomayo River A river in S central South America, rising in the Bolivian Andes and flowing generally SE, forming part of the Argentina-Paraguay border before joining the Paraguay River. Length: about 1000 mi (1600 km).

piles. *See* hemorrhoids.

Pilgrimage of Grace (1536) A revolt in N England against the government of Henry VIII. The rebels were united by their opposition to the recent *Reformation legislation and the dissolution of the monasteries as well as by economic grievances. Under Robert Ashe (c. 1500–37) they seized York but were persuaded by promises of pardon and a full hearing of their complaints to surrender. Some 230 men, however, including Ashe, were executed.

Pilgrim Fathers The 101 English colonists who established the first permanent European settlement in New England in 1620. Among these settlers was a group of 35 English Puritans led by William Bradford and William *Brewster that had lived in Holland for the previous decade in their attempt to escape religious persecution. Granted the right to settle within the American territory of the Virginia Company, the Puritans and other potential colonists set sail in the *Mayflower,* arriving off Cape Cod after a voyage of almost two months. Even though this was beyond the limits of the Virginia Company's possessions, the Pilgrims chose to remain in the area, establishing their first settlement, which they named Plymouth, after their port of departure in England. Although disease and the unexpectedly harsh conditions of the first winter drastically reduced the number of colonists, a sufficient number survived to sow the crops needed to maintain the Plymouth Colony and to reap their first harvest in November 1621 (*see* Thanksgiving Day).

Pill, the. *See* oral contraceptive.

Pillars of Hercules Two promontories at the entrance to the Mediterranean Sea, known in ancient times as Calpe (modern Gibraltar) and Abyla (modern Jebel Musa, at Ceuta, Morocco). According to one legend, the promontories were joined until Heracles tore them apart.

pilot fish A fish, *Naucrates ductor,* that has a pale-blue elongated body, up to 24 in (60 cm) long, marked with five to seven dark vertical bands. It is found in warm and tropical seas, accompanying ships and large fish, especially sharks, to feed on parasites and scraps of food. Family: *Carangidae*; order: *Perciformes.*

pilot whale A gregarious toothed *whale, *Globicephala melaena.* Growing up to 20 ft (6 m), pilot whales are black with a blunt head, narrow tapering flippers, and a broad dorsal fin. They were named by fishermen who found groups of them near herring shoals. Family: *Globicephalidae.*

Pilsen. *See* Plzeň.

Pilsudski, Józef Klemens (1867–1935) Polish statesman, who fought for Polish independence. Pilsudski formed three Polish legions, which fought against Russia in World War I. When Germany refused to guarantee Polish sovereignty, Pilsudski withdrew his support and was imprisoned. After Germany's defeat he declared Poland independent and served as head of state (1919–27). In 1926 he established a military dictatorship, remaining in power until his death.

Piltdown man Skeletal remains once thought to be those of a fossil *hominid, found on Piltdown Common, near Lewes (England), in 1912. In 1953–54 the "find" was shown to be a hoax or fraud. Analysis showed the skull to be made up of a human cranium and an ape's jaw, stained to simulate age. Extinct animal bones and tools had also been placed in the site.

pimento. *See* allspice.

pimpernel A slender annual or perennial herb of the genus *Anagallis* (about 20 species), found in Eurasia, Africa, and America, especially the annual scarlet pimpernel (*A. arvensis*). Growing 2–12 in (5–30 cm) tall, pimpernels have simple leaves and small red, pink, blue, or white bell-shaped flowers with five petals, borne individually on slender stalks. The fruit is a capsule, which opens by a round lid. The yellow pimpernel (*Lysimachia nemorum*) belongs to a closely related genus. Family: *Primulaceae*.

Pinchot, Gifford (1865–1946) US conservationist and politician. He was responsible for the first systematic approach to forest management in the US and became US Forest Service head in 1898. During his tenure (1898–1910) he established national forests and guidelines for privately owned forests. After unsuccessful bids for the Republican presidential nomination (1912) and the US Senate (1914), he served as commissioner of forestry in Pennsylvania (1920–22) and as governor of Pennsylvania (1923–27; 1931–35); he also taught forestry at Yale University (1903–36).

Pinckney, Charles (1757–1824) US statesman. He represented South Carolina in the *Constitutional Convention (1787) and his proposals for the new US government—the Pinckney plan—were included in the constitution. He served as governor of South Carolina (1789–92, 1796–98, 1806–08) and as a US senator (1798–1801) and a representative (1819–21). His cousins were **Charles Cotesworth Pinckney** (1746–1825), who was minister to France (1796), and **Thomas Pinckney** (1750–1828), who negotiated **Pinckney's Treaty** (the Treaty of San Lorenzo) with Spain in 1795, determining the boundary between US and Spanish possessions in America at latitude 31°N.

Pindar (518–438 BC) Greek poet. Born into an aristocratic family in Boeotia in central Greece, he was educated in Athens and lived in Sicily for two years from 476 BC. Of his 17 books of choral lyrics only four survive. These contain Epinician Odes written in honor of victors of athletic games and noted for their exalted style and deep religious feeling. He was acclaimed by the ancient Greeks as their greatest poet.

Pindus Mountains (Modern Greek name: Píndhos Óros) A range of mountains extending some 311 mi (500 km) NW–SE across W Greece and S Albania and rising to 8652 ft (2637 m) at Mount Smólikas.

pine A coniferous tree of the genus *Pinus* (about 80 species), widely distributed in the N hemisphere. Pines have long slender needles, usually in clusters of two, three, or five, and hanging cones, of variable shape, made up of overlapping woody scales. Pines are important softwoods: the timber is easily worked and yields turpentine, tar, pitch, and other resinous products. Commercially important and widely planted species include the Scots pine (*P. sylvestris*), of N and W Europe and Asia, up to 131 ft (40 m) high (□tree); the Monterey pine (*P. radiata*), from Monterey, California, up to 115 ft (35 m) high; the shore pine (*P. contorta*), of W North America, up to 80 ft (25 m) high; the Corsican pine (*P. nigra* var *maritima*), up to 148 ft (45 m) high; and the maritime pine (*P. pinaster*), of W Mediterranean regions and N Africa, up to 115 ft (35 m) high. These and other species are also planted for shelter and ornament and some species have edible seeds (*see* stone pine). Family: *Pinaceae*. *See also* bristlecone pine.

A number of other unrelated conifers are called pines, including species of **Araucaria,* the *cypress pine, and the *kauri pine.

pineal gland A small gland within the brain. In the 18th century it was supposed to be the site of the soul. In some lower animals, for example certain lizards, it is receptive to light and is visible externally as a third eye (pineal eye); in man its function is unknown, although it may help to regulate the onset of puberty.

pineapple A perennial herbaceous plant, *Ananas comosus,* native to tropical and subtropical America and cultivated in many warm and tropical regions for its fruit. It reaches a height of 40 in (1 m) and bears a rosette of 30–40 stiff succulent toothed leaves on a thick fleshy stem. Purplish flowers occur at the center of the rosette and—with their bracts—fuse to form the composite fruit, which ripens 5–6 months after flowering begins and can weigh up to 22 lb (10 kg). It takes nearly two years for a plant to bear its first marketable fruit. The major producing countries are the Hawaiian Islands, Brazil, Mexico, Cuba, and the Philippines. Family: *Bromeliaceae.*

pine marten A European carnivorous mammal, *Martes martes.* About 27.5 in (70 cm) long, it inhabits dense evergreen forests, preying on squirrels, birds, insects, and eggs. As with other *martens, the female has a litter (2–5 cubs) only every second year, a disadvantage for a species widely hunted for fur.

Pinero, Sir Arthur Wing (1855–1934) British dramatist. He abandoned his law studies to become an actor. His early plays, which included *The Magistrate* (1885) and *Dandy Dick* (1887), were hugely successful farces that exploited his professional knowledge of stagecraft. His later plays, notably *The Second Mrs. Tanqueray* (1893), were more serious treatments of contemporary social problems.

pink One of several usually perennial herbaceous plants derived from *Dianthus plumarius* and often grown as fragrant garden ornamentals. They have long slender leaves and showy white, pink, or red flowers, often with fringed petals. Family: *Caryophyllaceae.*

Pinkerton, Allan (1819–84) US detective, born in Scotland. He emigrated to the US in 1842. He founded the Pinkerton National Detective Agency in 1850 and organized an intelligence service for the Union during the Civil War.

pinkeye *See* conjunctivitis.

pink salmon A *salmon, *Oncorhynchus gorbuscha,* also called humpback salmon, found in the North Pacific. It is 16–20 in (40–50 cm) long and marked with large irregular spots. It undertakes the shortest migration of all the salmon and the male develops a lump on its back during the breeding season.

Pinochet, Augusto (1915–   ) Chilean general and head of state (1973–89). He led a military coup that overthrew the government of Salvador *Allende and became the head of a repressive military junta. After 1989, he retained his post as head of the armed forces.

Pinsk 52 08N 26 01E A port in Belarus, at the confluence of the Pina and Pripet Rivers. A medieval Russian principality, it came under Lithuania (13th century), Poland (16th century), Russia again (1793), and Poland again (1920–39); ceded to the Soviet Union, it was occupied by the Germans in World War II. It became part of independent Belarus in 1991. Timber, shipbuilding, and metalworking are the principal activities. Population (1988 est): 63,000.

pintail A *duck, *Anas acuta,* occurring in the N hemisphere, that breeds on inland waters and winters in coastal areas. The male is 28 in (70 cm) long and has a dark-brown head and neck with a white band down the neck, gray flanks, and long black central tail feathers. Females have mottled brown plumage and both sexes have a blue-gray bill.

Pinter, Harold (1930–   ) British dramatist. His first full-length play, *The Birthday Party* (1958), failed until he had established his reputation with his second, *The Caretaker* (1960), a study of suspicion between a tramp and two brothers. Later plays include *The Homecoming* (1965), *Old Times* (1971), *Betrayed* (1978), and *Mountain Language* (1988). He uses elliptical dialogue to evoke an atmosphere of tension and ambiguity that is rarely explicitly resolved. He has also written film scripts and directed plays.

pinto A horse whose coat consists of sharply defined patches of white and a darker color—either black (piebald pattern) or brown, bay, dun, or roan (skewbald pattern). A pinto may be predominantly white (tobiano pattern) or mainly dark with white splashes (overo pattern). Pintos were commonly used by American Indians. Height: 14 hands (5 ft; 1.42 m) minimum.

Pinturicchio (Bernardino di Betto; c. 1454–1513) Italian Renaissance painter, born in Perugia. He was influenced chiefly by *Perugino, whom he probably assisted on frescoes for the Sistine Chapel in the Vatican, where he later decorated the Borgia apartments (1492–94). His other major fresco cycle (1503–08) is in the cathedral library, Siena.

pinworm A slender parasitic *nematode worm, *Enterobius vermicularius,* also called seatworm or threadworm. Up to 0.4 in (1 cm) long, pinworms are white and inhabit the human intestine; they are common in Europe and America. Female worms migrate to the anus to lay thousands of eggs, causing itching, especially at night. The eggs are resistant to drying and to many disinfectants.

pinyin. *See* Chinese.

pion A group of three elementary particles (*see* particle physics) classified as *mesons (symbol: π). The charged pions (π^+ and π^-) have a mass of 139.6 MeV, the neutral pion (π°) a mass of 136 MeV. The *strong interaction can be represented by the exchange of virtual pions between particles (*see* virtual particle).

Pioneer probes A series of US solar-system space probes, first launched in 1958. Pioneers 4 to 9 went into solar orbit, monitoring solar activity in the 1960s and early 1970s. Pioneers 10 and 11 flew past and studied Jupiter in 1973 and 1974. Pioneer 11 approached Saturn in 1979. Two **Pioneeer Venus** probes reached Venus in 1978.

p'i-p'a An ancient Chinese *lute. It is short, with a shallow pear-shaped body and has four silk strings. It is held upright in the lap and played with a plectrum. Poets of the Tang dynasty (618–906 AD) played it to accompany their poems; it is still a popular instrument.

pipal. *See* bo tree.

pipefish One of several slender long-bodied fish belonging to the family *Syngnathidae* (*see also* sea horse); 1–20 in (2.5–50 cm) long, it has a long tubular snout with a small mouth and lives among aquatic plants mainly in warm marine waters, feeding on small organisms. The males carry the young until they hatch. Order: *Gasterosteiformes.*

Piper, John (1903–92) British painter and writer. Although he painted abstract works in the 1930s, he is best known for his watercolors and aquatints of architecture, such as Windsor Castle (1941–42). He has also designed stained glass, notably for Coventry Cathedral, and stage sets.

pipistrelle A small insect-eating *bat belonging to the genus *Pipistrellus* (50 species) with a worldwide distribution. The Eurasian pipistrelle (*P. pipistrellus*) is about 1.3 in (3.5 cm) long with an 8-in (20-cm) wingspan. It often flies near houses where insects are attracted to light. Pipistrelles have a prehensile tail, used when crawling into crevices to roost. Family: *Vespertilionidae.*

pipit A small insectivorous songbird of the genus *Anthus* (30 species), 5.5–6 in (14–16 cm) long with a brown-streaked plumage and paler speckled underparts. The meadow pipit (*A. pratensis*) occurs on moors and downs in Britain and is the chief prey of the *merlin. The water pipit (*A. spinoletta*) inhabits the high mountains of Eurasia and North America; it is also found in coastal regions, when it is known as the rock pipit. The Antarctic pipit (*A. antarcticus*) is the only passerine land bird in Antarctica. Family: *Motacillidae* (wagtails and pipits).

Piraeus (Modern Greek name: Piraiévs) 37 57N 23 42E The chief port of Greece, SW of Athens on the Saronic Gulf. It was founded during the 5th century BC as the port of Athens. Following the bombings of World War II extensive industrial renewal has taken place; industries include shipbuilding, oil refining, and chemicals. Its exports include wine and olive oil. Population (1971): 187,362.

Pirandello, Luigi (1867–1936) Italian dramatist and novelist. He was born in Sicily and studied philology in Germany. In 1903 his wife became insane, and his writing was greatly influenced by his life with her. He gained international success with his plays exploring the nature of reality and illusion, notably *Six Characters in Search of an Author* (1921) and *Henry IV* (1922). His other works include the novel *The Late Mattia Pascal* (1904) and the critical study *Humour* (1908). He won the Nobel Prize in 1934.

Piranesi, Giambattista (1720–78) Italian etcher, born in Venice. Initially trained as an architect and stage designer, he achieved a wide reputation with his prints of Rome and its ruins. As an archeologist and champion of the superiority of Roman architecture over Greek (*compare* Winckelmann, Johann Joachim), he was an important figure in early *neoclassicism, although his imaginative and dramatic style, particularly in the *Carceri d'invenzione* (*Imaginary Prisons*), anticipates *romanticism.

piranha A freshwater fish, also called caribe and piraya, belonging to a genus (*Serrasalmus*) found in South America. It has a deep body, up to 24 in (60 cm) long, ranging from silver to black in color, strong jaws, and razor-sharp teeth. Piranhas swim in groups and feed voraciously on other fish; they will also attack larger animals, including man. Family: *Characidae* (*see* characin).

Pirani gauge A pressure gauge used for measuring low gas pressures. It consists of an electrically heated wire placed in the gas. The rate at which the gas conducts heat away from the wire depends on its pressure; the pressure is measured by observing the resistance of the wire at a fixed voltage or observing the voltage at a fixed resistance.

Pisa 43 43N 10 24E A city in Italy, in Tuscany, on the Arno River. Dating from Etruscan times, it developed into a thriving maritime republic (11th–12th centuries) but declined in importance after it fell to the Florentines in 1509. It is the birthplace of Galileo, who taught at the university (founded in 1343). The most famous of its buildings is the Leaning Tower of Pisa, which is 180 ft (55 m) high and about 17 ft (5 m) out of perpendicular. Other notable buildings include the cathedral (11th–12th centuries) and the baptistry (12th–13th centuries). Its many historic monuments make it a popular tourist center. Machinery, textiles, bicycles, and glass are manufactured. Population (1991 est): 101,500.

Pisanello (Antonio Pisano; c. 1395–c. 1455) Italian *international gothic painter, draftsman, and medalist. He worked on frescoes, begun by *Gentile da Fabriano, in Venice and Rome. His portrait medals, influenced by Roman and Greek coins, were popular in court circles, particularly in Ferrara. In such paintings as the *Vision of St Eustace* (National Gallery, London) he recreated the world of chivalry.

Pisano, Andrea (Andrea de Pontedera; c. 1290–1348) Italian sculptor. Unrelated to Nicola and Giovanni *Pisano, Andrea worked chiefly in Florence, where he succeeded Giotto as architect of the cathedral (1336). His most important works are the bronze reliefs of the life of St John for the south doors of the Baptistry.

Pisano, Nicola (c. 1220–c. 1278) Italian sculptor. He initiated the revival of antique Roman forms that led eventually to Renaissance sculpture, beginning with his pulpit in the Baptistry, Pisa. Such later works as the pulpit in Siena Cathedral and the fountain in the main square of Perugia reveal the cooperation of his son **Giovanni Pisano** (c. 1250–1314). Giovanni introduced French gothic elements into his sculptures for the façade of Siena Cathedral and his pulpit for S Andrea, Pistoia. He returned to a more classical style in his pulpit for Pisa Cathedral.

Pisces (Latin: Fish) A large inconspicuous constellation that lies on the *zodiac between Aries and Aquarius, mainly in the N sky. It contains the vernal *equinox.

Pisistratus (c. 600–c. 528 BC) Athenian tyrant. After several ultimately abortive attempts to seize power in Athens, Pisistratus succeeded in 546 with a mercenary army. As tyrant, he diminished the power of landed aristocrats by instituting circuit judges to adjudicate local cases. Pisistratus encouraged Athenian agriculture and commerce and his benevolent tyranny promoted the national unity necessary for the later development of democracy.

Pissarro, Camille (1830–1903) French impressionist painter, born in the West Indies. After running away to Venezuela to become an artist, he was sent by his parents to Paris (1855). He trained in the École des Beaux-Arts, and the Académie Suisse, where he met *Monet. Chiefly influenced by *Corot, he was more interested in landscape structure than the other impressionists. He participated in all eight of the impressionist exhibitions (1874–86) and is noted for his encouragement of younger painters, especially *Cézanne and *Gauguin. In the 1880s he experimented with *pointillism. His son **Lucien Pissarro** (1863–1944) was also a painter.

pistachio A small aromatic tree, *Pistacia vera,* native to central Eurasia and widely cultivated in Mediterranean regions for its edible green kernels ("nuts"). Growing 23–33 ft (7–10 m) high, it has compound leaves with 1–5 pairs of leathery leaflets and drooping spikes of small male and female flowers, borne usually on separate trees. The oval white fruits, 0.6–0.8 in (1.5–2 cm) long, often split to expose the kernels, which are used as dessert nuts and for decorating and flavoring confectionery, cakes, etc. Family: *Anacardiaceae.*

pistil The part of a flower consisting of the female reproductive organs. It consists of one or more *carpels, which may be united into a single structure. Some plants, such as the cucumber, have separate male and female flowers: the latter are described as pistillate.

Pistoia 43 56N 10 55E A city in N central Italy, in Tuscany. *Catiline was killed in battle near there (62 BC). The 12th-century cathedral contains a famous silver altar. Population: 94,000.

pistol A short-range *small arm that can be used with one hand. It evolved from a small cavalry matchlock in the 15th century, later improvements following those of the □musket. The need to make a weapon that would fire more than once without reloading led to the division of pistols into two classes: the *revolver and the automatic. The first revolver (c. 1540) had multiple barrels, which were rotated by hand past the lock. However, the first successful revolver was the *Colt of 1835, in which a magazine chamber revolves behind a single barrel. The first automatics (1893) combined a box magazine in the butt with a recoil loading action. The *Luger 9 mm automatic went into service with the

German navy in 1904 and remained the standard weapon until 1938. Both re-volvers and automatics are still in military and police use throughout the world.

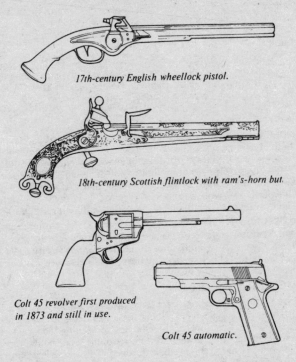

17th-century English wheellock pistol.

18th-century Scottish flintlock with ram's-horn but.

*Colt 45 revolver first produced
in 1873 and still in use.*

Colt 45 automatic.

PISTOL

Pitcairn Islands A small island group in the central S Pacific Ocean, a British dependent territory, consisting of Pitcairn Island and three uninhabited islands. Subsistence agriculture is the chief occupation; fruit, vegetables, and souvenirs are sold to passing ships. *History*: Pitcairn Island was occupied in 1790 by muti-neers from the *Bounty* and women from Tahiti. By 1856 the island was overpop-ulated and the inhabitants were moved to Norfolk Island; some later returned. Area: 1.75 sq mi (4.6 sq km). Chief town: Adamstown.

pitch (chemistry) A black or dark-brown residue resulting from the partial evaporation or fractional distillation of coal tars or tar products. The term is sometimes used for the residue obtained from petroleum distillation (bitumen) or for the naturally occurring petroleum residue (asphalt). Bitumen is a mixture of heavy hydrocarbons with a high proportion of free carbon. It is used as a binding agent (it is the main constituent of road tars), as a protective coating in bituminous paints, in roofing felts, and as a fuel.

pitch (music) The highness or lowness of a note, depending on the frequency of the vibrations producing it. Standard pitch has varied through the centuries: Handel's still extant *tuning fork gives A as 422.5 Hz. Modern **concert pitch** was standardized by international agreement in 1939, and the frequency of the note A was fixed at 440 Hz. **Perfect pitch** is the ability to recognize and name notes by ear alone; since notes have no absolute pitch value, even this depends on relative frequencies. *See also* temperament.

pitchblende The chief ore of uranium, a massive form of uraninite, UO_2, a black radioactive mineral found in hydrothermal veins and as an accessory mineral in acid igneous rocks. It occurs in North America, Africa, Australia, and central Europe.

Pitcher, Molly (Mary Ludwig Hays McCauley; 1754–1832) American Revolution heroine. Married to John Casper Hays, an artilleryman, she carried water to him and other troops during the Battle of Monmouth (1778) and took over her husband's cannon when he was wounded. After his death in 1789, she married George McCauley. It was not until 1822 that she was officially recognized as a heroine of the Revolution.

pitcher plant Any *carnivorous plant with pitcher-shaped leaves, belonging mainly to the families *Nepenthaceae* and *Sarraceniaceae*. The pitcher is often brightly colored and secretes nectar to attract insects, which often fall inside and drown in the digestive juices at the bottom of the pitcher. The *Nepenthaceae* comprises herbs and shrubs of the Old World, many of which are climbers. Their leaf tendrils are swollen to form the pitcher, 2–12 in (5–30 cm) long. The *Sarraceniaceae* are perennial herbs of the New World with rosettes of pitchers arising from a swollen underground stem.

Pithecanthropus A group of extinct Pleistocene *hominids, now generally called *Homo erectus* (*see* Homo). The name *Pithecanthropus* (literally apeman) was coined by *Haeckel before any supporting fossil evidence was found for the evolutionary link.

Pitman, Sir Isaac. *See* shorthand.

pitot tube A type of *anemometer for measuring the velocity of a fluid, invented by Henri Pitot (1695–1771). It consists of an L-shaped tube placed in the moving fluid; the vertical limb of the tube has an opening facing into the flow. The difference in pressure between the interior of the tube and the surroundings enables the velocity of the fluid to be calculated. The device is used to measure the velocity of liquids, aircraft airspeeds, etc.

Pittosporum A genus of small evergreen trees (about 150 species), called parchment-bark or Australian laurels, native to Australia and New Zealand and often grown as ornamentals. They have long pale leathery leaves and blue, white, yellow, or red flowers. *P. tenuifolium* is popular in flower arrangements. Family: *Pittosporaceae*.

Pittsburgh 40 26N 80 00W A city in Pennsylvania, at the confluence of the Allegheny and Monongahela Rivers, which here form the Ohio River. Settled in 1758, it was the site of Fort Pitt, completed by the British in 1761. The city was founded in 1764. It is the site of several colleges and universities, including the University of Pittsburgh (1787) and the famous Carnegie Institute, which contains a two-million-volume library, several museums, and the Carnegie Music Hall. Pittsburgh has grown as a major center of the steel industry and is the country's largest inland port. Other manufactures include machinery, petroleum, coal, glass, and chemicals. Population (1990): 369,879.

Pittsfield 42 27N 73 15W A city in W central Massachusetts, on the Housatonic River, in the Taconic Mountains. Settled in 1753, it is a popular resort and tourist attraction. The Shaker Village at Hancock is nearby. Population (1990): 48,622.

Pitt the Elder, William, 1st Earl of Chatham (1708–78) British statesman, known as the Great Commoner. Entering parliament in 1735, he established a reputation as an outstanding orator. In 1756 he became secretary of state and leader of the House of Commons but was dismissed in 1757 and then recalled to form a government with *Newcastle. In charge of foreign affairs, Pitt was largely responsible for Britain's victory in the *Seven Years' War. Forced to resign in 1761, he returned to form a new government in 1766. Plagued by ill health, he resigned in 1768.

His second son **William Pitt the Younger** (1759–1806) was twice prime minister (1783–1801, 1804–06), the youngest in British history. He entered Parliament in 1781 and became chancellor of the exchequer in 1782. As prime minister he inherited an enormous public debt, which he reduced by a fiscal policy influenced by Adam *Smith. He introduced new taxes, overhauled customs duties, and reformed the Indian administration. Pitt negotiated the first (1793) and second (1798) coalitions against France (*see* Revolutionary and Napoleonic Wars) and resolved the crisis caused by the Irish rebellion in 1798 by the union of Britain and Ireland in 1800. He resigned following George III's refusal to accept Catholic emancipation. His second ministry was marked by an alliance with Russia, Sweden, and Austria against Napoleon, which collapsed shortly before his death in office.

pituitary gland A small *endocrine gland, about 0.5 in by 0.3 in (12 mm by 8 mm), lying within the skull close to the center of the head. The anterior (front) lobe produces *growth hormone, *prolactin, and hormones that regulate the function of other glands, notably the *thyroid and *adrenal glands and the ovary and testis. The posterior (back) lobe is a downgrowth from the *hypothalamus and stores various neurohormones that are synthesized in this part of the brain. The pituitary is therefore the master endocrine gland, from which neural control of the entire endocrine system is effected.

pit viper A New World viper, belonging to the subfamily *Crotalinae,* that has a sensory pit between the eye and nostril used to detect the tiny changes in temperature caused by warm-blooded prey nearby. Pit vipers occur in habitats ranging from deserts to rain forests and are chiefly ground dwellers. *See also* bushmaster; copperhead; fer-de-lance; rattlesnake; sidewinder; water moccasin.

Pius II (Enea Silvio [*or* Aeneas Silvius] de' Piccolomini; 1405–64) Pope (1458–64), who was also a notable humanist. He served Emperor Frederick III as both imperial poet and secretary before becoming a priest (1446). On his election he attempted to restore papal authority by condemning the view that general councils had supreme authority in the Church. His proclamation of a crusade against the Turks after the fall of Constantinople (1453) was ignored by the secular powers and he died shortly after resolving to lead it in person.

Pius IV (Giovanni Angelo de' Medici; 1499–1565) Pope (1559–65). He continued papal support of the *Counter-Reformation, presiding over the last session of the Council of *Trent and reforming the Sacred College of cardinals.

Pius V, St (Michele Ghislieri; 1504–72) Pope (1566–72). A Dominican friar and noted for his asceticism, he was the greatest of the 16th-century reformer popes. Pius reedited a number of liturgical texts, including the breviary and missal, enforced the decrees of the Council of *Trent, and expanded the activities of the *Inquisition. He excommunicated the Protestant Elizabeth I of England in 1570. He was canonized in 1712. Feast day: May 6.

Pius VI (Giovanni Angelico Braschi; 1717–99) Pope (1775–99). His pontificate was marked by attempts to combat growing opposition to papal control from both national churches and states, especially in France, where he condemned the state church established during the French Revolution. Pius was captured in the Revolutionary Wars, during which the French attacked the papal states, and died a prisoner.

Pius VII (Gregorio Barnaba Chiaramonti; 1740–1823) Pope (1800–23), who made several unsuccessful attempts to preserve papal privileges in the face of Napoleon's demands. In 1804, under duress, he consecrated Napoleon emperor and in 1809, after the French conquest of Rome, was taken prisoner and forced to make extensive concessions in the Concordat of Fontainebleau (1813). After Napoleon's fall in 1815 Pius gained the restoration of the papal states and negotiated concordats with many of the victorious powers.

Pius IX (Giovanni Maria Mastai-Ferretti; 1792–1878) Pope (1846–78). At first sympathetic to liberal and nationalist movements, he abandoned radicalism for reaction after the Revolution of 1848, in which he fled Rome. He refused to acknowledge the newly established kingdom of Italy, into which Rome was incorporated in 1870. He defined the Immaculate Conception (1854) and papal infallibility (1869–70) and his encyclical *Quanta Cura* (1864), with its *Syllabus of Errors,* condemned modernism in theology and philosophy.

Pius X, St (Giuseppe Sarto; 1835–1914) Pope (1903–14). His pontificate was marked by his defense of the Church's independence against encroachment by the state, support of social reforms (especially in the Catholic Action movement), reform of the liturgy, and a new codification of canon law. He condemned theological modernism and revolutionary political movements. He was canonized in 1954. Feast day: Sept 3.

Pius XI (Achille Ratti; 1857–1939) Pope (1922–39). He attempted to extend the educational and social work of the Church, supporting the role of the laity in the Catholic Action movement. He signed the *Lateran Treaty (1929), establishing the Vatican City as a sovereign state.

Piux XII (Eugenio Pacelli; 1876–1958) Pope (1939–58). Pius's failure to condemn fascism during World War II caused controversy, although he attempted to prevent the outbreak of war, to curb atrocities, and to relieve suffering. He was a staunch conservative both in politics and doctrine, condemning communism and modernist theology.

Pizarro, Francisco (c. 1475–1541) Spanish conquistador. He accompanied Balboa on the expedition that discovered the Pacific (1513) and in the 1520s explored the NW coast of South America. In 1531 having gained Emperor Charles V's assent to the conquest of Peru and an assurance of the major part of the spoils, he crossed the Andes to Cajamarca. There he treacherously murdered the Inca king, Atahuallpa. Over the next nine years he consolidated the Spanish conquest of the Inca empire, founding Lima in 1535. He came into conflict with a fellow conquistador, Diego de Almagro (c. 1475–1538), who was defeated and put to death; his followers, however, subsequently murdered Pizzaro.

PK. *See* telekinesis.

placenta **1.** An organ formed within the womb of mammals and other viviparous animals during pregnancy, composed of fetal and maternal tissues. Within the placenta the blood vessels of the fetus and mother come into close contact, enabling exchange of substances in the blood. Thus the fetus receives nutrients, oxygen, and antibodies from the mother's blood and its waste products are absorbed into the mother's circulation. The fetus is attached to the placenta by the umbilical cord. The placenta also secretes hormones that contribute to the control of pregnancy. The placenta is expelled (as the afterbirth) shortly after the baby is delivered. **2.** A tissue in plants that connects the ovules (later the seeds) to the ovary (later the fruit wall).

Placodermi An extinct class of fish that lived from the Devonian to the Permian periods (415–240 million years ago). Their bodies, usually 4–16 in (10–40 cm) long, were covered with bony scales, particularly over the head and front half, and had a bony skeleton, primitive jaws, gill covers (opercula), and median and paired fins. Many species were bottom-dwelling carnivores.

plagioclase A group of *feldspar minerals with compositions varying between the two end-members albite ($NaAlSi_3O_8$) and anorthite ($CaAl_2Si_2O_8$). They are milky white or colorless, and occur both as phenocrysts and in the groundmass of most basic and intermediate igneous rocks and in many metamorphic rocks.

plague An infectious disease caused by the bacterium *Pasteurella pestis,* which is transmitted to man by rat fleas. There are three forms of the disease, the most common of which is bubonic plague, in which fever, vomiting, and headache are accompanied by swollen inflamed lymph nodes (buboes). The more severe pneumonic and septicemic plagues develop when the bacteria enter the lungs and bloodstream respectively. Plague is treated with antibiotics. Epidemics of plague afflicted Europe throughout the Middle Ages, the *Black Death of 1348 being the most devastating.

plaice A commercially important *flatfish, *Pleuronectes platessa,* that occurs in the N North Atlantic and British coastal waters. It is usually 10–16 in (25–40 cm) long, occasionally up to 35 in (90 cm), and is colored brown with bright red or orange spots above and white beneath. There are four to seven bony warts running backward from the eyes.

plainchant (*or* plainsong) The ritual music of the early Christian Church, as distinct from later polyphonic music. It consists of unaccompanied melodic lines deriving from natural intonation, with flexible rhythms to fit the Latin prose of the daily services. Probably initially influenced by Jewish liturgical chant, its melodic basis derived from the Greek system of *modes. At the end of the 6th century, during the papacy of Gregory I, it was codified as *Gregorian chant and flourished with few changes until the advent of harmonized melody in about 1000.

plains-wanderer An Australian bird, *Pedionomus torquatus,* of dry grassland regions; 4–5 in (10–13 cm) long, it has short rounded wings, a short tail, and a mottled red-brown plumage with a white throat and a collar of black spots. Largely ground-dwelling, it feeds on plant material and insects and is the only member of its family (*Pedionomidae*). Order: *Gruiformes* (cranes, rails, etc.).

planarian A free-living *flatworm of the order *Tricladida,* occurring in marine and freshwater habitats of temperate regions. Flattened and symmetrical, with simple eyespots and olfactory organs, planarians range from 0.08 in (2 mm) to 4 in (10 cm) in length. They glide smoothly by means of beating cilia (hairs) and use a long retractable feeding tube (pharynx) to consume small invertebrates. Class: *Turbellaria.*

Planck, Max Karl Ernst Ludwig (1858–1947) German physicist; the originator of *quantum theory, who was professor at Kiel University (1880–89) and then at the University of Berlin (1889–1926). Planck solved the problem of black-body radiation by assuming that the radiation was emitted in discrete amounts called quanta, the magnitude of a quanta being the product of the frequency of the radiation and a constant, now known as *Planck's constant. For this work he received the Nobel Prize in 1918. He remained in Germany during the Nazi period and attempted to intercede with Hitler on behalf of Jewish scientists. For this he was deprived of the presidency of the research institute that bears his name.

Planck's constant (*h*) A fundamental constant that relates the quantum of energy (*E*) of a photon to the frequency (*f*) of the corresponding electromagnetic radiation by the equation $E = hf$. Its value is $6.626,196 \times 10^{-34}$ joule second. Named for Max *Planck.

Planck's radiation law Electromagnetic radiation is emitted from and absorbed by matter in discrete amounts (quanta) known as *photons. The energy (*E*) of a photon is related to the frequency (*f*) of the radiation by the equation $E = hf$, where *h* is known as *Planck's constant. Max *Planck discovered the law (1900) while investigating the distribution of wavelengths of the radiation emitted by a *black body. It forms the basis of the *quantum theory.

planet A celestial body that moves around a star and shines by light reflected from its surface. The only known planets (*see* Barnard's star) are those orbiting the sun (□solar system): there are nine major planets and numerous *asteroids. The major planets in order from the sun are *Mercury, *Venus, *Earth, and *Mars (the **terrestrial planets**), *Jupiter, *Saturn, *Uranus, and *Neptune (the **giant planets**) and, usually outermost, *Pluto.

planetarium 1. A complex instrument that projects an artificial but accurate picture of the night sky, showing planets, stars, and other celestial bodies, on the interior of a hemispherical dome. The dome forms the upper part of an auditorium. The images of the celestial bodies are produced by a considerable number of small optical projectors in the instrument. By moving the individual projectors at the correct speed, the bodies are made to follow their natural paths through the sky. 2. A building housing such an instrument. There are some 60 planetariums in the US.

planetary nebula A luminous cloud of gas cast off and expanding away from a dying star. It is a type of emission *nebula, being ionized by radiation from the hot central star.

planetary probe An unmanned spacecraft that studies conditions on and near one or more planets and their satellites and in the interplanetary medium along the flight path. The information gathered is then transmitted to earth. The transmitters, TV cameras, and other instruments are powered by solar cells or, for deep-space probes, by thermoelectric generators, etc. Midflight course corrections and attitude adjustments can be made by rocket motors. *See* Mariner; Pioneer; Venera; Viking; Voyager probes.

plane tree A large tree of the genus *Platanus* (10 species), native to the N hemisphere and often grown for shade and ornament. Up to 165 ft (50 m) tall, the trees have patchy peeling bark, large lobed leaves, and separate round clusters (catkins) of male and female flowers: the female flowers give rise to bristly round fruits. The London plane (*P.* × *acerifolia*) is a hybrid between the Oriental plane (*P. orientalis*) and North American buttonwood (*P. occidentalis*). The timber is a valuable hardwood used in carpentry. Family: *Platanaceae.*

planimeter A device for measuring small irregular plane areas. A moving arm is traced around a closed curve. The enclosed area is calculated from the revolution of a small wheel attached to the arm.

plankton Minute or microscopic animals (zooplankton) and plants (phytoplankton) that float and drift in the open waters of a sea or lake. The phytoplankton (diatoms and other algae) carry out *photosynthesis in the surface waters and so provide the basic food source for all aquatic animals. The zooplankton include protozoa, small crustaceans, and larvae (e.g. barnacle and fish larvae). Plankton are of great ecological and economic importance as a food source for fish and whales and thus—indirectly—to man, whose fishing industry depends upon them. □oceans.

plant A living organism belonging to the kingdom *Plantae,* of which there are some 400,000 or so species. Plants are typically immobile and most manufacture their own food from simple inorganic nutrients by *photosynthesis, trapping the energy required for the process in the green pigment chlorophyll. (Plants that lack chlorophyll, notably fungi, feed on organic materials.) Plant cells have rigid cell walls, providing support, and growth occurs from specialized zones of tissue (*see* meristem), continuously or periodically throughout life. Plants lack specialized sense organs and a nervous system; response to external stimuli is usually slow and often permanent. Unlike animals, there is considerable variation in form between individuals of the same species. Green plants are the primary source of food and oxygen for all animals.

Plantagenet The surname of the Angevin, Lancastrian, and Yorkist kings of England (1154–1485). They were descended from Queen Matilda and Geoffrey Martel, Count of Anjou (d. 1151), who was nicknamed Plantagenet because he wore a sprig of broom (*plante genêt*) in his cap. The name was not formally adopted until the 15th century, when it was used by Richard Plantagenet, duke of *York, to further his claim to the throne in the Wars of the Roses.

Plantagenet, Richard, Duke of York. *See* York, Richard Plantagenet, 3rd duke of.

plantain 1. An annual or perennial herb of the genus *Plantago* (about 50 species), occurring in temperate regions and on mountains in the tropics, often as a troublesome weed. Plantains have a basal rosette of simple leaves from which arise a stalk, 1.2–27.5 in (3–70 cm) high, bearing a dense terminal head of inconspicuous green, white, yellow, or brown flowers with protruding stamens. The leaves of the greater plantain (*P. major*) of Eurasia are used to treat insect stings. Family: *Plantaginaceae.* **2.** *See* banana.

Plantation of Ireland (1556–1660) The government-sponsored settlement of British families in Ireland in the 16th and 17th centuries. Conceived as a method of subjugating the rebellious Irish, the first plantations were not noticeably successful but the Ulster plantation (1608–11), composed of English and Scots, survived and prospered.

plant bug A plant-eating insect belonging to the families *Myridae* (*see* capsid) and *Lygaeidae* (*see* ground bug). The term may also refer to any other herbivorous insect of the suborder *Heteroptera* (*see* Hemiptera).

plant hopper A plant-eating insect belonging to a family (*Fulgoridae;* over 5000 species) found mainly in tropical and subtropical regions. Plant hoppers are 0.40–2 in (10–50 mm) long and often brightly colored, with large unusually shaped heads. Some species are covered with a secretion of white waxy threads or powder. Suborder: *Homoptera*; order *Hemiptera. See also* lantern fly.

plasma (anatomy) The fluid constituent of *blood, in which the blood cells are suspended. Plasma consists of a solution of various salts, sugars, etc., and contains numerous proteins, including those involved in *blood clotting and the immunological response to infection (i.e. antibodies). It is obtained by centrifuging unclotted blood. *Compare* serum.

plasma (physics) A gas the atoms of which have been completely ionized. Sometimes called the fourth state of matter, plasmas occur at enormously high temperatures, such as those in the sun. Plasmas are also created in *thermonuclear reactors.

2022

PLANT

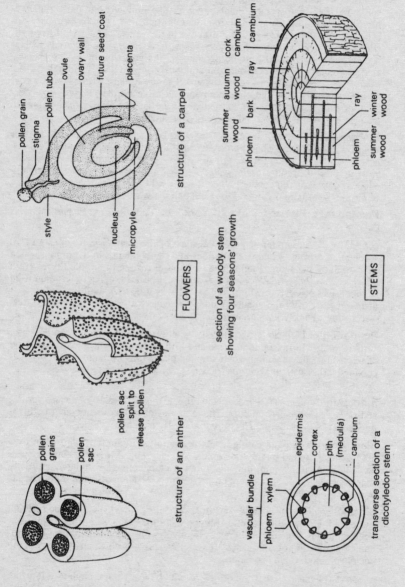

FLOWERS

pollen grains
pollen sac

structure of an anther

pollen sac split to release pollen

pollen grain
stigma
style
pollen tube
ovule
ovary wall
future seed coat
placenta
nucleus
micropyle

structure of a carpel

section of a woody stem
showing four seasons' growth

summer wood
bark
autumn wood
ray
cork
cambium
cambium
phloem
summer wood
ray
winter wood
phloem
summer wood

STEMS

vascular bundle
phloem
xylem
epidermis
cortex
pith (medulla)
cambium

transverse section of a
dicotyledon stem

PLANT

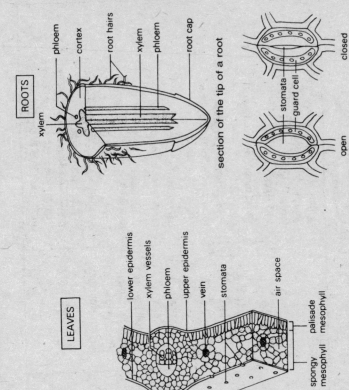

ROOTS

- phloem
- cortex
- root hairs
- xylem
- phloem
- root cap
- xylem

section of the tip of a root

- stomata
- guard cell

open   closed

LEAVES

- lower epidermis
- xylem vessels
- phloem
- upper epidermis
- vein
- stomata
- air space
- palisade mesophyll
- spongy mesophyll

transverse section of a leaf

- stamen
  - anther
  - filament
- petal
- receptacle
- carpel
- sepal
- lamina
- petiole
- vein
- midrib
- main (tap) root
- lateral root
- root hairs

broad category	major groups (usually divisions)	important classes	representative members
ALGAE	Chlorophyta Chrysophyta Phaeophyta Rhodophyta		green algae (*Spirogyra*, sea lettuce, etc.) yellow-green algae, diatoms brown algae (wracks, kelps, etc.) red algae
FUNGI	Myxomycophyta Eumycophyta	Phycomycetes Ascomycetes Basidiomycetes	slime fungi (clubroot, etc.) pin mold *Penicillium*, *Aspergillus* mushrooms, puffballs, bracket fungi
MOSSES and LIVERWORTS	Bryophyta	Hepaticae Musci	liverworts (e.g. *Pellia*) mosses (e.g. *Sphagnum*)
VASCULAR PLANTS (TRACHEOPHYTES)	Pteridophyta	Lycopsida Sphenopsida Pteropsida	clubmosses horsetails ferns
	Spermatophyta (seed plants)	Gymnospermae	cycads, *Ginkgo*, conifers (pines. larches, spruces, etc.)
		Angiospermae	monocotyledons (grasses, palms, orchids, lilies, etc.), dicotyledons (most trees and flowering plants)

PLANT *A simplified classification of the plant kingdom.*

plasmapheresis A laboratory technique used in blood transfusions in which the fluid constituent (plasma) is separated from the donor's blood and the blood cells are returned to the donor. This technique allows the donor to provide plasma more frequently than would be possible if whole blood were removed, since it is only the red cells that the body requires time to replace. Plasma transfusions are particularly useful for hemophiliacs, who require frequent transfusions, since it contains the blood-clotting factors that they lack.

Plasmodium A genus of parasitic single-celled animals (*see* Protozoa) that cause *malaria in man. *Plasmodium* undergoes the sexual phase of its development in bloodsucking mosquitoes of the genus *Anopheles,* through which it is transmitted to man. Asexual division of the parasite occurs in human liver and red blood cells. Four species cause different forms of malaria: *P. falciparum* (causing the most severe kind), *P. vivax, P. malariae,* and *P. ovale.* Class: **Sporozoa.*

Plassey, Battle of (June 23, 1757) The battle in West Bengal (India) in which Robert *Clive defeated the nawab of Bengal, Siraj-ud-Dawlah (c. 1728–57). Aided by the mutiny of the nawab's generals, Clive's victory made possible Britain's acquisition of Bengal.

plaster A paste used to give a smooth hard coating to ceilings, walls, etc. A number of formulations are in use, the traditional one being a mixture of lime, sand, and water, which hardens in air owing to drying and reaction with atmospheric carbon dioxide.

plaster of Paris A hydrated form of calcium sulfate ($CaSO_4 \cdot \frac{1}{2}H_2O$) made by partial dehydration of *gypsum by heating. When mixed with water it sets into a hard mass by formation of the dihydrate ($CaSO_4 \cdot 2H_2O$). It is used for casts for broken limbs and for modeling.

plasticity The permanent deformation of a substance after being subjected to a sufficiently large stress. Below a certain stress, called the elastic limit, most substances will recover their original shape when the stress is removed. Such substances are said to be elastic (*see* elasticity). However, single crystals of certain metals are plastic no matter how small the stress.

plastics Synthetic materials that consist of polymers (*see* polymerization) and are molded during manufacture. Plastics are made from synthetic *resins. **Thermosetting plastics** harden on heating to give a rigid product that cannot then be softened. *Polyurethanes, *polyesters, *silicones, and *epoxy resins all form thermosetting plastics. **Thermoplastic materials** soften when heated and harden again when cooled. These include derivatives of *cellulose and polymers such as *polyethylene, polystyrene, polyvinyl chloride, and polymethylmethacrylate, which contain a reactive double bond.

Natural polymers, such as *shellac and *rubber, have been known for many centuries. The first synthetic material was Celluloid, made in 1870 from cotton and camphor. This highly inflammable substance was replaced during World War I by cellulose acetate and casein products. These materials were all based on naturally occurring large molecules. The first polymers to be made by joining together smaller molecules were the phenol-formaldehyde resins (trade name Bakelite) invented in 1908 by Leo Baekeland (1863–1944). Since then a vast number of different resins have been synthesized.

plastic surgery The branch of surgery concerned with the correction of deformities, disfigurements, or other forms of damage to any part of the body. This includes the reconstruction of developmental defects, such as cleft palate, harelip, and club foot, and the repair of injuries (particularly those of the face) caused by fire, traffic accidents, or wounds. Great advances were made in this aspect of plastic surgery by Sir Archibald *McIndoe, during and after World War II. Cosmetic plastic surgery is performed simply to improve the appearance: an example is a face-lift to remove wrinkles.

Plata, Río de la (English name: Plate River) The estuary of the Paraná River and the Uruguay River, on the Atlantic coast of SE South America between Uruguay and Argentina. Its shores are densely populated; Montevideo, the capital of Uruguay, lies on the N shore and Buenos Aires, the capital of Argentina, is situated on the S shore. A naval battle was fought off its mouth in December 1939 (*see* World War II). Length: 171 mi (275 km). Width (at mouth): 140 mi (225 km).

Plataea An ancient city of Boeotia. Grateful for protection against Thebes, Plataea became Athens' permanent ally; Plataeans alone joined the Athenians at Marathon and they played a crucial role in the battle of Plataea (479 BC), where the allied Greek forces decisively defeated the Persians (*see* Greek-Persian Wars). During the Peloponnesian War Plataea suffered severely for its pro-Athenian policy, being besieged (429–427) and sacked by Sparta. Although rebuilt, it was again destroyed (by Thebes in 373) and then once more restored (by Philip of Macedon in the late 4th century BC).

Plate River. *See* Plata, Río de la.

plateau An extensive area of comparatively level elevated land, sometimes known as a tableland where it is bounded by steep slopes or scarps. It may be crossed by rivers and mountains. One of the world's highest is the Tibetan plateau.

platelet A small particle, 0.00004–0.00008 in (0.001–0.002 mm) in diameter, produced by the bone marrow and found in the ☐blood. Platelets are essential for *blood clotting, accumulating in large numbers at the site of an injured blood vessel. There are normally 150,000 to 400,000 platelets per cubic millimeter of blood. Absence of platelets causes severe bleeding and may occur in a variety of illnesses (e.g. liver disease).

platemaking The production of *printing plates. Original plates are made by hand engraving (for letterpress), drawing with wax crayons (for lithography), etc., or photographically. In one type of photographic process, metal with a photosensitive coating is exposed to light, usually through a film negative of the type, drawing, or photograph to be printed. The unexposed coating is then washed off and the bare metal underneath turned into nonprinting areas: with a letterpress plate it is etched away; with a typical lithographic plate it is wetted and made grease-repellent, while the exposed areas are inked to make them grease-receptive. A collotype plate has a photosensitive gelatin coating that is hardened, by exposure through a negative, in proportion to the amount of light falling on each area. Collotype can thus reproduce continuous tone, as in a photograph: the more any area is hardened, the less water it will absorb and the more ink it will accept and transfer to the paper. With gravure plates, the printing areas are etched away through an exposed gelatin layer. Continuous tone is simulated in letterpress and lithography by converting the image into a grid of dots of varying size called a half-tone and in gravure by varying the depth of the etched cells and thus the amount of ink that each transfers to the paper.

Duplicate (letterpress) plates are made from original plates by one of two methods. In **stereotyping**, a mold (*or* matrix) is made, in which the duplicate is cast in metal or molded from rubber or plastic. In **electrotyping**, a thin layer of copper is deposited electrolytically in a matrix similar to that used in stereotyping and then itself filled with molten metal to make it rigid when the metal cools.

plate tectonics The theory, developed mainly in the 1960s, that the earth's crust is divided into rigid plates (oceanic, continental, or a combination of both), which move about the earth's surface at rates of 0.4–3.5 in (1–9 cm) per annum. The edges of the plates are called plate margins. At constructive plate margins new oceanic crust is created where two plates are moving apart and magma rises to fill the gap; this occurs at midocean ridges (*see* sea-floor spreading). At destructive plate margins two plates collide and one dips beneath the other, producing deep-sea trenches and the associated volcanic island arcs. Where two continental plates collide, mountain chains are formed. All the major structural features of the earth's surface and almost all seismic and volcanic activity can be ascribed to plate movements.

Plath, Sylvia (1932–63) US poet and writer. After college, she married poet Ted *Hughes and moved with their family of two children to England in 1959. She committed suicide in 1963. Her writings, partly autobiographical, tell of rebellion and psychological conflict. Her poetry is collected in *The Colossus and Other Poems* (1960) and *Ariel* (posthumously; 1968); her novels include *The Bell Jar* (1962). Letters to her mother (*Letters Home*; 1975) and her journals (Pulitzer Prize; 1982) were published posthumously.

platinum (Pt) A precious silver-white noble metal, known to the South American Indians. It is malleable, ductile, and has a high melting point. Platinum is found in nature in nickel ore, as about one part in two million of ore. It can absorb large quantities of hydrogen and is used as a *catalyst, particularly in contact process for making sulfuric acid. It is also used in thermocouple wires and in jewelry. It dissolves in *aqua regia to form chloroplatinic acid (H_2PtCl_6). Although unreactive, platinum also forms other compounds, including the hexafluoride (PtF_6), one of the most powerful oxidizing agents known. At no 78; at wt 195.09; mp 3225°F (1772°C); bp 6895 ± 180°F (3827 ± 100°C).

platinum-iridium An alloy of platinum and iridium that is highly resistant to heat and is used in instruments for measuring high temperatures.

Plato (429–347 BC) Greek philosopher. An Athenian nobleman, he was early disillusioned by both democrats and aristocrats. Seeing no hope for man unless rulers became philosophers or philosophers rulers, he became a devoted follower of *Socrates. After Socrates' death he traveled widely, apparently becoming acquainted with many distinguished thinkers. In 387 he returned to Athens and founded his *Academy. To this he devoted the rest of his life, except that in 367 and again soon afterward, he visited Sicily to assist his friend, Dion, in his futile attempts to turn *Dionysius II, the young and unstable tyrant of Syracuse, into a philosopher, and Syracuse into a Platonic state. Some of Plato's poetry and all his prose works survive. Apart from 13 possibly spurious letters and the *Apology,* which purports to be Socrates' defense of himself before his judges, they are dramatic dialogues of outstanding literary merit. The early ones illustrate Socrates' character and philosophical methods, focusing especially on the question of whether virtue can be taught. The *Phaedo, Symposium,* and *Republic* of Plato's middle period develop Plato's mature views on such topics as metaphysics, love, and government, notably his theory of ideas (Forms), the perfect spiritual entities or prototypes of which the physical world is a feeble and imperfect copy. *See also* Platonism.

Platonism The philosophical tradition originating (c. 385 BC) in the Greek *Academy under *Plato. In the period of Middle Platonism (1st century BC–2nd century AD) interest centered on Plato's thought on God and the supersensible world. Subsequently the philosophers of Alexandria (*see* Plotinus) creatively systematized these and other aspects of their forerunners' work in *Neoplatonism. Works of Platonic character produced by such writers as St *Augustine of

Hippo, *Boethius, and Macrobius transmitted Platonism to the medieval West. The impact of *Aristotelianism in the 13th century brought a temporary eclipse, but at the Renaissance Platonism, promoted by such scholars as *Ficino and *Nicolas of Cusa, reasserted itself and exercised enormous influence on artists and writers, such as *Botticelli and *Spenser, as well as on philosophers and theologians (see also Cambridge Platonists). Despite modern science's final debunking of Platonic cosmology, elements of Platonism still permeate Western thought in areas as diverse as realist logic (see realism) and Christian *ethics.

Platt Amendment (1901) Legislation, part of the Army Appropriation Bill, that spelled out Cuban-American relations. Named for Connecticut Republican Sen. Orville H. Platt (1827–1905), it provided for a US naval base in Cuba, insured US intervention in Cuban affairs when deemed necessary, and prohibited Cuba from negotiating treaties with any country other than the US: It was made a part of the Cuban-American Treaty in 1903 and repealed in 1934, when a new treaty, granting full independence for Cuba, was negotiated.

Platte River A river in the central US. Formed by the confluence of the North Platte and South Platte Rivers at North Platte, Neb., it flows generally E to join the Missouri River. It is unnavigable but is a source of irrigation and hydroelectric power. Length: 310 mi (499 km).

Platyhelminthes. See flatworm.

platypus. See duck-billed platypus.

Plauen 50 30N 12 07E A city in S Germany, on the Weisse Elster River. Several old buildings remain despite damage done during World War II. Famous for lace making since the 15th century, Plauen is a center for textile manufacture and has a textile craft school. Population (1989 est): 77,500.

Plautus, Titus Maccius (c. 254–184 BC) Roman dramatist. He is traditionally believed to have worked as a craftsman in the theater before beginning, in middle age, his career as dramatist. His 21 surviving plays are all adapted from Greek *New Comedy writers, especially Menander and Philemon, and are noted for their robust humor and lively colloquial dialogue. His plays influenced the early development of comic drama by Shakespeare, Molière, and others.

player piano (or pianola) A mechanical piano in which the hammers are operated by an airflow produced by pedals or an electrically operated bellows and controlled by perforations on a rotating roll of paper. Rolls are either cut by a special machine attached to a piano and thus record an actual performance or they are produced mechanically. The player can control the volume and the speed by means of special levers.

playing cards Cards with pictures and symbols on one side, used in a wide variety of games, of which *bridge, *whist, *poker, *rummy, and *cribbage are the most popular. Modern cards derive from the *tarot pack; the 52-card French pack with suits of hearts, spades, diamonds, and clubs is now standard, the suits deriving from the tarot suits of cups, swords, money, and clubs respectively. Traditional German, Spanish, and Italian packs with variations in the number of cards and designs of the suits also derive from tarot cards. A connection has been suggested between the suits and the cup, sword, ring, and baton traditionally held by Hindu statues. Playing cards have long been used in divination and conjuring.

plebeians Romans other than the privileged *patricians. At first without civil rights, excluded from state and religious offices, and forbidden to marry patricians, in 493–92 the plebeians forced the Senate to appoint their own tribunes and an assembly. During the subsequent two centuries of conflict, the plebians gradually gained admission to all Roman offices and the wealthy and ambitious among them merged with the patricians. Thus, from later Republican times, the term plebeian implied low social class.

plebiscite A vote by the whole electorate on a particular issue. The term is usually used to refer to those *referendums held to decide to which state an area should belong. A plebiscite was first held by France in 1790–91 concerning the papal territory of Avignon.

Pléiade, La A group of seven French writers in the 16th century who sought to liberate French poetry from medieval tradition. Their principles, deriving from the study of Greek, Latin, and Italian literature, were expounded in *Défense et illustration de la langue française* (1549) by Joachim du *Bellay, and their innovations included the introduction of the sonnet, the ode, and the alexandrine. Led by Pierre de *Ronsard, the group included du Bellay, J.-A. de Baïf (1532–89), Étienne Jodelle (c. 1532–73), Rémy Belleau (c. 1528–77), Pontus de Tyard (c. 1522–1605), and Jacques Peletier (1517–82; for whom the name of Jean Dorat [1508–88] was occasionally substituted by contemporaries).

Pleiades A young open *star cluster in the constellation Taurus that contains several hundred stars, of which six are clearly visible to the naked eye. The brighter stars are surrounded by reflection *nebula. They were named for the seven daughters of *Atlas, who were changed by the gods into stars while being pursued by Orion.

Pleistocene epoch The epoch of geological time between the Pliocene and the Holocene, at the beginning of the Quaternary period. It lasted from about 1.8 million to 10,000 years ago. It is often called the *Ice Age because during this time the earth experienced great fluctuations in temperature: cold glacial periods, when the ice margins advanced toward the equator, separated by warmer interglacials, when temperatures at times were higher than today. Four main ice advances are recognized in the Pleistocene. Fossils from the Pleistocene include horses, pigs, and elephants.

Plekhanov, Georgi Valentinovich (1857–1918) Russian revolutionary and Marxist philosopher. Known as the "father of Russian Marxism," Plekhanov was instrumental in the creation (1898) of the Russian Social Democratic Workers' party. He believed that Russia must pass through industrialization and capitalism before reaching socialism and came to side with the *Mensheviks against Lenin. After the Bolshevik victory, he lived in Finland.

pleochroism The ability of certain crystals to transmit light vibrations in one plane only while absorbing those vibrations in other planes. Pleochroic crystals thus produce plane-*polarized light. If the effect occurs along only one axis of the crystal, the crystal is said to be dichroic. *Polaroid, for example, contains dichroic crystals. In trichroic crystals, the effect occurs along two axes perpendicular to each other.

plesiosaur A widely distributed marine reptile of the Jurassic and Cretaceous periods (200–65 million years ago). Up to about 39 ft (12 m) long, plesiosaurs had broad turtlelike bodies with paddlelike limbs, a long flexible neck, and jaws armed with sharp teeth used to catch fish.

Plessy v. Ferguson (1896) US Supreme Court case that upheld the "separate but equal" doctrine regarding segregation and that further defined the 14th Amendment. Plessy, of mixed race, was arrested because he refused to leave a "whites only" railroad car in Louisiana; his appeal against his conviction reached the Supreme Court, which ruled that as long as facilities were equal, segregation of races was constitutional. It also ruled that the 14th Amendment did not apply in this type of social situation and that states had the right to determine the race of a citizen.

pleurisy Inflammation of the pleura—the membrane that covers the lungs and lines the chest cavity. The commonest cause of pleurisy is bacterial or viral infection: pleurisy will often complicate *pneumonia. The patient will often have a fever, a pain in the chest that is worse on coughing or taking a deep breath, and a cough. Bacterial pleurisy is treated with antibiotics.

Pleurococcus A genus of common unicellular *green algae forming thin green powdery incrustations on the windward side of walls and tree trunks, particularly in tropical regions. The spherical cells are either solitary or form small flat aggregations; reproduction is by cell division.

Pleven 43 25N 24 40E A city in central N Bulgaria. The Russians and the Turks fought here in 1877. It has various industries and serves a mixed agricultural area. Population (1991 est): 138,323.

Plexiglas (polymethyl methacrylate) A colorless transparent thermoplastic material made by *polymerization of methyl methacrylate. It can be extruded and molded and colored, for use in light fittings, including colored signals, aircraft parts, and car parts. It is resistant to ultraviolet radiation from fluorescent lights and is widely used as an unbreakable substitute for glass.

Plimsoll line A series of lines painted on the outside of a cargo ship's hull showing the various safe levels to which the ship can be loaded. Typically, the loading levels are marked for ships loaded and unloaded, in sea and fresh water, winter and summer, and tropical or northern waters.

Pliny the Elder (Gaius Plinius Secundus; 23–79 AD) Roman scholar, whose universal encyclopedia, *Natural History,* was a major source of scientific knowledge until the 17th century. During his military career, Pliny assembled material from numerous sources on a wide range of disciplines, including astrology, geography, agriculture, medicine, precious stones, and—most notably—zoology and botany. Pliny did not discriminate fact from fiction and included much folklore and superstitition. He finally completed this work of 37 volumes in 77 AD.

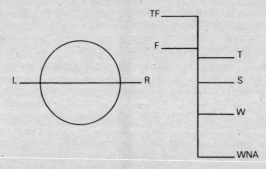

PLIMSOLL LINE *The lines and letters mark the waterline under various conditions. TF=fresh water in the tropics; F=fresh water; T=salt water in the tropics; S=salt water in the summer; W=salt water in the winter; WNA=winter in the N Atlantic. LR represents Lloyd's Register.*

Pliny the Younger (Gaius Plinius Caecilius Secundus; c. 61–c. 113 AD) Roman writer, nephew and adopted son of the encyclopedist Pliny the Elder. He held various administrative posts including that of consul in 100 AD and was a prominent legal orator. His 10 volumes of private letters constitute an intimate unofficial history of his time.

Pliocene epoch. *See* Tertiary period.

pliosaur An extinct marine reptile that evolved from the *plesiosaurs but had a shorter neck and a longer head with stronger jaws, giving it a more streamlined appearance. It was a powerful swimmer and fed on cuttlefish, squid, etc.

PLO. *See* Palestine Liberation Organization.

Plock 52 32N 19 40E A city in central Poland, on the Vistula River. Its 12th-century cathedral contains the tombs of Polish kings. Industries include oil refining. Population (1992 est): 124,500.

Ploiesti 44 57N 26 01E A city in SE Romania, at the foot of the Transylvanian Alps. It is the center for the country's oil production. Population (1992): 252,073.

Plotinus (205–70 AD) Greek philosopher and founder of *Neoplatonism. Born in Egypt, he studied at Alexandria, visited Persia (242–43), and finally settled in Rome, becoming the focus of an intellectural circle. Developing *Plato's mysticism, he taught that the immaterial impersonal indescribable "One" is the ground of all existence and value. From it emanate successively mind, soul, and nature. Mind contemplates and organizes within itself the Platonic Forms; soul thinks less coherently, thus creating time and space; nature "dreams" the chaotic material world, the source of all evil. Man partakes of all these; by rejecting material nature and cultivating the intellect he may briefly become mystically united with the One.

Plovdiv (former name: Philippopoli) 42 08N 24 45E A city in S central Bulgaria, on the Maritsa River. It is Bulgaria's second largest city and has the remains of the Roman walls. Its industries include food processing and carpet manufacture. Population (1991 est): 379,083.

plover A bird belonging to a widely distributed family (*Charadriidae;* 56 species) occurring in open regions and along shores; 6–12 in (15–30 cm) long, plovers have brown or gray plumage, often mottled, with white underparts, which become black in summer for some species. They feed on insects and other small invertebrates and nest on the ground. Order: *Charadriiformes* (gulls, plovers, etc.). *See also* lapwing.

Plowright, Joan (1929–   ) British actress. Her reputation is based on her performances in both classical and modern plays, the latter including the first productions of Osborne's *The Entertainer* (1957) and Wesker's *Roots* (1959). She married Laurence *Olivier in 1963.

plum A small tree, *Prunus domestica*—a natural hybrid between the *blackthorn and the cherry plum (*P. cerasifera*) native to SW Asia and cultivated in most Mediterranean and N temperate regions for its □fruit; 20–33 ft (6–10 m) tall, it has oval toothed leaves and clusters of attractive white flowers. The fruit is round or oval and has a dark-red to blue-black skin (when ripe), enclosing a sweet greenish-yellow pulp and a central oval stony seed. Plums are eaten fresh, cooked in desserts, canned, or dried as prunes. Family: *Rosaceae. See also* bullace; damson.

plumbago. *See* graphite.

Plumbago A genus of herbaceous plants, shrubs, and climbers (12 species), native to warm regions and including a number of ornamentals. They have simple leaves and terminal clusters of white, blue, violet, pink, or red flowers, with five petals arranged to form a narrow tube with spreading lobes. *P. auriculata,* with pale-blue flowers, and *P. rosea,* with red flowers, are popular greenhouse plants. Some species are used for medicinal purposes and some yield a juice that causes blistering. Family: *Plumbaginaceae.*

pluralism. *See* dualism.

Plutarch (c. 46–c. 120 AD) Greek biographer and essayist. He was a citizen of both Athens and Rome, a priest of Delphi, and director of a school in his native town of Chaeronea in Boeotia in central Greece. His *Parallel Lives* consists of biographies of 23 pairs of Greek and Roman statesmen and soldiers. The *Moralia* contain 83 essays on ethical, scientific, and literary topics. His works had a great influence in Europe in the 16th and 17th centuries. The English translation by Sir Thomas North of the *Lives* (1579) was the source of Shakespeare's Roman plays. The *Moralia* served as models for the essays of both Montaigne and Francis Bacon.

Pluto (astronomy) The smallest and usually outermost planet, orbiting the sun every 248 years at a mean distance of 3660 million miles (5893 million km). Its eccentric orbit has brought it inside Neptune's orbit for the period 1979–99. Pluto was discovered in 1930 but little was known about it until its satellite was discovered in 1978. It is apparently a low-density body (relative density 1.3), about 1550 mi (2500 km) in diameter. It is possible that Pluto was once a satellite of Neptune.

Pluto (mythology). *See* Hades.

plutonic rock. *See* igneous rock.

plutonium (Pu) An important synthetic transuranic element discovered in 1940. Trace quantities exist in natural uranium ores. It is produced in large quantities in nuclear reactors by beta-decay from uranium 239. Plutonium is fissile and was used in the atomic bomb dropped on Nagasaki in 1945 (*see* nuclear weapons). It is absorbed into bone marrow and is one of the most toxic substances known. It forms oxides (PuO, PuO_2), halides (for example PuF_3), and other compounds. It is used in *fast reactors and small power units for spacecraft. At no 94; at wt (244); mp 1187°F (641°C); bp 5861°F (3235°C).

Plymouth 50 23N 4 10W A port in SW England, in Devon on Plymouth Sound. The *Mayflower* embarked from here for America in 1620. Severely damaged by bombing during World War II, much of the city center has been rebuilt. Plymouth is an important naval base with associated marine industries. More recent industries include the manufacture of clothing, radio equipment, and processed foods. Population (1981): 243,895.

Plymouth 41 58N 70 40W A town in Massachusetts, on Plymouth Bay. The first European settlement in New England, it was founded by the Pilgrims from the *Mayflower* (1620). Industries include fisheries, boatyards, and tourism. Population (1990): 45,608.

Plymouth Brethren An austere Protestant sect founded at Plymouth in 1830 by a former Anglican priest, J. N. Darby (1800–82). The Brethren have strict standards of behavior and shun many secular trades and professions. They insist on the spiritual priesthood of believers and celebrate communion weekly. Small groups exist throughout the world, often as active missionaries.

Plymouth Colony A settlement of English colonists seeking religious freedom in Plymouth, Mass. Pilgrims from the *Mayflower,* destined for Virginia, landed on New England's shores in 1620 and established Plymouth Colony, also known as New Plymouth. Governed by the Mayflower Compact, the colony expanded but was merged in 1691 with Massachusetts Bay Colony and Maine.

Plymouth Patent Land title (patent) granted to the Pilgrims in *Plymouth Colony from the Council of New England in 1621. A second patent (1630) defined the colony's boundaries from SE Massachusetts to E Rhode Island.

Plymouth Rock A breed of domestic fowl developed and widely used for meat production. It has a deep compact body with large thighs. The plumage can be of various colors, including white with black bars and pure white. Weight: 9 lb (4.3 kg) (cocks); 7 lb (3.4 kg) (hens).

Plzeň (German name: Pilsen) 49 45N 13 25E A city in the Czech Republic, in W Bohemia. It has been famous for its beer (Pilsener lager) since the Middle Ages. Local coal and iron ore resources have led to the development of heavy industry, including engineering and chemicals. Population (1991): 173,129.

pneumococcus A spherical baceterium, *Streptococcus pneumoniae,* that is commonly found in the throat and causes pneumonia if it infects the lungs. Pneumococci typically exist in pairs and often form capsules, the composition of which is used to identify different strains (pneumococcal typing).

pneumoconiosis Chronic lung disease caused by inhaling dust, most commonly coal dust (causing coal workers' pneumoconiosis) and silica (causing *silicosis). Considerable coal dust may be taken into the lungs without causing much damage, but later progressive massive fibrosis may develop and the coal worker is disabled by breathlessness. Lung cancer may also complicate pneumoconiosis. There is no effective treatment and prevention is all-important. *See also* asbestosis.

pneumonia Inflammation of the lungs, most commonly caused by infection. Pneumonia may arise on only one lobe of the lung (lobar pneumonia) or in patches in both lungs (bronchopneumonia). The infective organisms may be streptococci, viruses (causing a mild disease), tubercle bacilli, or other organisms, such as mycoplasmas. The patient has a fever, cough, and pain in the chest and may be breathless. Treatment is with antibiotics and physiotherapy.

pneumothorax The presence of air in the pleural cavity, which causes the lung to collapse. This may happen for no apparent reason or it may develop in *emphysema or after a penetrating injury of the chest. The patient has pain in the chest and may be breathless. The lung will slowly expand itself or a tube may be inserted into the pleural cavity to allow the trapped air to escape.

Po River (Latin name: Padus) The longest river in Italy rising in the Cottian Alps and flowing mainly ENE through Turin to enter the Adriatic Sea by way of a large delta in the E. The Po Valley is the most fertile and economically important region in Italy. Length: 405 mi (652 km).

Pocahontas (c. 1595–1617) American Indian woman. Daughter of the Indian chief Powhatan, Pocahontas is said to have saved the life of Capt. John *Smith from her father's warriors. She married the English colonist John Rolfe (1585–1622) and was entertained as a princess at the English court; she died of smallpox on her return to America.

pochard A large-headed *duck, *Aythya ferina,* occurring in temperate inland waters of Eurasia. It is 18 in (45 cm) long and has gray legs and a gray-blue bill; males have a reddish head, black breast, and gray body; females are brown. It feeds on water plants and small aquatic invertebrates.

Po Chü-i. *See* Bo Zhu Yi.

pocket gopher A *rodent belonging to the subfamily *Geomyinae* (39 species), of North and Central America. Pocket gophers are 4–10 in (10–25 cm) in length and brownish in color. They inhabit open dry country, where they dig extensive burrows, and feed on roots, seeds, insects, and mice. Their large cheek pouches have an outside opening like a pocket.

Pocono Mountains A low mountain range in NE Pennsylvania, part of the Catskills, which are part of the Appalachian Mountains. The highest points are about 2000 ft (600 m). A popular year-round vacation area because of its forests, lakes, and recreation facilities, the Poconos are easily accessible from eastern cities.

Podgorica. *See* Titograd.

Podgorny, N(ikolai) V(iktorovich) (1903–83) Soviet statesman. Podgorny was president of the Soviet Union from 1965 to 1977, when he resigned under pressure and was replaced by Brezhnev.

Podocarpus. *See* yellowwood.

Podolsk 55 23N 37 32E A city in W central Russia 26 mi (42 km) S of Moscow. Lenin and his Bolshevik colleagues often met there before the Russian Revolution. Industries include oil refining, machinery manufacturing, and railroad engineering. Population (1991 est): 208,500.

podzol A type of *soil typical of many cool temperate humid zones especially with coniferous vegetation, as in the taiga of Russia and North America. It is characterized by an ashen-colored upper layer (A horizon) and an underlying layer (B horizon) of redeposition humus and iron, which may develop into an impermeable pan.

Poe, Edgar Allan (1809–49) US poet, short-story writer, and critic. He was brought up by foster parents after the death of his mother in 1811. He briefly attended Virginia University and West Point. After publishing two volumes of poetry (1827, 1829), he began to contribute to and work for literary magazines. Among his many prose tales and horror stories are "The Fall of the House of Usher" (1839), "The Purloined Letter" (1842), "The Black Cat" (1843), "The Cask of Amontillado" (1846), and the first detective story ever written, "The Murders in the Rue Morgue" (1841). His best-known poems are "The Raven" (1845), and "The Bells" (1849) and his most influential critical work is "The Philosophy of Composition" (1846).

poet laureate A title bestowed by the British monarch on a contemporary poet, whose traditional duties include the writing of commemorative odes on important public occasions. The first official poet laureate was John Dryden, who served from 1668 to 1688. The US has had a poet laureate since 1986.

poetry A form of literature distinguished from prose by the deliberate employment of *meter, rhythm, *rhyme, sound, and figurative language. Poetry probably originated as a form of language distinct from ordinary speech in religious ritual and is an earlier development than prose. The earliest poetic landmarks in Western literature are Homer's *Odyssey* and *Iliad,* which developed out of a primitive oral tradition and became models for the epic poems of Virgil and numerous later poets. Poetry was associated with drama from its appearance in the dramatic choruses of ancient Greece until the 19th century; verse drama was revived by T. S. Eliot in the 20th century. The early forms of lyric poetry derived from the dithyrambic poetry of religious ritual; they are characterized by the repetition of songlike elements arranged in stanzas. The sonnet, one of the most popular of all poetic forms, evolved in Renaissance Italy. Narrative poetry, like the epic, derived from oral tradition; the ballad combines lyrical and narrative qualities. A tradition of didactic verse, stretching from Hesiod to Cowper, employed rhyme or meter as an aid to the expression of ideas. Poetry has been used as a medium for satire (Pope), religious and philosophical statement (Lucretius and Wordsworth), and even for scientific classification (Erasmus Darwin). While the poetry of ancient Greece and Rome depended on the variation of fixed metrical patterns, the early poetry of N Europe was characterized by alliteration. Blank verse was evolved by the Earl of Surrey and became the main medium for drama in the works of Shakespeare and his contemporaries and in much subsequent serious poetry. In the 19th and 20th centuries some poets adopted free verse, to avoid the constraints of regularity in meter or rhyme.

EDGAR ALLAN POE *Writer whose poems, especially "The Raven," and short stories are internationally acclaimed.*

Poggio Bracciolini, Giovanni Francesco (1380–1459) Italian humanist. A pupil of Manuel *Chrysoloras, Poggio recovered the manuscripts of Lucretius, Quintilian, Silius, and other classical writers. His books include a *History of Florence* and the *Liber Facetiarum,* a collection of humorous tales.

Pogonophora. *See* beardworm.

pogrom (Russian: devastation) An attack on Jews and Jewish property, especially in the Russian Empire. Russian pogroms, which were condoned by the government, were particularly common in the years immediately after the assassination of Alexander II in 1881 and again from 1903 to 1906, though mob persecution of Jews continued until the Russian Revolution (1917).

Po Hai. *See* Chihli, Gulf of.

poikilothermy The condition of being cold-blooded. Invertebrate animals, fishes, amphibians, and reptiles have no physiological mechanism for the control of their body temperature, which therefore fluctuates with that of the environment. They are therefore restricted to environments with a suitable temperature range. *Compare* homoiothermy.

Poincaré, Jules Henri (1854–1912) French mathematician; cousin of Raymond *Poincaré. He is regarded by some as the last universal mathematician because he made important contributions to all fields of mathematics as well as to physics and astronomy. A gifted writer, Poincaré in later life wrote important treatises on the nature of mathematical creativity, emphasizing its intuitional aspects.

Poincaré, Raymond (1860–1934) French statesman; president (1913–20) and prime minister (1912–13, 1922–24; 1926–29). His foreign policy aimed to prevent French isolation in the face of possible German aggression and when, after World War I, Germany delayed in the payment of reparations he ordered French troops to occupy the Ruhr. His postwar economic policy brought a period of stability to France.

poinciana A tropical shrub or small tree of the genera *Caesalpinia* or *Delonix* (both formerly called *Poinciana*), often grown for ornament. Up to 50 ft (15 m) tall, they have large feathery compound leaves and clusters of showy orange or scarlet flowers. Popular species include the Barbados pride (*C. pulcherrima*) and the *flamboyant tree (*or* royal poinciana). Family: *Leguminosae.*

poinsettia An ornamental shrub, *Euphorbia pulcherrima,* native to Mexico and tropical America and a popular pot plant at Christmas in Europe and North America. Growing 2–10 ft (0.6–3 m) tall, it has simple dark-green leaves and clusters of tiny greenish-yellow flowers surrounded by large scarlet bracts, up to 5.5 in (14 cm) long, which resemble petals. Family: *Euphorbiaceae.*

point 1. A unit of weight for precious stones, especially diamonds, equal to two milligrams. **2.** A unit of type size.

Pointe-à Pitre 16 14N 61 32W The chief town and port of Guadeloupe. It possesses a good harbor and is the chief commercial center for the island. Population (1990): 26,083.

Pointe-Noire 4 46S 11 53E A port in the People's Republic of Congo, on the Atlantic coast. Its port was completed in 1939 and has a considerable entrepôt trade. Population (1992 est): 576,206.

pointer A breed of sporting □dog originating in England and named for its habit of pointing its nose toward game. It is lithely built with a long tapering tail, a long slightly concave muzzle, and drooping ears. The short smooth coat is white combined with yellow, orange, liver, or black. Height: 25–27 in (63–68 cm) (dogs); 24–26 in (61–66 cm) (bitches).

Point Four Program (1950) US program of foreign aid. Named for the fourth point in Pres. Harry S. Truman's inaugural address (1949), the program helped developing nations by sending experts, equipment, and funds to modernize industry and agriculture. By 1953 it became a part of the general US foreign aid program.

pointillism A style of painting using dots of pure color. The pointillists applied primary colors to the canvas in dots and allowed the colors to be mixed by the eye, thus achieving an intense luminosity. Also called divisionism and neoimpressionism, it was developed by *Seurat in France in the 1880s and carried into the 20th century by his disciple *Signac.

poise A unit of viscosity in the *c.g.s. system equal to the tangential force per unit area, in dynes per square centimeter, required to maintain unit difference in velocity, in centimeters per second, between two parallel planes in a fluid one centimeter apart.

poison ivy An extremely poisonous woody vine or shrub, *Rhus toxicodendron* (or *Toxicodendron radicans*), native to North America. It has compound leaves with three broad leaflets and clusters of small round whitish-green flowers, which give rise to whitish berries. All parts contain a poison that causes severe skin inflammation on contact. Family: *Anacardiaceae*.

poisons Substances that injure health or cause death when introduced into the body. The term is often restricted to those substances that are fatal in small doses (e.g. strychnine, cyanide) but can also be applied to those that are harmful when small doses are taken over long periods (cumulative poisons, e.g. lead) and to otherwise safe drugs taken in large doses. Poisons may be classified in various ways, one of which is according to use: i.e. agricultural (pesticides, herbicides, etc.); industrial (poisonous elements and gases, etc.); medicinal (dangerous drugs, e.g. opiates); and natural (bacterial toxins, poisonous plants, animal venoms, etc.). Another way is to group them according to activity: corrosives (acids, alkalis, etc.); blood poisons (e.g. carbon monoxide, warfarin); nerve poisons (e.g. strychnine, cocaine); poisons that interfere with cell function (e.g. cytotoxic drugs, nitrogen mustard, methotrexate); etc.

Toxicology is the study of poisons, which deals with their chemical nature and origin, the pathological changes they induce, their recognition in a poisoned patient, and the determination of specific antidotes.

Poisson, Siméon Dénis (1781–1840) French mathematician, who became professor at the École Polytechnique in 1806. He made important contributions to the mathematical theory of electricity, magnetism, and mechanics. His work on electricity led him in 1837 to discover Poisson's equation, which describes the electric field created by an arbitrary charge density. Poisson's distribution is widely used in probability calculations and **Poisson's ratio** (the ratio of the lateral strain to the longitudinal strain in a stretched wire) is used by engineers in studying the elongation of structural members.

Poitiers (Latin name: Limonum) 46 35N 0 20E A town in W central France, the capital of the Vienne department. The former capital of Poitou, it dates back to Roman times and was the site of a battle (1356) in which the English under the Black Prince defeated the French under John the Good. Notable buildings include the 4th-century baptistry of St John, the cathedral (11th–12th centuries), and the university (1432). Metallurgy, textiles, and brewing are the chief industries. Population (1982): 82,885.

poker A card game, usually for five to seven players, using a single deck of cards. There are many variants but in the standard game of draw poker each player receives five cards, with an option to discard up to three of them and receive replacements. The objective is to make the best hand or to bluff one's opponents into believing one has the best hand. The best hand is (in ascending order) the one containing the highest card; highest pair of cards of the same denomination (irrespective of suit); two pairs; three cards of the same denomination; a straight (a sequence of denominations irrespective of suit); a flush (all of the same suit, irrespective of denomination); a full house (a pair and three of the same denomination); four cards of the same denomination; or a straight flush. Each player makes bets on his hand before and after discarding and the betting continues until the limit (if there is one) is reached or until no one wishes to bet further. Although poker is a game of chance there is an element of skill in the opportunity it provides for bluffing one's opponents into thinking one has the best hand.

Pola. *See* Pula.

Poland, People's Republic of A country in N Europe, on the Baltic Sea. Extensive plains in the N rise to the Carpathian Mountains in the S, which reach heights of over 8000 ft (2500 m). Following the reorganization of the population after World War II, when Poles were transferred from the area ceded to the Soviet Union to that gained from Germany, forcing out the Germans, the majority of the inhabitants are now Polish. Approximately 70% are Roman Catholic. *Economy*: since World War II there has been a significant shift in the balance of the economy from agriculture to industry, but Poland remains one of the world's leading agricultural nations. Until 1989, much of the land was organized into collectives and state farms. The chief crops are rye, wheat, oats, sugar beets, and potatoes. Its mineral wealth includes rich deposits of copper and sulfur; natural gas has been found, as well as some oil. Poland is among the world's leading exporters of ships. Other important industries include textiles, engineering, steel, cement, chemicals, and food products. Tourism is an important source of revenue. *History*: Poland first appeared as a separate state in the 10th century, which also saw the introduction of Christianity. From the 14th to 16th centuries its power was extended under the *Jagiellon dynasty, which was succeeded by elected kings. Poland declined in the 17th century, although it was able, under John III Sobieski, to defeat the Turks in 1683. Foreign intervention in the 18th century culminated in partition by Russia, Austria, and Prussia (in 1772, 1793, and 1795), and at the Congress of Vienna in 1815 the *Congress Kingdom of Poland was created under the Russian crown. After the defeat of the Central Powers in World War I, independence was declared under Józef Piłsudski. In 1939 Poland was invaded by Germany, the *casus belli* of World War II, and then by the Soviet Union, being partitioned between them. Some six million Poles, including three million Jews, died during the occupation. Polish resistance to Germany, both within Poland and abroad, directed by Sikorski's government in exile, contributed to the Allied victory, and in 1945 Poland was liberated by the Russians. The *Oder-Neisse line became its W frontier. The first postwar elections, in 1948, brought a communist-controlled government to power under *Gomułka. He was demoted in 1948 for asserting independence from the Soviet Union but returned to power after the *Poznań Riots. Further unrest in 1970 led to his enforced resignation and he was succeeded by Edward *Gierek. Gierek was dismissed in 1980 and succeeded by Stanisław Kania. The political and economic situation in Poland worsened and Kania resigned (1981) to be replaced by Gen. Wojciech Jaruzelski. In December 1981, the independent labor union Solidarity, led by Lech Walesa, was accused of attempting to overthrow the government, its leaders were detained, and a state of martial law was declared under a military council led by Jaruzelski. Martial law was lifted in 1983, and political prisoners were released, but unrest continued, sometimes expressed through the church's resistance to Communist control of religious and educational matters. Solidarity was legalized in 1989, and a more democratic legislature and presidency were established. Unable to put together a government, the Communists gave way to Solidarity leaders, and in 1990 elections Walesa became president. Amid the reforms sweeping Eastern Europe, he took control of the stormy transition to a multiparty democracy and a free market economy. Official language: Polish. Official currency: złoty of 100 groszy. Area: 120,624 sq mi (312,677 sq km). Population (1990 est): 38,363,000. Capital: Warsaw. Main port: Gdańsk.

Polanski, Roman (1933–) Polish film director, born in Paris. After his first full-length film, *Knife in the Water* (1961), he worked in Britain and the

US. His later films include *Repulsion* (1965), *Cul de Sac* (1966), *Rosemary's Baby* (1968), *The Tenant* (1976), *Pirates* (1986), *Metamorphosis* (1988), and *Frantic* (1988), in all of which he skillfully created an atmosphere of tension and menace.

polar bear A white bear, *Thalarctos maritimus,* living on the shores of the Arctic Ocean. Up to 8 ft (2.5 m) long and weighing 1100–1550 lb (500–700 kg) (depending on the season), polar bears prey mainly on seals, also taking some fish and birds. Males move southward in winter but females sleep in dens prior to the birth of their young in early December. ▢mammal.

Polaris (*or* North Star) A remote cream supergiant, apparent magnitude 2.0 and about 650 light years distant, that is the brightest star in the constellation Ursa Minor. It is the present *pole star, lying about 1° from the N celestial pole; its position is found using the Pointers in the Plow. It is a *Cepheid variable and is the primary component of a *multiple star.

Polaris missile A US navy two-stage solid-fueled nuclear strategic missile launched from a submarine and having a range of 2800 miles (4500 km). Traveling at speeds of over mach 10, some versions (Poseidon) are capable of delivering 10 separately guided 15-*kiloton warheads. When fired from below the surface, the missile is ejected from the vessel by compressed gas, its rocket firing at the surface. Its inertial guidance system is programmed to the launching vessel's exact position. Firing is by two-key control, linked directly to Washington.

polarized light Light in which the direction of vibration is restricted. In ordinary light (and other types of *electromagnetic radiation) the transverse vibrations of the electric and magnetic fields are at right angles to each other in all possible planes. In **plane-polarized light** the vibrations of the electric field are confined to one plane and the magnetic field to one at right angles to it. Plane-polarized light can be produced by reflection at a certain angle (*see* Brewster's law) or by passing light through such doubly refracting substances as *Polaroid. **Circularly** and **elliptically polarized light** occur when the electric vector describes a circle or an ellipse around the direction of the light beam.

Polaroid A trade name for a plastic sheet impregnated with many tiny crystals of a dichroic substance (*see* pleochroism) oriented parallel to each other. The crystals only transmit light vibrating in one plane and absorb all other light. Polaroid is used for reducing glare in sunglasses, camera filters, etc., by removing stray beams of plane-polarized light.

polder An area of low-lying land reclaimed from the sea or other water, often for agricultural purposes. Polders are usually formed by constructing dikes around the area, which is then drained. Land lying below low-tide mark must be pumped clear of water, while that above may be drained by means of tide gates, which close as the tide rises. The most notable polders are those of Holland, next to the IJsselmeer.

Pole, Reginald, Cardinal (1500–58) English Roman Catholic churchman; archbishop of Canterbury. He opposed Henry VIII's divorce and in 1532 went to Italy. There he wrote *Pro ecclesiasticae unitatis defensione* (1536), an attack on Henry's claims of supremacy over the English Church. He was a leading advocate of reform within the Roman Catholic Church and presided at the Council of *Trent. Returning to England on Mary's accession, he became archbishop of Canterbury in 1556.

polecat A carnivorous mammal, *Mustela putorius,* found in woods and grassland throughout Europe, Asia, and N Africa. About 20 in (50 cm) long, it has a dark-brown coat with yellowish patches on the face and ears. Polecats are nocturnal, foraging for rodents and insects. They eject a pungent fluid when alarmed and were once called "foul martens." Family: *Mustelidae* (weasels, etc.). *See also* ferret, skunk.

Poles, North and South The most northerly and southerly points of the earth's surface and the ends of the earth's axis, about which it rotates. The magnetic north and south poles are the points to which a magnetic compass needle points and where the lines of force of the earth's magnetic field are vertical. They do not coincide with the geographical poles and their positions slowly change. *See also* Arctic Circle; Antarctica.

pole star Either of two bright stars that are nearest the N or S celestial pole. The poles are not fixed in position but, owing to *precession of the earth's axis, trace out two circles in the sky over a period of 25,800 years. There is thus a sequence of stars that slowly, in turn, become the N or S pole star. *See also* Polaris.

pole vault A field event for men in athletics, in which competitors use a fiberglass pole to lever themselves over a horizontal bar. A competitor is allowed three tries at each height and is eliminated if he fails to clear it. The height is increased until only one competitor is left.

Polignac, Auguste Jules Armand Marie, Prince de (1780–1847) French statesman. As chief minister to Charles X (1829–30) he supported the absolute authority assumed by the king, thus helping to bring about the *July Revolution. Arrested and imprisoned until 1836, he was then exiled until 1845.

poliomyelitis A viral infection of the central nervous system that may result in muscle paralysis. It was formerly known as infantile paralysis, because children were most commonly affected. In most cases the infection is mild, with only a nonspecific fever, but sometimes a more severe illness develops three to seven days later, which may lead to severe pain in the limbs followed by permanent paralysis. There is no specific treatment, but an Australian nurse, Elizabeth Kenny (1886–1952), developed the practice of actively exercising affected limbs rather than immobilizing them. Polio is now uncommon in developed countries and a vaccine is available that gives complete protection (*see* Sabin vaccine; Salk vaccine).

Polish (*or* Lekhitic) A West Slavonic language spoken in Poland and closely related to *Czech, *Slovak, and Sorbian. It is written in a Latin alphabet and the standard form is based on the dialect of Poznań.

Polish Corridor A belt of land that separated E Prussia from the rest of Germany and was granted to Poland in the Treaty of Versailles (1919). It allowed Poland access to the sea of Danzig (now Gdańsk). It was annexed by Germany in 1939 and returned to Poland in 1945, after World War II.

Polish Succession, War of the (1733–35) A European war precipitated by the election of rival claimants to the Polish throne in succession to Augustus the Strong: *Stanisław I Lesczyński, supported by France, Spain, and subsequently Sardinia, and Augustus' son, Frederick Augustus III (1696–1763), supported by Russia and Austria. After the fall of Danzig to the Russians (1734) Stanisław fled and the subsequent Treaty of Vienna (1735) recognized Frederick Augustus as king.

Poliziano (*or* Politian; 1454–94) Italian poet and scholar, born Angelo Ambrogini. He gained the patronage of Lorenzo de' *Medici and later of Cardinal Francesco Gonzago in Mantua. His major work is *Stanze per la giostra* (1475–78), an unfinished poem expressing humanist ideals in classical style. His other works include *Orfeo* (1480), a dramatic court entertainment, as well as many translations and Latin poems.

Polk, James Knox (1795–1849) US statesman; 11th president of the United States (1845–49). Beginning his political career as a member of the Tennessee legislature, Polk was later elected to the US House of Representatives, where he became one of the national leaders of the Democratic party and speaker of the House (1835–39). After serving a single term as governor of Tennessee (1839–41), he received the Democratic presidential nomination in 1844. Polk defeated Henry *Clay in the general election and began his term of office with four distinct aims, all of which he achieved. He established an independent federal treasury; lowered tariffs; resolved the Oregon boundary dispute with Great Britain, placing its border at the 49th parallel; and significantly expanded American territorial possessions in the Far West. As a result of the US victory in the *Mexican War, Texas, New Mexico, and California became part of the US. Because of poor health, Polk chose not to seek reelection in 1848.

Polk, Leonidas Lafayette (1806–64) US churchman and Confederate general. A bishop in the Episcopal Church, he served in the SW and in Louisiana and was responsible for the establishment of the University of the South (1860) at Sewanee, Tenn. He had graduated from West Point (1827) and resigned his commission shortly after graduation. He accepted a commission in the Confederate Army during the Civil War, defeated Gen. Ulysses S. Grant at Belmont, Mo., and saw action at *Shiloh, Murfreesboro, and *Chickamauga before dying of wounds at Pine Mountain (1864).

polka A Bohemian folk dance in $\frac{2}{4}$ time, which became a ballroom dance in 19th-century Europe and rivaled the *waltz in popularity. It is characterized by three steps and a hop.

pollack A popular game fish, *Pollachius* (or *Gadus*) *pollachius,* related to cod, with a protruding lower jaw and no chin barbel. Its elongated body, usually up to 40 in (1 m) long, is brown or olive, sometimes with yellow or orange markings above, and paler below. It occurs in European coastal waters down to 650 ft (200 m).

Pollaiuolo, Antonio (c. 1432–98) Florentine Renaissance artist. He and his brother **Piero Pollaiuolo** (c. 1441–96) trained as goldsmiths and often collaborated on paintings and sculptures. Antonio is famous for his bronze sculptures, the painting of the *Martyrdom of St Sebastian* (National Gallery, London), and the influential engraving *Battle of the Nudes* (Uffizi), which is remarkable for its depiction of movement. He was reputedly the first artist to make anatomical dissections. Piero painted a series of *Virtues* (Uffizi) and *The Coronation of the Virgin* (Duomo, Florence).

pollen The male gametes of seed plants, which are produced in the *stamens of flowering plants and in the male *cones of conifers and other gymnosperms. To ensure fertilization, the pollen must be transferred to the stigma (in flowering plants) or the female cone (in conifers)—the process of **pollination**. Many flowers are cross-pollinated, i.e. the pollen from one plant is deposited on the stigma of another of the same species by means of animal carriers (usually insects), wind, or water. Some flowers are self-pollinated, the pollen being transferred from the anthers to the stigma of the same plant: the stamens are usually bent over the stigma to assist the process. After pollination, a pollen tube grows down from the pollen grain into the pistil of the pollinated flower until it reaches the ovule. Two pollen nuclei travel down this tube: one fertilizes the egg cell, which develops into the embryo plant in the seed; the other fuses with a nucleus in the ovule to become a food source for the seed.

pollen analysis. *See* palynology.

Pollock, Jackson (1912–56) US painter. He trained in New York under Thomas Hart *Benton but early in his career he was influenced by *Orozco and *surrealism. By 1947 he had developed an abstract style (*see* action painting) by which he attempted to express feelings and unconscious thoughts through the act of painting itself. He poured and dripped commercial and metallic paints onto very large canvases to form patterns of interweaving lines. Shortly before his early death in a car crash, he abandoned the use of color, painting only in black and white.

poll tax A levy on every individual (*poll,* head), regardless of means. First levied regularly in England in 1377, it was a direct cause of the *Peasants' Revolt in 1381 and was abolished in 1698. Originally preferred in the US to property-based taxes, the poll tax as a voting qualification was abused as a means of disenfranchising African Americans and was constitutionally banned.

pollution The addition to the environmnet of substances that cannot be rendered harmless by normal biological processes. Modern industrial and agricultural activities have led to the pollution of land, rivers, seas, and the atmosphere by either man-made toxic substances (such as pesticides and fertilizers) or by the overproduction of naturally occurring substances (such as carbon dioxide gas). Pesticides, such as *DDT, can build up in the environment and in the bodies of living organisms until they reach toxic levels. Other forms of pollution may have long-term effects on the health of living things, including man. Current problems include the disposal of radioactive wastes; increasing amounts of heavy metals (such as lead) in the atmosphere; atmospheric pollution by carbon dioxide, carbon monoxide, etc.; the disposal of human refuse and sewage; and unacceptable noise levels. In many cases a technical solution to these problems is available but cannot be implemented because the cost is too high or because of conflict with minority interests. *See also* conservation.

Pollux An orange giant, apparent magnitude 1.15 and 35 light years distant, that is the brightest star in the constellation Gemini.

polo A four-a-side stick-and-ball game in which the players are mounted on ponies (*see* polo pony). It was played in Persia by 600 BC and spread E but had almost died out when it was rediscovered by British officers in India in the 19th century. The riders use long sticks with mallet heads to hit a solid wooden ball, with the object of scoring goals. Several balls are worn out in a game. A game consists of up to eight seven-minute periods, or "chukkas," after each of which mounts are changed. After every goal the teams change ends. It is presided over by two mounted umpires and a referee. Since World War II Argentina has become the leading polo-playing nation but the game has long had an enthusiastic following in the US.

Polo, Marco (c. 1254–1324) Venetian traveler. His father Niccolò Polo and uncle Maffeo Polo undertook a trading expedition to Peking (1260–69) and in 1271 they returned at the request of the Mongol emperor, Kublai Khan, taking Marco with them. Having learned Mongolian, he entered Kublai's service, conducting missions as far as S India, until leaving China in 1292. He subsequently fought for the Venetians against the Genoese and was captured. In prison (1296–98) he dictated an account of his travels, which remained almost the only source of information about the Far East until the 19th century.

polonaise A Polish dance in triple time, with characteristic rhythmic stresses and cadences. Originally a processional folk dance, it evolved into a courtly dance in 18th century Europe; it also became a purely instrumental form, as in Chopin's polonaises for the piano.

polonium (Po) A highly radioactive element discovered in 1898 by Marie Curie in minute amounts in pitchblende. It is 5000 times as radioactive as *radium and liberates considerable amounts of heat. Polonium has 27 isotopes, more than any other element. It is used in compact radiation and thermoelectric power sources. At no 84; at wt (209); mp 490°F (254°C); bp 1765°F (962°C).

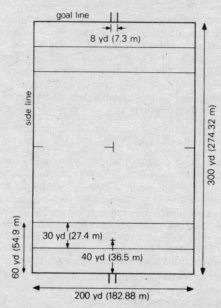

POLO *The dimensions of the field. If the sidelines are boarded, the width is 160 yd (146.4 m) and there is a safety area extending 10 yd (9 m) beyond each sideline and 30 yd (27 m) beyond each goal line.*

polo pony A pony bred and selected as a mount for polo. Polo demands speed, agility, stamina, and courage and the ponies ideally have a strong back, broad deep chest, powerful shoulders and hindquarters, a long flexible neck, and hard legs and feet. Some of the best polo ponies come from Argentina, where they have been specially developed since about 1900. Height: 14½–16 hands (1.47–1.63 m).

Poltava 49 35N 34 35E A city in E Ukraine. The center of a fertile agricultural region, it has food-processing industries as well as factories producing machinery, building materials, and consumer goods. *History*: it is one of the oldest Ukrainian towns (dating to the 8th century) and was a Cossack center in the 17th century. Peter the Great defeated Charles XII of Sweden there (1709) during the Great *Northern War. Population (1991 est): 320,000.

poltergeist A noisy, mischievous, and frequently destructive invisible agent that persecutes the occupants of a house, most commonly by throwing or moving objects.

polyanthus A hardy perennial, *Primula × polyanthus,* derived from a cross between the common primrose and the cowslip. There are many varieties, with yellow, brown, blue, or red flowers, grown as garden ornamentals. *See also* Primula.

Polybius (c. 200–c. 120 BC) Greek historian. While he was a political hostage in Rome from 168 to 150 BC he became a friend of the general and literary patron Scipio Aemilianus. His major work was a history of Rome from 220 to 145 BC in 40 books, of which only the first 5 survive intact.

Polycarp, St (c. 69–c. 155) Greek martyr and bishop of Smyrna. He was reputedly converted to Christianity and made a bishop by St John the Apostle. His fame rests on his *Epistle to the Philippians*, explaining St Paul's teachings and defending Christianity against the leading heresies of his age. The *Martyrdom of Polycarp* is an anonymous letter describing his death and is the earliest of its kind. Feast day: Jan 26.

Polyclitus (5th century BC) Greek sculptor, born at *Argos. A very popular and much copied artist, he was primarily a sculptor of athletes in relaxed poses, combining naturalism with beauty of proportion. His works, as known from later copies, seem less majestic and more individual than those of his contemporary *Phidias.

Polycrates (died c. 522) Tyrant of Samos, whose naval campaigns made Samos an important power in the eastern Mediterranean. Deceived into believing he was joining a revolt against the Persians, Polycrates was captured and crucified by the Persian governor of Lydia, Oroetes.

polycythemia An excessive accumulation of red cells in the blood. This may occur in response to a chronic shortage of oxygen (e.g. in people living at high altitudes) or for no obvious reason (polycythemia vera). The blood becomes much thicker and both *thrombosis and hemorrhage are more common in affected people. Treatment is often with radioactive phosphorus.

polyesters Synthetic resins or *plastics that are polymers of *esters. Saturated polyesters (those with no double bonds), made by a condensation reaction, are widely used in such synthetic fibers as Dacron. Unsaturated polyesters are used as resins to make thermosetting plastics.

polyethylene (polythene) A white translucent thermoplastic material made by *polymerization of *ethylene. **Low-density polyethylene** is made at high pressure and is a soft material used for flexible pipes, sheets, and bags. **High-density polyethylene** is made at lower pressures, is more rigid, and softens at a higher temperature. It is used for molded articles.

polygamy. *See* marriage.

polygon A plane straight-sided geometrical figure with three or more sides; for example a pentagon, which has five sides. A regular polygon has all sides equal and all interior angles equal.

Polygonum A genus of annual or perennial herbs (about 75 species), found worldwide, especially in temperate regions. Ranging usually from 4–80 in (10–200 cm) in height, they bear simple leaves and small five-lobed white or pink flowers, clustered into dense terminal heads or loose branching clusters. Species include the *knotgrass, *bistort, and persicaria (*P. persicaria*)—a creeping weed. Several others are grown in rock gardens and borders. Family: *Polygonaceae*.

polygraph An instrument designed to detect whether a person is lying by measuring such factors as blood pressure, respiration rate, skin conductivity, and pulse rate. A sudden change in these factors in a person being questioned is taken to indicate that he is under stress and may be telling a lie. Lie detectors are not usually accepted in a court of law.

polyhedron A solid bounded by plane *polygons called the faces. Two faces intersect at an edge and three or more at a vertex. In a regular polyhedron all the faces are equal regular polygons. The five regular polyhedrons, called the Platonic solids, are the regular tetrahedron, hexahedron, octahedron, dodecahedron, and icosahedron with 4, 6, 8, 12, and 20 sides respectively.

polymerization The chemical combination of simpler molecules (monomers) to form long chain molecules (**polymers**) of repeating units. In **addition polymerization**, the monomers simply add together and no other compound is formed. Polyethylene is made from ethylene in this way. In **condensation polymerization**, water, alcohol, or some other small molecule is formed in the reaction, as in the production of *nylon.

polymorphism In biology, the functional or structural variation between two or more members of a species, determined by differences in either genetic constitution, environmental conditions, or both. It is a widespread phenomenon in animals and plants. In **transient polymorphism** two different forms exist together temporarily, while one form is replacing the other. This occurs in industrial melanism in moths: with industrial pollution of the environment, the black variety has an advantage over the normal pale form and eventually replaces it. In **balanced polymorphism** the different forms continue to coexist, as in the *castes in social insects.

Polyneices In Greek legend, a son of Oedipus. Having succeeded to the Theban throne, Polyneices and his brother Eteocles agreed to rule the city in alternate years. At the end of his term Eteocles refused to yield to Polyneices, who then laid siege to the city (*see* Seven Against Thebes). Eteocles and Polyneices killed each other in the war, fulfilling Oedipus' curse on his sons. *See also* Antigone.

Polynesia A division of Oceania in the S and central Pacific Ocean. The volcanic and coral islands include those of French Polynesia, Hawaii, Samoa, Tonga, Tuvalu, Kiribati, and the Line and Cook Islands. *See also* Melanesia; Micronesia.

Polynesian The people of the Pacific islands contained within the roughly triangular area between and including Hawaii, New Zealand, and Easter Island. They are seafarers, with considerable skill in navigation. Fishing and cultivating are also important. There is considerable uniformity in culture throughout this huge area but social organization varies greatly. Kinship is important everywhere. The degree of political centralization and hierarchy varies between the smaller and larger islands. The Polynesian languages belong to the Oceanic branch of the *Austronesian family and include Samoan, *Maori, Tongan, Tahitian, and Hawaiian.

polyp (biology) A sedentary form that occurs during the life cycle of many animals of the phylum *Coelenterata*. It has a cylindrical stalklike body attached at the base, with the mouth at the free end surrounded by tentacles bearing stinging cells (nematocysts). Polyps occur singly or in colonies; colonial polyps are modified for different functions, such as feeding, reproduction, and protection. Polyps reproduce asexually to form new polyps or *medusae or sexually to form polyps.

polyp (medicine) A growth that has a narrow base or stalk. Polyps may occur in the bowel, the nose, the womb, the larynx, and other sites. They often cause obstruction or infection and some forms may become cancerous: for this reason they are best removed by surgery or cauterization.

polypeptide. *See* peptide.

Polyphemus In Greek mythology, a one-eyed giant, one of the *Cyclops. He lived in Sicily and was an unrequited lover of the nymph *Galatea. Odysseus and his companions escaped from imprisonment in his cave by making him drunk and then blinding him.

polyphony (Greek: many voices) Music that consists of a horizontal combination of melodic strands rather than a series of vertical chords. In its earliest form (9th to 11th centuries) it consisted of voices moving in parallel fourths, fifths, and octaves, called *organum, a development of *plainchant. The true polyphonic period began when the voices became independent, moving in contrary motion and having different note values. The high point of the polyphonic style was reached in the 16th century with *Palestrina's church music, the Italian *madrigal, the compositions of the English madrigalists, and the church music of Tallis and Byrd. The music of later polyphonic composers completed the transition from modal polyphony to the system of major and minor keys and stands at the threshold of the harmonic period. *See* counterpoint; harmony; modes.

polyploidy A condition in which the number of sets of chromosomes in a cell is greater than normal. Most organisms have two representatives of each chromosome in their body cells—the diploid state. With three of each the cell is triploid, with four—tetraploid, five—pentaploid, and so on. Polyploidy may arise naturally, for example when a sterile hybrid doubles its chromosome number. This results in a fertile organism and is thought to be the means by which many species of plants arose, including wheat. Polyploid plants often show improved size and vigor, and the condition has been induced in crop plants by treating them with chemicals.

polypody A *fern of the genus *Polypodium,* especially *P. vulgare,* which grows on walls, rocks, and trees in temperate regions. It has a creeping slender scaly rhizome with numerous roots, and the tapering branched fronds, 2–30 in (5–75 cm) long, are made up of paired leaflets. The spore capsules are grouped in rounded yellow or orange clusters (sori) and usually occur in two rows on the undersides of the upper leaflets. Family: *Polypodiaceae.*

polypropylene A thermoplastic material made by *polymerization of propylene ($CH_2:CHCH_3$). It is similar to high-density *polyethylene but stronger, lighter, and more rigid. Polypropylene products, such as beer crates, luggage, and hinges, are injection molded. Fibers, which are used to make sacks and carpet backings, are made by extrusion.

polysaccharide A carbohydrate comprising chains of between three and several thousand linked *monosaccharide units. Polysaccharides, such as *starch, *glycogen, and *cellulose, are important as energy reserves and structural components of plants and animals.

polytechnics Institutes of higher education concentrating on courses with vocational relevance while maintaining high academic standards. The first polytechnic was established in Paris in 1794 to provide technical training for artillery and engineering officers. Polytechnics were established in Germany during the first half of the 19th century, while the development of the polytechnic movement in the UK began in 1880.

polytetrafluoroethylene (PTFE) A synthetic material produced by the *polymerization of tetrafluoroethylene ($F_2C:CF_2$). It can withstand temperatures of up to 750°F (400°C) and has a very slippery surface. PTFE is used to coat nonstick cooking utensils and in gaskets, bearings, and electrical insulation. It is sold under the trade names Teflon and Fluon.

polytheism Belief in more than one god (*compare* monotheism). Polytheism characterized the religions of the ancient Indo-European peoples (*see* Greek religion; Roman religion) and survives today in *Hinduism.

Polytrichum A genus of *mosses (over 100 species), known as pigeon wheat and hair-cap mosses, that form large mats in peat bogs, old fields, and acid soils. *P. commune* is the most widely distributed species and grows up to 6 in (15 cm) high. *Polytrichum* has been used in brooms, baskets, and in stuffing mattresses. Family: *Polytrichaceae*.

polyurethane A synthetic polymer the molecules of which contain the NHCOO group. Some polyurethanes form thermosetting resins and others, thermoplastic resins. They have a wide range of properties and are used in paints, adhesives, molded articles, rubbers, lacquers, and foams. Polyurethane foam is manufactured from *urethane and can be made flexible or rigid.

polyvinyl acetate (PVA) A vinyl *resin produced by *polymerization of vinyl acetate (CH_2:CHOOCCH$_3$). It is a soft material, used in paints and adhesives.

polyvinyl chloride (PVC) A vinyl *resin or plastic produced by *polymerization of vinyl chloride (chloroethene; CH_2:CHCl), a toxic gas. Rigid PVC products are made by molding. The addition of a plasticizer produces flexible PVC. PVC is tough, nonflammable, resistant to moisture, and a good electrical insulator. It is widely used in sheets, pipes, electrical insulators, and clothing.

Pombal, Sebastião José de Carvalho e Mello, Marquês de (1699–1782) Portuguese statesman, who was the virtual ruler of Portugal from 1750 to 1777 as the chief minister of José I (1715–77; reigned 1750–77). A proponent of enlightened despotism (*see* Enlightenment), he reformed government administration, encouraged manufacturing, and modernized education. He also directed the rebuilding of Lisbon following the earthquake of 1755. His reforms did not achieve lasting success and his unpopular methods caused his downfall after José's death.

pomegranate A shrub or small tree, *Punica granatum,* native to W Asia and widely cultivated in the tropics and subtropics for its fruit; 16–23 ft (5–7 m) tall, it has narrow pointed leaves, about 3 in (7.5 cm) long, and orange-red flowers growing in the leaf axils. The large round fruit has a thick leathery yellowish-reddish skin and contains several chambers, each containing many seeds coated with a pinkish acid-sweet juicy pulp. Pomegranates are eaten fresh or used in beverages or wines. The seeds are used in preserves and syrups. Family: *Punicaceae*.

Pomerania A region of NE Europe on the Baltic Sea between the Oder and Vistula Rivers. Pomerania was Polish territory until the 17th century, when the western and central regions were acquired by Brandenburg (later Prussia). Sweden gained W Pomerania in 1648 but by 1815 it had been reacquired by Prussia, which in 1772 had annexed E Pomerania. Territorial redistribution after World Wars I and II restored Pomerania E of the Oder River to Poland; W Pomerania became part of East Germany and, from 1990, of reunited Germany.

Pomeranian A breed of toy dog, developed in Pomerania, whose ancestors are thought to have been Scandinavian sled dogs. The Pomeranian has a compact body and foxlike head with small erect ears. The short undercoat is covered by a long straight outercoat and the fluffy tail is held over the back. The coat may be any recognized color, including white, black, brown, or reddish. Height: 5.5–7 in (14–18 cm).

Pomona (mythology) A Roman goddess of fruit to whom a sacred precinct outside Rome was dedicated. She was married to Vertumnus, a god who controlled the change of seasons.

Pomona (Orkneys). *See* Mainland.

MME DE POMPADOUR *Portrait by François Boucher of the mistress of Louis XV.*

Pompadour, Mme de (Jeanne Antoinette Poisson, Marquise de P.; 1721–64) The mistress of Louis XV, who exerted considerable political influence from 1745 until her death. She influenced the negotiation of an Austrian alliance against Prussia and was blamed for French defeats in the subsequent *Seven Years' War. She was a notable patron of artists and scholars.

pompano A valuable food fish of the genus *Trachinotus*. It has a deep body, usually up to 20 in (50 cm) long, colored silvery blue or gray. Pompanos are carnivorous and live in fast-swimming groups, usually around rocks in warm coastal waters. Family: *Carangidae*; order: *Perciformes*.

Pompeii An ancient city near Naples, in Italy. It was buried 12–18 ft (4–6 m) deep under volcanic ash by the eruption of Mount *Vesuvius (79 AD). Its rediscovery (1748) stimulated general interest in classical archeology. Pompeii, now about three-quarters excavated, provides unparalleled evidence for daily life in Roman times: buildings, often standing to the second floor and with extensive wall paintings and graffiti; normally perishable objects including food, wooden furniture, and paintings, preserved by the ash; and personal possessions abandoned by the fleeing inhabitants.

Pompey (Gnaeus Pompeius; 106–48 BC) Roman general and statesman, called Pompeius Magnus (Pompey the Great). Granted extraordinary powers (67–66) to destroy marauding pirates and then to wage war in Asia, Pompey returned a popular hero. In 60 he joined Julius Caesar and Crassus in the first *Triumvirate, marrying Caesar's daughter Julia (d. 54) in 59, but in 50 he supported the Senate's demand for Caesar to resign his armies. In the civil war that followed Pompey was defeated by Caesar at Pharsalus (48) and fled to Egypt, where he was murdered.

Pompidou, Georges (Jean Raymond) (1911–74) French statesman; prime minister (1962, 1962–66, 1966–67, 1967–68) and president (1969–74). He served under de Gaulle during World War II and was his personal assistant in 1958–59, when he helped draft the constitution of the Fifth Republic. He negoti-

ated a settlement with the Algerians (1961) and with the students in the revolt of
May 1968. He succeeded de Gaulle as president.

Ponce 18 01N 66 36W A major city and port in S Puerto Rico, on the
Caribbean Sea. Industries include iron processing, sugar refining, and canning.
Population (1990): 187,749.

Ponce de Leon, Juan (1460–1521) Spanish explorer. He accompanied
Columbus on his second voyage to Central America (1493–96) and in 1508–09
founded the first settlement in Puerto Rico, of which he became governor
(1510). In 1512, searching for the legendary fountain of eternal youth, he dis-
covered Florida. He died while attempting to colonize it, from a wound received
from an Indian's poisoned arrow. The port of Ponce is named for him.

Pondicherry A Union Territory in SE India, on the Coromandel Coast.
Founded by the French in 1674, it was their chief settlement in India until
transferred to Indian administration in 1954. Rice and millet are the chief prod-
ucts. Area: 185 sq mi (479 sq km). Population (1991): 202,648. Capital:
Pondicherry.

pond skater A *water bug belonging to the family *Gerridae* (about 350
species). Pond skaters, or water striders, have a dark slender body and long legs.
They are found mainly in fresh water, running or skating across the surface and
feeding on small insects.

pond turtle Either of two species of turtle found in ponds and other still wa-
ters. The Pacific pond turtle (*Clemmys marmorata*), of the W coast of North
America, is 6–7 in (15–18 cm) long and brown with yellow spots; it is widely
sold for food. The European pond turtle (*Emys orbicularis*) of Europe, N Africa,
and W Asia, is 4.7–5.1 in (12–13 cm) long and brown with yellow speckles.
Family: *Emydidae*.

pondweed A usually perennial aquatic herb of the genus *Potamogeton* (100
species), found worldwide in fresh water. It has submerged or floating oblong or
pointed leaves, 0.8–8 in (2–20 cm) long, and stalked heads of tiny four-lobed
greenish flowers. Family: *Potamogetonaceae*.

The Canadian pondweed (*Elodea canadensis*) has submerged stems, up to
10 ft (3 m) long, with whorls of narrow backward-curving dark-green leaves.
Native to North America, it is naturalized in Europe. Family: *Hydrocharitaceae*.

Poniatowski, Józef (1763–1813) Marshal of France, born in Austria, who
served consecutively in the Austrian and Polish armies before becoming com-
mander of the Duchy of Warsaw, established by Napoleon in 1807. He fought in
Napoleon's Russian campaign (1812–13) and died at *Leipzig.

Ponta Delgada 37 29N 25 40W A city in the Azores, Portugal, the capital of
São Miguel Island. Important since 1540, it is a tourist resort and the main com-
mercial center of the Azores. Population: 146,600.

Pontchartrain, Lake A coastal lake in SE Louisiana, just NW of New Or-
leans. It is connected to the Mississippi River and the Gulf of Mexico by lakes
and canals and receives excess water from the Mississippi River by way of spill-
ways. The largest lake in Louisiana, it is a popular resort area. Area: 625 sq mi
(1620 sq km).

Ponte Vecchio A bridge over the Arno River in Florence. Topped by build-
ings, it was designed by Taddeo *Gaddi and finished in 1345. It was a highly ad-
vanced structure for its period.

Pontevedra 42 25N 8 39W A port in NW Spain, in Galicia. It has a 16th-century cathedral and an episcopal palace. Its manufactures include cloth, leather, and pottery. Population: 52,452.

Pontiac (c. 1720–c. 1769) American Indian chief, who organized local tribes to resist white migration to the NW. In **Pontiac's Conspiracy** (1763–66) the Indians took all but three of the British fortified posts. Fighting continued until 1765, when the posts were all recaptured, and peace was signed at Oswego in 1766.

Pontianak 0 05S 109 16E A port in Indonesia, in W Kalimantan on the Kapuas delta. Formerly Borneo's main gold town, its chief industries are shipbuilding and rubber, palm oil, sugar, and timber processing. Its university was established in 1963. Population (1980): 304,778.

Pontine Marshes (Italian name: Agro Pontino) A reclaimed marshland area in S central Italy, bordering on the Tyrrhenian Sea. An extensive program to drain the marshes was begun in 1928; several towns including Littoria (now Latina) were established and it has become one of the most productive agricultural areas in Italy.

pontoon bridge A type of temporary bridge in which the deck (or roadway) rests on floating flat-bottomed vessels (pontoons). Pontoons were often used in the earliest military campaigns as they could be preassembled, floated into position, and did not need to last forever. Modern pontoon bridges often have a movable section to allow boats to pass; they are useful where the earth is unsuitable for heavy pier foundations or the traffic is too light to justify a piered bridge.

Pontormo, Jacopo da (J. Carrucci; 1494–1557) Italian mannerist painter, born in Pontormo (*see* mannerism). He settled in Florence, where he trained under *Andrea del Sarto. He painted mythological scenes in the Medici villa at Poggio a Caiano (1521) and scenes of the Passion (1522–25) at the Certosa, near Florence, but his major work is the *Deposition* (Sta Felicità, Florence).

Pontus The coastal region S of the Black Sea in NE Asia Minor. Pontus was a kingdom from the 4th century BC, becoming prominent in the 1st century BC under *Mithridates VI Eupator. Pompey conquered Pontus in 64, after which the region was administered by Rome.

pony A *horse that does not exceed $14\frac{1}{2}$ hands (5 ft; 1.47 m) in height at maturity, measured from the top of the shoulders (withers). The many modern breeds of pony are throught to have developed from one or two original types, which may have resembled *Przewalski's horse. Ponies have traditionally been used by man as pack animals and for riding. Today, they are especially popular as children's mounts.

poodle A breed of □dog of uncertain origins but long associated with France and Germany. The poodle is an active intelligent dog with a long straight muzzle, drooping ears, and a docked tail. The dense coat, which was originally clipped to enable them to swim and retrieve in water, may be any recognized color, including gray, white, black, brown, or cream. The miniature poodle and toy poodle are derivative breeds of the standard poodle. Height: 15 in (38 cm) minimum (standard); 11–15 in (28–38 cm) (miniature); under 11 in (28 cm) (toy).

pool A form of *billiards played on a table usually 4.5 × 9 ft (1.4 × 2.7 m) with six pockets. The object is to use a white cue ball to sink the 15 colored balls into the pockets.

Poole 50 43N 1 59W A resort in SW England, in Dorset on Poole Harbour. It is a minor port, with boat building, engineering, pottery (using local clays), and chemical industries. Population (1981): 118,922.

Poona (*or* Pune) 18 34N 73 58E A city in India, in Maharashtra. Capital of the Marathas in the late 18th century, it was taken by the British in 1817. It is the site of a university (1949) and a renowned Oriental research institute (1919). A commercial, manufacturing, and military center, it has cotton textiles, rubber, paper, and munitions industries. Population (1991): 1,559,558.

Poor Laws The laws that governed assistance to the poor in Britain. From the 16th century parishes were responsible for providing for their poor and from 1572 levied a tax for poor relief. The Poor Law Amendment Act of 1834 abolished outdoor relief and those seeking assistance had to enter a workhouse. The Poor Law system was not abolished until 1947.

pop art A modern art movement dominant in the US and Britain in the 1960s. Pop art is strongly influenced by the mass media—television, comics, advertising, etc.—in its subject matter and techniques. Also characteristic is the use of silkscreen *printing, *collage, and the *ready-made. Pioneered in the 1950s by Jasper *Johns and Robert *Rauschenberg, it was influenced by the early 20th-century *dada movement and developed as a reaction to *action painting. Leading pop artists are Andy *Warhol, Roy *Lichtenstein, Claes *Oldenburg, Richard *Hamilton, George Segal, and Peter *Blake.

pope. *See* papacy.

Pope, Alexander (1688–1744) British poet. A severe childhood illness left him a cripple for life. He established his reputation as a poet of biting wit and skill, especially in his masterly use of the heroic couplet, with *An Essay on Criticism* (1711) and the mock epic *The Rape of the Lock* (1712–14). The financial gains from his translations of Homer's *Iliad* (1715–20) and *Odyssey* (1725–26) enabled him to move in 1719 to a comfortable house in Twickenham. There he wrote the mock epic *The Dunciad* (1728; revised 1742–43), the philosophical poem *An Essay on Man* (1733–34), and poems modeled on the satires of Horace.

Pope, John (1822–92) US Union general. A graduate of West Point, he served in the *Mexican War and during the Civil War. As head of the Army of Virginia (1862) he was defeated at the second battle of *Bull Run. Later, he was in command of the Department of Missouri (1870–83).

Popish Plot (1678) A conspiracy in England, invented by Titus Oates (1649–1705) and Israel Tonge. They alleged the existence of a plot to assassinate Charles II and place his Roman Catholic brother, James, on the throne. The anti-Catholic passions Oates and Tonge thus aroused led to the execution of 35 suspects and the exclusion of Catholics from Parliament (*see* Test Acts).

poplar A shrub or tree of the genus *Populus* (about 30 species), native to N temperate regions and grown for wood pulp, shade, and ornament. Up to 130 ft (40 m) tall, the trees may have a broad spreading crown, as in the European black poplar (*P. nigra*), or a tall slender one, as in the Lombardy poplar (*P. nigra* var. *italica*). The oval, triangular, or heart-shaped leaves may have striking autumn colors and the drooping male and female catkins are usually borne on separate trees. The seeds have tufts of silky white hairs. Family: *Salicaceae. See also* aspen.

pop music Any music that is general in its appeal, especially among young people; it includes folk, country and western, and, predominantly, *rock music. It is distinguished from classical music and pure jazz by its lack of sophistication. Pop emerged as a distinctive genre in the 1950s with the emergence of small groups using electronically amplified instruments, simple harmonies, and heavy rhythms. Pop songs are generally about basic human emotions, such as love, happiness, and grief. The emergence of youth movements in the early 1960s lent pop a rebelliousness that expressed itself in the lifestyles of pop musicians, the lyrics of pop songs, and unconventional styles of dress and performance. The multiplicity of styles in the 1960s, 1970s, and 1980s reflected the development of rock, the predominance of individual performers and groups, and the emergence of disco music. The term **popular music** is generally applied to light music of a romantic or sentimental kind.

Popocatépetl, Mount 19 02N 93 38W A dormant volcano in central Mexico, near Mexico City. Its crater contains sulfur deposits. Height: 17,887 ft (5452 m).

Popov, Aleksandr Stepanovich (1859–1905) Russian physicist, who studied the transmission of radio waves. Popov's work preceded that of *Marconi and in 1897 he succeeded in transmitting over a distance of three miles (five kilometers). However, he failed to pursue the use of radio waves for communication, using them instead to study thunderstorms.

Popper, Sir Karl Raimund (1902–) Austrian-born philosopher. Forced by the Nazi threat to emigrate, Popper was a professor at the London School of Economics (1949–69). His interests were mainly scientific and political. In *The Logic of Scientific Discovery* (1935) he cast doubt upon time-honored methods of establishing scientific laws by observation and experiment: "all crows are black" is an unrestricted generalization that can never be verified (we can never hope to observe *all* crows), but it could be falsified by the observation of one white crow. *The Open Society and its Enemies* (1945) and *The Poverty of Historicism* (1957) promote "methodological individualism," the restoration of the historical importance of the individual against collective doctrinaire systems such as Marxism.

poppy An annual, biennial, or perennial plant of the genus *Papaver* (about 120 species), native mainly to the N hemisphere and often grown for ornament; 6–40 in (15–100 cm) high, it yields a milky sap (latex) and bears large lobed or divided leaves and showy white, pink, or red flowers, sometimes with a dark center, with 4–6 petals surrounding a dense whorl of stamens. The □fruit is a capsule with pores through which the seeds are dispersed. Species include the *corn poppy and *opium poppy. Family: *Papaveraceae. See also* horned poppy; prickly poppy; Welsh poppy.

popular front A coalition of left-wing and moderate political groups. Increasingly concerned by the rise of fascism in the mid-1930s, many Communist parties, with Soviet encouragement, sought political alliances with socialist and liberal groups. In 1936 a popular-front government was elected in France; but generally the different parties were too divided to oppose fascism effectively. *See also* United Fronts.

populism US farm movement, active in the 1890s. The Populist party, organized in 1892, evolved from individual farmers' alliances, action groups formed in the West and South in the 1880s to protest poor economic conditions for farmers. Their platform demanded *free silver coinage, government-controlled railroads, and a graduated income tax, among other things—all meant to equalize farmers' power with that of business and industry. Although the party made inroads in the elections of 1892 and 1894, it was absorbed into the Democratic party by 1896.

porbeagle A *mackerel shark, *Lamna nasus,* commonly called the Atlantic mackerel shark, that lives mainly in N temperate shallow waters. It has a dark-blue robust body, 5–10 ft (1.5–3 m) long, with a white belly and may occur in small groups, feeding principally on shoals of fish, especially mackerel.

porcelain White vitrified ceramic evolved by Chinese potters about 900 AD. It was not invented but developed out of stoneware pottery. There are three kinds of porcelain: hard-paste or true porcelain, soft-paste or artificial, and English bone china. Hard-paste porcelain consists of china clay (kaolin) and fusible feldspathic rock (petuntse) finely mixed and fired to about 2550°F (1400°C). This forms a translucent white resonant vitreous body, which is usually glazed with pure petuntse during the firing. Hard-paste porcelain was made in Japan about 1500 AD but the secret of its manufacture defied discovery elsewhere until the early 18th century when the alchemist Böttger (1682–1719) succeeded, after exhaustive secret experiments, in making it at *Meissen. Soft-paste porcelain differs from hard-paste in that the clay or kaolin is mixed with an artificial flux. This might be sand with lime, or flint, soda, etc., depending on the factory. The mixture is fired at about 2015°F (1100°C) and the glaze, usually of glass, is applied in a second firing at about 1835°F (1000°C). Bone porcelain is an 18th-century English invention using bone ash as a flux.

porcupine A large herbivorous spiny *rodent belonging to either of the families *Erethizontidae* (New World porcupines; 11 species) or *Hystricidae* (Old World porcupines; 15 species). American porcupines tend to be arboreal and have prehensile tails. The North American porcupine (*Erethizion dorsatum*) is about 30 in (75 cm) long and grows a soft winter coat that almost conceals its covering of quills. Old World porcupines are mainly ground-dwelling. The Indian crested porcupine (*Hystrix indica*) grows to 40 in (1 m) in length and may have spines 14 in (35 cm) long. Porcupines respond to a threat by turning their backs and raising their spines or even running backward at an attacker. □mammal.

porcupine fish A fish, also called sea porcupine, belonging to a family (*Diodontidae*) related to *puffers, especially *Diodon hystrix,* found in tropical seas. It has a short broad body, up to about 35 in (90 cm) long, which it inflates when provoked, erecting numerous spines in the skin.

porgy. *See* sea bream.

Pori (Swedish name: Björneborg) 61 28N 21 45E A seaport in S Finland, on the Gulf of Bothnia. Its industries include copper refining, textiles, wood processing, steel, and chemicals. Population (1980): 79,405.

porphyria A group of genetic disorders in which there is an accumulation in the body of one or more porphyrins—precursors of the red blood pigment—due to an enzyme defect. The disease affects the digestive tract, causing abdominal pain, vomiting, and diarrhea; the nervous system, causing psychotic disorder, epilepsy, and weakness; the circulatory system, causing high blood pressure; and the skin, causing photosensitivity. There is no specific treatment. The madness of George III is now known to have been due to porphyria.

porphyry An igneous rock, usually hypabyssal, containing numerous large crystals called phenocrysts set in a finer-grained, or sometimes glassy, groundmass. The term porphyry is often given with the name of the prophyritic mineral, for example quartz porphyry.

Porphyry (235–305 AD) Syrian-born philosopher and devoted disciple, editor, and biographer of *Plotinus. Among nearly 80 titles attributed to him are religious and philosophical works, including a *Treatise against Christians,* banned 448 AD but still partly extant, and commentaries on philosophical authors. He also wrote on literary, grammatical, and scientific topics.

porpoise A small toothed *whale belonging to the family *Phocoenidae* (7 species), of coastal waters. Porpoises are 5–7 ft (1.5–2 m) long and have no beak. The common, or harbor, porpoise (*Phocoena phocoena*) of the N Atlantic and Pacific, has a rounded body, tapering toward the tail, blue-gray above and pale gray beneath. It lives in large groups called schools, feeding on fish, squid, and crustaceans.

port A fortified usually dessert *wine from Oporto (N Portugal). The grapes grown on the Douro hillsides are trodden in stone presses. Fermentation is halted by adding brandy. Subsequently the wine is taken to the lodges near Oporto, where it matures in wood. Port-type wines are made in other countries, such as South Africa.

Port Arthur 29 55N 93 56W A city in S Texas. Situated in an oil region known as the Golden Triangle, Port Arthur is a major shipping outlet for oil and has large petrochemical industries. Population (1990): 58,724.

Port Arthur. *See* Lüda; Thunder Bay.

Port-au-Prince 18 40N 72 20W The capital of Haiti, a port in the SW on the Gulf of Gonaïves. Its main exports are coffee and sugar. The University of Haiti was founded there in 1944. Population (1992 est): 752,600.

Port Elizabeth 33 58S 25 36E A city in South Africa, in S Cape Province on Algoa Bay. It was founded in 1820 by British settlers. The university was founded in 1964. Nearby is the Addo Elephant National Park. It is a major port, ore being the chief export, and industries include automobile assembly, fruit canning, and flour milling. Population (1985): 272,844.

Porter, Cole (Albert) (1893–1964) US composer of musical comedies and popular songs. He wrote a series of musicals, including *The Gay Divorcée* (1932), *Anything Goes* (1934), *Kiss Me Kate* (1948), and *Can Can* (1953). His songs included "Night and Day" and "Begin the Beguine."

Porter, Katherine Anne (1890–1980) US short-story writer and novelist. As a journalist she traveled in Mexico and Spain. *Flowering Judas,* her first collection of stories, was published in 1930. Her stories, especially those in *Pale Horse, Pale Rider* (1939), are mostly delicate explorations of autobiographical material. Her only novel was the allegorical *Ship of Fools* (1962), which won a Pulitzer Prize.

Port Harcourt 4 43N 7 05E A port in S Nigeria. Founded in 1912, it developed as a port following the arrival of the railroad (1916) from the Enugu coal fields. It now exports coal, tin, and palm oil. It is the major industrial center of the Niger delta oil fields. It has a university (1975). Population (1990 est): 352,000.

Portile de Fier. *See* Iron Gate.

Port Klang (name until 1971: Port Swettenham) 3 01N 101 25E A port in W Peninsular Malaysia, on the Strait of Malacca. Exporting chiefly rubber, it serves the Klang Valley, Malaysia's chief industrial area. Population (1980): 192,000.

Portland 45 32N 122 40W A city in Oregon, on the Willamette River. It was founded in 1829 and its growth was stimulated by several gold rushes along the Oregon Trail. The state's largest city, it is a deepwater port, with shipbuilding, timber, and metallurgical industries. It is the site of the University of Portland (1901). Population (1990): 437,319.

Portland 43 41N 70 18W A city in SW Maine, on Casco Bay. Destroyed by Indians, French, and British, it was the state capital (1820–32). It is a major petroleum port and commercial center. Industries include timber, textiles, and chemicals. Population (1990): 64,358.

Portland, William Henry Cavendish Bentinck, 3rd Duke of (1738–1809) British statesman; prime minister (1783, 1807–09). He was nominal head of the coalition between Lord North and Charles James Fox (1783) and was subsequently home secretary (1794–1801).

Portland vase A Roman vase (c. 1st century AD) of dark blue glass with a white glass relief of figures, discovered in Italy in 1644. It once belonged to the duke of Portland but is now in the British Museum.

Port Louis 20 10S 57 30E The capital of Mauritius, in the NW of the island. Founded in about 1736, it is the site of two cathedrals. Sugar is exported. Population (1990 est): 141,870.

Port Lyautey. *See* Kenitra.

Port Moresby 9 30S 147 07E The capital and main port of Papua New Guinea, on the Gulf of Papua. It was an important Allied base in World War II and since then the port has been considerably modernized. The University of Papua New Guinea was founded in 1965. Population (1987): 152,000.

Pôrto. *See* Oporto.

Pôrto Alegre 30 03S 51 10W A city in S Brazil, the capital of Rio Grande do Sul state on the Lagôa (Lagoon) dos Patos. It is a major commercial and industrial center; industries are chiefly related to agriculture and include meat processing, tanning, and the manufacture of textiles. It is the seat of two universities. Population (1986): 2,705,000.

Port-of-Spain 10 38N 61 31W The capital and main port of Trinidad and Tobago since 1783, on the W coast of Trinidad. It was the capital of the short-lived Federation of the West Indies from 1958 until 1962. Notable buildings include the Anglican and Roman Catholic cathedrals. Petroleum products, sugar, and rum are among the main exports. Population (1990 est): 50,900.

Porto Novo 6 30N 2 47E The capital of Benin, on the Gulf of Guinea. A former center of the slave trade with the Portuguese, it came under French rule in the late 19th century. Trade includes palm oil and cotton. Population (1982 est): 208,000.

Port Royal A former Cistercian nunnery originally situated a short distance SW of Paris; also called Port Royal des Champs. In the 17th century it became a center of *Jansenism under Abbess Angélique Arnauld (1591–1661), sister of Antoine *Arnauld. After persecution the nuns were dispersed (1709).

Port Said (*or* Bur Said) 31 17N 32 18E A major port in Egypt, situated at the Mediterranean entrance to the Suez Canal. Founded in 1859, it became an important fueling point but suffered from the closure of the Suez Canal (1967–75) and Israeli occupation of the E bank. Population (1986 est): 382,000.

Portsmouth 50 48N 1 05W A port in S England, at the entrance to Portsmouth Harbour. Notable landmarks include Admiral Nelson's flagship HMS *Victory* and Charles Dickens' birthplace (now a museum). The chief naval base in the UK, Portsmouth is also a commercial port with shipbuilding, ship-maintenance, electronics, and aircraft-engineering industries. Population (1991): 174,700.

Portsmouth 36 50N 76 20W A city and port in Virginia, on Hampton Roads. Founded in 1752, it is the site of the Norfolk Naval Yard, abandoned by Federal troops (1861) during the US Civil War and used by the Confederates to transform the scuttled USS *Merrimack* into the *ironclad *Virginia*. The main industry is shipbuilding and ship repairing. Population (1990): 103,907.

Portsmouth 43 03N 70 47W A city in New Hampshire, on the Atlantic coast. It has several notable buildings, including the John Paul Jones House (1758). The state's only seaport, it is the site of the Portsmouth Naval Yard (established in 1800); it is an important submarine base. Population (1990): 25,925.

Portsmouth Peace Conference (1905) US-sponsored meeting in Portsmouth, NH, to work out peace terms to end the *Russo-Japanese War.

Port Sudan 19 38N 37 07E A port in the Sudan, on the Red Sea. It handles much of the country's trade; exports include cotton, gum arabic, and sesame seeds. It also has an important salt-panning industry. Population (1983): 206,727.

Portugal, Republic of A country in SW Europe, occupying the W section of the Iberian Peninsula and bordering on the Atlantic Ocean. The *Madeira Islands are an integral part of Portugal. Coastal plains rise to mountains, reaching 6352 ft (1935 m) in the N. The main rivers are the Douro, Miño, and Tagus. *Economy*: traditionally agricultural, Portugal's principal exports are textiles, clothing, cork, wood products, sardines, and fortified wines. However, recent political upheavals, an inefficient farming system, and drought, combined with loss of cheap raw materials following the independence of former colonies, have led to many economic difficulties. Tourism, an important source of foreign currency, virtually ceased for a while but was being revived by the late 1970s. Rich mineral resources include coal, copper pyrites, kaolin, and hematite, and hydroelectricity is a valuable source of power. *History*: the early history of the region is that of the rest of the Iberian Peninsula (*see* Spain, Kingdom of). Portugal as a distinct Christian territory dates from 868. It became a kingdom in 1139 under Alfonso I and its position was consolidated in the 13th century by the conquest of Muslim territory. Portugal's long alliance with England began in the 14th century. From the 15th century Portuguese explorers opened up new trade routes, allowing for the establishment of an extensive overseas empire that included Angola, Mozambique, and Brazil. In 1580 Portugal came under Spanish domination, which lasted until 1640, after which the Portuguese monarchy became increasingly reactionary, a trend that *Pombal's reforms attempted to reverse. In 1807 Portugal was invaded by the French, who were defeated in the subsequent *Peninsular War. A revolution in 1910 overthrew the monarchy and established a republic. A long period of political instability culminated in a military coup in 1926. A prominent role in the new government was played by *Salazar, who became prime minister in 1932 and established the corporatist New State. His long dictatorship also witnessed bitter colonial wars in Africa. In April 1974, the government of Salazar's successor, Marcello Caetano, was overthrown in a military coup led by Gen. Antonio de Spinola. Spinola granted independence to Portugal's remaining African colonies before falling from power later the same year. The military revolutionary council was abolished in 1982, and in 1983, parliamentary elections were held. Portugal became a member of the European Community in 1986, which made the transition to democracy progress smoothly and bolstered the economy. President: Mario Alberto Soares. Prime minister: Anibal Cavaco Silva. Official language: Portuguese. Official religion: Roman Catholic. Official currency: escudo of 100 centavos. Area: 34,861 sq mi (91,631 sq km). Population (1990 est): 10,528,000. Capital and main port: Lisbon.

Portuguese A *Romance language spoken in Portugal, Galicia (Spain), Brazil, Madeira, and the Azores. It emerged as a distinct language during the early medieval period. The standard form is based on the dialect of Lisbon. Brazilian Portuguese differs slightly in grammar and sound system. A notable characteristic of Portuguese is the use of nasal vowel sounds.

Portuguese literature Literature in the Portuguese language commences with the lyrics of a school of poets who flourished under the kings Alfonso III (1248–79) and Dinis (1279–1325) and are preserved in three collections of *cancioneiros*. In a later collection, the *Cancioneiro Geral* (1516), the influence of Provençal poetry was replaced by that of Spanish and Italian models. During the

16th century, the golden age of Portuguese literature, Gil Vicente wrote pioneering works of drama, Sá de Miranda (c. 1481–1558) introduced many new poetic forms from Italy, and Luís de Camões composed the national epic poem, *Os Lusíadas* (1572). The subsequent period of decline lasted until the influence of romanticism in the early 19th century inspired the works of João Baptista da Silva Leitão Almeida-Garrett (1799–1854) and Alexandre Herculano (1810–77). Further stimulation was provided by a reaction against the pseudoclassicism of Feliciano de Castilho led by Antero de Quental (1842–91) and by the influence of French symbolism. Outstanding individual writers of the 20th century include the poet Fernando Pessoa (1888–1935) and the novelist Manual Ribeiro (1879–1941).

Portuguese man-of-war A colonial marine invertebrate animal belonging to a genus (*Physalia*) of *coelenterates found mainly in warm seas. It has a translucent bladder-like float (pneumatophore), pink, blue, or violet in color, which acts like a sail in the wind. Attached underneath are clusters of *polyps bearing stinging tentacles, up to 165 ft (50 m) long, used to paralyze fish and other prey. The sting can also have a serious effect on humans. Order: *Siphonophora*; class: *Hydrozoa*. □oceans.

Poseidon The Greek god of the sea and earthquakes, son of Cronus and Rhea and brother of Zeus and Hades. He used his ability to change his form mainly to further his amorous desires, and his many offspring included Theseus, Polyphemus, and the winged horse Pegasus. He was usually portrayed with a trident and dolphin. He was identified with the Roman *Neptune.

positivism The philosophical doctrine of *Comte and his successors. It asserts that knowledge of reality can be achieved *only* through the particular sciences and ordinary observation. Positivism rejects all metaphysical propositions, but it has been pointed out (with regard to later *logical positivism) that this rejection itself constitutes a metaphysical proposition. *Hobbes was an earlier positivist with regard to the status of the law. The only law is positive law, the law that is actually enforced; there is no "higher" law such as natural law. *Existentialism, especially in France, has been a reaction against positivism.

positron The antiparticle of the *electron, having the same mass and *spin as the electron but opposite electric charge. A positron and an electron annihilate each other on collision, producing two gamma-ray photons.

possum The most common Australian *marsupial, *Trichosurus vulpecula,* also called brush-tailed phalanger. Nocturnal and arboreal, it is cat-sized and has a soft grayish coat and tail. It feeds mainly on buds, leaves, and fruit, and occasionally fledgling birds. The name possum is often used for other members of the family *Phalangeridae.*

Postal Service, United States Independent agency that provides mail processing and delivery services to individuals and businesses within the US. It protects the mails from loss or theft and apprehends those who violate postal laws. It is headed by the postmaster general, who is appointed by a board of nine governors appointed by the president.

poster art The design of public notices for advertising and propaganda purposes. Poster design originated in the mid-19th century, the first major poster artist being the Frenchman Jules Chéret (1836–1933). Its development was facilitated by the use of lithography (*see* printing), an inexpensive and easy printing process. Leading painters of the period who designed posters included *Toulouse-Lautrec and Aubrey *Beardsley.

postimpressionism The art of the late 19th-century French painters *Cézanne, *Seurat, *Van Gogh, *Gauguin, *Toulouse-Lautrec, and their followers whose work developed out of and, to some extent, in reaction to *impressionism. The term was coined by the British art critic, Roger *Fry. Many of them painted impressionist works early in their careers but later rejected the objectivity and fleeting light effects of impressionism. Cézanne was the forerunner of *cubism and Van Gogh of *expressionism, while Gauguin developed a style known as *synthetism, and Seurat introduced *pointillism. The postimpressionists were not an organized group with a coherent style or fixed program.

POSTIMPRESSIONISM Bathers, Asniéres *(1883–84) by Georges Seurat in his pointillism style.*

postmortem. *See* autopsy.

potassium (K) A reactive alkali metal discovered by Sir Humphry Davy in 1807. It is a common constituent of the earth's crust; forming *feldspars ($KAlSi_3O_8$), clays, and evaporite minerals (for example sylvite; KCl). The metal is prepared by electrolysis of the molten hydroxide. It is soft, easily cut with a knife, and reacts readily with water, catching fire and liberating hydrogen. It oxidizes rapidly in air and must therefore be stored under oil. The element is highly electropositive and its chemistry is dominated by its ability to form ionic salts (for example KCl, KNO_3, K_2CO_3, KBr, K_2SO_4, and KCN). Its largest use is in fertilizers, potassium being essential for plant growth. Alloys of potassium and sodium have been proposed as heat transfer media in nuclear reactors, since the lowest melting alloy melts at 9.9°F (-12.3°C). One of the three isotopes (^{40}K) is radioactive with a half-life of 1.3×10^9 years and is used in *potassium-argon dating. The metal and its salts impart a lilac color to flames. At no 19; at wt 39.102; mp 147°F (63.65°C); bp 1427°F (774°C).

potassium-argon dating A method of *radiometric dating of geological specimens based on the decay of the radioactive isotope potassium 40, which is present to a small extent in all naturally occurring potassium. Its half-life is 1.3×10^9 years and it decays to argon 40; thus an estimate of the ratio of the two isotopes in a specimen of rock gives an indication of its age.

potato A perennial herbaceous plant, *Solanum tuberosum,* native to the Andes but cultivated throughout the world, especially in temperate regions, as an important vegetable crop. Potatoes were introduced to England in the late 16th century by Sir Walter Raleigh; they reached Spain and Portugal earlier. The plants grow to a height of 20–40 in (50–100 cm), with compound leaves and clusters of white and purple flowers. The tubers (swollen tips of underground stems) have a thin brownish-white, white, yellow, or pinkish skin and are rich in starch; there

are several varieties, up to 3.3 lb (1.5 kg) in weight, and they are eaten cooked or ground into flour. Commercial potatoes are grown from small tubers termed "seed" potatoes. Potatoes are vulnerable to a number of diseases, the most notorious being the potato *blight that ravished Ireland in 1845–47 (*see also* Irish famine). Family: *Solanaceae. See also* sweet potato.

Potawatomi North American Algonkian-speaking Indian tribe, related to the *Ojibwa and the *Ottawa and found in S Michigan. Basically hunters and farmers, they were driven S by the *Sioux Indians and then W by white settlers and the US Army. Known as the Fire Nation (Potawatomi means "People of the Place of Fire"), they warred successfully against the *Pawnee over land in Kansas. Today, about 2000 Potawatomi live on a Kansas reservation.

Potchefstroom 26 42S 27 06E A city in South Africa, in the S Transvaal. Founded by Voortrekkers (1838), it is the oldest town in the Transvaal. Gold mining and agriculture are important. Population: 60,000.

Potemkin, Grigori Aleksandrovich (1739–91) Russian field marshal and favorite of *Catherine the Great. Potemkin distinguished himself in Catherine's first Turkish War (1768–74) and became her lover for two years as well as her chief adviser. Potemkin retained his political influence, especially in foreign affairs, until his death.

potential, electric A measure of electrical work. The potential at a point in an *electric field is one volt when one joule of energy is needed to bring a positive charge of one coulomb to that point from infinity. Usually the potential difference between two points, rather than the absolute potential, is used. *See also* electromotive force.

potential energy *Energy stored in a body by virtue of its position or configuration. Thus a body, mass m, at a height h above the ground has a potential energy equal to mgh, where g is the *acceleration of free fall, relative to the ground. A compressed spring and an electrically charged body also store potential energy.

Potentilla A genus of mostly perennial herbs (500 species), found mainly in N temperate and arctic regions. It includes several species and hybrids grown as ornamentals. They have erect or creeping stems, 2–27.5 in (5–70 cm) long, bearing compound leaves and yellow, white, or red four- or five-petaled flowers with many stamens. The fruit is a group of seedlike achenes. Family: *Rosaceae. See also* cinquefoil; tormentil.

potentiometer A variable electrical *resistance in which a sliding contact can be adjusted to any position along its length so that a variable proportion of the resistance can be included in a circuit. Potentiometers are used for measuring unknown voltages and as a potential divider, producing a voltage output corresponding to calibrated positions of the sliding contact.

potlatch The ceremonial distribution of gifts, practiced by the American Indians of the NW Pacific coast region, in order to affirm claims to rank and status at lavish feasts, to which rivals were invited. Gifts had to be returned with interest at subsequent potlatches to avoid humiliation and loss of status; competition to exceed others in generosity was intense. Among the *Kwakiutl, potlatching developed to an exaggerated extent often involving the ostentatious destruction of property to demonstrate power and rank.

pot marigold A herb, *Calendula officinalis,* native to S Europe and cultivated in temperate regions as an ornamental. About 12–14 in (30–35 cm) tall, it bears simple oblong leaves and yellow or orange daisylike flowers, often double in cultivated varieties. The fresh petals may be eaten in salads or puddings or are dried and used in medicines. Family: **Compositae.*

Potomac River A river in the E central US, rising in the Appalachian Mountains of W Virginia and flowing generally NE through Washington, D.C., to Chesapeake Bay. Length: 287 mi (462 km).

Potosí 19 34S 65 45W A city in S Bolivia, at an altitude of 13,340 ft (4066 m). It is the chief industrial center of Bolivia. Mining is important; minerals extracted include tin, copper, and zinc. Its university was founded in 1892. Population (1987 est): 111,000.

Potsdam 52 19N 13 15E A city in E central Germany, on the Havel River adjoining Berlin. It was the residence of Prussian kings and German emperors. The city was severely damaged by air raids during World War II but extensive restoration has been carried out. Notable buildings include the Brandenburg Gate (1770) and the Sanssouci Palace (1745–47) built by Frederick II. An industrial city, Potsdam has many scientific institutes and is a center of the German film industry. Population (1990 est): 140,000.

Potsdam Conference (1945) The conference attended by Truman (US), Stalin (Soviet Union), and Churchill (later Attlee; UK) after the conclusion of World War II in Europe. Its objectives were to confirm the conclusions of the *Yalta Conference, to establish a political and economic program for Allied-occupied Germany, and to decide upon action toward Japan. The Conference was marked by the conflict of interests between the communist and noncommunist powers that developed into the *Cold War.

Potter, Beatrix (1866–1943) British children's writer and illustrator. During a solitary childhood she became a skilled artist and observer of nature. *The Tale of Peter Rabbit* (1900) was the first of a series of famous children's books concerning the domestic lives of such animals as Jemima Puddle-Duck and Mrs. Tittlemouse.

Potter, Paul (1624–54) Dutch animal painter and etcher, born in Enkhuizen, the son and pupil of a landscape artist. Working successively in Delft, The Hague, and Amsterdam, he was painting as early as 1640. His best works, such as *The Bull,* were executed in 1647.

Potter, Stephen (1900–70) British humorist and critic. He wrote critical studies of D. H. Lawrence (1930) and Coleridge (1935) but is best remembered for his series of humorous books on the art of establishing personal superiority. These include *Gamesmanship* (1947), *Lifemanship* (1950), and *One-Upmanship* (1952).

potter wasp A solitary *wasp belonging to the genus *Eumerus,* common in North America and Europe. It constructs juglike nests of mud or clay, cemented by saliva and attached to plant stems. A single egg is laid in each nest and paralyzed caterpillars are provided as food for the developing larva.

pottery Generally, all *ceramics other than porcelain, but especially clay that has been shaped into containers (*compare* terra-cotta) and baked at varying temperatures over 753°F (400°C). Usually thrown on a potter's wheel, pottery can also be coiled and molded. Being opaque and porous, it is often glazed with an impervious glassy layer. Pottery making is worldwide and of great antiquity. It was being made about 10,000 BC in Japan; from about 3500 BC the fast wheel was used in Mesopotamia. Pottery styles and decorative techniques are important aids to archeologists in identifying and dating cultures. The ancient Greeks (*see* Greek art) and Renaissance Italians (*see* majolica) were among those who raised pottery making to high aesthetic levels, but since the 18th-century advent of porcelain in Europe it has been mainly utilitarian.

potto A *loris, *Perodictus potto,* of African forests. It is about 16 in (40 cm) long with a short tail, a catlike face, stout legs, and strong grasping hands. Pottos have a row of spines on the neck and shoulders, used for butting in self-defense.

pouched rat An African rodent characterized by cheek pouches used for carrying food. They range in size from the African giant pouched rat (*Cricetomys gambianus*), 9.4–18 in (24–45 cm) long excluding the tail (14–18 in; 36–46 cm), to the Cape pouched mouse (*Saccostomus campes-tris*), 5–6 in (12–15 cm) long, excluding the tail (1.2–2.4 in; 3–6 cm). All are vegetarians.

Poughkeepsie 41 42N 73 56W A city in SE New York, on the E bank of the Hudson River, S of Albany. Vassar College was founded there in 1861. Industries include computers and business machines, dairy farming equipment, chemicals, and ball bearings. Population (1990): 28,844.

Poulenc, Francis (1899–1963) French composer, a member of Les *Six. He was influenced by Ravel and Satie and produced a wide variety of compositions, including the song cycle *Le Bestiaire* (1919), a concerto for piano (1950) and one for two pianos (1932), the operas *Les Mamelles de Tirésias* (1944) and *Les Dialogues des Carmélites* (1953–56), and the ballet *Les Biches* (1923). As a pianist he frequently accompanied the French tenor Pierre Bernac (1899–   ).

poultry, domestic 1. Domesticated birds, especially chickens, turkeys, ducks, and geese, that are bred and reared chiefly for eggs and meat but in some cases also for feathers and down. *See* livestock farming. 2. A domesticated form of the red *jungle fowl, *Gallus gallus,* native to Asian forests. It was first domesticated about 4000 years ago as a religious and sacrificial animal and was used by the Romans for food. Since the 19th century, a large number of breeds and varieties have been selected for size, resistance to disease, egg production, shell color, fertility, and food conversion efficiency. Immature males are castrated and reared for meat as capons. In many countries, males (cockerels) are still used for cockfighting.

Pound, Ezra (1885–1972) US poet and critic. After studying Romance languages, he went to Europe in 1908 and became a dynamic propagandist for modernist literary and artistic movements in London (*see* imagism; vorticism). His early poetry included *A Lume Spento* (1908), his first volume, the long poems *Homage to Sextus Propertius* (1917), and *Hugh Selwyn Mauberly* (1920). *The Spirit of Romance* (1910) was a collection of literary criticism. He moved to Paris and, in 1924, to Italy, where he worked on the *Cantos* (1925–69). His support for Mussolini and his broadcasts of fascist propaganda during World War II led to his confinement in a mental hospital in the US (1946–58), after which he returned to Italy.

Pound, Roscoe (1870–1964) US jurist, teacher, and botanist. He directed a botanical survey for Nebraska (1892–1903), during which time a rare moss, *Roscopoundia,* was named for him. He attended Harvard Law School (1889–90), passed the Nebraska bar exam (1890), and began teaching at Harvard in 1910. He served as dean of its law school (1916–36). He was best known for his legal theory of sociological jurisprudence—adapting laws to social conditions—and for his theories on reform of court administration. His works include *The Spirit of the Common Law* (1921), *Law and Morals* (1924), and *Jurisprudence* (5 vols; 1959).

Poussin, Nicolas (1594–1665) French painter, regarded as one of the greatest exponents of *classicism. Poussin lived in Rome from 1624 until his death, apart from two years (1640–42) as painter to the French king Louis XIII. His representation of religious themes, such as *The Martyrdom of St Erasmus*

(1628), gave way in the 1630s to an interest in mythology and the Old Testament, for example *The Worship of the Golden Calf* (c. 1635). The pure classicism of his second Roman period is exemplified in such landscapes as *Landscape with Diogenes* (1648).

Powderly, Terence Vincent (1849–1924) US labor leader. A machinist, he rose in the ranks of the Knights of Labor to become its head (1879–93). He believed in arbitration and cooperation and worked against strikes and violence. He also served as mayor of Scranton, Pa. (1878–84), US commissioner general of immigration (1897–1902), and head of the information department of the Bureau of Immigration (1907–21).

powder metallurgy The shaping of metals by pressing powdered metal into blocks, heating (*see* sintering), and then shaping it by stamping. Often pressing and sintering are done together in a mold to produce the finished article in one operation. The method is used for working metals, such as platinum and tungsten (used in lightbulb filaments) that are difficult to shape by other means. It has the advantages of leaving no scrap and being suitable for intricate shapes. Nonmetal additives can be easily included, such as the graphite lubricant in self-lubricating bearings.

Powell, Anthony (1905–   ) British novelist. His novel sequence *A Dance to the Music of Time* comprises 12 social satires beginning with *A Question of Upbringing* (1951) and ending with *Hearing Secret Harmonies* (1975). He has also written a biography of John Aubrey (1948) and two volumes of memoirs.

Powell, Cecil Frank (1903–69) British physicist, who became professor at Bristol University. Powell pioneered the technique of observing particles by the tracks that they leave on specially prepared photographic plates. In 1947 he exposed his plates to *cosmic rays high up in the Andes and discovered the *pion. He was awarded the 1950 Nobel Prize for this work.

Powell, Colin Luther (1937–   ) US Army officer and chairman of the Joint Chiefs of Staff (1989–93). A member of the Reserve Officers Training Corps in college, he became a second lieutenant upon graduation (1958). His Army assignments alternated between combat units, including two tours in Vietnam, and staff positions, including a tour as the senior military advisor to the secretary of defense. Appointed a corps commander in West Germany in 1986, Powell was soon ordered to Washington, D.C., to work on the National Security Council and to serve as national security advisor (1987–89). After being named commander of the Army Forces Command and promoted to full general in early 1989, he was chosen to head the Joint Chiefs of Staff, the first African American to hold the post. As chairman he helped to direct the US invasion of Panama in 1989 and the operations of the Persian Gulf War in 1990–91.

Powell, Lewis Franklin, Jr. (1907–   ) US jurist; associate justice of the Supreme Court (1971–87). He was instrumental in achieving desegregation of the Richmond, Va., school system during the 1950s. He served as president of the American Bar Association (1964–65) and the American Bar Foundation (1969–71) and was appointed to the Supreme Court in 1971 by Pres. Richard M. *Nixon. Although generally a conservative he sometimes holds liberal opinions on social and racial issues.

Powell v. Alabama (1972) US Supreme Court decision that established right to counsel in state criminal cases, as provided in due process of law. Seven African Americans, accused of raping two white women on a train in Alabama, were tried, convicted, and sentenced to die. The Supreme Court upheld the prisoners' appeal that they had been denied right to counsel, a fair trial, and an unbi-

ased jury (African Americans were excluded), fundamental rights accorded in
the 14th Amendment.

power The rate at which a body or system does work. It is measured in watts
or horsepower.

power station An electricity generating plant that forms part of the *electric-
ity supply system. In **thermal power stations**, heat from the burning of fossil
fuels (oil, coal, and gas) or from *thermal nuclear reactors is used to generate
steam. The steam drives *turbines connected to alternating-current generators
(turbo-alternators), thus converting heat via mechanical energy into electricity.
Gas turbines are also used, eliminating the steam-generation stage. They are
easy to build and flexible to run, but have an efficiency of only about 25%.
Sometimes the exhaust gas is used to help generate steam for a steam turbine, in
order to increase the station's overall efficiency. Usually in a steam-turbine ther-
mal station about 30 to 40% of the heat is converted to electricity, most of the
rest being lost when steam is condensed to water before it is returned to the boil-
ers. ***Hydroelectric power stations** are more efficient (up to 90%) and provide
a significant proportion of electricity supplies. *See also* energy.

Powhatan A confederation of Algonkian-speaking North American Indian
tribes of Virginia. It was founded by the chief known to the European settlers as
Powhatan (?1550–1618), the father of *Pocahontas. Although he resented the
colonists, violence was avoided when Pocahontas married colonist John Rolfe.
The Powhatans were corn cultivators and hunters living in palisaded villages.

Powys, John Cowper (1872–1963) British novelist. He lectured for many
years in the US. He wrote poetry, philosophy, and criticism, but his best-known
books are his long novels. These include *Wolf Solent* (1929) and *A Glastonbury
Romance* (1932), the historical novels *Owen Glendower* (1940), and *Porius*
(1951).

Poyang, Lake An area of marsh and lakes in SE China, drained by the
Yangtze River. In summer the whole area is flooded. Area (summer): about
1073 sq mi (2780 sq km).

Poyning's Law (1495) A measure introduced by Sir Edward Poynings
(1459–1521), lord deputy of Ireland, which ensured that the Irish Parliament
could legislate only in accordance with proposals previously approved by the
English crown. A further act applied all English laws to Ireland.

Poznań (German name: Posen) 52 55N 16 53E A city in W Poland, on the
Warta River. One of the oldest cities in Poland, it became the first Polish bish-
opric in 968 AD. It possesses an 18th-century cathedral, rebuilt following exten-
sive damage in World War II; its university was founded in 1919. An important
industrial and commercial center, its manufactures include railroad rolling
stock, chemicals, and glass. Population (1992 est): 590,100.

Poznań Riots (1956) Labor disturbances in Poland. They began when work-
ers at a steel plant in Poznań staged a strike to protest against the country's polit-
ical restrictions and economic problems. The ensuing riots were ruthlessly sup-
pressed, with the death of 53 people, but they forced the appointment of a
reformist leader, Władysław Gomułka.

Prado An art gallery in the Prado Avenue, Madrid. Designed originally as a
natural-history museum by the neoclassical architect Juan de Villanueva (1739–
1811), the art gallery was founded in 1818 by Ferdinand VII. Most of its
collection consists of paintings collected by the Spanish monarchs from the 16th century on-
ward. Its works by *Vélazquez, *Goya, *El Greco, *Titian, and *Bosch are among
the finest in the world.

Praesepe An open *star cluster in the constellation Cancer, just visible to the naked eye.

praetor In ancient Rome, originally a consul as leader of an army and subsequently a magistrate responsible for the administration of justice. From about 242 BC a second praetor assisted with lawsuits involving foreigners. Later more praetors were appointed to administer the increasing number of provinces and numbered 18 under Emperor Nerva (96–98 AD).

Praetorian Guard The official bodyguard of the Roman emperors created by Augustus in 27 BC. Composed of up to 16 long-serving cohorts (infantry divisions) each of 500–1000 men, and stationed as a single unit in Rome, the Guard and its commanders developed great political influence; as senatorial power diminished emperors came to rely upon Praetorian support for election and in later imperial times the emperor's position and even his life depended on the Guard's favor.

Praetorius, Michael (M. Schultheiss; 1571–1621) German composer. He studied the organ, worked in the service of Julius Heinrich, duke of Brunswick (1564–1613), and was kapellmeister in Wolfsbüttel (1612–21). He composed a large number of motets, hymns, madrigals, and dance pieces, as well as writing *Syntagma musicum* (1615–20), a valuable account of the musical theory and instruments of the time.

pragmatic sanction A royal edict establishing a fundamental principle of government. Historically the term is usually applied to the edict of Emperor Charles VI (1713) settling the succession to his Austrian territories on his daughter Maria Theresa. Disregard of this edict by European powers provoked the War of the *Austrian Succession (1740–48). The Edict of Bourges, issued by Charles VII of France in 1438 and limiting papal authority over the French Church, was also a pragmatic sanction.

pragmatism A philosophical movement initiated by William James (*see* James, Henry) and C. S. *Peirce in the US. It asserts that the truth of a theory can be judged only by its practical consequences, so the question is: what difference would it make if it were true? The comprehensive metaphysical schemes of European philosophers were thus found to have no meaning, since their truth or falsity did not affect human experience. In science, a theory was true if it "worked"—if its expected consequences occurred. In ethics and theology a principle or belief was true if it satisfied its holders. *See also* Dewey, John.

Prague (Czech name: Praha) 50 8N 14 25E The capital of the Czech Republic, on the Vltava River. The industrial and commercial center of the republic, its various manufactures include machinery, cars, aircraft, processed foods, clothing, and chemicals. A leading cultural center, Prague is the site of Charles University (1348) and a technical university (1707). Notable buildings include Hradčany Castle and the mainly gothic Cathedral of St Vitus. *History*: in the Middle Ages it was the seat of the Přemyslid kings of Bohemia. Following rivalry between the Czechs and Germans, it became the center of the religious reform movement of Jan *Hus. Under Hapsburg rule from the 16th century, it was made the capital of newly independent Czechoslovakia in 1918. In 1968 the city was occupied by Soviet troops following Soviet opposition to the liberal Dubček government. Population (1991): 1,212,000.

Prague School A group of language scholars based in Prague during the 1920s and 1930s, including N. S. Trubetskoy and Roman Jakobson. Their work was chiefly in the field of Saussurean structural *linguistics. They originated aspects of modern phonological theory, drew sociolinguistic distinctions between various aspects of language use (for example, between everyday and poetic language), and devised the concept of analyzing both speech sounds and word meanings into ultimate components transcending individual languages.

prairie dog A large *ground squirrel, *Cynomys ludovicanis,* of North America, also called black-tailed prairie marmot. Heavily built animals, about 12 in (30 cm) long, prairie dogs live in large colonies called "towns." They feed on grass and have been treated as pests by cattle ranchers. Prairie dogs raise a firm rim of soil round their burrows so that the surface water will not enter. □mammal.

Prairie Provinces The Canadian provinces of *Alberta, *Manitoba, and *Saskatchewan. They lie chiefly in the Great Plains and are major producers of wheat and oil.

prairies The extensive grasslands of the interior of North America. They occupy a broad N–S belt extending from Alberta and Saskatchewan through the Midwest into Texas, reaching as far W as the Rocky Mountains. Little of the original true prairie now remains, having been extensively plowed for wheat production. *See also* steppes.

prairie wolf. *See* coyote.

Prakrit Ancient *Indo-Aryan languages of N India, which were considerably simpler than the standard written form of *Sanskrit. From these spoken forms are derived a number of literary styles and the modern languages of N India. *Pali, the language of the Jain scriptures, is included among the Prakrits.

Prandtl, Ludwig (1875–1953) German physicist, whose discovery of the boundary layer adjoining the surface of a solid over which a fluid flows led to the foundation of aerodynamics. His major studies were on the effects of streamlining and the properties of aircraft wings. He also made important improvements to such constructions as wind tunnels and his name is remembered in the **Prandtl number**, a dimensionless group used in the study of convection.

Prasad, Rajendra (1884–1963) Indian statesman; the first president of India (1950–1962). He gave up his legal practice to join *Gandhi's movement of noncooperation with the British and was several times president of the *Indian National Congress (1934, 1939, 1947–48). He helped draft the new Indian constitution.

praseodymium (Pr) A *lanthanide element, which was separated from its mixture with neodyminium by von Welsbach in 1885. It forms trihalides (for example $PrCl_3$) and an oxide (Pr_2O_3), which is used to give a strong yellow color to glass. At no 59; at wt 140.9077; mp 1709°F (931°C); bp 6360°F (3512°C).

pratincole A bird belonging to an Old World subfamily (*Glareolinae;* 6 species); 7–9 in (17–22 cm) long, pratincoles have a forked tail, long pointed wings, and a small bill with a wide gape for catching insects. The common pratincole (*Glareola pratincola*) has red-brown underwings and a yellow throat outlined by a black band. Family: *Glareolidae* (pratincoles and coursers); order: *Charadriiformes* (gulls, plovers, etc.).

Prato (*or* Prato in Toscana) 43 53N 11 06E A city in central Italy, in Tuscany on the Bisenzio River. It has a cathedral (dating from the 12th century) and is an important center of the woolen industry. Population (1991 est): 166,688.

prawn A large shrimplike *crustacean (up to 8 in [20 cm] long), belonging to the suborder *Natantia.* The antennae are longer than the body and a forward projection of the carapace forms a spike (rostrum) between the eyes, bearing six or more teeth. The second pair of appendages are enlarged to form pincers (*compare* shrimp). The common edible prawn (*Leander serratus*) occurs in temperate coastal waters and is 2–3 in (5–8 cm) long. Large shrimps are often mistakenly called prawns.

Praxiteles (mid-4th century BC) Athenian sculptor, renowned for his handling of marble. His statue of Hermes, discovered at *Olympia in 1877, exemplifies the sensuous grace and repose for which his work was noted. Most of his statues have perished, but some, such as the famous Aphrodite of Cnidos, are known from Roman copies.

Precambrian Geological time from the formation of the earth's crust, about 4500 million years ago, to about 590 million years ago when the Paleozoic era began. Precambrian rocks lie below the Cambrian system and fossils are rare and often obscure. The rocks have been subjected to much alteration because of their great age. Most are metamorphosed and have undergone one or more Precambrian mountain-building periods as well as later ones. The largest areas of exposed Precambrian rocks are the *shield areas. Correlation of successive strata is done where possible by radiocative *dating. *See also* Cryptozoic time.

precession The rotation about an axis of a line that is itself the axis of a rotating body. The effect may be observed in a spinning top, of which the axis of rotation is initially vertical but, as the top slows down, begins to precess about its original position. *See also* precession of the equinoxes.

precession of the equinoxes The gradual westward motion of the *equinoxes around the *ecliptic in a period of about 25,800 years. It is caused by the *precession of the earth's axis of rotation, which results mainly from the gravitational pull of the sun and moon on the equatorial bulge of the nonspherical earth. As the axis precesses, slowly tracing out a circle in the sky, the celestial equator (lying in a plane perpendicular to the axis) moves relative to the ecliptic. The points of intersection, i.e. the equinoxes, thus continuously change.

predestination In Christian doctrine, God's foreordaining of salvation for certain people. The idea is explicitly propagated by St *Paul in the Epistles. It raises enormous problems about the nature of divine justice and the role of the human will and endeavors, problems that Christian philosophers have never satisfactorily solved. St *Augustine of Hippo, *Origen, and St Thomas *Aquinas were among those who produced influential approaches to the difficulties. An extreme form of predestination was integral to *Calvinism, with salvation for the elect and eternal damnation for everyone else, whatever their virtues or faults. Modern thinking on the subject tends to stress the universality of God's will to save mankind.

prefect A high-ranking French government official. Created in 1800 by Napoleon's reorganization of provincial government, prefects are responsible for general administration, public law and order, and the enforcement of central government policies in their own departments. Although dependence on the government in power and a centralized bureaucracy weakens their position, prefects still have considerable civil authority.

pregnancy The period during which a fetus develops within the womb, usually lasting for about 280 days from conception to delivery of the baby. Pregnancy is signaled by cessation of the menstrual periods, tenderness and discomfort in the breasts, and—sometimes—an increase in appetite, nausea, and vomiting. These changes are brought about by the activity of hormones secreted by the *corpus luteum (in the ovary) and *placenta. In the early weeks pregnancy can be definitely diagnosed only by means of pregnancy tests. A commonly used test is based on the detection of the hormone chorionic *gonadotrophin in the urine. *See also* childbirth; prenatal diagnosis.

Pregnancy in animals is usually called gestation, and the period varies between species. In elephants, for instance, it is 18 months and in rats 3 weeks.

Preminger, Otto (Ludwig) (1906–86) US film director, born in Austria. He went to the US in 1935 and became a naturalized citizen in 1943. His films range from literary adaptations to large-scale epics and include *Laura* (1944), *Anatomy of a Murder* (1959), and *Exodus* (1960).

premise One of the statements in an argument or chain of reasoning from which the conclusion follows or is said to follow. For example, from the premises "only dogs bark" and "Fido barks," the conclusion is that "Fido is a dog."

Premonstratensians A Roman Catholic order of monks, also called Norbertines after St Norbert (c. 1080–1134), who founded them in 1120 at Prémontré (N France). They originally followed an austere rule, which included total abstinence from meat. The order spread all over Europe but was nearly annihilated during the French Revolution. Belgium is now its main base.

prenatal diagnosis Tests made on pregnant women in order to diagnose genetic or developmental abnormalities in the developing fetus. If the tests reveal severe malformation or gross malfunctioning in the fetus the possibility of an *abortion is considered. The investigations include X-rays, scanning using ultrasonic rays, *amniocentesis (involving analysis of a sample of the amniotic fluid surrounding the fetus), and fetoscopy, in which a sample of fetal blood is withdrawn from the placenta and examined for abnormal cells (indicating blood disorders, such as *thalassemia). Some of the techniques may involve risks to the health of the mother or fetus and are not undertaken without good cause.

Preparedness Movement (1915–16) Campaign to bolster the US armed forces in anticipation of involvement in *World War I. Advocated by Theodore *Roosevelt and other national figures when it became obvious that the neutrality of the US was being violated, the movement sponsored legislation to increase national defense.

pre-Raphaelite Brotherhood The 19th-century British painters Dante Gabriel *Rossetti, John Everett *Millais, and William Holman *Hunt, who joined together in 1848 in reaction to the banality of contemporary British painting and its enthusiasm for *Raphael. Signing all their works PRB, they sought to emulate Italian painters earlier than Raphael and to paint subjects of a moral or religious character, many of their subjects being drawn from medieval literature. Although initially attacked for their lack of idealism, particularly in religious subjects, by 1851 the PRB had won the support of the art critic John *Ruskin. Although the group disbanded soon afterward (Hunt being the only member to remain faithful to PRB ideas), the PRB had a strong influence on such artists as William *Morris and Edward *Burne-Jones, as well as subsequent painting styles.

Presbyterianism A form of Protestant Church organization based on government by elders (*compare* episcopacy). These elders comprise the ministers and certain laymen from each congregation and all have equal rank; they enforce a strict code of ethics and make decisions on Church policy through a hierarchical system of presbyteries, synods, and general assemblies. Presbyterianism originated with the 16th-century followers of *Calvin who believed that they were returning to a system of the primitive Church. In Scotland the tenets of Presbyterianism were formulated (1560) by *Knox and it became the established Church in 1696. A pan-Presbyterian alliance (founded 1875) embraces the Presbyterian Churches in the US and elsewhere.

Prescott, William Hickling (1796–1859) US historian. Prescott established his reputation with a major work, *The History of the Reign of Ferdinand and Isabella* (1837). There followed *The Conquest of Mexico* (1843), *The Conquest of*

Peru (1847), and *The History of Philip II* (1855–58). Although his critical insight was not outstanding, Prescott combined factual accuracy with a vivid narrative style. His discursive memory compensated for his partial blindness.

president In most republics, the executive head of state. In the US the president is the head of the executive branch of government, which was established together with the legislature (*see* Congress) and the judiciary (*see* Supreme Court) by the US constitution (1789). In modern times the president is a member of the *Democratic party or the *Republican party and is elected every four years; no one may hold the office for more than eight years. The president is head of the *cabinet. In some other countries (e.g. Germany and Italy) the president fulfills the nonexecutive function of a monarch.

presidential powers Those powers invested in the head of a country that enable the country's laws to be carried out. Included in the powers of the US president are command of the armed forces; appointment of cabinet members, agency heads, ambassadors, and Supreme Court justices; and declaring war with the consent of Congress.

presidential succession US procedure for transferral of the presidency in cases of emergency, such as death, inability to function, or resignation. Provided for in the US Constitution and amended by the Presidential Succession Act of 1947 and the 25th Amendment (1967), the line of succession is the vice president, the speaker of the House of Representatives, the president pro tempore of the Senate, and the secretary of state.

President of the United States. *See* president.

President Pro Tempore of the Senate The presiding officer of the US Senate when the vice president is not available. The position is filled by a senator who is elected by fellow senators.

Presley, Elvis (Aaron) (1935–77) US popular singer, whose first big hit, "Heartbreak Hotel" (1956), was followed by "Hound Dog" and "Don't Be Cruel." His suggestive performances earned him the nickname "Elvis the Pelvis." Presley also appeared in numerous films and television programs and was long one of the most popular entertainers in the US and the world. His death, probably a result of drug dependence, resulted in his becoming a cult figure.

preSocratics Greek philosophers who lived in Ionia and S Italy (Magna Graecia) during the 6th and early 5th centuries BC, before the time of *Socrates. They were responsible for the earliest philosophical—as opposed to magical and religious—speculation about the universe. The Ionians were *Thales, *Anaximander, and *Anaximenes, all of Miletus, *Xenophanes of Colophon, and *Heraclitus of Ephesus. Notable figures in Italy were *Parmenides and *Zeno, both of Elea (*see* Eleatics), and *Pythagoras.

Pressburg, Treaties of 1. (1491) The treaty in which Maximilian, Hapsburg heir to the Holy Roman Empire, recognized Vladislav II of Bohemia (1456–1516) as king of Hungary, renouncing his own claim in return for the restoration of Austria, Styria, and Carinthia, which had been annexed by Matthias I Corvinus in 1486. **2.** (1805) The treaty between Austria and France following Napoleon's defeat of Austria at Austerlitz. Austria surrendered territory and paid a large indemnity.

press gang A band of men employed to force paupers, tramps, or criminals into the army or navy. This system of impressment (recruits were paid imprest money), common throughout the world in the 18th century, ceased when improved pay and conditions in the army and navy increased voluntary recruitment.

ELVIS PRESLEY *In a scene from* Girl Happy (1965).

pressure Force per unit area. For a liquid, density d, the pressure at a depth h is hdg, where g is the *acceleration of free fall. Pressure is usually measured in pascals, millimeters of mercury, or millibars.

pressure gauge An instrument for measuring the pressure of a fluid. Atmospheric pressure is measured with a mercury *barometer or an aneroid barometer. Pressures above atmospheric pressure are usually measured with a Bourdon gauge, which consists of a flattened curved tube that tends to straighten under pressure. As it straightens it moves a pointer around a scale. Low pressures are measured with such vacuum gauges as the *McLeod gauge or *Pirani gauge.

Prestel. *See* viewdata.

Prester John A legendary Christian priest-king. First mentioned in 12th-century chronicles, he became famous as the hero destined to help the Crusaders against Islam. He was sometimes identified as a Chinese prince but more commonly as the king of Ethiopa.

Preston 53 46N 2 42W A city and port in NW England, on the Ribble River. It was the site of a major battle in the English *Civil War. It has plastics, chemical, motor-vehicle and aircraft construction, and electronics industries as well as the traditional cotton and engineering works. Population (1981): 143,734.

Pretender, Old. *See* James Edward Stuart, the Old Pretender.

Pretender, Young. *See* Charles Edward Stuart, the Young Pretender.

Pretoria 25 36S 28 12E The administrative capital of South Africa and the capital of the Transvaal. Founded in 1855, it became the capital of the Union of South Africa in 1910. The University of South Africa was founded there in 1873; other important institutions are the University of Pretoria (1930) and the Onderstepoort Veterinary Research Institute. Pretoria is noted for its jacarandalined avenues and Voortrekker monument. Its industries include iron and steel processing, engineering, and food processing. Population (1991): 443,059.

Pretoria Convention (1881) The peace treaty between Britain and the Transvaal that ended the first *Boer War. The Transvaal acquired self-government under the British crown, which, however, retained control of foreign relations and the power to veto legislation regarding Africans.

Pretorius, Andries (Wilhelmus Jacobus) (1799–1853) Afrikaner leader in the *Great Trek to Natal and then in the Transvaal. He defeated (1840) the Zulu king Dingane and fought the British in Natal (1842) and then in the Transvaal (1848), establishing Transvaal's independence as the South African Republic (1852). The city of Pretoria is named for him. His son **Marthinus Wessel Pretorius** (1819–1901) was president of the South African Republic (formerly and subsequently the Transvaal) from 1857 to 1871 and of the Orange Free State from 1859 to 1863. He returned to politics after Britain's annexation of the Transvaal, finally retiring after Afrikaner victory in the first *Boer War (1880–81).

Prévert, Jacques (1900–77) French poet. He was associated with the surrealist movement in the 1920s. His best-known poems about the street life of Paris, written with anarchic humor, are collected in *Paroles* (1946); later volumes include *Spectacle* (1951) and *Hebromadaires* (1972). He also wrote film scripts, notably for *Les Enfants du paradis* (1944).

Previn, André (Andreas Ludwig Priwin; 1929–) German-born US conductor, pianist, and composer. Active in Hollywood in his youth as a film composer and jazz pianist, he was subsequently conductor of the London Symphony Orchestra (1969–79), and the Pittsburgh Symphony Orchestra (1976–86); director of the Royal Philharmonic Orchestra (1985), and conductor of the Los Angeles Philharmonic (1986–89). He has done much to popularize classical music through television performances.

Prévost d'Exiles, Antoine François, Abbé (1697–1763) French novelist. His unsettled career included periods of military service, of religious retreat as a Benedictine monk, and of exile in England and Holland. Of his many novels and translations, mostly written to pay off debts, the best known is *Manon Lescaut* (1731), the story of a young nobleman ruined by his love for a courtesan, which was used by both Massenet and Puccini as the basis for operas.

Priam In Greek legend, the last king of Troy, husband of Hecuba. As an old man he witnessed the deaths of many of his 50 sons in the *Trojan War and he pleaded with Achilles for the body of Hector. He was killed at the altar of Zeus by Neoptelemus.

Priapus A Greek fertility god associated with gardens, son of Dionysus and Aphrodite. He was usually portrayed as a comic ugly figure with an enormous phallus. The donkey, symbol of lust, was sacrificed to him.

Pribilof Islands Four US islands in the Bering Sea. They are the breeding ground of the northern fur seal. Since 1911 the seals have been protected by agreements between the US, Russia or the Soviet Union, Japan, and Canada. Area: about 65 sq mi (8 sq km).

Price, (Mary) Leontine (1927–) US soprano. After studying at New York City's Juilliard School of Music, she toured internationally as Bess in *Porgy and Bess* (1952–54). She made her debut with the Metropolitan Opera in 1961, singing the role of Leonora in *Il Trovatore*.

price index A single figure used to measure the average percentage change in the price of a set of goods over a period of time, taking a base figure of 100 for a specified year. Thus if a particular price index, in January 1985, stands at 156

(January 1975 = 100), there has been a 56% increase in the average prices over the 10-year period. The best-known indexes are the Wholesale Price Index and the Retail Price Index, the latter providing a reliable guide to the *cost of living. Some wages, salaries, and costs are **index-linked** (i.e. increase in proportion to a specified price index) to cover the devaluation of money as a result of *inflation. **Indexation** is commonly used in agreements that extend over a long period during which inflation is expected to be a significant factor.

prickly heat A disorder that occurs most commonly in the tropics due to obstruction of the ducts of the sweat glands. It causes itching and a red rash and often leads to secondary infection.

prickly pear A *cactus of the genus *Opuntia,* native to North and South America and sometimes cultivated for food or ornament. Introduced to Australia and South Africa, it has become a troublesome weed. It has flat jointed spiny stems bearing large orange or yellow flowers, which give rise to edible pear-shaped fruits. The seeds are used to produce an oil and the shoots are eaten as vegetables or used as animal feed.

prickly poppy A plant of the genus *Argemone,* especially *A. mexicana,* also called devil's fig, native to North America and the West Indies and cultivated as a garden ornamental. Growing 12–35 in (30–90 cm) tall, its blue-green bristly stems bear spiny lobed leaves and orange or pale-yellow flowers, with five pointed petals and numerous long stamens. Family: *Papaveraceae.*

Pride, Thomas (d. 1658) English parliamentary soldier during the Civil War, famous for effecting "Pride's Purge" of Parliament in 1648. He excluded over a hundred Presbyterian representatives suspected of wanting to negotiate with Charles I, leaving the Rump of the *Long Parliament. He was a signatory of Charles's death warrant.

Priestley, J(ohn) B(oynton) (1894–1984) British novelist and dramatist. He first won popular success with his picaresque novel *The Good Companions* (1929). His plays include social comedies, such as *Dangerous Corner* (1932) and *Laburnum Grove* (1933), and several mildly experimental expressionist dramas, including *The Glass Cage* (1957). A traditionalist by temperament and conviction, he published many volumes of criticism and memoirs and was a popular broadcaster during World War II.

Priestley, Joseph (1733–1804) British chemist and one of the discoverers of oxygen (together with Carl *Scheele). Priestley, being a firm believer in the *phlogiston theory, named his gas dephlogisticated air and first prepared it in 1774 by heating mercuric oxide. In 1778–79 *Lavoisier demolished the phlogiston theory and named the gas oxygen. Priestley also produced and studied several other gases, including ammonia, sulfur dioxide, and hydrogen chloride. He invented the method of collecting them over mercury, since some of these gases dissolved in water.

primary colors The minimum number of *colors that, when mixed in the correct proportions, are capable of giving all the other colors in the visible spectrum. When light of three **primary additive colors** (usually red, green, and blue) is mixed in equal intensities, white light results. This principle is used in color television and *color photography. Any particular color can also be obtained by subtracting from white light a mixture of three **primary subtractive colors**, usually cyan (blue-green), magenta (purplish red), and yellow, which are complementary to red, green, and blue. Adding pigments of these in equal proportions gives black pigment.

primate A mammal belonging to the order *Primates* (about 195 species), which includes *prosimians, *monkeys, *apes, and man. Primates probably evolved from insectivorous climbing creatures like *tree shrews and have many adaptations for climbing, including five fingers and five toes with opposable first digits (except in the feet of humans). They have well-developed sight and hearing and—most importantly—enlarged cerebral hemispheres of the brain, most marked in higher primates. Most forms are arboreal but the great apes and man are largely terrestrial.

prime minister A head of government. The best-known example is in the UK, where the post developed in the 18th century with the growth of the *cabinet. Sir Robert *Walpole is generally regarded as the first prime minister (1721–42) but the post was not formally recognized until 1905. The prime minister is customarily a member of the House of Commons and is head of government by virtue of being the leader of the dominant political party in the Commons. The monarch makes all governmental appointments on the advice of the prime minister.

prime number An integer greater than one that has no integral factors except itself and one; for example 2, 3, 5, 7, 11, 13, 17. Every natural number can be expressed uniquely as a product of prime numbers; for example $1260 = 2^2 \times 3^2 \times 5 \times 7$. Prime numbers are of major interest in number theory.

primitivism In art, the style of untrained artists who ignore or are ignorant of both traditional aesthetic standards and avant-garde trends. Its chief characteristics are meticulous detail, brilliant colors, childlike representation, and faulty perspective. Among the first primitives were 17th- and 18th-century American painters who developed in cultural isolation from European artistic trends, but the best known is the French painter Henri *Rousseau. Recent primitives include the Yugoslav peasants Ivan Generalič (1914–) and Mijo Kovačič (1935–) and the American Grandma *Moses. The term is also sometimes applied to African and Polynesian indigenous art.

Primo de Rivera, Miguel (1870–1930) Spanish general, who led a successful coup on Sept 13, 1923, and was dictator of Spain until 1930. He brought the Moroccan War to a victorious end (1927) but dissatisfaction with his absolute rule, exacerbated by the Depression, caused his downfall. *Alfonso XIII's support of Primo de Rivera discredited the monarchy, which was overthrown a year later. His son **José Antonio Primo de Rivera** (1903–36) founded the Falange, the Spanish fascist party. Executed by the Republic shortly after the start of the Spanish Civil War, his memory was honored by Franco's National Movement.

primrose A perennial herbaceous plant, *Primula vulgaris, growing in woodlands and hedge banks in Europe and N Africa. It has a basal rosette of puckered spoon-shaped leaves, with solitary pale-yellow flowers on slender stalks, up to 4 in (10 cm) high. Bird's-eye primrose (P. farinosa) has pale-purple flowers with yellow centers. Family: Primulaceae. See also evening primrose.

Primula A genus of perennial plants (about 500 species), native mainly to N temperate regions and often grown as ornamentals. They have a basal rosette of oval to spoon-shaped leaves and erect flower stalks bearing erect or nodding five-petaled flowers, red, pink, purple, blue, white, or yellow in color and usually with a different colored center. The fruit is a capsule. The genus also includes the *cowslip and *primrose. Family: Primulaceae. See also auricula.

Prince Albert National Park A national park in S Canada, in central Saskatchewan. Established in 1927, the park offers a wide variety of plants, animals, and birds. At an average elevation of 1800 ft (550 m), black and white spruce, as well as aspens and grasslands, are found. The many lakes in the park have made it popular for summer vacations. Area: 1496 sq mi (3875 sq km).

Prince Edward Island An island province of E Canada, in the S Gulf of St Lawrence. Its gentle rolling hills and mild climate support small farms producing potatoes, grains, dairy cattle, and other livestock. Tourism and fishing are also important. *History:* discovered (1534) and colonized (1720) by France, the island was captured (1758) and resettled by Britain. In 1873 it joined Canada. Area: 5657 sq km (2184 sq mi). Population (1991): 129,765. Capital: Charlottetown.

Prince of Wales A title customarily conferred on the eldest son of the British sovereign. It was a native Welsh title until 1301, when Edward I, following his annexation of Wales, bestowed it on his son, the future Edward II. The present holder of the title is Prince *Charles.

Princeton 40 21N 74 40W A city in New Jersey. George Washington defeated the British there on Jan 3, 1777. It is the site of Princeton University (1746) and the Rockefeller Institute for Scientific Research. Population (1990): 12,016.

Princeton University One of the oldest universities in the US, it was founded in 1746 by Presbyterians. A private institution, it has been situated at Princeton, N.J., since 1756. Women were first admitted to the university in 1969.

princewood A dark wood with lighter veins, obtained from two tropical trees found in the West Indies, *Hamelia ventricosa,* also called Spanish elm (family *Rubiaceae*), and *Cordia gerascanthoides* (family *Ehretiaceae*). It is used for furniture, doors, boats, etc.

Príncipe Island. *See* São Tomé and Príncipe.

printed circuit An electronic circuit in which the connections between components are formed by a pattern of conducting film on a board, instead of by wires. The method greatly facilitates mass-production. An insulating board is coated with a conducting material, such as copper, and a protective pattern is deposited on it using photographic techniques. The unprotected metal is then etched away and components are soldered in place. In television receivers, the replacement of thermionic valves by plug-in printed-circuit boards has made maintenance easier. A faulty circuit board can be quickly replaced without tracing the individual failed component.

printing The production of multiple copies of text or pictures, usually on paper. The oldest method, in use in China and Japan before 800 AD, is **letter-press**, in which the raised surfaces of etched, engraved, or cast material are inked and pressed onto the paper. This method was revolutionized by the invention of movable type (*see* typesetting) in the 15th century, but printing itself remained fundamentally unchanged for four centuries until other methods of mechanization were introduced. Early printing presses were of the hand-operated platen variety in which the type stands on a horizontal surface and the paper is pressed onto it from above. Faster production became possible on the power-driven presses of the 19th century: first the cylinder press, in which the paper is rolled by a cylinder over a flat printing surface, and later the rotary press, in which the printing surface is also a cylinder. Different types of rotary press print either on separate sheets or on a web (*see* paper), which makes for still faster printing—up to 35,000 impressions per hour.

In **lithography**, a method invented by Aloys *Senefelder in 1798, the printing surface is plane (originally a polished stone but now usually an aluminum sheet), the printing and nonprinting areas being made grease-receptive and grease-repellent respectively (*see* platemaking). Greasy ink is rolled over the entire area but is taken only by the grease-receptive areas; the ink is then transferred by rolling onto the paper. **Offset printing**, most commonly lithography, involves an intermediate rubber-covered cylinder that transfers the ink from plate to paper. In **gravure printing**, the small square etched holes (cells) in the

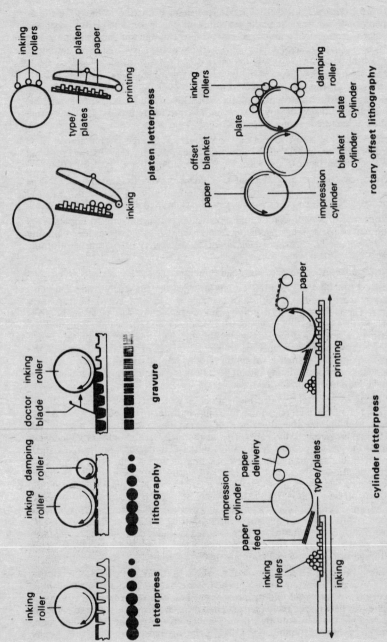

PRINTING *Principles of three major printing processes and the three major designs of printing presses.*

copper printing plate are filled with a free-flowing ink, the rest of the plate is wiped clean, and the plate is rolled against the paper, which absorbs the ink out of the cells. Nearly all gravure and offset lithography is done on rotary presses.

Letterpress and offset lithography are used for almost all types of printing jobs; because of the expensive copper plates gravure is limited to long runs, such as cheap illustrated magazines, postage stamps, and packaging. Direct lithography has been used almost exclusively by artists—*Goya and *Manet, for example— and was the principal medium for *poster art in the 19th century. **Flexography** is a widespread form of (usually rotary) letterpress printing using fluid volatile ink and a rubber printing surface. It is used for paperback books, packaging materials, and for printing on nonabsorbent surfaces, such as plastic foil. In **silk-screen printing** (screen-process printing *or* serigraphy), a piece of taut open-weave silk, metal, or synthetic fabric carries the negative of the desired image in an impervious substance, such as glue; ink is forced through the clear (printing) areas by a squeegee onto the paper, glass, fabric, or other material, behind. It is used for printing posters, electronic circuit boards, labeling on bottles, and anything that requires a thick layer of ink or other material. For example pop artists, such as Andy *Warhol, use it to make painted photographic transfers. **Collotype** is a method of printing short runs of high-quality illustrations from gelatin plates; it is not widely used but it is the only method by which continuous tone can be reproduced (*see* platemaking).

Full-color reproduction is achieved by **color-process printing**, in which all colors can be produced from combinations of three primary colors—yellow, cyan (blue-green), and magenta. Four separate printing plates are made, one for each primary and one for black; each is printed in succession in exactly the same place. In letterpress and lithography, half-tones are used instead of printing plates (*see* platemaking). At the normal viewing distance for any piece of color-process printing, the dots are imperceptible, and the effect is of varying shades.

prion A *petrel belonging to a genus (*Pachyptila*; 4 species) found in Antarctica and nearby islands; 8–11 in (20–27 cm) long, prions have a blue-gray plumage with white underparts. The flattened bill has a fringe of strainers with the floor of the mouth forming a small pouch; it feeds by skimming over the sea and straining out small invertebrates.

Prior, Matthew (1664–1721) British poet. He became a member of Parliament in 1700 and served as a diplomat in France and Holland. He wrote several long philosophical poems but is best known for *Poems on Several Occasions* (1709).

Pripet River (Russian name: Pripyat) A river rising in NW Ukraine, it flows mainly ENE through Belarus and joins the Dnepr River near Kiev. The **Pripet Marshes** that lie along its course were the scene of extensive fighting in World War II. Length: 500 mi (800 km).

Priscian (6th century AD) Latin grammarian, born at Caesarea (now Cherchell, Algeria). He taught at Constantinople and was the last considerable Latin scholar in antiquity. His *Institutiones Grammaticae*, in 18 books, which sum up the researches of all previous grammarians, remained a standard work throughout the Middle Ages.

prism A piece of glass or other transparent material having parallel polygonal ends, with a number of rectangular surfaces meeting them at right angles. They are used in optical instruments, such as cameras and binoculars, for changing the direction of light, either by refraction or by reflection from its walls. They are also used for splitting light into its component colors as a result of double refraction, once on entering the prism and again on leaving it.

prisoner of war A soldier captured by a belligerent in war. Guerrillas are so categorized provided that they have a commander, wear distinctive clothing, carry arms openly, and obey the laws and customs of war. The rights of a prisoner of war, which are defined in the *Geneva Conventions of 1929 and 1949 and are supervised by the International *Red Cross, include: withholding all information except name, rank, and number; receiving adequate amounts of food, drink, and medical care; engaging in correspondence and receiving parcels; and attempting to escape without being punished for so doing. In addition, prison camps must be open for inspection by the representatives of neutral powers.

prisons Institutions for confining convicted criminals (*see* criminal law). In primitive societies, and throughout much of history, offenders were either banished, executed, or physically punished; such prisons as existed were primarily places in which people were held until these punishments could be carried out. It was not until the 18th century that the main purpose of prisons became custodial. The appalling prison conditions at this time led to both reform movements and large-scale prison-building programs in the US in the late 19th century. Reforms since the 19th century have changed the emphasis in penal institutions from retribution to correction and rehabilitation. These have included halfway houses and other measures that prepare prisoners for reentry into society. Overcrowding, however, has remained a feature of US prisons and became particularly severe in the 1980s and 1990s.

Pritchett, V(ictor) S(awden) (1900–   ) British short-story writer and critic. He traveled widely in Europe during the 1920s and has written frequently about Spain. He has published critical works, such as *A Man of Letters* (1986); volumes of stories including *Collected Stories* (1956), *Selected Stories of V. S. Pritchett* (1978), *Collected Stories* (1982), *More Collected Stories* (1983), and *A Careless Widow and Other Stories* (1989); biographies, including *The Gentle Barbarian* (1977) and *Chekhov* (1988); and two much acclaimed autobiographical books, *A Cab at the Door* (1968) and *Midnight Oil* (1971).

private enterprise. *See* capitalism.

privateering The practice of permitting, under government license, private individuals to equip ships to attack and capture enemy merchantmen. Such action constituted piracy without the privateers' official authorization—"letters of marque." Although a useful complement to regular navies and common during the 17th and 18th centuries, privateering frequently degenerated into piracy because these formalities were disregarded; all European countries, except Spain, renounced privateering in 1856. The US abandoned it after the Civil War. *See also* buccaneers.

privet An evergreen or deciduous shrub or small tree of the genus *Ligustrum* (40–50 species), native to Eurasia and Australia and widely used for ornamental hedges, especially the European common privet (*L. vulgare*). Growing up to about 16 ft (5 m) high, it has simple oval leaves and terminal clusters of small creamy four-lobed flowers, which give rise to black berries. Family: *Oleaceae*.

Privy Council A body advising the British monarch, now having chiefly formal functions. It grew out of the Curia Regis (King's Court), forming a distinct group of royal advisers in the 14th century. The emergence of the *cabinet system of government in the 18th century led to a lessening of its power. By convention, it consists of all cabinet ministers, the archbishops of Canterbury and York, the Speaker of the House of Commons, and a number of senior British and Commonwealth statesmen.

probability The mathematical concept concerned with the effects of chance on an event, experiment, or observation. It originated in 1654, when the mathematicians *Pascal and *Fermat worked on problems sent to them by a gambler.

If an event can occur in n ways and r is the number of ways it can occur in a specified way, then the **mathematical probability** of it occurring in the specified way is r/n. For example, the probability of the number 5 coming up on a six-faced dice in one throw is $\frac{1}{6}$. The probability of a 5 coming up x times in x throws is obtained by multiplication, i.e. it is $(\frac{1}{6})^x$. Probabilities are expressed as numbers between 1 (a certainty) and 0 (an impossibility).

If in a number of experiments an event has occurred n times and failed m times, the **empirical probability** of success in the next trial is $n/(n + m)$. Actuarial tables of life expectancy are based on empirical probabilities.

proboscis monkey A large leaf-eating *Old World monkey, *Nasalis larvatus*, of Borneo. Up to 5 ft (1.5 m) tall, proboscis monkeys have a protruding nose and live in groups in forests, feeding on young palm leaves. They can swim as well as climb.

processionary caterpillar The caterpillar of a moth of Old World genus *Thaumetopoea*. The caterpillars move in columns, guided by a leader, keeping head and tail contact with each other. Resting in nests by day, they feed at night and can be very destructive.

Proclus (410–85 AD) Neoplatonist philosopher, head of *Plato's Academy at Athens. Indefatigable in commenting on, and explaining, earlier philosophers, Proclus integrated pagan religion, philosophy, and mathematics into a single system. His works, translated into Latin and Arabic, transmitted *Neoplatonism to the medieval world.

Procne. *See* Philomela and Procne.

Proconsul A genus of extinct apes whose remains have been found in E Africa. They lived 20 million years ago and were probably ground dwellers but could not stand erect. *Proconsul* apes were ancestors of modern apes.

Procopius (6th century AD) Byzantine historian. He accompanied the military commander Belisarius on several campaigns and worked in Constantinople from about 540 AD. His works include histories of the wars and of the public works undertaken during the reign of the Emperor Justinian I.

Procrustes A lengendary Greek robber. He tortured his victims by stretching them or cutting off their limbs so that they fitted the exact length of his bed. He was killed by Theseus.

Procyon A conspicuous star, apparent magnitude 0.35 and 11.4 light years distant, that is the brightest star in the constellation Canis Minor and one of the nearest stars to the sun. It is part of a *multiple star, forming a visual *binary star with a *white dwarf.

producer gas A fuel gas containing nitrogen and carbon monoxide, as well as small amounts of hydrogen and hydrocarbons. It is produced by passing air (mixed with a little steam) over incandescent coke. The calorific value is low but heat is also obtained from the heat of reaction. *See also* water gas.

productivity The output of goods and services in a factory, country, etc., in relation to inputs (workers, machines, land) used to produce them. It is difficult to produce a single measure of productivity, but output per manhour can be used as a rough approximation. Increases in productivity are largely responsible for the large increases in output in Western economies since World War II; these increases are probably largely due to increased *investment in new machines and the higher levels of education and skill in the workforce. Two causes of low productivity may be distinguished: overmanning, the use of too many workers to produce a given level of output, and underproduction, a given number of workers producing less output than they should. **Productivity bargaining** is a form of *collective bargaining in which wage increases are agreed subject to a corresponding increase in productivity.

profit sharing Any program for sharing the profits of a firm between employees as well as shareholders. The aim is to give employees an interest in the profitability of a firm both as an incentive to productivity and to promote good *industrial relations. Profits may be shared in the form of bonuses or by making employees shareholders.

progesterone A steroid hormone secreted mainly by the *corpus luteum of the mammalian ovary following ovulation. It prepares the womb for implantation of the embryo and maintains this state during pregnancy. Progestogens—synthetic steroids with progesterone-like actions—are constituents of *oral contraceptives; they are also used to treat menstrual disorders. Progesterone preparations have been used in cattle breeding to suspend the estrous cycle and to enable the mating of the whole herd to be synchronized.

program, computer A series of instructions, written in a special programming language, enabling a *computer to perform a particular function. In a large computer there are several levels of programming. Low-level programming languages are those that resemble more closely the logic of the machine itself. High-level languages, such as *FORTRAN, *ALGOL, and *COBOL, are used for the first stage of passing instructions from the human operator to the machine. *See also* software.

program music Music that is based on a literary, descriptive, or emotional subject, in contrast to **absolute music**, which has no overt associations outside the music itself. Programmatic elements are found in music of almost all periods; one of the first major works of program music was Vivaldi's set of violin concertos entitled *The Four Seasons* (1725), based on four sonnets by the composer. The development of the *symphonic poem and the concert *overture in the 19th century resulted in such well-known programmatic compositions as Mussorgsky's *Night on Bald Mountain* (a depiction of a witches' sabbath), Liszt's *Les Préludes* (based on Lamartine's *Méditations poétiques*), and Richard Strauss's *Alpine Symphony* (a description of the ascent and descent of a mountain).

Progressive party (1912–16) US political party; also called the Bull Moose party. A progressive faction of the Republican party tried to nominate Theodore *Roosevelt as its presidential candidate in 1912. Defeated at the Republican convention, the faction split from the Republican party, and Roosevelt became the candidate of the new Progressive party. Espousing restrictions on business, aid to farmers, and reform in labor and industry, Roosevelt attracted enough votes to cause a loss for Republican presidental candidate William Howard *Taft in 1912. By 1916 it had rejoined the Republican party to unite behind Charles Evans *Hughes for president.

progressive taxation. *See* taxation.

Prohibition (1919–33) The period during which the manufacture, sale, and transportation of alcoholic drinks were prohibited in the US by the 18th Amendment to the constitution. The *temperance movement, which attributed crime and poverty to alcohol, combined with the wartime need to divert grain from distilleries to food manufacture, led to national prohibition. It proved impossible to enforce, not least because prohibition agents were outnumbered by gangsters and others profiting from illicit alcohol, and in 1933 prohibition was repealed by the 21st Amendment. *See* bootlegging.

projection (geometry) A mapping of a figure in one plane onto its image in another, called the image plane or plane of projection. A map of the earth's surface is an example of a projection (*see* map projection). The image of each point in the figure is the intersection of a straight line (the projector) and the image plane. In central projection a projector is the straight line drawn though the point and a fixed point (the center of projection). In orthogonal projection a projector is the perpendicular from the point to the image plane. The set of image points makes up the image figure.

projection (psychology) The process of attributing one's own qualities to other people or things. In *psychoanalysis this is a *defense mechanism; people who cannot tolerate their own emotions may cope by believing that other people have them. In projective tests, such as the *Rorschach test, a person's character is assessed from his descriptions of ambiguous objects.

projector, film A device for viewing photographic transparencies by shining a light through them to produce an enlarged image on a screen. Its principal use is in *cinematography although still pictures are also often viewed on slide projectors, particularly for viewing by a number of people together. Motion picture projectors and some home-movie projectors also contain equipment for reproducing sound from the track on the edge of the film.

Prokofiev, Sergei (1891–1953) Soviet composer and pianist. He studied at the St Petersburg conservatory under Rimsky-Korsakov. He won the Anton Rubinstein Prize in 1914, playing his first piano concerto. He lived abroad from 1918 to 1933 and in 1948 was officially condemned for "undemocratic tendencies" in his music. His work includes seven symphonies (the first of which is the *Classical Symphony*; 1916–17), five piano concertos, two violin concertos, the operas *Love for Three Oranges* (1919) and *War and Peace* (1941; revised 1952), the ballet *Romeo and Juliet* (1935–36), music for the films *Lieutenant Kijé* (1934) and *Alexander Nevsky* (1938), and *Peter and the Wolf* (1936) for speaker and orchestra.

Prokop (*or* Procop; c. 1380–1434) Bohemian priest and leader of the *Hussites. In the 1420s Prokop successfully led the Hussites against the imperial armies detached to destroy them but, after joining the radical (Taborite) Hussites against the moderates (1434), he was killed in the ensuing battle of Lipany.

Prokopyevsk 53 55N 86 45E A city in S Russia. Located in the Kuznetsk Basin, it is an important coal-mining center. Population (1991 est): 273,100.

prolactin A protein hormone, produced by the pituitary gland, that initiates and maintains lactation in mammals. In other animals, it has a variety of functions, being involved in growth and the balance of water and salts, as well as reproduction. *See also* gonadotrophin.

proletariat Originally, the lower class of Rome and other ancient states, the term was later used to refer to the lower class of any community. *Marx defined the proletariat as the wage laborers of capitalist economies, who depended on the sale of their labor to live and who owned no property; the struggle between this class and the *bourgeoisie would eventually lead to revolution. *See* Marxism.

Prometheus (Greek: forethought) In Greek mythology, the son of a Titan and Themis who created man and endowed him with reason. He also stole fire from heaven to give to man. Zeus chained him to a rock in the Caucasus and sent an eagle each day to devour his liver, which grew again by night. After thousands of years he was rescued by Heracles.

promethium (Pm) A radioactive element, not known on earth but identified by its spectrum in the light from stars, in which it is continuously being formed by nuclear reactions. The most stable isotope has a half-life of 17.7 years. Promethium salts exhibit bluish-green *luminescence and can be used in photoelectric cells. It is obtained from nuclear reactors. At no 61; at wt (145); mp about 1975°F (1080°C).

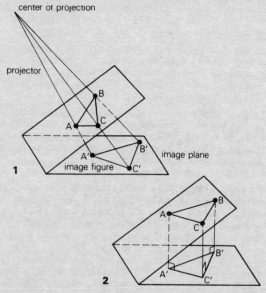

PROJECTION *The mapping of a triangle by* (1) *central and* (2) *orthogonal projections.*

pronghorn A hoofed mammal, *Antilocapra americana,* resembling an antelope and found in rocky deserts of the W US. Up to 40 in (100 cm) high at the shoulder, pronghorns are not true antelopes, shedding the horny sheath of their branched horns every year; the bony core is permanent. Brown above and white beneath with white chevrons under the neck, they have brilliant-white rump hairs used for signaling. They are the only surviving members of the family *Antilocapridae.*

proof alcohol *See* alcohol strength.

propellant 1. A solid or liquid substance used to provide thrust in a rocket engine or gun. Propellants utilize very fast exothermic chemical reactions to produce large quantities of expanding gas quickly. Generally, they are explosive substances or mixtures. A single unstable substance (such as nitrocellulose) or mixture of combustible material and oxidant (such as alcohol and hydrogen peroxide) is termed a **monopropellant**. If the combustible material and oxidant are mixed in a combustion chamber the mixture forms a **bipropellant**. Generally, bipropellants are hypergolic systems, i.e. systems that ignite spontaneously when mixed. **2.** The pressurized inert liquids used to drive an *aerosol from its container.

propeller A device for converting the rotation of a shaft into thrust in the direction of its axis. A **marine propeller** is attached to a shaft connected to the ship's engine and has between two and six blades, shaped as part of a helical surface. It acts as a screw, accelerating a column of water rearward. An **air propeller** (*or* airscrew), moving in a thinner medium, has longer thinner blades (usually two or four) and a higher rotational speed. It, too, accelerates a mass of air rearward thrusting the aircraft forward by reaction.

proper motion The rate at which a star is observed to move on the *celestial sphere, i.e. perpendicular to the line of sight. Values are very small, often negligible.

Propertius, Sextus (c. 50–c. 16 BC) Roman poet. Born in Assisi in Umbria, he went to Rome as a young man and established himself in literary circles. *Cynthia,* the first of his four surviving books, contains highly personal love poems addressed to his mistress Hostia. His later books contain more generalized poems on various topics, including the psychology of love, written in a style noted for its bold originality.

prophets Ancient Israelite religious leaders and visionaries. The books of the prophets make up the second of the three divisions of the Hebrew *Bible and are grouped into the "Former Prophets" (Joshua, Judges, Samuel, and Kings) and the "Latter Prophets" (Isaiah, Jeremiah, Ezekiel, and the 12 Minor Prophets). Moses is regarded by Jews as the first and greatest of the prophets, and the gift of prophecy is thought to have ceased in the 5th century BC. In Islam, however, Jesus and Mohammed are also regarded as prophets.

proportional representation (PR) A voting system that aims accurately to reflect the wishes of the electorate and to ensure that votes for candidates of minority parties are not wasted. In the system of PR known as the **single transferable vote**, electors indicate their preferences among the candidates by numbering them on their ballot paper (1, 2, 3, etc.). Those candidates who are named as a first choice and who obtain the required quota are elected. First-choice votes for an unsuccessful candidate are then redistributed to second-choice votes for that candidate, and so on until the requisite number of candidates has been elected (the system requires multimember constituencies). In the **party-list system** (widely used in Europe) electors vote for a party, which is then allocated seats in proportion to its total vote.

propositional calculus A system of formal logic that assigns truth or falsehood to compound propositions or statements on the basis of the rules governing the connective words between them. Examples of such connective words are "and," "or," or "if . . . then. . . ." For example, the rule for "and" is that a statement containing it is true only if both the simple statements it connects are true; for "or" it is sufficient that only one of the statements be true. Thus "pigs fly and birds sing" is false, while "either pigs fly or birds sing" is true.

propylaea Ancient Greek monumental gateways, generally the ceremonial entrances to the *acropolis of a town. The best-preserved example is that on the Acropolis of Athens.

proscenium The arch at the front of a □theater stage through which the audience views the play. It became a standard feature of theater architecture following its first use in Italy in the 17th century but has been dispensed with in many theaters built during the 20th century.

Proserpine. *See* Persephone.

prosimian A *primate of the suborder *Prosimii* (53 species), including the *lemurs, *indris, *sifakas, *lorises, *bushbabies, *tarsiers, *tree shrews, and the *aye-aye. Prosimians are the most primitive of the primates and are mainly arboreal. Tree shrews have claws instead of fingernails and only partly opposable thumbs.

prostaglandins Compounds derived from long-chain (essential) fatty acids and found in mammalian body tissues. Their effects include stimulation of contraction in the womb, dilation of blood vessels, and modification of hormonal activity. They are released at sites of inflammation following tissue damage and the pain-relieving properties of such drugs as aspirin are due to their inhibition of prostaglandin synthesis. Synthetic prostaglandins are used to induce labor and abortion in women.

prostate gland A gland in men, situated just beneath the bladder. It secretes an alkaline fluid during ejaculation that forms part of the semen. Enlargement of the prostate commonly occurs in elderly men, obstructing the bladder and preventing urination. It is usually treated by surgically removing the gland in the operation of prostatectomy.

prostitution The practice of offering sexual gratification in return for money or other return. It has always been common, especially in societies in which legitimate sexual relations are closely regulated. Attitudes to prostitution differ greatly in different societies. Sometimes a bride earns her dowry in this way with general approval. It was practiced in ancient Mesopotamia by priestesses for religious reasons. In modern societies it is generally controlled by legislation, usually with the object of preventing the spread of venereal diseases and of making it more difficult for pimps (men who live off the earnings of prostitutes) to introduce young girls into the profession. Male prostitution is less common than female and largely confined to homosexual relations.

protactinium (Pa) A radioactive *actinide element, first identified by K. Fajans and O. H. Göhring in 1913. It is present in pitchblende as a member of the uranium decay series. The oxide (Pa_2O_5) and iodide (PaI_5) have been produced. The latter decomposes on heating to give the metal. At no 91; at wt (231); mp <2900°F (<1600°C).

Protagoras (c. 485–415 BC) Greek *Sophist. He claimed to teach virtue (more accurately interpreted as "success") and was himself successful and respected for more than 40 years. His says, "Man is the measure of all things," shows his skeptical and subjectivist attitude to knowledge. His skepticism extended to religion, but not, apparently, to morality.

Protea A genus of evergreen shrubs and trees (over 100 species), native to S and central Africa. They have broad simple leaves and small white, pink, yellow, or orange flowers that are grouped into showy cup-shaped clusters, up to 12 in (30 cm) across, and surrounded by whorls of colored bracts. The flowers are a national emblem of South Africa. Family: *Proteaceae.*

Protectorate (1653–59) The period during which England was governed by Oliver *Cromwell. The Instrument of Government (1653) vested executive authority in the Lord Protector (Cromwell) and a state council and legislative authority in the Protector and a triennial Parliament. As modified in 1657, the Instrument gave more power to Parliament and less to the state council. Cromwell's relations with Parliament subsequently deteriorated and he dismissed it in 1658. Following his death, his son Richard *Cromwell was Protector until his abdication in 1659.

protein A complex organic compound that consists of one or more chains of *amino acids linked by *peptide bonds (−NH−CO−). These chains are variously coiled, wound, and cross-linked to form a three-dimensional molecular structure, revealed by such techniques as *X-ray diffraction, that determines the biological properties of the protein. This structure is irreversibly damaged at temperatures above 140°F (60°C). Proteins are manufactured by cells according to the genetic information carried in the chromosomes and the specific function of the cell (*see* DNA; RNA). Proteins fulfill many important biological roles: some, including *collagen and *keratin, are important structural materials of body tissues, while the proteins of *muscle—actin and myosin—are responsible for its contractile properties. Proteins vital to the functioning of the body include enzymes—the biological catalysts of metabolic reactions; *antibodies—important in the body's defense mechanisms; and many *hormones—the chemical messengers of the body.

Protestant Episcopal Church Church of England, or Anglican Communion, Christian denomination in the US. Formed and named in 1789, it established seminaries, missionaries, and parish Sunday schools in the early 1800s. Administered by diocesan bishops, local parishes are led by priests who are assisted by curates and the laity. A national General Convention at which a presiding bishop, the national executive officer, is elected, is held every three years. The doctrine of scriptural faith in the Apostles' and Nicene creeds is followed. In 1976 the ordination of women priests was formally accepted.

Protestantism The movement for Catholic Church reform that arose in the Western Church in the 16th century and led to the establishment of the Reformed Churches. The word derives from the *protestatio* of the dissident reforming minority at the Diet of *Speyer (1529). The early leaders of the *Reformation—*Luther, *Calvin, and *Zwingli—each promoted his own brand of Protestantism.

There are many doctrinal divisions among Protestants, but all reject a varying number of tenets and practices retained in Catholicism. In general Protestants rely less upon ecclesiastical tradition, believing the Bible to be the sole source of truth. They deny papal authority and admit a variety of forms of Church government (*see* episcopacy; Presbyterianism); in some sects the spiritual priesthood of all the faithful is emphasized. *Transubstantiation, *purgatory, special veneration of the Virgin Mary, and invocation of saints are all repudiated. The importance of the sacraments is minimized, with only baptism and the *Eucharist being accorded widespread acceptance, and some groups, such as the *Quakers, reject even these. The preaching and studying of God's word in the Bible is conversely important. Church furnishings, vestments, and music are more austere than their Roman Catholic equivalents. The 20th-century ecumenical movement has gone some way toward reconciling the Roman Catholic and Protestant Churches, but there are still serious doctrinal and other differences, while fresh issues, such as the ordination of women, introduce new elements of divisiveness.

Proteus (bacteria) A genus of motile rod-shaped bacteria found mainly in soil and sewage, where they decompose organic matter, but also in the wounds of animals and man. Some species cause enteritis and urinary-tract infections.

Proteus (mythology) A Greek sea god who served Poseidon as a shepherd of seals. He is usually portrayed as an old man. He had prophetic powers but used his ability to change his form to avoid communicating his knowledge.

Protista A taxonomic group or kingdom that comprises all microscopic organisms, i.e. the algae, some fungi, protozoa, and bacteria.

Protoceratops A dinosaur that lived during the late Cretaceous period (about 100–65 million years ago). It was a short-legged squat quadruped, 7 ft (2 m) long and weighing 1.5 tons, and had long sharp teeth and huge jaw muscles attached to a bony neck frill. Its diet probably consisted of palm fronds. Order: *Ornithischia.*

protochordate Any animal of the subphylum *Chordata* that does not possess a backbone. Protochordates, which include the *tunicates and *amphioxus, may represent the ancestors of the first vertebrates.

Protocols of Zion A document published in 1903 purporting to contain Jewish plans to overthrow Christian civilization. Although conclusively proved a forgery in 1921, Hitler, like earlier anti-Semitic agitators, used it to justify his persecution of the Jews.

proton A positively charged elementary particle classified as a baryon (*see* particle physics). It forms part of all atomic nuclei, a single proton being the nucleus of the hydrogen atom. It is a stable particle, 1836 times heavier than the electron.

protostar An embryonic star that has formed out of a contracting cloud of interstellar gas and dust. It continues to contract, the density and temperature at its center rising slowly at first and then increasingly rapidly until they are sufficiently high to cause energy-releasing thermonuclear reactions to begin in the central core. The collapse is then halted, and the object becomes a luminous star.

Protozoa A phylum of typically microscopic single-celled organisms (about 30,000 species), usually classified as simple animals and widely distributed in moist and watery places, including mud, soil, fresh waters, and oceans. Protozoans range in size from 0.0039 in (0.1 mm) to several centimeters. They may have one or several nuclei and a variety of specialized structures, including a contractile vacuole for regulating the water content of the cell and cilia flagella for movement and feeding. The cell may be fairly rigid, with a stiff cell wall (pellicle) or skeletal elements, or flexible and variable. Some protozoans contain pigment and obtain food by photosynthesis in the same way as plants. However, most forms take in dissolved nutrients or solid food particles (detritus, bacteria, etc.). Asexual reproduction is by means of simple division of the parent cell (binary fission) or by budding to form new cells; various forms of sexual reproduction occur, including *conjugation. Protozoans can survive dry or adverse conditions by forming resistant cysts or spores. Some are important parasites of man and animals, including species of *Plasmodium,* which cause malaria, and trypanosomes, which cause sleeping sickness. The phylum includes the classes *Sarcodina, *Ciliata, *Flagellata,* and *Sporozoa.*

Protura A worldwide order of primitive wingless insects (150 species) that live in humus and soil, feeding on decaying organic materials. They have a pale cylindrical body (0.02–0.08 in [0.5–2 mm] long), which tapers to a simple tail (telson) and lacks eyes and antennae.

Proudhon, Pierre Joseph (1809–65) French socialist and political theorist. Proudhon was largely self-educated. In his treatises *Qu'est-ce que la propriété?* (1840) and the *Système des contradictions économiques ou philosophie de la misère* (1846), he argued that all property was theft and that in a just society orderly anarchy would replace oppressive government.

Proust, Joseph-Louis (1754–1826) French chemist, who demonstrated by accurate analysis that compounds always contain fixed proportions of elements. This is now known as the law of definite proportion or sometimes as Proust's law. This work contributed to *Dalton's atomic theory.

Proust, Marcel (1871–1922) French novelist. The son of rich bourgeois parents, he suffered from asthma from childhood and was devotedly cared for by his mother. He studied at the Lycée Condorcet and the Sorbonne and in the 1890s became a socialite in the most fashionable aristocratic circles in Paris. After the deaths of his parents (1903, 1905), he dedicated his life to writing and, because of asthma, lived as an invalid recluse in a cork-lined room in an apartment on the Boulevard Haussmann. In 1912 he financed the publication of the first volume (*Swann's Way*) of what was to become his masterpiece, *Remembrance of Things Past*. He then set to work expanding his original conception,

2085

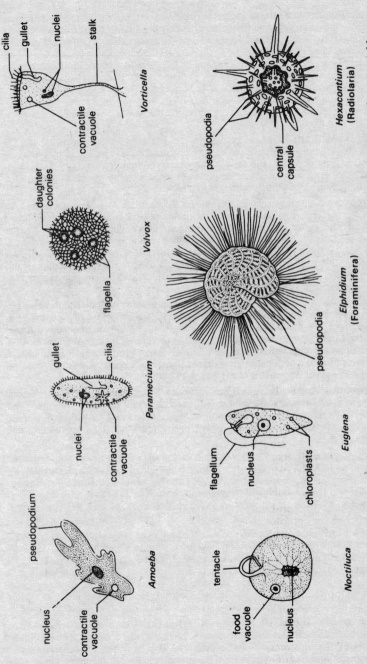

PROTOZOA *Although consisting only of single cells, these primitive animals show a surprising complexity of structure. Many have organs of locomotion (pseudopodia, flagella, or cilia) and some have gullets, through which food is channelled.*

realizing that his time was limited because of his ill health. The second volume, *Within a Budding Grove* (1919), won the Prix Goncourt; it was followed by *The Guermantes Way* (1920–21) and *Cities of the Plain* (1921–22). Proust managed to complete but not revise the final volumes, *The Captive* (1923), *The Sweet Cheat Gone* (1925), and *Time Regained* (1927), before his death. Written in an elaborate style and influenced by the philosophy of *Bergson, *Remembrance of Things Past* is a detailed portrait of the society that Proust had abandoned, recreated through the involuntary workings of memory. There is a strong autobiographical element in the narration and in the theme of homosexuality that plays a large part in several sections.

Prout, William (1785–1850) British chemist and physiologist, who in 1824 discovered the presence of hydrochloric acid in the stomach. He was also the first to classify foods in terms of what are now called proteins, fats, and carbohydrates. He also formulated the idea that atomic weights are all multiples of the atomic weight of hydrogen (Prout's hypothesis).

Provençal A *Romance language, strictly the dialect of *Provence, but also used to refer to the dialects of various regions of S France and in this broad sense often called Occitan. These dialects are also collectively described as the *langue d'oc*, in contrast to the *langue d'oïl* spoken in northern and central areas of France (*oc* and *oïl* being the medieval forms for *yes* in these two dialect areas). The primary literary use of Provençal was by the *troubadours; it fell into disuse as a literary language during the later Middle Ages. About nine million people still speak it.

Provence A former province in SE France, bordering on Italy and the Mediterranean Sea. A kingdom during the 9th century AD, it became part of France in 1481 and now forms the modern planning region of **Provence-Côte d'Azur**. Chiefly mountainous, its fertile river valleys produce grapes, olives, and mulberries. The perfume industry, centered on Grasse, is important. It contains the French *Riviera, a popular tourist area, along the S coast. Area: 12,134 sq mi (31,435 sq km). Population (1991 est): 4,194,400.

Proverbs An Old Testament book that is a collection of moral and religious maxims, traditionally ascribed to Solomon. Its chief theme is the nature and value of wisdom, which is the result of "fear of the Lord." Also prominent are maxims relating to justice, self-control, purity, industry, friends and family, and life and death.

Providence 41 50N 71 25W A seaport and the capital city of Rhode Island, on Narragansett Bay. Founded in 1636, it is the site of many historical buildings, including the First Baptist Church (1775), the First Unitarian Church, two cathedrals, and Brown University (founded in Warren in 1764 and moved to Providence in 1770). A major outlet for much of New England's oil, its manufactures include jewelry, machinery, and rubber goods. Population (1990): 160,728.

province A territorial subdivision of the empire of ancient Rome administered by a Roman governor. Provincial governors, who in Republican times (510–27 BC) were appointed by the Senate, commanded the garrisons, levied taxes, administered justice, and in wartime recruited troops. Under the Empire (after 27 BC), the Senate continued to provide governors for the 10 more peaceful provinces while the emperors through their legates controlled those provinces still requiring military occupation. *See also* Roman Republic; Roman Empire.

Provo 40 14N 111 39W A city in N central Utah, on the Provo River, SW of Salt Lake City, E of Utah Lake, and W of the Wasatch Range. The Mormons founded the city in 1849 and established Brigham Young Academy (now Brigham Young University) in 1875. Economic activities include a major steel industry, as well as mining and the production of foodstuffs, electronics, machinery, and clothing. Population (1990): 86,835.

Proxima Centauri. *See* Alpha Centauri.

Prudhoe Bay A small inlet of the Arctic Ocean on the coast of N Alaska. Since the discovery of vast oil deposits in the area (1968) it has been a center of drilling activity. A pipeline transfers oil from Prudhoe Bay to the S.

Prud'hon, Pierre Paul (1758–1823) French painter and draftsman, born at Cluny. He trained in the Dijon Academy and in Rome (1784–7), where he was influenced by the works of *Correggio and *Leonardo. The style of his court portraits, for example *Empress Josephine* (Louvre), and his famous *Crime Pursued by Vengeance and Justice* (Saint-Omer, N France) display a romantic feeling distinctly different from the current neoclassical vogue (*see* neoclassicism).

Prunus A genus of deciduous or evergreen shrubs and trees (over 200 species), mostly native to N temperate regions. It includes the *plums, *almonds, *apricots, *peaches, and *cherries as well as many ornamental species. They have oval toothed leaves, often rolled in the bud, and white or pink flowers, about 0.4 in (1 cm) across, with five petals and many stamens. They produce stone fruits (*see* drupe), often with edible flesh or kernels. Family: *Rosaceae*.

Prussia A former state in N Germany on the NE Baltic coast. Established in the 13th century by the Teutonic Knights, Prussia became a duchy in 1525 under *Hohenzollern rule. United with Brandenburg in 1618, under *Frederick William, the Great Elector, it became the most powerful N German state. In 1701 his son took the title king of Prussia. In the 18th century, under *Frederick the Great, Prussia annexed Silesia and parts of Poland and became a major European power. Following Napoleon's defeat, it made important territorial gains at the Congress of Vienna (1815). Under *Bismarck's ambitious leadership, Prussia defeated Austria and Austria's German allies (1866), acquiring *Schleswig-Holstein and forming the *North German Confederation. Following victory in the *Franco-Prussian War (1870–71) the German Empire was proclaimed under Prussian leadership. In 1918 Prussia became a republic and was abolished by the Allies after World War II.

prussic acid. *See* hydrocyanic acid.

Przemyśl 49 48N 22 48E A city in SE Poland. During World War I it withstood a five-month siege by Russian armies before surrendering. Its industries are varied and include flour milling, tanning, and the manufacture of machinery. Population: 54,800.

Przewalski's horse The single surviving species of wild horse, *Equus przewalskii*, discovered in Mongolia in about 1880 by the Russian explorer Nicolai Mikhailovich Przewalski (1839–88). It is sturdily built with a relatively large head and has a short erect dark-brown mane and a dark dorsal stripe. The coat is reddish brown, becoming paler in winter. Height: 12–14 hands (4–5 ft; 1.22–1.42 m).

Psalms An Old Testament book, also known as the Psalter, containing 150 spiritual songs. They were formerly all attributed to David but are now generally believed to be by a number of different authors; some of them may date from the early period of the Jewish monarchy. They were intended to be sung with musical accompaniment and used in the liturgy of the Temple at Jerusalem; they continue to be used in both public and private worship by Jews and Christians. The majority are expressions of praise and worship of God and his works. A large number deal with aspects of a believer's experience, such as penitence, trust, doubt, fear, and suffering.

psaltery A medieval musical instrument, a type of *zither. It was plucked by the fingers of both hands or by two plectra.

Psamtik I King of Egypt (664–610 BC); the founder of the 26th dynasty. Appointed viceroy of Egypt by *Ashurbanipal of Assyria in 663, he took advantage of Assyria's weakness to repudiate its suzerainty, while remaining its ally. Psamtik encouraged trade with Greece and employed Greek mercenaries (the "brazen men"). During his reign Egyptian national sentiment revived the art and institutions of the pyramid age.

Pseudo-Dionysius the Areopagite (early 6th century AD) Mystical theologian, probably born in Syria, whose real name is unknown. His fame rests on several Greek treatises and letters, which greatly influenced leading medieval scholars. They attempt to combine Christianity with *Neoplatonism and include *The Celestial Hierarchy, The Ecclesiastical Hierarchy, The Divine Names,* and *The Mystical Theology.* They were formerly attributed to St *Dionysius the Areopagite.

pseudopodium A temporary extension of the cytoplasm found in some *Protozoa and used for locomotion and for engulfing food particles. In *Amoeba,* the pseudopodia are blunt lobular processes but in other protozoa they may be slender, filamentous, or branching.

Psilocybe A genus of mushrooms growing in soil and dung. The Mexican species *P. mexicana* contains the hallucinogenic compounds psilocin and psilocybin, which have effects similar to those of *LSD. It was regarded as a sacred mushroom in Mexico and eaten during religious ceremonies. Mushrooms of the liberty cap fungus (*P. semilanceolata*) are common in pastures and lawns, having grayish-brown or olive-green conical caps, 0.4–0.8 in (1–2 cm) in diameter.

psi particle An elementary particle discovered in 1974 and classified as a meson. Its unusually long lifetime led to the extension of the quark model (*see* particle physics) to include a quark (and its antiquark) having a new property called *charm. The psi particle itself is not charmed as it consists of a charmed quark and its antiquark.

psittacosis (*or* parrot disease) An infectious illness caused by a microorganism of the *Chlamydia* group, which is caught from birds, particularly parrots. The severity of the disease varies, but usually it causes pneumonia. Tetracycline antibiotics are used to treat the disease.

Pskov 57 48N 28 26E A city in NW Russia, on the Velikaya River, SE of Lake Pskov. Nicholas II abdicated at the railroad station there in 1917. Industries include food processing and tourism, Pskov having many historic buildings. Population (1991 est): 207,500.

Pskov school A school of Russian *icon and mural painting that flourished in the city of Pskov between the late 12th and early 16th centuries. It developed in isolation from other cultural centers since most other parts of Russia were occupied by the Mongols during this period. Characteristics of the school's style were the influence of *Byzantine art, monumental forms, brilliant colors, emotional intensity, and the persistence of archaic methods of representation.

psoriasis A chronic recurring skin disease marked by excessive scaling of the skin. The disease is very common, begins with small red patches covered with scales, and may spread extensively. The knees, elbows, lower back, scalp, and nails are most commonly affected. There is no known cure, but steroid creams and ultraviolet light are used to alleviate the condition.

Psyche In Greek mythology, a personification of the soul, portrayed as a beautiful mortal girl. *Apuleius tells the allegorical story of how she lost her divine lover, Cupid, and of her subsequent quest and suffering before she was finally reunited with him in marriage in heaven.

psychedelic drugs. *See* hallucinogens.

psychiatry The study and treatment of mental disorders. A psychiatrist is a medically qualified physician specializing in mental illness. Modern psychiatry also involves those of other professional disciplines, including nurses, social workers, and psychologists. The range of mental disorders includes *psychosis, *neurosis, *psychosomatic disorders, *drug dependence, and *mental retardation. Within psychiatry there are several specialties, notably child psychiatry, *psychotherapy, forensic psychiatry (which deals with those who have broken the law), and geriatric psychiatry (psychogeriatrics), which cares for the mentally disordered elderly.

psychoanalysis A school of *psychology and a method of treating mental disorders based upon the teachings of Sigmund *Freud (*see also* Adler, Alfred; Jung, Carl). Psychoanalysis stresses the dynamic interplay of unconscious mental forces and the way in which the adult personality is determined by the course of sexual development in childhood. The chief techniques of psychoanalysis are free *association and the recall of *dreams in the course of intensive psychotherapy, which usually requires several 50-minutes sessions each week for up to three years. In the course of this treatment transference takes place, in which aspects of the patient's past experiences and relationships are transferred to the analyst, the object being to bring repressed conflicts into consciousness so that they can be resolved. Although analysis was originally intended as a treatment for neurosis, it has been extended to some psychotic conditions by W. R. Bion, Herbert Rosenfeld, and others. Among those who have made significant contributions to the field are Carl Jung, Alfred Adler, Karen Horney, Carl Rogers, Harry Stock Sullivan, Otto Rank, Wilhelm Reich, and Eric Fromm. The work of Melanie *Klein was devoted to exploring early infantile experiences on a Freudian basis, while some of Freud's underlying concepts were challenged by other analysts. *See also* defense mechanisms; ego; id; Oedipus complex; repression; superego; unconscious.

psychokinesis. *See* telekinesis.

psychology The scientific study of the behavior of man and animals. Different schools of psychology use differing methods and theories. These include *behaviorism; experimental psychology, in which laboratory experiments are used to investigate factors influencing behavior (particularly *memory, perception, and learning); *Gestalt psychology; associationist psychology (*see* association); and *psychoanalysis. Clinical psychology applies these approaches to the understanding and treatment of mental illness (*see also* psychiatry). Educational psychology studies the ways in which children learn, in order to intervene as problems arise. Occupational psychology studies people in their working environment. *See also* ethology.

psychopath A person who behaves violently or antisocially and shows neither guilt nor any feeling for others. Psychopathy can be caused by a constitutional abnormality or an emotionally deprived upbringing.

psychosis A severe mental illness in which the sufferer loses contact with reality. Organic psychoses are caused by diseases affecting the brain, such as epilepsy, alcoholism, and dementia; functional psychoses have no known physical cause. The major functional psychoses are *schizophrenia and *manic-depressive psychosis. All psychoses can cause *hallucinations, delusions, and altered thought processes. They are common and disabling illnesses that account for the occupation of more hospital beds than any other illness.

psychosomatic disorder An illness in which physical symptoms are caused or exacerbated by mental factors. Certain physical illnesses, including asthma, eczema, and peptic ulcer, are thought to be partly a response to psychological and social *stress.

psychosurgery Surgical operations performed on the brain in order to relieve psychological symptoms. The commonest operation is *leukotomy. In lobectomy a whole lobe of the *brain is removed, often because of epilepsy. In amygdalectomy a lesion is made in a small part of the limbic system of the brain to reduce pathological aggression. These are all irreversible treatments and are reserved for the most severe forms of mental illness that are resistant to other therapies.

psychotherapy Psychological methods of treatment for mental disorders. There are many different approaches to psychotherapy, including *psychoanalysis and *group therapy. In client-centered therapy the therapist refrains from giving any direct advice. Family therapy involves several members of a family meeting together with a therapist to improve their relationships. All these approaches share the goal of helping self-understanding and personal development through the relationship between the client and the therapist. *See also* behavior therapy; hypnosis.

Ptah In ancient Egyptian mythology, the creator god. A local deity of *Memphis, he was proclaimed the supreme god when Egypt was first unified (c. 3100 BC), but was later identified with *Osiris and became the patron of craftsmen. He is always shown in the form of a *mummy.

ptarmigan A grouse, *Lagopus lagopus,* found in Arctic tundra and mountain regions; 17 in (35 cm) long, it has white wings and a mottled blackish-brown body that changes to white in winter. Its feet are covered with feathers and it feeds on shoots and fruits in summer and on lichens and leaves dug from the snow in winter.

Pteranodon An extinct flying reptile of the Cretaceous period (135–65 million years ago); 10 ft (3 m) long with a wingspan of 25 ft (7.5 m), it had an enormous bony crest that balanced its large head. It lived around sea cliffs, clinging to them with its long hind claws and gliding over the sea to catch fish in its long toothless beak.

Pteraspis An extinct genus of jawless fishlike vertebrates, belonging to the class *Ostracodermi,* that lived from the Ordovician to the Devonian periods (about 500–370 million years ago). The head and anterior part of the body were covered by a heavy bony shield, the remainder by small scales, and there was an upturned beaklike extension of the head (rostrum). Fins were placed singly, not in pairs. Subphylum: *Agnatha.*

pteridophyte A flowerless perennial vascular plant of the division *Pteridophyta,* which shows a distinct *alternation of generations with the asexual spore-bearing (sporophyte) generation predominating. The sporophyte plant consists typically of leaves, stems, and roots and bears spores in special capsules (sporangia), which are often arranged in clusters (sori) on the leaves. Pteridophytes are subdivided into *Lycopsida* (e.g. *clubmosses), *Sphenopsida* (e.g. *horsetails), *Psilopsida,* or *Psilotopsida* (mostly extinct), and *Pteropsida* (*see* fern).

pterodactyl. *See* pterosaur.

pterosaur An extinct flying reptile, also called pterodactyl, that lived during the Jurassic and Cretaceous periods (200–65 million years ago). A thin wing membrane stretched from the elongated fourth finger of the fore limb along the body to the knee; a second membrane stretched to the neck. It had a compact body and long slender hind limbs, probably used to cling, batlike, to rocks and trees. Its light bones, toothless beaked jaw, large eyes, and large brain resembled those of modern birds. ▢fossil.

Ptolemaic system A theory concerning the motions of the sun, moon, and planets that was originally advanced in Greece in the 3rd century BC and was completed by Claudius *Ptolemy in the 2nd century AD. It was a geocentric system in which the moon, Mercury, Venus, Sun, Mars, Jupiter, and Saturn were thought to move around the earth. Prediction agreed reasonably well with observation. To achieve this Ptolemy had to propose that each orbiting body moved in a small circle (an epicycle) the center of which moved in a larger circle (a deferent) around the earth. A sphere of stars lay beyond the seven deferents. The Ptolemaic system was finally abandoned when the *heliocentric system of *Copernicus was accepted.

Ptolemies A Macedonian dynasty that ruled Egypt from 323 BC, when *Ptolemy I Soter became governor of Egypt, until 30 BC, when Ptolemy XV Caesar (47–30 BC; reigned 44–30 BC), nicknamed Caesarion, the son of Cleopatra and, perhaps, Caesar, was executed by Octavian (later *Augustus).

Ptolemy (*or* Claudius Ptolemaeus; 2nd century AD) Egyptian mathematician, astronomer, and geographer. Little is known of his life except that he lived and worked in Alexandria, probably publishing his major works between 127 and 145. The foremost of these outlines the *Ptolemaic system of astronomy and was originally known as *He mathematike syntasis* (*The Mathematical Collection*) but was known to Arab astronomers by the Greek superlative *Megiste,* which took the Arab form *Almagest,* the name by which it is still known. His other works include *Analemma* and *Planisphaerium* on geometry, *Harmonica* on music, and *Geographike hyphegesis,* an extensive guide to geography.

Ptolemy I Soter (?367–283? BC) The first Macedonian king of Egypt and founder of the Ptolemaic dynasty (*see* Ptolemies). He was a general of Alexander the Great, after whose death he became governor of Egypt as his share of the Macedonian empire. He conquered Palestine, Cyprus, and much of Asia Minor, taking the title of king in 304. He founded the Library of *Alexandria, which he made his capital, and wrote a history of Alexander's campaigns.

Ptolemy II Philadelphus (308–246 BC) King of Egypt (285–246); the son and successor of Ptolemy I. He and his second wife and sister *Arsinoe II were engaged unsuccessfully in war with Syria. He completed the public buildings of *Alexandria, restored the Nile–Red Sea canal, and introduced camels into Egypt.

Ptolemy XIII Theos Philopator (63–47 BC) King of Egypt (51–47), ruling jointly with his sister and wife *Cleopatra VII until he and his advisers expelled her (48). He murdered *Pompey after his defeat by *Caesar, hoping for Caesar's favor, but when Caesar reinstated Cleopatra, Ptolemy opposed him and was killed.

ptomaines Compounds formed during the bacterial decomposition of proteins in animal and plant tissues. Most are amines, such as diethylamine, putrescine, and cadaverine, and they may be poisonous, although the symptoms ascribed to "ptomaine poisoning" are usually due to bacterial toxins in contaminated food (*see* food poisoning).

puberty The onset of sexual maturity. The age at which this occurs is very variable but is usually between 12 and 17 in boys and between 10 and 16 in girls. The sexual organs develop to their adult form and pubic hair starts to grow; in girls the menstrual periods begin (menarche). The secondary sexual characteristics develop: in girls the breasts enlarge and in boys the muscles enlarge, the voice deepens, and facial hair grows. Psychological changes include an increase in the sexual drive and often in anxiety and insecurity.

Public Health Service (PHS) US agency, part of the Department of *Health and Human Services, that is charged with promoting the protection and advancement of the country's physical and mental health. Its functions include implementation of a national health policy, coordination of research programs, and enforcement of safety and drug laws. The National Center for Health Statistics; the Alcohol, Drug Abuse, and Mental Health Administration; and the Food and Drug Administration are among its divisions. It was established in 1798 to oversee marine hospitals.

public relations Efforts by firms, organizations, individuals, etc., to present a good public image. Good public relations are achieved by prompt servicing of complaints and questions from the public, involvement in local affairs, sponsorship of charities, etc. A public relations firm may be hired by a company or an individual to ensure that these tasks are carried out and to promote his employer by such means as obtaining free mention of him or his products in the media.

Public Safety, Committee of A governing body during the French Revolution. When a coalition of European powers attacked France following the king's execution in 1793, the Committee of Public Safety was established to meet the emergency. Coming under the influence of Robespierre, it conducted the *Reign of Terror. After Robespierre's fall in July 1794, its powers were curtailed.

public sector Those parts of the productive and nonproductive sectors of the economy that are financed out of taxation, are under state control, or both. It embraces all the employees and activities of central and local government, public institutions and utilities, and nationalized industries.

Public Works Administration (PWA) US federal agency established by the National Industrial Recovery Act of 1933 to stimulate the economy and provide jobs for the unemployed. Part of the *New Deal, roads were laid; housing, schools, and hospitals were built; and electrical power and sewage systems were constructed. Secretary of the Interior Harold L. Ickes managed the agency until it was absorbed into the Federal Works Agency in 1939.

publishing The commissioning, production, and distribution of books, *periodicals, and *newspapers. Before the invention of printing, reading matter was produced by hand in the form of papyrus rolls in ancient Egypt, Greece, and Rome, and later in the form of manuscripts copied by hand. With the invention of printing by *Gutenberg, early printed books (*see* incunabula) were sold by the printer, who also functioned as publisher and bookseller. During the 15th and 16th centuries these functions began to separate; the Netherlands was one of the earliest centers of book publishing and the house founded by Louis Elzevir (1540–1617) is still active in Haarlem. After the introduction of the Copyright Act (1709), book publishing, which had previously been financed largely by rich patrons, expanded in the UK and the US as an independent industry.

The growth of libraries, the spread of literacy, and technical innovations in printing and papermaking during the 19th century enabled the independent publisher to flourish. During the 20th century the main innovation in publishing has been the growth of inexpensive paperbacks. The introduction of book clubs has also expanded the market for books.

Puccini, Giacomo (1858–1924) Italian opera composer. He was a church organist before studying at the Milan conservatory with Amilcare Ponchielli (1834–86). His first major success was *Manon Lescaut* (1893). The operas that followed established Puccini as the master of the Italian stage and of the *verismo* (Italian: realism) style: *La Bohème* (1896), *Tosca* (1900), and *Madame Butterfly*

(1904). An opera on an American subject, *La fanciulla del West* (1910) and the three one-act operas of *Il Trittico* (1918) were less successful; his final masterpiece, *Turandot,* was produced posthumously in 1926, having been completed by Franco Alfano (1876–1954).

Pucelle, Jean (?1300–1355?) French miniature painter and manuscript illuminator. His best-known works are the *Belleville Breviary* and *The Hours of Jeanne d'Évreux* (Metropolitan Museum, New York), the latter being a prayer book commissioned by the French queen.

puck In English folklore, a household spirit, malicious fairy, or demon. The famous Puck of Shakespeare's *A Midsummer Night's Dream* is identified with the mischievous fairy Robin Goodfellow.

puddling process A method of making pure iron from *pig iron. The pig iron is melted in a furnace and powdered iron oxide is stirred in to drive off the slag. As the iron becomes purer, its melting point increases and eventually it forms a pasty mass, which is removed and hammered or rolled into shape. Puddling superseded *wrought-iron working by hand and its introduction was an important contribution to the industrial revolution, although it is now little used.

Pudovkin, Vsevolod (1893–1953) Russian film director. He is best known for his early silent films, especially *Mother* (1926), *The End of St Petersburg* (1927), and *Storm Over Asia* (1928). He published influential lectures concerning the technique of montage.

Puebla (*or* Puebla de Zaragoza) 19 03N 98 10W A city in S Mexico. Strategically situated on the route between Mexico City and Veracruz. it was an important fortress city for several centuries. Notable buildings include an ornate cathedral (1649) and the Teatro Principal (1790). A major agricultural and industrial center, Puebla is famous for its onyx products. Population (1980): 835,759.

Pueblo 38 17N 104 38W A city in Colorado, on the Arkansas River. Established in 1842, it has important steel industries, which use local coal. Other industrial activities include oil refining and meat packing. Population (1990): 98,640.

Pueblo Indians North American Indian tribes of the SW region including the Tewa, Keres, *Hopi, and Zuni. Their collective name derives from the Spanish term for their villages—*pueblos.* They began to abandon their hunting existence and adopt their present farming economy about 1600 years ago. They were always extremely peaceful peoples, much given to ritual and ceremonial pursuits. Their villages are often constructed around a central courtyard; the buildings, made from mudbrick blocks, have several stories, each set back from the one below. Communities were traditionally governed by a council of the heads of the various secret religious societies, which met in underground rooms called kivas. The diversity of Pueblo languages indicates different origins.

puerperal fever Persistent fever occurring in a woman soon after childbirth, most commonly caused by infection of the genital tract, particularly of the lining of the womb. The infection may be serious and progress to blood poisoning. Formerly many women died of puerperal fever, but with improved hygiene and antibiotics the disease is now rare and can be cured by prompt treatment with antibiotics.

Puerto Rico, Commonwealth of (name from 1898 until 1932: Porto Rico) An island and self-governing commonwealth in association with the US. It is in the West Indies, the smallest and most easterly island in the Greater Antilles. It is largely mountainous, rising over 3937 ft (1200 m) and supports one of the densest populations in the world. *Economy*: rapid industrialization has taken place since the 1940s, transforming the economy from a basically agricultural one to a mixed one. Manufacture (chemicals, textiles, plastics, food processing) is the main source of income, while in the agricultural sector income from dairy and livestock farming has overtaken that of sugar, the principal crop. Tourism is an increasingly important source of revenue. *History*: discovered by Columbus in 1508, it was under Spanish rule for nearly 400 years until ceded to the US in 1898. Full US citizenship was granted in 1917 and it attained its present status in 1952, which was ratified by a plebiscite (1967). During the 1940s and 1950s emigration to the US was high, a trend that later moderated. In 1976 the New Progressive party regained governorship and legislative control, led by Carlos Romero Barceló, who is an advocate of the incorporation of Puerto Rico as a US state. Since 1974, however, there has been growing militant pressure for the independence of Puerto Rico and in August 1978, the UN special committee on decolonization reaffirmed the "inalienable right of the people of Puerto Rico" to self-determination. Official language: Spanish; English is also widely spoken. Official currency: US dollar of 100 cents. Area: 3349 sq mi (8674 sq km). Population (1992 est): 3,581,000. Capital: San Juan.

Pufendorf, Samuel von (1632–94) German jurist, philosopher, and historian, known for his contribution to natural and international law. A professor at Heidelberg and later at Lund, he became historiographer to the Swedish court in 1677 and to the Elector of Brandenburg in 1688. In his best-known work, *De Jure naturae et gentium* (1672), influenced by *Grotius and *Hobbes, he argued that all men are entitled to be free and equal and that international law is not restricted to Christendom but is common to all nationalities. His *De habitu religionis christianae ad vitam civilem* (1687) advocated state superiority over the church in civil affairs.

puff adder A large stout-bodied highly venomous *adder belonging to the genus *Bitis* (8 species), occurring in semiarid areas of Africa and characterized by its habit of hissing loudly and inflating its body in a threatening posture; 1–7 ft (0.3–2 m) long, puff adders are brown or gray with yellow chevron patterning.

puffball The globular or pear-shaped fruiting body of certain fungi. As it matures, the outer layer cracks and sloughs off; the spongy interior produces powdery spores, which are released either through a pore (genus *Lycoperdon*) or from the upper surface (genus *Calvatia*). The grayish-white giant puffball (*C. giganteum*) occurs in pastures, woodlands, and roadsides and may reach over 40 in (1 m) across. It is attached to the ground by a short cord. Class: *Basidiomycetes*.

puffer A ▢fish, also called globe fish, belonging to the family *Tetraodontidae*, that inflates its body with air or water when disturbed. The tough spiny skin contains a highly toxic chemical (tetraodontoxin), which can be fatal. Up to 20 in (50 cm) long, puffers live mainly in tropical and subtropical seas, using their beaklike snouts to feed on corals, mollusks, and crustaceans. They are edible if expertly prepared. Order: *Tetraodontiformes*.

puffin A N Atlantic seabird, *Fratercula arctica*; 11.5 in (29 cm) long, it is black with a white face and underparts, red legs, and a blue ring around the eye. Its large triangular bill is striped red, yellow, and blue in the breeding season. It feeds at sea on fish and mollusks and breeds in disused rabbit burrows. Family: *Alcidae* (auks).

pug A breed of toy ▢dog originating in China and introduced to Holland and the West by Dutch traders in the 17th century. It is stockily built, with the tail curled over the back, and has a wrinkled skin and a large head with a short square muzzle. The short smooth coat can be silver, black, or apricot-fawn with a black mask on the face and a black line along the back. Height: 10–11 in (25–28 cm).

Pugachov, Yemelyan Ivanovich (1726–75) The leader of a Cossack rebellion in Russia, the Pugachov Rebellion (1773–74). Claiming to be the assassinated Tsar Peter III (1728–62; reigned 1762), Pugachov raised a revolt against the government of *Catherine the Great. The revolt collapsed and Pugachov was beheaded.

Puglia. *See* Apulia.

Pugwash Conferences International conferences on science and world affairs, convened at the suggestion of, among others, Albert Einstein and Bertrand Russell, that discuss the problems of *disarmament and the social responsibility of scientists. The first conference was held in the village of Pugwash, Nova Scotia (Canada), in 1957.

PUFFIN *The puffin, which breeds in large colonies, has a bill that is armed with serrations that enable it to carry 30–40 fish at a time. Puffins will continue to bring food to the nest even after the young have left.*

Pulci, Luigi (1432–84) Italian poet. He lived mostly at the court of Lorenzo de' *Medici and wrote all his works in Italian. His major work is the epic poem *Morgante* (1483), a colloquial and irreverently comic treatment of French chivalric material concerning Roland (*see* Charlemagne).

puli A Hungarian breed of sheepdog whose unique coat hangs to the ground in long tight cords. The puli is agile and lively; its tail is held over the back and its coat is usually black but may be bronze-black, gray, or white. Height: 16–18 in (41–46 cm) (dogs); 14–16 in (36–41 cm) (bitches).

Pulitzer Prizes Annual awards endowed by editor and publisher Joseph Pulitzer (1847–1911) and first awarded in 1917. Pulitzer stipulated that $500,000 left to Columbia University be used to recognize achievements in journalism and literature. The $1,000 prizes for journalism include local, national, and international reporting, public service and investigative reporting, editorial writing, editorial cartooning, news photography, feature photography, commentary, criticism, and feature writing. The five $500 prizes for literature are fiction, poetry, history, drama, biography, and nonfiction. A prize for musical composition has also been awarded.

Pullman, George Mortimer (1831–97) US businessman and inventor. In 1865, Pullman produced a prototype of a luxurious railroad sleeping car, which he called "The Pioneer" and which proved to be enormously successful. He later founded the Pullman Palace Car Co. for the manufacture of similar sleeping cars and experimented with new types of factory organization, including a planned residential town for his employees. His relations with his employees were not always peaceful, however. In 1894 the *Pullman Strike led to a national boycott of all railroads that used his cars and sporadic violence that was ended only by the intervention of federal troops.

Pullman Strike (1894) US railroad labor strike. A strike over wage cuts by workers in the Pullman car factory near Chicago initiated a union boycott against all Pullman cars. When management fired some union leaders, the American Railway Union, under Eugene V. *Debs, struck the railroads nationwide. The government received an injunction against interference, and federal troops were necessary to quell outbreaks of violence. The railroads were kept running with nonunion help and military guard. Debs was arrested for violating the injunction.

pulsar A celestial object that emits extremely regular pulses of radiation and is almost certainly a rotating *neutron star. Pulsars were originally discovered, in 1967, at radio wavelengths. The Crab and Vela pulsars also emit pulses at optical and gamma-ray wavelengths. The pulses arise when a beam of radio waves emitted by the rotating star sweeps past the earth, similar to the way in which lighthouse flashes are produced. The radiation (synchrotron radiation) is generated by electrons moving in the star's strong magnetic field; the emission site is still uncertain. The pulsation periods, ranging from 0.033–4 seconds, are all very gradually increasing. Pulsars are thought to originate in *supernovae. X-ray pulsars also exist but apparently involve a neutron star as a component of a close binary star.

pulsating stars. *See* variable stars.

pulse The rhythmic contraction and expansion of the elastic walls of the arteries caused by the pressure of blood pumped from the heart. The pulse therefore reflects the heart rate and can be readily felt in arteries just beneath the skin: it is usually measured at the radial artery in the wrist. The average pulse rate of a resting adult is 60–80 per minute; it increases with exercise and emotion. The pulse also changes in disease, becoming faster during a fever and irregular in heart-rhythm disorders. A reduction in blood pressure (e.g. after hemorrhage) will cause a fast feeble pulse.

puma. *See* cougar.

pumice A volcanic rock derived from acidic lava. It resembles sponge in having many cavities produced by bubbles of gas trapped on rapid solidification, often during submarine eruptions. Pumice is light in color and weight and often floats on water.

pumpkin The fruit of certain varieties of *Cucurbita pepo* and *C. maxima*, small bushes or trailing vines cultivated in North America and Europe. The fruit is large and round, up to 66 lb (30 kg) in weight with a lightly furrowed yellow rind surrounding an edible fleshy pulp and numerous seeds. It is cooked and eaten as a vegetable, in pies, puddings, and soups or used as animal feed. Family: *Cucurbitaceae*.

pumps Machines designed to transfer mechanical energy to a fluid. This energy may be required to move the fluid from one place to another, raise its level, increase its pressure, or provide circulation. Pumps are of three kinds: reciprocating, centrifugal, and rotary displacement. The reciprocating pump consists essentially of a piston moving to and fro; liquid is drawn in through one valve on the down stroke, and expelled through an exhaust valve on the upstroke. The centrifugal pump draws liquid into the center of a rotating impeller, which thrusts it out of the exit. Rotating pumps consist of shaped gears or rotors, which move the liquid around a close-fitting chamber.

Punch and Judy A puppet show performed with glove puppets and featuring the violent quarrels of the heartless Punch and his wife Judy. The character of Punch, who wears a striped costume and has a hooked nose and a humped back, derives from the Italian *commedia dell'arte.

Punic Wars Three wars between Rome and Carthage, which gave Rome control of the Mediterranean. The first Punic (from the Latin *Punicus*, Carthaginian) War (264–241 BC) was provoked by Roman intervention in Sicily and was marked by the emergence of Roman naval power: its newly built fleet was victorious off Mylae (260) and again off the Aegates Insulae (241), which brought the war to an end with Carthage's evacuation of Sicily. The second Punic War (218–201) was instigated by *Hannibal's capture (219) of Saguntum, a Roman ally in Spain. His advance into Italy was eventually checked, after disastrous Roman losses at Trebia (218), Trasimene (217), and *Cannae (216), by *Fabius Maximus. Ultimate victory, however, was achieved by *Scipio Africanus, who defeated Hannibal at *Zama (202). Carthage gave up its Spanish conquests and became a dependent ally of Rome. Roman fears of a resurgence of Carthaginian power caused the third Punic War (149–146), in which Carthage was destroyed and its territory became the Roman province of Africa.

Punjab A region of the NW Indian subcontinent, in India and Pakistan below the Himalayan foothills on the flat alluvial plain of five Indus tributaries. Hot and dry, it produces grain surpluses with irrigation. Pulses, cotton, sugarcane, oilseeds, fruit, and vegetables are also grown. Industries include textiles, bicycles, electrical and metal goods, machinery, and food products. The region is comparatively urbanized. Its population is 60% Sikh in India's Punjab state, and almost entirely Muslim in Pakistan's Punjab province. *History*: on the invasion route into India, the Punjab passed successively under different rulers. It was conquered by Muslims (11th century) but eventually became a Sikh stronghold until Britain established control (19th century). On the partition of India and Pakistan (1947), the Punjab was divided on a religious basis. This led to a massacre of minorities and mass migration. The W section became the Pakistan province of West Punjab (renamed Punjab in 1949), with an area of 79,284 sq mi (205,346 sq km) and its capital at Lahore; its population in 1983 was 50,460,000. The Indian section was reorganized in 1956 and again in 1966 on a linguistic basis when the Punjabi-speaking state of Punjab was created, 19,445 sq mi (50,376 sq km), with its capital at Chandigarh; its population in 1991 was 20,190,795.

Punjabi An *Indo-Aryan language of the Punjab (NW India, SE Pakistan). It is similar to *Hindi and written in the Devanagari script or in the Gumurki script of the Sikh scriptures.

Punt, land of A country with which the ancient Egyptians traded from 2750 BC for gold, ivory, incense, and spices. It was probably situated on the Somali coast of NE Africa.

Punta Arenas 53 10S 70 56W A port in S Chile, on the Strait of Magellan. It serves a large sheep-rearing area. Exports include hides, wool, mutton, lumber, and oil. Population (1991 est): 125,030.

pupa A stage in the life cycle of certain insects, including flies, butterflies (in which it is the chrysalis), ants, bees, and beetles, during which complete *metamorphosis from larva to adult takes place. The adult emerges by cutting or digesting the pupal case after a period of a few days to several months.

pupil. *See* eye; iris.

puppetry The art of manipulating puppets or marionettes in a dramatic performance. Puppets were used in religious ritual and folk drama in many early civilizations. In Japan, the form of puppet theater known as *Joruri* and developed by Chikamatsu Monzaemon (1653–1724) is still actively maintained. Introduced into the rest of Europe from Italy in the late 17th century, puppet theater flourished throughout Europe during the 18th century and enjoyed an artistic revival in the late 19th and early 20th centuries.

Purbeck, Isle of A peninsula in S England, in Dorset between the English Channel and Poole Harbour. Purbeck marble, a limestone used in building, is quarried here.

Purcell, Edward Mills (1912–) US physicist, who shared the 1952 Nobel Prize with Felix *Bloch for their independent measurements of the magnetic moments of nuclei in solids and liquids. He also worked in astronomy, discovering an important emission by interstellar hydrogen in the microwave region.

Purcell, Henry (1659–95) English composer and organist. He became organist of Westminster Abbey in 1679. In 1677 he was appointed composer to the orchestra of the Chapel Royal and, in 1682, organist there. He wrote keyboard pieces, sonatas, anthems, songs, cantatas, and much music for the stage, including incidental music for *King Arthur* (1691) and *The Fairy Queen* (1692) and one opera, *Dido and Aeneas* (1689).

Pure Food and Drug Act (1906) US law that banned interstate transport of adulterated packaged food and drugs. It also required accurate labeling of contents. The law is enforced by the Department of Agriculture. It was amended in 1912, 1913, and 1923 to cover false cure claims regarding medicines, accurate weight markings, and milk requirements.

Pure Land Buddhism A popular E Asian devotional form of Mahayana Buddhism, originating in China in the 4th century AD. Its adherents, following the Sukhavativyuha sutras, believe that by reciting the name of Amitabha, the Buddha of Infinite Light, they will be reborn in the Pure Land in the West (Sukhavati), which he has created.

purgatives. *See* laxatives.

purgatory In Roman Catholic doctrine, the state in which souls are purified after death to make them fit for heaven. Masses or prayers for the dead are believed to shorten a soul's purgatorial sufferings. The doctrine of purgatory was officially adopted by the Church in the late 6th century, but at the Reformation the Protestants rejected the concept, holding that souls either go directly to heaven or hell or sleep until the Last Judgment.

Puri 19 49N 85 54E A port in India, in Orissa on the Bay of Bengal. A major religious center, it holds many festivals and has an exceptional 12th-century temple. Population (1991): 124,835.

Purim A Jewish festival, commemorating the frustration of an attempt to exterminate the Jews of the Persian Empire (473 BC), as narrated in the book of Esther. It is celebrated on the 14th Adar (Feb–Mar), with lighthearted festivities and charitable gifts. The scroll (*megillah*) of Esther is read in synagogues.

purine An organic nitrogenous base ($C_5H_4N_4$) consisting of a two-ringed molecule of carbon and nitrogen atoms. The derivatives adenine and guanine are constituents of the nucleic acids *DNA and *RNA. *Uric acid and *caffeine are also purines.

purism An art movement launched in 1918 by the manifesto, *Après le Cubisme,* of the painter Amédée Ozenfant (1886–1966) and the architect and painter *Le Corbusier. Their aim was to purify *cubism by stripping it of its decorative features and basing their austere geometrical shapes on machine forms.

Puritanism A movement among Protestants in 16th- and 17th-century England. The term originally denoted members of the Church of England in Elizabeth I's reign who wished to eliminate elements in the Church's liturgy and hierarchy that were reminiscent of Roman Catholicism. In the 17th century, Puritan criticism of the Anglican episcopacy was intensified and the Puritans, many of them now forming extremist sects, became associated with the parliamentarian party in the Civil War. Many Puritans emigrated to the American colonies, several of which were governed according to Puritan principles.

Purple Heart Oldest US military decoration, established as the Badge of Military Merit by George Washington in 1782 and awarded during the American Revolution. Reinstituted in 1932, it is awarded to those wounded in battle. It is a purple heart of cloth, bordered by bronze.

purpura Localized limited bleeding into the skin, causing a rash of purple spots. This is a common and harmless condition of the elderly (senile purpura). Purpura may also result from reactions to drugs and infections, scurvy, and an allergic disease of childhood called Henoch-Schönlein purpura. A deficiency of blood platelets (important in clotting) also leads to purpura.

purslane An annual herbaceous plant, *Portulaca oleracea,* with prostrate reddish stems bearing fleshy oval leaves and dense terminal clusters of tiny pink flowers. It is widespread as a weed and has been used as a culinary herb. Family: *Portulacaceae.*

Sea purslane (*Halimione portulacoides*) is a shrubby perennial of temperate salt marshes, with grayish oval leaves and knobbly heads of tiny golden flowers. Family: *Chenopodiaceae. Honkenya peploides,* also called sea purslane, is a creeping perennial plant of N temperate sandy beaches. It has pointed fleshy leaves and small five-petaled white flowers on short stalks, surrounded by fleshy sepals. Family: *Caryophyllaceae.*

Purus River (Spanish name: Río Purús) A river in NW South America, rising in SE Peru and flowing generally NE through Brazil to the Amazon River. Length: about 2000 mi (3200 km).

pus Thick yellow fluid that arises in infected areas and contains dead bacteria, dead white blood cells, serum, and damaged tissue. It is formed as a result of the body's defensive action against invading bacteria and other particles. Pus is present in boils and similar skin conditions but can be formed anywhere in the body (*see* abscess). *See also* inflammation.

Pusan 35 05N 129 02E A port in SE South Korea, on the Korea Strait, capital of South Kyongsang province and South Korea's second largest city. It is the site of a state and a private university. Refugees gathered there during the Korean War (1950–53). Its varied industries include shipbuilding. Population (1990): 3,797,566.

Pushkin (name from 1708 until 1937: Tsarskoye Selo) 59 43N 30 22E A city in Russia, 14 mi (24 km) S of St Petersburg, with which it was joined by Russia's first railroad (1837). Founded in 1708 by Peter the Great, it was the site of the imperial summer residence; Catherine the Great's palace (1748–62) is still to

Pushkin, Aleksandr

2100

be seen. In 1937 it was renamed for the Russian poet, who studied there. It has varied manufacturing industries and a botanical institute. Population (1989 est): 80,000.

Pushkin, Aleksandr (1799–1837) Russian poet, novelist, and dramatist. In 1820 he was exiled to the southern provinces for his political verse, which was considered revolutionary by the government. In exile he wrote two long romantic poems strongly influenced by Byron and began the epic verse novel *Eugene Onegin* (1833), on which Tchaikovsky based his opera (1877–78). In 1824 he was transferred to NW Russia, where he wrote the historical drama *Boris Godunov* (1831), which became the basis of Mussorgsky's opera (1874). After his return to Moscow in 1826 he was still hindered by censorship, but during his last years he wrote the epic poem *The Bronze Horseman* (1837) as well as lyrical poetry and several prose works. He was killed in a duel. Pushkin was the most versatile and influential of Russian writers; he broke with a number of artificial conventions of the 18th and 19th centuries, established new literary genres and themes, and made the Russian language a highly adaptable literary medium.

Pushtu. *See* Pashto.

puss moth A moth, *Cerura vinula*, of Europe, Asia, and N Africa. The adult has a fat white hairy body with black spots. The caterpillar is green with black markings and when alarmed it presents a grotesque appearance with the head and tail appendages raised up. It feeds on sallow, willow, and poplar.

putrefaction The decomposition of organic matter, particularly of proteins by bacteria under anaerobic conditions (i.e. in the absence of oxygen). Putrefaction is associated with a characteristic bad smell, produced by the amines, ammonia, hydrogen sulfide, and other compounds that are formed.

putty A mixture of boiled linseed oil and powdered calcium carbonate (whiting) used as a cement. Of doughlike consistency, it is used for cementing sheets of glass into windows.

Putumayo, Río A river in South America. Rising in the Colombian Andes, it flows generally SE forming most of the border between Colombia and Peru. On entering Brazil it is known as the Rio Içá before joining the Amazon River. Length: 980 mi (1578 km).

Puvis de Chavannes, Pierre (Cécile) (1824–98) French painter, born in Lyons. He was an independent artistic figure but also an important influence on such painters as *Seurat and *Gauguin. He is famous for his murals for public buildings, notably *The Life of S Genevieve* (Panthéon, Paris) and his painting *The Poor Fisherman* (Louvre). Imitating in oil the pale colors and simplified forms of frescoes, he chiefly painted allegorical subjects.

Pu Yi, Henry (*or* H. P'u-i; 1906–67) The last emperor of China (1908–12) as Xuan-tong (*or* Hsuan-t'ung). He became emperor at the age of two and abdicated four years later after the republican revolution of 1911. He was allowed to live in the summer palace on a government pension until the Japanese made him ruler, as Kang-de (*or* K'ang-te), of *Manchukuo (1934–45).

PVC. *See* polyvinyl chloride.

Pycnogonida. *See* sea spider.

pyelitis Infection of the central part of the kidney, where the urine collects before passing to the ureter. Infection may spread through the blood or up to the kidney from the bladder. The patient usually has a fever and loin pain and produces urine containing protein, white blood cells, and sometimes red blood cells. In some cases the infection spreads to the rest of the kidney (**pyelonephri-**

tis). The infection will normally settle with antibiotics, but repeated low-grade infections may lead to kidney failure and *uremia.

Pygmalion In Greek mythology, a legendary king of Cyprus who made an ivory statue (known as Galatea in modern versions of the story) and fell in love with it. When he prayed for a wife who would be as beautiful as the statue, Aphrodite gave the statue life and Pygmalion married her.

Pygmies Peoples of the tropical forest region of Africa, who are much smaller in stature than their Bantu neighbors. The males are less than 4 ft 11 in (150 cm) in height. They are nomadic hunters and gatherers, wandering in small and basically patrilineal exogamous bands of around 30 members. They use either the bow and arrow or, more usually, nets and spears. There are no chiefs, decisions being made by general consensus. They speak various Bantu languages.

pygmy hippopotamus A small *hippopotamus, *Choeropsis liberiensis,* of West African forests. Up to 40 in (100 cm) high at the shoulder and weighing about 441 lb (200 kg), pygmy hippos are less aquatic and more solitary than their larger relatives. They frequent river banks, sleeping during the day and feeding in the forest at night.

pygmy owl A very small *owl belonging to a widely distributed genus (*Glaucidium*; 12 species). About 6 in (16 cm) long, pygmy owls hunt small mammals, birds, and insects, which may be larger than themselves.

Pylos (Greek name: Pílos) 36 55N 21 42E A seaport (also called Navarino) in W Greece, on the Peloponnesian coast. It lies at the S end of Órmos Navarínou (Bay of Navarino), scene of two important battles: the Athenian victory over the Spartans during the Peloponnesian War (425 BC) and the decisive battle of *Navarino (1827) in the War of Greek Independence. The Mycenaean town associated with the legendary King *Nestor lies N of the modern town. Excavations there revealed a well-preserved palace and archive of *Linear B tablets.

Pynchon, Thomas (1937–   ) US novelist. He was acclaimed as one of the most original and ambitious writers to emerge in the 1960s. A common theme of his first three novels, *V* (1963), *The Crying of Lot 49* (1967), and *Gravity's Rainbow* (1973), is the protagonists' wandering quest through a bizarre and unpredictable landscape. He also wrote *Vineland* (1990). His short stories are collected in *Slow Learner* (1984).

pyorrhea. *See* periodontal disease.

Pyracantha A genus of thorny evergreen shrubs (about 10 species), known as firethorns, native to SE Eurasia and widely cultivated as garden shrubs in hedges or against walls. A commonly grown species is *P. coccinea.* It has finely toothed leaves and flat-topped clusters of white or pinkish-yellow flowers. The round scarlet berries may last all winter. Family: *Rosaceae.*

pyralid moth A moth of the widespread family *Pyralidae.* The adults have generally narrow forewings and broader hindwings. Both pairs are fringed. The larvae feed on a variety of substances, including dried stored products. They can be serious economic pests, especially the *corn borer, *wax moth, and meal moth (*Pyralis farinalis*). Many larvae spin silken tunnels in which they live.

pyramids Royal funerary monuments in ancient Egypt. The greatest are the pyramids of *Khufu, *Khafre, and Menkaura (Greek name: Mycerinus) at Giza (built c. 2600–2500 BC), the only survivors of the *Seven Wonders of the World. Their tombs were all robbed in antiquity but they nevertheless remain extraordinary feats of engineering. For over four millenniums the pyramid of Khufu, now 453 ft (138 m) high, was the highest building in the world. Pyramids were also built in ancient Mexico.

Pyramids, Battle of the (July 21, 1798) The battle in which Napoleon with some 25,000 troops defeated about 40,000 Egyptians near Imbaba on the W bank of the Nile. The battle was followed by Napoleon's defeat of the Ottoman Turks at *Aboukir Bay.

Pyramus and Thisbe Legendary lovers in a Babylonian story retold by *Ovid. The couple were forbidden to marry by their parents but exchanged vows through a chink in the wall between their houses. They arranged a secret meeting. Thisbe arrived first at the meeting place, which was near a mulberry tree; but she was frightened by a lion and fled, dropping her veil. Pyramus, finding her veil and thinking her dead, stabbed himself, and when Thisbe returned she killed herself also. The mulberry tree has borne blood-red fruit ever since. The rustics' farce in Shakespeare's *A Midsummer Night's Dream* is based on this story.

Pyrenean mountain dog (*or* Great Pyrenees) A breed of large dog, possibly of Asian origin, used in Europe for over 3000 years to guard shepherds and their flocks. They are massively built with drooping ears and an ambling gait. The long thick slightly wavy coat is white, with or without gray or brown patches. Height: 28 in (71 cm) (dogs); 26 in (66 cm) (bitches).

Pyrenees (French name: Pyrénées; Spanish name: Pirineos) A mountain range in SW Europe. It extends between the Bay of Biscay in the W and the Mediterranean Sea in the E, forming a barrier between France and Spain. The entire republic of Andorra lies within the range, which rises to 11,168 ft (3404 m) at Pico de Aneto, close to the source of the Garonne River in the center.

Pyrenees, Treaty of the (1659) The treaty that ended the war of 1648–59 between France and Spain and marked the rise of French predominance in Europe. Spain lost Artois and the Catalan counties of Rousillon and Cerdana. Maria-Theresa, the daughter of Philip IV of Spain, was married to Louis XIV of France.

pyrethrum A perennial plant, *Chrysanthemum coccineum* (or *Pyrethrum roseum*), with finely divided leaves and showy red, pink, lilac, or white flowers. It is native to Persia and the Caucasus and widely cultivated for ornament in temperate regions. The name is also given to an insecticide prepared from the dried flower heads of this and related species. Family: *Compositae*.

Pyrex The trade name for a heat-resistant glass containing borosilicate. It is also resistant to many chemicals and is an electrical insulator. Pyrex is used in laboratory glassware, ovenware, and large telescopes.

pyridine (C_6H_5N) A hygroscopic colorless liquid, with a strong odor, which boils at 239°F (115°C). It is a basic aromatic compound with a six-membered heterocyclic molecule, made by passing tetrahydrofurfuryl alcohol and ammonia over a catalyst at 933°F (500°C). It is used as an industrial solvent and in the manufacture of various drugs and pesticides.

pyridoxine. *See* vitamin B complex.

pyrimidine An organic base ($C_4H_4N_2$) consisting of a six-membered ring of carbon and nitrogen atoms. Its derivatives cytosine, thymine, and uracil are constituents of the nucleic acids *RNA and *DNA.

pyrite (*or* iron pyrites) A pale brassy yellow mineral, FeS_2, the most common sulfide mineral. It occurs as an accessory mineral in igneous rocks, in hydrothermal veins, in contact metamorphic rocks, and in sediments laid down in anaerobic conditions. It is usually mined for its sulfur, used for the manufacture of sulfuric acid, or for the gold and copper found in association with it. Because of its color it has been called fool's gold. The term is sometimes used for other sulfides, for example copper pyrites, but if used alone it refers to iron pyrites.

pyroclastic rock Rock formed from fragments thrown out by volcanic explosions, in either the solid or molten state. Fragments less than 0.08 in (2 mm) in diameter are known as ash or, when consolidated, tuff. Lapilli are larger fragments and bombs are even larger, often spindle-shaped. Blocks are large angular fragments ejected in the solid state.

pyroelectricity The development of opposite electric charges on opposite faces of asymmetric crystals when they are heated. The charges occur on those faces that are responsible for the crystal's asymmetry. Quartz and tourmaline have pyroelectric properties. *See also* piezoelectric effect.

pyrogallol (*or* pyrogallic acid; $C_6H_3(OH)_3$) A white soluble crystalline solid. It is a powerful reducing agent, used in developing photographs and to absorb oxygen in gas analysis.

pyrolysis A chemical reaction produced by high temperatures. Common examples include the charring of wood and firing of pottery. Pyrolysis has many industrial applications, a recent one being the recovery of hydrocarbon fuels from waste organic materials.

pyrometer An instrument used for measuring high temperatures. The two most important types are the optical pyrometer and the radiation pyrometer. In the optical pyrometer a filament, heated to a known temperature, is viewed with the hot body in the background. The temperature of the filament is adjusted until it appears to vanish, at which point its temperature is the same as the temperature to be measured. In the radiation pyrometer, radiant heat from the hot body is focused into a *thermopile, which develops a potential difference proportional to the temperature.

P'yŏngyang 39 00N 125 47E The capital of North Korea, in the NW on the Taedong River. Reputedly the oldest city in Korea, it suffered severely from successive Japanese and Chinese attacks over the centuries and was almost destroyed by US bombing in the Korean War (1950–53). It is a major industrial as well as administrative and commercial center. Its three universities include the Kim Il Sung University, founded in 1946. Population (1987 est): 2,350,000.

pyrope. *See* garnet.

pyroxenes A group of ferromagnesian rock-forming silicate minerals. They usually occur in basic and ultrabasic igneous rocks but also in some metamorphosed rocks. Those of orthorhombic crystal structure are orthopyroxenes and those of monoclinic structure are clinopyroxenes. Orthopyroxenes vary in composition between the end-members enstatite ($MgSiO_3$) and orthoferrosilite ($FeSiO_3$). Clinopyroxenes, the larger group, include diopside, hedenbergite, augite, pigeonite, aegirine, jadeite, and spodumene (a source of lithium).

Pyrrhon (c. 360–c. 270 BC) Greek philosopher, born at Elis, who was the founder of *skepticism. Pyrrhon believed that objective knowledge was impossible, the limitations of knowledge being explored by later skeptics. He sought a way of achieving mental tranquility by suspension of judgment.

Pyrrhus (319–272 BC) King of Epirus (307–303, 297–272). Having secured his throne (297), Pyrrhus pursued an adventurous policy of expansion but his empire was short-lived: in support of Tarentum against Rome he won victories that cost much in loss of life ("Pyrrhic" victories), especially at Asculum (279), and he was forced to withdraw.

pyruvic acid An organic acid ($C_3H_4O_3$). Its anion, pyruvate ($C_3H_3O_3$) is an important intermediate compound in the carbohydrate metabolism of living organisms.

Pythagoras (6th century BC) Greek philosopher and religious leader. Born at *Samos, he migrated in about 530 BC to Crotone (S Italy), where he founded a religious society that governed Crotone for many years until its suppression (460–440 BC). Its members followed an ascetic regime of dietary taboos, self-examination, and study aimed at purifying the soul and releasing it from "entombment" in successive bodies. Pythagoras probably discovered the geometrical theorem named for him and certainly discovered the arithmetical ratios governing musical intervals, which led him to interpret the universe in terms of mathematics alone. Pythagoreans were pioneers in several branches of science. *See also* Alcmaeon; Archytas; Pythagoreanism.

Pythagoreanism The philosophy of the followers of *Pythagoras, who developed the two main strands in their master's thought: mysticism and mathematics. The former was fostered by an ascetic religious order founded by Pythagoras at Crotone, Italy, the rules of which included silence and vegetarianism. Other disciples extended Pythagoras' interpretation of the physical world through numbers and made substantial advances in geometry. In astronomy they evolved a model of the universe that anticipated the heliocentric system of *Copernicus. An eclectic form of Pythagoreanism, known as Neopythagoreanism, developed in Alexandria during the 1st century BC.

Pytheas (4th century BC) Greek navigator. From Marseilles he made a voyage along the coasts of Spain, France, and E Britain and seems to have reached as far N as Iceland. His narrative is lost but was later used by the Greek geographer *Strabo.

Pythian Games The ancient Greek festival at Delphi in honor of Apollo. Second only to the Olympic Games in importance, the festival originally consisted of musical competitions but from 582 BC also included athletic and equestrian events, taking place every four years.

python A large *constrictor snake belonging to the Old World subfamily *Pythoninae* (20–25 species), occurring in tropical and temperate regions. Pythons usually live near water and tend to be sluggish, catching prey—which may include goats, pigs, and deer—by ambush. The reticulated python (*Python reticulatus*) is the largest of all constrictors, reaching 33 ft (10 m) in length. Many pythons are killed for their meat and skin. Family: *Boidae.* ◻reptile.

Q

Qaboos ibn Sa'id (1940–) Sultan of Oman (1970–). He became sultan after deposing, with British support, his reactionary father Sa'id ibn Taymur. With Omani oil revenues Qaboos has initiated modernization programs. His rule has been threatened by guerrillas.

Qaddafi, Moammar al-. *See* Gaddafi, Moammar al-.

Qajars. *See* Agha Mohammad Khan.

Qatar, State of A country in the Middle East, in *Arabia occupying a peninsula on the W coast of the Persian Gulf. It is the smallest Arabian state. The native population is mainly Arab and Wahhabi Sunnite Muslim, but over 80% of workers are immigrants from other countries, including Iran and Pakistan. *Economy*: oil extraction accounts for over 90% of the national income and has led to the development of other industries, such as fertilizer production and water desalination. During the 1980s Qatar experienced sharp declines in oil revenues. Qatar is a member of OPEC. There is also some fishing. *History*: Qatar relied on Britain for most of the 19th and 20th centuries, becoming a protectorate in 1916; it became independent when Britain withdrew in 1971. A member of the UN since 1971 and a long-time ally of Saudi Arabia, Qatar participated in the UN-coalition forces during the Persian Gulf War in 1991. Head of state: Emir Sheik Khalifa bin Hamad Al-Thani. Official language: Arabic. Official currency: Qatar riyal of 100 dirhams. Area: 4246 sq mi (11,000 sq km). Population (1990 est): 498,000. Capital: Doha.

Qattara Depression An area in NE Egypt descending to 436 ft (133 m) below sea level. Its steep N side proved a defense for the S flank of the British army in the battle of El Alamein. Area: about 7000 sq mi (18,000 sq km).

Q fever An infection with the microorganism *Coxiella burnetti,* first described in Queensland, Australia (hence *Q* fever) in 1937. The disease affects cattle and sheep but can be transmitted to man through contaminated milk. The incubation period is two to four weeks and the disease usually takes the form of a viral *pneumonia. Treatment is with tetracycline antibiotics.

Qian Long (*or* Ch'ien-lung; 1711–99) The title of Hong-li (*or* Hung-li), Chinese emperor (1736–96) of the Qing dynasty. During his reign the Chinese empire saw its greatest period of expansion through continuing wars of conquest, which, however, undermined China's economy. His government was further weakened by the corruption of his minister He-shen (*or* Ho-shen). Qian Long was a distinguished patron of the arts. He abdicated in favor of his son.

Qin (*or* Ch'in; 221–206 BC) The dynasty under which China became a unified empire. The first Qin emperor, Shi Huangdi (*or* Shih Huang Ti; c. 259–210 BC), consolidated his vast conquest by unifying weights, measures, and coinage and by creating one system of writing for the whole empire. He ordered the burning of all books in China, except for practical handbooks and the history of his own dynasty. Believing in the absolute power of the ruler, his government was so harsh that the dynasty outlasted him by only four years. It was during the Qin reign that much of the *Great Wall of China was built. Excavations in the vicinity of his tomb in the late 1970s revealed several thousand life-size terra-cotta men and horses.

Qing (*or* Ch'ing; 1644–1911) A Manchu dynasty, founded by *Nurhachi, that ruled China from the fall of the Ming dynasty until the revolution of 1911. The Manchus, living on the borders of Chinese civilization, gradually conquered Chinese territory as the Ming government weakened. The Qing (pure) dynasty was declared in 1636 but Peking was not captured until 1644. At its height in the 18th century under *Qian Long, the Qing ruled a vast empire that included Outer Mongolia, Tibet, and Turkistan. Trade and commerce flourished, as did cultural life and learning. In over two and a half centuries, however, there was little change in the social order, with dangerous results. Bureaucratic conservatism resisted modernization, corruption became rife, and China suffered a series of defeats by foreign powers (e.g. *Opium Wars) as well as internal rebellions (e.g. the *Taiping Rebellion) that culminated in the overthrow of the Qing in 1911.

Qingdao (Ch'ing-tao *or* Tsingtao) 36 04N 120 22E A port in E China, in Shandong province on the Yellow Sea. From 1898 to 1922 it was under German and then Japanese control. It is a center of heavy industry. Population (1991 est): 1,459,000.

Qinghai (Ch'ing-hai *or* Tsinghai) A mountainous province in NW China. Tibetan and Mongol nomadic herdsmen keep yaks, sheep, and cattle, and it is famed for its horses. The monastery near Xining is an important center of Tibetan Buddhism. Salt, oil, coal, and iron are produced. Area: 278,400 sq mi (721,000 sq km). Population (1990): 4,456,956. Capital: Xining.

Qinghai, Lake (*or* Koko Nor) A shallow salt lake of N central China, in the mountains of Qinghai province, the largest lake in China. Area: about 1600 sq mi (4100 sq km).

Qom 34 39N 50 57E A city in central Iran, S of Tehran. It is the burial place of many Islamic saints and a pilgrimage center of Shiite Muslims. Population (1986): 543,139.

quadratic equation An algebraic *equation in which the greatest power of the *variable is two. It is usually written in the form $ax^2 + bx + c = 0$, in which the two *roots, or possible solutions, are given by $x = [-b \pm \sqrt{(b^2 - 4ac)}]/2a$. Both roots are real *numbers when the quantity under the square-root sign is greater than or equal to zero. They are equal when that quantity is zero. If it is less than zero the roots are complex numbers. The sum of the roots is $-b/a$ and their product is c/a.

quadrature The position of a celestial body in the solar system when its angular distance from the sun, as measured from earth (i.e. the angle body–earth–sun), is 90°.

quadriplegia. *See* paralysis.

Quadruple Alliances 1. (1718) The alliance formed by Britain, France, the Holy Roman Emperor, and the Netherlands to maintain the Treaties of *Utrecht (1713–14), which had been repudiated by Spain. **2.** (1814) The alliance formed by Britain, Austria, Prussia, and Russia against Napoleon. It was confirmed at the Congress of *Vienna after Napoleon's fall. **3.** (1834) The alliance between Britain, France, Spain, and Portugal that sought to maintain constitutional monarchy in Spain and Portugal.

quaestors Ancient Roman financial officers. Originally two were elected annually; more were appointed as Rome expanded. Two stayed in Rome in charge of the state treasury and records; others supervised Rome's corn supply and the financial administration of the provinces and military campaigns.

quagga An extinct wild horse, *Equus quagga,* that lived on the plains of South Africa. Up to 6 ft (180 cm) high at the shoulder, quaggas had a neck and head striped like a zebra with sandy-colored hindquarters and white legs and tail. The last quagga died in Amsterdam Zoo in 1883.

Quai d'Orsay A street in Paris, on the Left Bank of the Seine River, on which the French Ministry of Foreign Affairs is situated.

quail A round-bodied short-tailed gamebird of open grassland and farmland. Old World quail (subfamily *Perdicinae*; 95 species) are 5–8 in (13–20 cm) long and characterized by a smooth-edged bill and leg spurs; they are stocky and usually sandy in color. New World quail (subfamily *Odontophorinae*; 36 species) are up to 12 in (30 cm) long and have a strong serrated bill, no leg spurs, and are brightly colored and patterned, often with crests; males and females differ markedly. Quail feed on seeds, berries, and leaves. Family: *Phasianidae* (pheasants, partridges, and quail).

Quakers The Christian sect, formally known as the Society of Friends, founded in England by George *Fox in the late 1640s. They suffered violent persecution for many years and in 1682 William *Penn led a colony of Friends to *Pennsylvania. In the US they were leaders in the fight against *slavery, emancipating their own slaves. The early Quakers adopted an unostentatious dress and way of life. They were (and remain) pacifists, refused to take oaths, and rejected the use of titles. In speech they used the old singular form "thou" in preference to the plural form "you" for one person, as more suited to the truth. They rejected the ministry and sacraments of the established church. They worship in meetings, which start with a period of silence until one member is moved by the "inner light," which they believe to be their guide, to address the congregation or to pray.

quaking grass An annual or perennial *grass of the genus *Briza* (about 20 species), mostly native to South America. Their long slender flower stalks bear spikelets of open flower clusters, which quiver in the wind. *B. media* is native to temperate Eurasia and grows 8–20 in (20–50 cm) high. It is sometimes planted for ornament.

quandong A small shrubby Australian tree, *Fusanus acuminatus,* with simple leaves and heads of small inconspicuous flowers. The fruit is fleshy and edible, with a hard stony pitted edible seed. Family: *Santalaceae.*

Quant, Mary (1934–   ) British fashion designer, one of the first to become known for ready-to-wear rather than *haute couture* clothes. Her miniskirts, created especially for the young, made London a leading fashion center in the 1960s.

quantity theory of money A theory that seeks to explain how the money supply (*see* money) affects the economy. Originally put forward in the 17th century, it has been restated in its modern form by the US economist Milton *Friedman. It states that if there is a change in the money supply, either the price level will change or the supply of goods in the economy will alter. The monetarists (*see* monetarism) assert, on the basis of the quantity theory, that if there is full employment it is the price level that will be affected by altering the money supply.

Quantrill, William Clarke (1837–65) US Confederate guerrilla fighter. After leading a guerrilla band in Kansas and Missouri, he was made a captain in the Confederate army. He continued his raids, the best-known of which was the sacking of Lawrence, Kans. (1863), in which nearly 200 inhabitants were killed and the town was burned down. He was captured by Union forces and died in prison.

quantum number An integral or half-integral number (0, ½, 1, 1½, 2, . . .) that gives the possible values of a property of a system according to the *quantum theory. For example, in Bohr's atomic theory the angular momentum of an electron moving in orbit around an atomic nucleus can only have the values $nh/2\pi$, where n is a quantum number specifying these values and h is Planck's constant. Bohr's theory has now been replaced by the more versatile *wave mechanics, but the concept of quantum numbers is useful in some contexts. It is also used to quantify the properties of elementary particles (*see* particle physics). For example spin is characterized by the quantum numbers $+\frac{1}{2}$ or $-\frac{1}{2}$ for an electron, depending on whether it is parallel or antiparallel to a specified direction. *Parity, *electric charge, *strangeness, *charm, *isotopic spin, etc., are other properties of elementary particles expressed by quantum numbers.

quantum theory The theory first developed by Max *Planck in 1900 to explain the distribution of wavelengths of electromagnetic radiation emitted by a *black body. The experimental observations could only be explained when Planck assumed that the radiation was emitted and absorbed in discrete amounts, which he called quanta. The energy of each quantum has the value hf, where h is a universal constant (now known as the Planck constant) and f is the frequency of the radiation. Planck's quantum theory was used by *Einstein to explain the *photoelectric effect and in 1913 by Niels *Bohr to explain the spectrum of hydrogen. Quantum theory has since become an essential part of modern physics. **Quantum mechanics** is the application of quantum theory to the mechanics of atomic systems; **quantum electrodynamics** is the theory of *electromagnetic interactions between elementary particles; **quantum statistics** is the application of statistical methods to many-particle quantum systems. *See also* wave mechanics.

quarantine The period during which a person or animal suspected of carrying an infectious disease is kept in isolation. The term was originally applied to the 40-day period (French: *quarantaine*) during which ships suspected of carrying infected people were prevented from communicating with the shore. The quarantine period is now slightly longer than the incubation period of the disease; if no symptoms appear during quarantine the individual is considered free of the infection.

quarks. *See* particle physics.

quarrying. *See* mining and quarrying.

quarter horse A breed of horse developed in colonial America from both local and English stock for racing over short distances, popularly a quarter of a mile. It has a deep compact muscular body and, with its speed and agility, is widely used for ranch work. Quarter horses may be any color. Height: $14\frac{1}{4}$–$15\frac{1}{2}$ hands (1.45–1.57 m).

quartz The commonest of all minerals, consisting of crystalline *silica. It is stable over a wide range of conditions and consequently occurs in many rocks, particularly acid igneous rocks (such as granite), many metamorphic rocks (such as gneisses), and in sands and gravels, which form sandstones on consolidation. It is commonly milky white in color. Pure quartz is colorless and is known as rock crystal; it is used in glassmaking, in jewelry, and (because of its piezoelectric properties) in making electrical oscillators. Some colored varieties, such as amethyst (violet), rose quartz (pink), and citrine (yellow), are used as gemstones. In the form of sand it is used as an abrasive and in cement.

quartzite A resistant pale-colored rock consisting almost wholly of quartz. It is formed by the metamorphism of a pure sandstone, the original quartz grains being recrystallized and interlocking.

quasar (*quasi*-stell*ar* object; *or* QSO) A class of celestial objects discovered in 1964–65, lying far beyond our galaxy. They appear as starlike points of light but are each emitting more energy than a hundred giant galaxies. Quasar *red-shifts are extremely large and indicate that quasars are the most distant and hence the youngest extragalactic objects known. They must therefore be extremely luminous to be visible at such distances. The energy-producing region is compact, and it is thought that the prodigious energy could result from matter spiraling into a supermassive *black hole (maybe 10^9 solar masses) at the center of a galaxy.

Quasimodo, Salvatore (1901–68) Italian poet. His early work, such as *And Suddenly It's Night* (1942), was evocative and private, but after World War II poetry, such as *Il falso e vero verde* (1956), expressed his active concern for social issues. He won the Nobel Prize in 1959.

Quassia A genus of tropical Asian trees and shrubs (40 species). Bitterwood (*Q. amara*) is an attractive shrub or small tree. The heartwood is a source of quassiin, a bitter substance used in medicine. Family: *Simaroubaceae*.

Quaternary period The most recent period of geological time, from the end of the *Tertiary (about 1.8 million years ago) to the present day. It includes the *Pleistocene (Ice Age) and *Holocene epochs. Some authorities consider the Quaternary to be a division of the Tertiary.

Quayle, Dan (James Danforth Q. III) (1947–   ) US politician and statesman, vice president (1989–93). While a law student at Indiana University, he held several positions in state government (1970–74) and served in the US Coast Guard (1969–75). From 1974–76 he worked on a family-owned newspaper. He was a Republican US representative (1977–81) and a US senator (1981–89) from Indiana. Known for his conservative views, he served as vice president under Pres. George *Bush. In 1992, he unsuccessfully ran for reelection with Bush.

Quebec The largest province of Canada, stretching from the *St Lawrence River N to Hudson Bay and Strait. The rocky forested Canadian Shield covers 90% of the N. Most of the population lives in the St Lawrence valley, which has dominated the history and economy of the province. The SE strip of Quebec enters the fertile Appalachian Highlands. The province's highly industrialized economy is based on its abundant natural resources, especially forests, minerals, and water power. Quebec is a major source of the world's paper. Asbestos, the rich iron-ore deposits at Ungava, copper, zinc, gold, and other minerals are mined. Cheap hydroelectricity aids smelting, refining, food processing, and the manufacture of metal and electrical products, textiles, machinery, and chemicals. Fishing, farming, and tourism are also economically important. *History*: claimed by France (1534), Quebec or New France was a French colony (1608–1763) until ceded to Britain. French-Canadian culture was preserved and nationalism increased steadily after the formation of Canada (1867). The Quiet Revolution (1960s) led to the victory of the secessionist Parti Québecois in the 1977 provincial election, but a referendum on secession was defeated in 1980. Area: 523,858 sq mi (1,356,791 sq km). Population (1991): 6,895,963; over 80% are French speaking. Capital: Quebec. *See also* Montreal.

Quebec 46 50N 71 15W A city and port in E Canada, the capital of Quebec. First settled in 1608, it is strategically located above a sudden narrowing of the St Lawrence River. Quebec was the key to New France until captured by Britain (1759). It remains a cultural center of French-speaking Canada, housing Laval University. Most of the workforce is employed by government and service industries but textiles, leather goods, printing, publishing, and pulp and paper are also important. Quebec is a major tourist attraction. The Plains of *Abraham lie to the SW of the city. Population (1991): 167,577.

Quebec Act (1774). *See* Intolerable Acts.

quebracho A tropical or subtropical tree of the genus *Schinopsis*, especially *S. lorentzii* and *S. balansae*. Their reddish-brown wood is an important commercial source of tannin, while *S. quebracho-colorado* is an important timber tree. Family: *Anacardiaceae*.

Quechua The language of the *Incas and of the present-day American Indian peoples of the central Andean highlands. These peoples, having now mainly lost their lands to Spanish settlers, form an impoverished peasantry. Crops are potatoes, corn, and quinoa. Llamas and alpacas are herded. The people are nominally Roman Catholic but many pagan beliefs and rituals survive.

Queen Anne style An English architectural and decorative style with some baroque elements, dating from about 1700 to 1715. It was characterized by increasing restraint in the decorative elements. Beautiful walnut-veneered furniture was made; it was curvilinear in outline, exhibiting well-chosen figured woods, and enhanced by the restrained use of herringbone inlays. Gilt and lacquer continued in vogue but in a less flamboyant manner. Chairs became lighter, more comfortable, and invariably had cabriole legs. Plate-glass wall mirrors in gilt frames decorated paneled rooms.

Queen Anne's War (1702–13) US colonial war between England and France; it is the counterpart of Europe's War of the *Spanish Succession. The British captured Spanish-held St Augustine, Florida (1702); Indians, allied with the French, attacked New England from Canada, destroying Deerfield, Mass. (1704); and the British took French-held Port Royal in Nova Scotia. By 1712 an armistice was declared, and terms were spelled out in the Treaty of *Utrecht (1713). England gained Nova Scotia, Newfoundland, and Hudson Bay.

Queen Charlotte Islands An archipelago of W Canada, in British Columbia 100 mi (160 km) off the Pacific coast. Mountainous with lush vegetation (especially forests), the islands are mostly inhabited by Haida Indians engaged in fishing and forestry. Area: 3705 sq mi (9596 sq km).

Queen Maud Land. *See* Norwegian Antarctic Territory.

Queens 40 45N 73 50W One of the five boroughs of New York city, on Long Island. It is both residential and industrial and is the site of La Guardia and John F. Kennedy airports. Area: 118 sq mi (307 sq km). Population (1990): 1,951,598.

Queensland The second largest state of Australia, situated in the NE. The *Great Dividing Range separates the hilly coastlands from the vast inland plain and the *Great Barrier Reef runs parallel to the Pacific coast. The area is rich in natural resources, with coal the most important mineral. Other important minerals extracted include copper, bauxite, lead, silver, zinc, oil, and natural gas. Manufactures include metals, machinery, chemicals, motor vehicles, textiles, and food. Agricultural activities are also important; large quantities of sugar cane are produced in the E, while elsewhere bananas, pineapples, cotton, and tobacco are grown. Beef and wool are major industries. Another growing industry is tourism. Area: 667,000 sq mi (1,728,000 sq km). Population (1992 est): 3,068,100. Capital: Brisbane.

Queenstown. *See* Cóbh.

quelea A small brown African weaverbird, *Quelea quelea,* about 6 in (13 cm) long, also called the red-billed dioch and labeled the most destructive bird in the world. Queleas live in vast colonies: they destroy grain crops, frequently causing famine, and also damage the trees in which they roost by their combined weight. Attempts to control them by poisoning, introducing disease, and by dynamiting their colonies have had little success.

Quemoy. *See* Jinmen.

Queneau, Raymond (1903–79) French novelist and poet. He was involved in the surrealist movement in the 1920s and subsequently wrote a series of parodies and other literary exercises the surface humor of which is founded on profound erudition. Notable among these is *Exercices du style* (1947), in which the same episode is rendered in many different styles. His novels include *Le Chiendent* (1933), *Rude hiver* (1939), *Pierrot mon ami* (1942), and *Zazie dans le métro* (1959).

Quercia, Jacopo della. *See* Jacopo della Quercia.

Querétaro 30 38N 100 23W A city in central Mexico. The movement for Mexican independence was begun there (1810). There are many Spanish colonial buildings, notably the cathedral and federal palace. Industries include cotton textiles and potteries. Population (1980): 215,976.

Quesnay, François (1694–1774) French economist. Originally the physician of Louis XV, Quesnay devoted himself to the study of economics after 1756. He was founder and leader of the *Physiocrats, a school of economic theorists. He contributed articles to Diderot's *Encyclopédie* and published such books as *Tableau économique* (1758).

Quesnel, Pasquier (1634–1719) French Jansenist theologian (*see* Jansenism). He was a priest of the French Oratory (*see* Oratorians) until expelled from the society in 1684 for his views. He settled in Brussels but was imprisoned there in 1703 and finally escaped to Holland. His *Nouveau Testament en français avec des réflexions morales* (1692) was condemned by the pope in 1713.

Quetta 30 15N 67 00E A city in W central Pakistan, at an altitude of 5500 ft (1650 m). The chief town of Baluchistan, it was badly damaged by an earthquake in 1935. Quetta is a trading center and summer resort. The University of Baluchistan was established in 1970. Population (1981): 285,719.

quetzal A Central American bird, *Pharomachus mocinno,* that lives in cloud forests and feeds on fruit, insects, tree frogs, and lizards. The male reaches 4.3 ft (1.3 m) in length, including its curved ornamental tail feathers; its plumage is iridescent green, red, and white and the long outer wing feathers curl over the flight feathers. Family: *Trogonidae* (trogons).

Quetzalcoatl A Mexican wind and fertility god, usually portrayed as a feathered snake. During the Aztec period (14th–16th centuries) he was identified with the planet Venus, symbol of death and resurrection. He was also a creator god, having made humans by sprinkling blood on bones he brought from the underworld.

Quezon City 14 39N 121 01E A city in the N Philippines, in S Luzon near to Manila. It was the nation's former capital (1948–76). The University of the Philippines was established in 1908. Mainly residential, its chief industry is textiles. Population (1990): 1,632,000.

Quiberon 47 29N 3 07W A peninsula in NW France, on the S coast of Brittany. In 1759, during the Seven Years' War, a naval battle in which the French were defeated by the English was fought off its coast, in Quiberon Bay.

quicksand A mass of soft unconsolidated sand that, when saturated with water, becomes semiliquid and unable to support any appreciable weight.

Quicksands occur where conditions permit large amounts of water to remain in the sand.

QUETZAL *These magnificent birds construct nest holes in tree trunks, both parents taking part in nest building, egg incubation, and feeding the young.*

Quietism A form of mystical passivity that discounts all human effort of will or activity and sees perfection in total dependence upon God. Quietism is associated with certain 17th-century theologians, notably the Spanish priest Miguel de *Molinos. It was condemned by the pope (1687) on account of its practical and philosophical implications.

Quiller-Couch, Sir Arthur Thomas (1863–1944) British critic and novelist who published under the pseudonym "Q." He wrote several adventure novels, many of them set in his native Cornwall, but is best known as compiler of the influential *Oxford Book of English Verse* (1900).

quillwort A small perennial *pteridophyte plant of the genus *Isoetes* (about 60 species), which grows in water or on land, mainly in swampy cooler regions of N North America and Eurasia. Tufts of stiff spiky quill-like leaves, about 2–7 in (5–18 cm) long, grow from a short stout rhizome that bears numerous roots. The spore capsules are embedded in the expanded bases of the leaves. The common Eurasian quillwort (*I. lacustris*) is aquatic. Class: *Lycopsida* (clubmosses, etc.).

Quimper 48 00N 4 06W A city in NW France, the capital of the Finistère department. A tourist center, it has a gothic cathedral and is famous for its Breton pottery. Industries include textiles and furniture. Population (1975): 60,510.

quince A small tree or shrub, *Cydonia vulgaris*, probably native to W Asia but cultivated in temperate regions for its fruit; 15–20 ft (4.5–6 m) high, it has oval leaves (which are woolly beneath) and white or pink flowers, 2 in (5 cm) across. The pear-shaped fruit is 3–4 in (7.5–10 cm) long with a golden-yellow skin and many pips. When cooked, its flesh turns pink, giving a distinctive color and flavor to preserves and jellies. Family: *Rosaceae.*

Quincy, Josiah (1772–1864) US politician, reformer, and educator. A Federalist from Massachusetts, he served in the US House of Representatives (1805–13), where he was strongly opposed to the Embargo Act (1807), acceptance of Louisiana as a state, and the War of 1812. While mayor of Boston (1823–28), he instituted many reforms in government and housing. His term as president of Harvard University (1829–45) brought about growth, especially in building, faculty, and the curriculum.

Quincy 42 15N 71 00W A city in Massachusetts, on Boston Harbor. It is the birthplace of two US presidents, John Adams and his son John Quincy Adams. Industries include shipbuilding and the manufacture of machinery. Population (1990): 84,985.

Quine, Willard van Orman (1908–   ) US philosopher. He became professor of philosophy at Harvard in 1955. His philosophy was largely concerned with language and logic. He argued that linguistic adjustments could make any statement valid. His works include *Word and Object* (1960), *Set Theory and Its Logic* (1963), *Philosophy of Logic* (1970), and *The Roots of Reference* (1973).

Qui Nhon 13 47N 109 11E A port in S Vietnam, on the South China Sea. The site of ancient ruins, it was a naval base during the Vietnam War. Its main industry is fishing. Population (1989): 160,091.

quinine The first drug used to treat malaria. Quinine, which is obtained from the bark of *Cinchona* trees, has now been largely replaced by other drugs (e.g. *chloroquine), which have fewer side effects and are less toxic. Quinine-like compounds (e.g. quinidine) are used to treat abnormal heart rhythms. Quinine may produce allergic reactions in susceptible patients.

quinone ($O:C_6H_4:O$) An *aromatic compound with two hydrogen atoms in the benzene ring replaced by two oxygen atoms. Quinones are used in photography and dye manufacture. They are also found in plants.

quinsy An abscess in the tissue surrounding a tonsil. This arises from infection of the tonsils and may be a complication of tonsillitis. The patient has a sore throat and difficulty in swallowing. Quinsy is sometimes treated by surgical draining of the abscess.

Quintilian (Marcus Fabius Quintilianus; c. 35–c. 100 AD) Roman rhetorician. He was born in Spain and educated in Rome, where he worked as an advocate and teacher of rhetoric. The emperor Domitian appointed him tutor to his heirs. His *Institutio oratoria,* a practical treatise on rhetoric, includes a comparative survey of Greek and Latin literature and many original observations on the education of children.

Quisling, Vidkun (Abraham Lauritz Jonsson) (1887–1945) Norwegian army officer and Nazi collaborator, whose name is a synonym for "traitor." After serving with the army in Russia, Quisling formed (1933) the fascist National Union party in Norway. He encouraged the Nazi occupation of Norway (1940), and as "minister president" in the occupation government, sent a thousand Jews to concentration camps. Arrested in 1945, he was found guilty of war crimes and executed.

Quito 0 20S 78 45W The capital of Ecuador, on the slopes of the volcano Pichincha at an altitude of 9350 ft (2850 m). Originally settled by Quito Indians, it became the capital of the Inca kingdom of Quito until 1534, when it was captured by the Spanish. It contains many Spanish-colonial churches with fine wooden sculptures and paintings; its two universities were founded in 1769 and 1946. Population (1990): 1,100,847.

Qumran, Khirbat The site on the NW shore of the Dead Sea in Jordan, where a Jewish sect called the *Essenes lived from about 125 BC to 68 AD. The community produced the written documents known as the *Dead Sea Scrolls, which were concealed in nearby caves. Excavations from 1951 revealed a complex of buildings.

quotas, import Limits set by a government to the quantity of specified goods that can be imported from abroad (or sometimes from a specified country) in a given period. Quotas are usually operated by a licensing system, importers being granted licenses authorizing them to import a certain quantity of a product and to purchase the requisite amount of foreign exchange. Quotas are used to remedy a weak *balance of payments or to protect domestic manufacturers but they must be used with discretion to avoid provoking retaliation from other countries. *See also* free trade; tariffs.

Qu Qiu Bai (*or* Ch'ü Ch'iu-pai; 1889–1935) Chinese communist leader. He was a leading literary figure in the communist movement and became general secretary of the Chinese Communist party in 1927. He was captured and executed by *Guomindang (Nationalist) forces in Shanghai.

Quran. *See* Koran.

Qwaqwa. *See* Bantu Homelands.

R

Ra (*or* Re) The Egyptian sun god and lord of creation, usually portrayed with a falcon's head bearing a solar disk. He sailed across the sky by day in his sun boat and through the underworld by night. His center of worship was at Heliopolis. During the 18th dynasty (1567–1320 BC) he became identified with the Theban god *Amon as Amon-Ra.

Rabat (Arabic name: Ribat) 34 00N 6 42W The capital of Morocco, near the Atlantic coast. Founded as a military post in the 12th century, it became the capital under the French protectorate in the early 20th century. It has a university (1957) and its notable buildings include the 12th-century Hassan Tower. It has an important textile industry. Population (1982): 519,000.

Rabaul 4 13S 152 11E A city in Papua New Guinea, the chief town on the island of New Britain. The capital until 1941 of the Territory of New Guinea, it was evacuated in 1937 because of a volcanic eruption and heavily bombed during World War II. Copra is exported. Population (1980): 14,954.

rabbi A Jewish scholar and religious authority. The term came into use in the 1st century AD, and the Judaism of the following centuries is often called "rabbinic Judaism." For a long time the rabbinate was not a salaried office; the title indicated scholarly achievement and legal competence. In modern Jewish communities rabbis are communal leaders, preachers, and pastoral workers.

rabbit A burrowing *mammal belonging to the family *Leporidae* (which also includes the *hares). The rabbit from which domestic breeds derive, (*Oryctolagus cuniculus*), grows to about 18 in (45 cm); it has long ears, a short tail, and soft gray-brown fur. The North American cottontail rabbit (*Sylvilagus floridanus*) has a fluffy white tail, gray-brown fur, and white undersides. It grows to about 15 in (38 cm). Rabbits are gregarious, living in large warrens and feeding on grasses and vegetation. They mature at three months and females can produce a litter of up to 10 young (kittens) every month. Rabbits can become a serious agricultural pest although populations have been depleted by myxomatosis. Order: *Lagomorpha*.

Rabelais, François (1483–1553) French humanist and satirist. He became a Franciscan and then a Benedictine monk, left the monastery to study and practice medicine, and visited Italy with his patron, Cardinal Jean du Bellay (1492–1560). His humanist philosophy is expressed in his works of richly inventive and often frankly coarse comic satire, *Pantagruel* (1532), *Gargantua* (1534), *Tiers Livre* (1546), and *Quart Livre* (1552). The authenticity of the posthumous *Cinquiesme Livre* (1564) has been debated. His attacks on superstition and scholasticism were condemned by theologians but gained him wide popularity. The classic English translation of his works is by Sir Thomas Urquhart (1653).

Rabi, Isidor Isaac (1898–1988) US physicist, born in Austria, who invented a highly accurate technique for measuring the nuclear magnetic movements of atoms. For this work he was awarded the Nobel Prize in 1944. During World War II Rabi worked on the development of the atom bomb.

rabies An acute viral infection of the brain that can affect all warm-blooded animals and may be transmitted to man through the bite of an infected animal ·(usually a dog). Symptoms, which appear after an incubation period of from 10 days to two years, include painful spasms of the throat on swallowing. Later, the very sight of water induces convulsions and paralysis (hence the alternative name of the disease—hydrophobia, literally "fear of water") and the patient eventually dies in a coma. There is no treatment for the established disease, but antirabies vaccine and rabies antiserum given to patients immediately after they have been bitten may prevent the infection from developing.

Rabin, Yitzhak (1922–) Israeli prime minister (1974–77; 1992–), who worked to settle the conflicts between Israelis and Palestinians. He served as Israeli chief of staff (1964–68) and was Israel's ambassador to the US (1968–73) before becoming Israel's first native-born prime minister in 1974. During his first term, he was responsible for a peace accord between Israel and Egypt. In 1984, he became defense minister and was responsible for dealing with the uprising (*intifada*) that began in 1987, in the occupied territories. During his second term as prime minister, he showed a willingness to negotiate with the Palestinians and in 1993 concluded an historic agreement with Yasir Arafat, head of the Palestine Liberation Organization (PLO).

raccoon An omnivorous mammal belonging to the genus *Procyon* (7 species), of the Americas. About 40 in (1 m) long, raccoons are stockily built, with long hind legs and short forelegs. A masklike black patch across the eyes and a striped tail contrast with the thick gray coat. Raccoons forage at night for nuts, roots, snails, mammals, and birds and take aquatic prey, such as crustaceans, mollusks, and fish. Family: *Procyonidae*; order: *Carnivora*.

raccoon dog A short-legged wild *dog, *Nyctereutes procyonides*, of Asia. It is golden-brown, about 24 in (60 cm) long, with black eye patches (like a raccoon). It lives near water and feeds on frogs. Its fur is known as Japanese fox.

Rachel (Élisa Félix; 1820–58) French actress. She made her debut at the Comédie-Française in 1838 and gained an international reputation as a leading tragic actress. She was particularly effective in productions of Racine and Corneille. She died of tuberculosis.

SERGEI RACHMANINOV *In London, 1924.*

Rachmaninov, Sergei (1873–1943) Russian composer, pianist, and conductor. He studied in St Petersburg and Moscow, where he became famous as a pianist, particularly with his own compositions. He left Russia in 1917 and spent most of the rest of his life in the US. His works include four operas, three symphonies, four piano concertos (which he also recorded), the *Rhapsody on a Theme of Paganini* (for piano and orchestra; 1934), and *The Bells* (for soloists, chorus, and orchestra; 1910). One of his most popular pieces for piano is the prelude in C-sharp minor (1892).

racial discrimination The practice of making unfavorable distinctions between the members of different races. In the US relations were established as slavery grew during the 17th and 18th centuries, with different laws for slaves (African Americans). Although conditions improved through the efforts of the *Abolition Movement and emancipation (during the *Civil War), discrimination is still a part of American life despite legislation (*see* Civil Rights Acts and Constitution) and the *civil rights movement. A similar tradition characterizes South Africa (*see* apartheid), where race relations were long governed by an inflexible tradition, which led to the legal and economic separation of peoples on the basis of their ethnic backgrounds. The circumstances that lead to prejudice are many and diverse and much has been written attributing inferiority to particular races (*see* social Darwinism); however, no scientifically accepted work exists to support these contentions.

Racine, Jean (1639–99) French dramatist. He received a Jansenist education at the convent of Port-Royal but was attracted by the Parisian world of theater and began writing plays in 1664. His major classical verse tragedies, influenced initially by those of *Corneille but eventually surpassing them, include *Andromaque* (1667), *Britannicus* (1669), *Bérénice* (1670), and *Phèdre* (1677). In 1677 he retired from the theater, married a young pious girl, and accepted a post at the court of Louis XIV. His final works were two religious dramas based on Old Testament subjects, *Esther* (1689) and *Athalie* (1691). Racine was the outstanding tragedian of the French classical period.

rad The unit of absorbed dose of ionizing radiation in the *c.g.s. system equal to an energy absorption of 100 ergs per gram of irradiated material.

radar (*ra*dio *d*etection *a*nd *r*anging) A method of locating distant objects used in military surveillance, air traffic control, and marine and air navigation; it was first developed during the years before World War II by a British team led by Sir Robert *Watson-Watt. High-frequency (300 to 30,000 megahertz) radio waves are sent out in pulses from a powerful rotating transmitter and are reflected back by any object they encounter. The reflected signal is picked up by a receiver antenna and is used to deflect the electron beam in a *cathode-ray tube. The beam scans the screen of the tube by rotating at the same speed as the antenna, so that its angular position indicates the direction of the located object. Brightness indicates the strength of the reflected signal, i.e. strong for solid objects, weak for water. The distance from the center of the screen shows the delay between transmission and reception of the reflected signal, i.e. the distance of the object. The screen continues to glow for a short time after the beam has passed so that a picture is built up with each successive rotation. Radar is now fitted to most aircraft and ships to provide a means of navigation in the dark, cloud, or fog.

Radcliffe, Ann (Ward) (1764–1823) British novelist. Despite their technical clumsiness and lack of characterization, her gothic novels, such as *The Mysteries of Udolfo* (1794) and *The Italian* (1797), were important influences in the change of literary taste and the increasing interest in romantic characters, description, etc.

Radcliffe-Brown, Alfred Reginald (1881–1955) British anthropologist. A pioneer of social anthropology, Radcliffe-Brown held professorships at Chicago, Sydney, Cape Town, and Oxford Universities. His specific contribu-

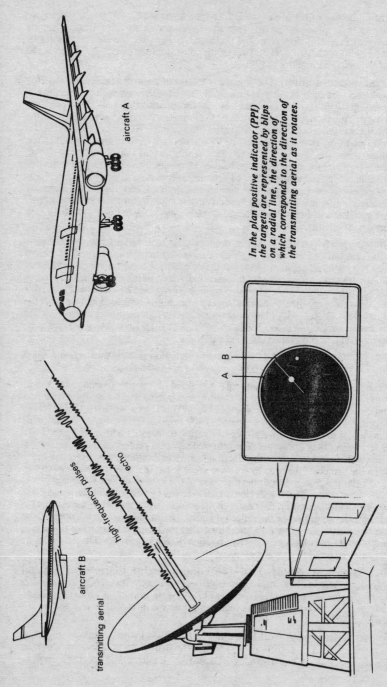

aircraft A

In the plan positive indicator (PPI) the targets are represented by blips on a radial line, the direction of which corresponds to the direction of the transmitting aerial as it rotates.

A B

echo

high-frequency pulses

aircraft B

transmitting aerial

RADAR *The high-frequency pulses sent out by the transmitting aerial are reflected back by the target and displayed on a PPI.*

tion to anthropology lies in his studies of *kinship and society, for which he did field work in Australia and the Andaman Islands.

Radek, Karl (1885–1939?) Soviet politician and journalist. Radek participated in the Russian Revolutions of 1905 and 1917. In 1920 he became secretary of Comintern and served until 1924. Accused of being a Trotskyite, Radek was expelled from the Communist party in 1927. After recanting in 1929, he wrote for the newspaper *Izvestia* and helped to draft the 1936 constitution. Accused of treason in 1937, he probably died in a Siberian labor camp.

radial velocity The velocity of a star, etc., along the line of sight, i.e. toward or away from the earth. It is calculated from the Doppler shift of the lines of the star's spectrum (*see* Doppler effect).

radian (rad) The *SI unit of plane angle equal to the angle subtended at the center of a circle by an arc equal in length to the radius of the circle.

radiation The propagation of energy by means of beams of particles or waves. It includes all electromagnetic waves, beams of elementary particles, ions, etc., and sound waves.

radiation sickness Illness caused by exposure to *ionizing radiation, either naturally occurring or from nuclear weapons, X-ray machines, etc. The radiation affects the cells of the body in various ways depending on its intensity. Short-term effects include nausea and diarrhea, while long-term effects include sterility, hemorrhage, loss of hair, and cancer. However, sufficiently intense radiation can kill cancer cells or prevent them from reproducing, hence its use in *radiotherapy.

Radić, Stjepan (1871–1928) Croatian statesman. Founder of the Croatian Peasant party (1904), Radić advocated a federated Yugoslavia with Croatian autonomy and opposed *Pašić's centralized Yugoslav government. In 1925, however, he became minister of education but resigned a year later. He was assassinated in Parliament.

radical A group of atoms in a chemical compound that behaves as a unit in chemical reactions. For example, the methanol molecule (CH_3OH) can be considered as a methyl radical (CH_3.) and a hydroxyl radical (.OH). In this sense, radicals are often simply referred to as groups, a functional group being one responsible for the characteristic reactions of a class of compounds. Thus, the hydroxyl group is thße functional group of alcohols. **Free radicals** are groups existing independently. Because they have unpaired electrons they are usually extremely reactive transient species. They can be produced by *pyrolysis or *photolysis and are important intermediates in many reactions, particularly photochemical, combustion, and polymerization reactions.

Radiguet, Raymond (1903–23) French novelist. His precocious talent was recognized by several prominent literary and artistic figures, especially Jean Cocteau. His two novels were *Le Diable au corps* (1923), a story of adolescent passion and cruelty, and *Le Bal du Comte d'Orgel* (1924).

radio The transmission of sound or other information by radio-frequency (3 kilohertz to 300 gigahertz) electromagnetic waves. The use of radio waves for communication was pioneered by *Marconi in 1895, although their existence had been postulated by *Maxwell in 1873 and demonstrated by *Hertz in 1888.

A **radio transmitter** generates a radio-frequency electrical signal (carrier wave) in an oscillator and superimposes the sound signal on it by a *modulation process. The composite signal is then fed to an aerial, which transmits electromagnetic waves. Although the waves travel in straight lines, transmission beyond the horizon is made possible by the ionosphere, a layer of the upper atmosphere

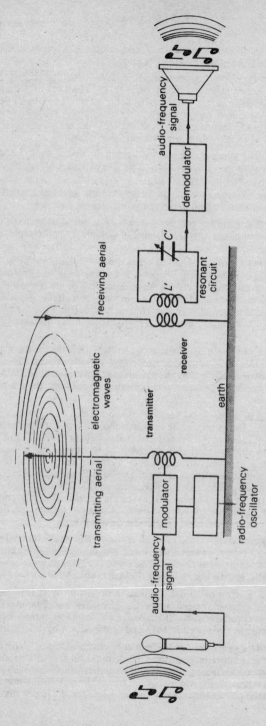

RADIO *The transmission and reception of sound broadcasts.*

2121   **radio beacon**

that reflects radio waves in the long and medium wavebands. Long-wave (30–300 kilohertz) and medium-wave (300–3000 kilohertz) radio is used for direct (ground-wave) transmission in amplitude-modulated (AM) sound broadcasting. Short-wave radio is used for AM sound broadcasting over longer distances using the ionosphere (sky waves) and for communication to ships and aircraft. VHF (very high frequency; 30–300 megahertz) is used for *stereophonic sound broadcasting in frequency modulated (FM) transmissions. Television uses mostly UHF (ultrahigh frequency). Neither VHF nor UHF are reflected by the ionosphere, but can be relayed by *communications satellites. All **radio receivers**, from the pocket transistor radio to the most sophisticated and sensitive systems, consist of an *aerial, which detects the signal and converts it to an electrical current; a resonant circuit, which selects the required frequency band; a demodulator to retrieve the audio-frequency signal from the modulated carrier wave; an amplification system; and one or more *loudspeakers to reproduce the sound.

radioactive tracer A radioactive *isotope used for following the course of a substance during a physical, biological, or chemical process. A nonradioactive isotope in the substance is replaced by a radioactive isotope of the same element, which can then be detected by observing its emitted radiation with, for example, a *Geiger counter. Substances containing such radioisotopes are called labeled compounds. Radioactive tracing is a sensitive technique used in medical, scientific, and industrial research.

radioactive waste Waste products from nuclear reactors, uranium-processing plants, etc., that have become radioactive. The disposal of these waste products, which include solids, liquids, and gases, constitutes a major problem as some materials have a very long *mean life. At present solid waste is either stored in tanks underground or placed in drums weighted with concrete and sunk in deep sea water. Liquid waste represents the most difficult problems owing to the possibility of leakage. Gaseous waste is usually released into the atmosphere in small quantities.

radioactivity The spontaneous emission of a particle by an atomic nucleus. The emitted particle may be an alpha particle (a helium nucleus consisting of two protons and two neutrons), in which case the process is known as *alpha decay; or it may be a beta particle (an *electron), when the process is known as *beta decay. Highly energetic X-rays (*see* gamma radiation) may also be emitted simultaneously. In both alpha and beta decay the nucleus changes into that of another element. A less common method of decay is the emission of a *positron, the antiparticle of the electron, the process being similar to that of beta decay. Radioactive decay is a random process and its occurrence for a single nucleus can be neither predicted nor controlled. However, for a large number of nuclei the time taken for a certain fraction of nuclei to decay can be accurately predicted as either its *mean life or *half-life. These quantities vary from about 10^{-8} second to 10^{10} years, depending on the isotope. The phenomenon was first discovered in 1898 by *Becquerel in uranium and elucidated by the *Curies, *Rutherford, and *Soddy.

radio astronomy The study of celestial objects by means of the radio waves they emit. This radio emission was first noticed by K. G. *Jansky in the US in 1932 and it now forms an important branch of *astronomy. *See* radio telescope.

radio beacon An automatic navigational beacon that broadcasts a coded radio signal. The angular position of the source of the signal can be determined by a vessel or aircraft carrying a radio direction finder or radio compass and can be identified by its code, usually given in Morse. Where two such radio beacons can be received, the exact position of the receiver can be determined by triangulation.

radiocarbon dating A method of estimating the age of a material, such as wood, that was once living. Atmospheric carbon dioxide contains a small proportion of the radioisotope carbon 14. As all living things absorb carbon from atmospheric carbon dioxide, either directly or indirectly, they too contain a constant proportion of carbon 14. However, once dead, the level of carbon 14 falls as a result of *beta decay. By measuring the radioactivity of a material, the concentration of carbon 14 and hence its age can be estimated. The method is accurate within stated limits for ages up to 4500 years. *See also* radiometric dating.

radiochemistry The branch of chemistry concerned with compounds containing radioactive *isotopes of elements. It includes chemical techniques for isotope separation, and the use of *radioactive tracers for investigating the mechanisms of chemical reactions.

radio galaxy A *radio source that lies beyond our galaxy, is identified with an optical *galaxy, and the radio-power output of which greatly exceeds that of a normal galaxy. The size can be immense. A massive *black hole at the galaxy center has been postulated as a possible energy source.

radiography The technique of examining the internal structure of a solid body by passing *X-rays or *gamma radiation through it to produce an image on a photographic plate or fluorescent screen. Radiography is used in medicine for the diagnosis of disease (*see* radiology) and in industry to examine objects, etc., for structural defects.

radio interferometer. *See* radio telescope.

radioisotope (*or* radioactive isotope) An *isotope that is radioactive. Radioisotopes are used in the production of *nuclear energy, in *radiotherapy, as *radioactive tracers, and in *dating techniques. Some are naturally occurring (those with mass numbers in excess of 208) while others can be made radioactive by neutron bombardment.

Radiolaria An order of single-celled animals (*see* Protozoa) found chiefly in the sea, as a component of plankton. Radiolarians are typically spherical, 0.004 in (0.1 mm) to several millimeters in diameter, with a silicaceous skeleton of radiating spines from which lone thin pseudopodia extend to capture food particles. The skeletal remains of dead radiolarians sink to the ocean floor to form a deposit called radiolarian ooze. Class: *Sarcodina.* □Protozoa.

radiology The branch of medicine concerned with the use of X-rays and other forms of radiation and radioactive substances in the diagnosis and treatment of disease. *Radiography is used to diagnose a wide range of disorders, including fractures, ulcers, and cancer: hollow organs are often visualized by injecting a fluid that is opaque to X-rays. A radiologist is a doctor specialized in the interpretation of X-ray photographs and films. Recent advances in radiology include the CAT scan, the use of computer-aided tomography, in which X-ray "slices" of the body are recorded with an X-ray scanner and integrated by a computer to produce a cross-sectional image. *See also* radiotherapy.

radiometric dating A method of dating rocks, developed mainly in the 1950s, by observing the extent to which a radioactive (parent) element in a rock has decayed to form a stable daughter element. Since the half-life or rate of decay of the radioactive element chosen is known, the age of the rock can be calculated from the ratio of parent to daughter isotopes present. The most frequently used methods are *radiocarbon dating, *potassium-argon dating, and *rubidium-strontium dating. Methods based on uranium-lead and thorium-lead decays are also sometimes used.

radio source A celestial object that emits radio waves and can be detected by a *radio telescope. The sun and Jupiter are solar-system sources. Other radio sources within our galaxy are pulsars, supernova remnants, interstellar hydrogen clouds, and the galactic center. Extragalactic sources include spiral galaxies, radio galaxies, and some quasars. The spatial distribution and intensity of the radio emission can be shown on a contour map.

radio telescope An instrument for detecting and measuring the radio emissions from celestial *radio sources. It consists of an antenna, or system of antennae, the radio-frequency signals of which are carried by wires or waveguides to one or more receivers. The receiver output signal is finally displayed on a graph, stored on magnetic tape, etc. The antenna may be a large metal parabolic or spherical dish, usually steerable, that brings radio waves from a radio source to a focus on a secondary antenna. Alternatively simple dipole antennae may be used. An antenna system may consist of two separate units the signals of which are fed to a common receiver. This radio interferometer has a very much greater resolving power than a single antenna.

radiotherapy The use of X-rays and other forms of radiation, either produced by machines or emitted by radioactive isotopes, for treating disease. The radiation may be directed at the target organ from a distance or radioactive needles, wires, pellets, etc., may be implanted in the body. Radiation is particularly destructive to rapidly dividing cells: it is therefore used in treating various forms of *cancer and certain other tumors as well as overactivity of the thyroid gland.

radish An annual or biennial herb, *Raphanus sativus,* widely grown for its edible fleshy hot-tasting root, which may be red, white, or purple. Spring varieties are quick-growing while winter varieties may be stored. The plant bears white flowers. Family: *Cruciferae.*

radium (Ra) A metallic element, discovered in pitchblende in 1898 by Pierre and Marie Curie. It is a divalent alkaline-earth element, forming a number of simple salts, such as the chloride ($RaCl_2$). It decays to form the noble gas radon and is used in radiotherapy for the treatment of cancers. At no 88; at wt 226; mp 1293°F (700°C); bp 2086°f (1140°C).

radius. *See* arm.

Radom 51 26N 21 10E An industrial city in SE central Poland. Founded in 1340, it was held successively by Austria and Russia before returning to Poland in 1918. Industries include leather, glass, and chemicals. Population (1992 est): 230,000.

radon (Rn) The heaviest noble gas, produced by the decay of radium, thorium, and actinium. It is radioactive, the longest-lived isotope (^{222}Rn) having a half-life of 3.825 days. Like the other noble gases, Rn forms clathrates and fluorides. Increased radon levels have been noted in ground water shortly before earthquakes. At no 86; at wt 222; mp −96°F (−71°C); bp −79°F (−61.8°C).

Raeder, Erich (1876–1960) German admiral; commander in chief of the navy (1928–43). In contravention of the Treaty of Versailles, he rebuilt the German navy in the years before World War II but was dismissed after disagreeing with Hitler over strategy. He was sentenced to life imprisonment for war crimes but was released in 1955.

raffia (*or* raphia) A *palm tree of the genus *Raphia,* especially *R. pedunculata* (or *R. ruffia*), native to Madagascar and cultivated for its fiber. Its leaves, up to 65 ft (20 m) long, are composed of 80–100 leaflets from which the fiber is torn in thin strips and dried in the sun. Raffia is soft, strong, pliable, and resistant to shrinking; it is woven into mats and baskets and used in horticulture, etc.

Raffles, Sir Thomas Stamford (1781–1826) British colonial administrator and Oriental scholar, who acquired Singapore for the East India Company (1819). In 1805 he became assistant secretary to the governor of Penang and was lieutenant governor of Java (1811–16) while it was under British rule and then of Bengkulu (1818–23) in W Sumatra.

Rafflesia A genus of Malaysian parasitic herbs (12 species), the vegetative parts of which are reduced to fungus-like threads that extract food from the roots and stems of other plants. The monster plant (*R. arnoldii*) has the world's largest flower—up to 18 in (45 cm) across and weighing up to 22 lb (10 kg). It smells of rotten meat and attracts carrion flies, which act as pollinators. The genus was named for Sir Stamford *Raffles. Family: *Rafflesiaceae*.

Rafsanjani, Ali Akbar Hashemi (1934–   ) Iranian religious and political leader; president of Iran (1989–   ). As a protégé of Ayatollah Khomeini, Iran's future leader, Rafsanjani opposed the opposition to the autocratic Shah of Iran and was imprisoned (1975–77) for his views. When the Shah was overthrown in 1979, Rafsanjani became a member of Iran's Revolutionary Council and later led Iran's legislature as a loyal Khomeini supporter. After Khomeini's death in 1989, Rafsanjani assumed the presidency in the face of challenges by more conservative leaders. He tried to modernize Iran and bring it back into the world community without offending religious conservatives, and he adopted a neutral stance during the Persian Gulf War in 1991. He was reelected in 1993.

raga (Sanskrit: color) In Indian music, a type of *scale used as the basis for improvisation. There are many different ragas, some of which are associated with particular moods, feelings, times of day, etc.

ragged robin A Eurasian perennial herb, *Lychnis flos-cuculi*. Growing to a height of 30 in (75 cm), it has rose-red flowers with five deeply divided ragged petals. It is common in damp places and has been introduced to North America. Family: *Caryophyllaceae*.

Raglan, FitzRoy James Henry Somerset, 1st baron (1788–1855) British field marshal. After service in the Napoleonic Wars (in which he lost his sword arm at Waterloo), he became secretary to Wellington, whom he succeeded as master general of the ordnance in 1852. In 1854 he became commander in the *Crimean War and, in spite of success at *Inkerman, his strategy was much criticized (*see also* Balaclava, Battle of). The raglan sleeve, extending to the neck without shoulder seams, is named for him.

RAGNARÖK *The gods struggle against the evil progeny of Loki at the end of the world. Thor (right) battles with the serpent Jörmungandr, Odin with the wolf Fenris, and Frey with the fire-giant Surtr. Bifrost, the rainbow bridge connecting Asgard and earth, is in the background.*

Ragnarök In Norse mythology, doomsday, when a catastrophic battle between the gods and the forces of evil will occur. It will be preceded by warning signals: three years of perpetual winter will be followed by three years of moral decline

2125 rain

among men. After the defeat of the gods by the forces of evil, led by *Loki, everyone will be destroyed except for *Lif and Lifthrasir.

ragtime A precursor of *New Orleans style jazz. Ragtime developed from minstrel-band music, but many rags were published as piano compositions. Ragtime was characterized by syncopation in the melody against a regular march-like accompaniment and was popular from the 1890s until around 1920. Famous rags include "Harlem Rag" (1895) and "Maple Leaf Rag" (1899), written by Scott *Joplin, the first ragtime composer to write down his music.

ragweed An annual plant, *Ambrosia,* that grows up to 12 ft (3.7 m) high and has green flowers atop thin clustered stems with large leaves. Found mainly in North America, the ragweed's pollen, especially that of the common ragweed (*Ambrosia elatior*), causes hay fever, an allergic reaction. Family: *Compositae.*

ragworm A marine *annelid worm, *Nereis cultrifera,* also called chainworm, of European coastal waters; 2–4 in (5–10 cm) long, ragworms swim by means of paddlelike structures occurring in pairs on each body segment. Most live in burrows in sand or mud or among stones, feeding on dead organisms and detritus using a pair of horny jaws inside a protrudable mouth tube. Class: *Polychaeta.*

ragwort A perennial or biennial herb, *Senecio jacobaea,* that grows up to 60 in (150 cm) high and has much-divided leaves and dense flat-topped heads of yellow flowers. It is found on dunes, waste places, and pastures of Eurasia and N Africa and has been introduced to New Zealand and North America. When eaten in large quantities it is poisonous to livestock. Family: *Compositae.*

rail A slender secretive ground-dwelling bird belonging to a widely distributed family (*Rallidae*; about 300 species), occurring mostly in swamps, marshes, and fresh waters; 4.3–18 in (11–45 cm) long, rails have short rounded wings, a short tail, and typically a dull gray or brown plumage, often barred for camouflage. They feed on plant material, invertebrates, and birds' eggs. Order: *Gruiformes* (cranes, rails, etc.). *See also* coot; corncrake; gallinule.

railroad A permanent track, consisting of parallel rails, on which □locomotives draw wagons or cars for transporting goods or passengers. Wooden rails have been in use in mines since the 14th century, but flanged wheels running on cast-iron rails were not introduced until 1789. Thereafter they were quite widely used in the mining and metallurgical industries, although cars were horse-drawn until the invention of the steam locomotive at the beginning of the 19th century. The first effective railroad in the world opened in England in 1825 and ran between Stockton and Darlington, using *Stephenson's *Locomotion* as the locomotive. The US railroad boom began in the 1830s, and systems grew rapidly before the Civil War. After the war, the system expanded greatly, symbolized by the completion of the transcontinental railroad in 1869.

Since World War II the growth of internal air services, the development of efficient trucking services, and the spread of private automobiles have led to the decline of the railroads in industrial countries, causing services to be reduced. The introduction of high-speed trains, however, has enabled them to survive. In developing countries they still play an essential role in transporting goods and passengers over long distances.

rain A form of precipitation composed of liquid water drops ranging in size from about 0.02 to 0.20 in (0.5 to 5 mm) diameter. Minute droplets of water in clouds may coalesce to form larger drops; if these are sufficiently heavy they will fall as rain. The amount of rain, together with other forms of precipitation, that falls in a specific time is usually measured with a **rain gauge**. This is a cylindrical container with a funnel of standard diameter into which the rain falls.

The water collected is periodically measured and recorded in inches or millimeters; some rain gauges are designed to record automatically.

rainbow An optical phenomenon consisting of an arc of light across the sky composed of the colors of the spectrum. It is caused by the refraction of sunlight through falling water drops; the larger the drops the more spectacular are the colors.

Raine, Kathleen (1908–) British poet. Her volumes of poetry, which include *Stone and Flower* (1943) and *The Lost Country* (1971), are noted for their visionary lyricism. She has also published several studies of William Blake, notably *Blake and Tradition* (1969).

Rainier, Mount A mountain in the US, the highest peak in Washington state and the Cascade Mountains. It is noted for its many glaciers. Height: 14,408 ft (4392 m).

Rainier III (1923–) Prince of Monaco (1949–). He repudiated the principle of the *divine right of kings in a new constitution (1962). In 1956 he married Grace *Kelly. Their three children are Prince Albert (1958–), Princess Caroline (1957–), and Princess Stephanie (1965–).

Rais, Gilles de (*or* G. de Retz; 1404–40) French marshal, who fought with *Joan of Arc. After her capture he retired to his estates in Brittany and dabbled in alchemy and witchcraft. In 1440 he was sentenced to death for the torture and murder of over 140 children. He was later associated with the story of Bluebeard, immortalized by Charles *Perrault.

Rajasthan A state in NW India, extending from the Thar Desert along Pakistan's border SE into forested hills. The economy depends primarily on grain and livestock farming, as well as cotton, sugarcane, and pulses. Coal, phosphates, gypsum, marble, mica, and salt are mined. Industries include textiles, cement, and glass. *History*: Rajasthan flourished in the Harappan period (3rd–2nd millenniums BC). Under Rajput princes (from the 7th century AD), it withstood Muslim invaders but succumbed to British expansion (19th century). Area: 132,095 sq mi (342,214 sq km). Population (1991): 43,880,000. Capital: Jaipur.

Rajput A group of clans in N and central India, now numbering about 11 million people. They appeared in about the 5th century AD and are believed to have been descended from invading tribes from Central Asia, although they claim descent from more ancient Indian tribes. Because of their warfaring occupation they were at some time included within the Ksatriya (warrior) caste of Hindu society. The Rajput states fought vigorously against the Muslim invaders, maintaining their independence in Rajasthan. They acknowledged the overlordship of the Moguls in the 16th century, the Marathas in the 18th century, and the British in 1808. Rajput dynasties were responsible for building many fine temples.

Rákóczy II, Ferenc (1676–1735) Hungarian revolutionary. In 1703 Rákóczy led a peasant uprising against Austria and in 1704 he was elected Prince of Transylvania. After two serious defeats in 1708 and 1710, Hungary signed the Peace of Szatmár (1711) with Austria. Rákóczy rejected it and went abroad, dying in Turkey.

Raleigh 35 46N 78 39W The capital of North Carolina. Named for Sir Walter Raleigh, its industries include the manufacture of computers and textiles. North Carolina State University (1887) and Shaw University (1865) are situated there. Population (1990): 207,951.

Raleigh, Sir Walter (1554–1618) British explorer and writer; half-brother of Humphrey *Gilbert. He became a favorite of Elizabeth I. He was unsuccessful in his attempts (1584–89) to found a colony in Virginia (now North Carolina) but brought back the potato and tobacco plant from America. In 1595–96 he led an expedition to South America, which he described in *The Discoverie of Guiana* (1596), and in 1596 took part in the sack of Cádiz. At James I's accession (1603) he stood trial for treason, but the death sentence was commuted to imprisonment; while in the Tower of London he wrote *The History of the World* (1614). He was released in 1616 to search for gold along the Orinoco but his mission was a failure and after his return his death sentence was invoked and he was executed.

rally 1. A competitive automobile racing event, in which drivers have to reach checkpoints by certain times. The routes are normally over public roads, but rallies often also include speed or other tests after the route has been completed. Major events, such as the Monte Carlo Rally (first held in 1911), require extensively modified cars. **2.** A similar event for motorcycles, but usually with more emphasis on the social and touring aspects than the competitive.

Rama The seventh incarnation of *Vishnu, appearing as a hero in the epics the *Ramayana* and *Mahabharata*. In the *Upanishads* and elsewhere he appears as a god. Since about the 15th century he has been widely worshiped as the supreme deity, epitomizing reason and virtue. He is usually represented holding a bow and arrow and attended by his wife.

Ramadan The ninth month of the Muslim year. It is a time of atonement, and every Muslim is required to observe a strict fast daily from dawn to dusk until the new moon of the next month is visible.

Ramakrishna (1836–86) Hindu saint and religious teacher. Son of an impoverished Brahmin family, he had little formal education, but he gathered a following throughout the world. He condemned greed, lust, and the caste system, teaching the essential unity and truth of all religions.

Raman, Sir Chandrasekhara Venkata (1888–1970) Indian physicist, who was professor at Calcutta University. He won the Nobel Prize in 1930 for his discovery that there is a change in the wavelength of light or ultraviolet radiation when scattered by certain molecules (**Raman effect**). This discovery was used to determine some of the finer details of molecular structure.

Ramanuja (11th century AD) Hindu philosopher and theologian, born in Kanchipuram (S India). He diverged sharply from the tradition in *Vedanta associated with *Sankara, insisting upon the value and reality of the physical world. In religion he provided an influential philosophical basis for devotional worship (*bhakti*), based upon his concept of a personal God epitomized by the god *Vishnu.

Ramapithecus A genus of fossil *hominids that lived during the late Miocene and early Pliocene. It is represented by fossil remains found in India in 1934. They were about the size of a gibbon, possibly walked erect, and may represent the earliest ancestors of modern man after the divergence of his evolutionary line from the apes.

Ramat Gan 32 04N 34 48E A city in central Israel, just E of Tel Aviv-Yafo. It has some manufacturing and is the seat of Bar-Ilan University. Population (1990 est): 116,000.

Ramayana (Sanskrit: romance of Rama) Hindu epic poem in seven books. Probably composed in its present form after the 4th century BC, it tells the story of *Rama and his devoted wife Sita, her abduction by the demon king Ravana, and Rama's struggle to recover her with the aid of *Hanuman. The *Ramayana* and *Mahabharata* are the two great classics of Sanskrit literature.

Rambert, Dame Marie (Cyvia Rabbam, later Miriam Rambach; 1888–1982) British ballet dancer and choreographer, born in Poland. She worked with Diaghilev's Ballets Russes in 1913 and was naturalized as a British citizen in 1918. As director of the Carmargo Society, which in 1935 became the Ballet Rambert, she trained and encouraged many young British dancers and choreographers.

Rambouillet 48 39N 1 50E A city in N France, in the Yvelines department. Its chateau (14th–18th centuries) is now the summer residence of French presidents. Population: 20,056.

rambutan A Malaysian tree, *Nephelium lappaceum,* that grows 65 ft (20 m) high and produces edible plum-sized red or yellow spiny fruit. It is cultivated in moist tropical lowlands. Family: *Sapindaceae.*

Rameau, Jean Philippe (1683–1764) French composer. He held several posts as organist and wrote a *Traité de l'harmonie* (1722), a significant contribution to modern musical theory, before beginning to compose. His works include chamber, keyboard, and vocal music, as well as 24 operas, including the opera *Hippolyte et Aricie* (1733), and opera-ballets, including *Les Indes galantes* (1735) and *Castor et Pollux* (1737). There was great rivalry between his adherents and those of Lully and Pergolesi.

ramie A perennial plant, *Boehmeria nivea,* also called China grass, native to E Asia and cultivated, chiefly in China, for its stem fibers. Each plant produces several stalks, up to 7.9 ft (2.4 m) high, with clusters of greenish-white flowers in the leaf axils. Although strong and durable, ramie fiber is not widely used due to difficulties in extraction, spinning, and weaving. Family: *Urticaceae* (nettle family).

Ramillies, Battle of (May 23, 1706) The battle in the War of the *Spanish Succession in which British, Dutch, and Danish forces under Marlborough defeated the French 13 mi (21 km) N of Namur. The victory gave much of the Spanish Netherlands to the allies.

Ramón y Cajal, Santiago (1852–1934) Spanish histologist, who established the neuron (nerve cell) as the basic unit of the nervous system. Ramón improved staining techniques to distinguish the complex connections between neurons in the brain, spinal tissue, and the retina of the eye. He was awarded the 1906 Nobel Prize with Camillo *Golgi.

Ramsay, Sir William (1852–1916) Scottish chemist, whose work on the *noble gases earned him the 1904 Nobel Prize in chemistry. His interest was kindled when *Rayleigh discovered that atmospheric nitrogen was slightly heavier than laboratory-prepared nitrogen. In 1894, Ramsay, working with Rayleigh, removed all known gases from some air and discovered a small residue, which they identified spectroscopically as a new element, naming it argon (inert). By fractionally distilling argon, Ramsay isolated neon, xenon, and krypton in 1898. In 1895 he had discovered the inert gas helium, being given off by the mineral cleveite.

Ramses (II) the Great King of Egypt (1304–1237 BC) of the 19th dynasty. He fortified the coast road to repel nomads and pirates. His more serious, though indecisive, warfare against the Hittites, whose success at Qadesh (c. 1300) unsettled Egypt's Palestinian subjects, ended in lasting peace around 1284. Ramses built, or enlarged, more temples than any other pharaoh and built the temple complex of *Abu Simbel. He is probably the pharaoh who oppressed the Israelites.

Ramses III King of Egypt (1198–1166 BC) of the 20th dynasty, famous for two victories against the invading Sea Peoples. The first recorded strike in history occurred during his reign, when workers building a necropolis protested against the government's failure to deliver grain rations.

Ram Singh (1816–85) Indian Sikh leader. He organized a new, severely puritanical, sect of Sikhs, the Kukas, and worked to oust the British from India. His men were brutally punished for their attacks on Muslims and Ram Singh died after a long exile in Burma.

Rance River A river in NW France, rising in Brittany and flowing generally E and N to the Gulf of St Malo. It powers the world's first successful tidal power station, opened in 1966. Length: 62 mi (100 km).

Rand, Ayn (1905–82) US author; born in Russia. She began her writing career as a screenwriter (1932–34; 1944–49). Her first book, *We, the Living*, was published in 1936 and the works that followed promoted her doctrine, objectivism, which advocated self-interest and fulfillment in a capitalist world. Her works include *Anthem* (1938), *The Fountainhead* (1943), *Atlas Shrugged* (1957), *The Virtue of Selfishness* (1965), and *Philosophy: Who Needs It?* (1982).

Rand, The. *See* Witwatersrand.

Randolph, A(sa) Philip (1889–1979) US labor and civil-rights leader. He founded the *Messenger*, a radical magazine for African Americans, in 1917, and by 1925 was urging unionization of railroad porters. He organized the Brotherhood of Sleeping Car Porters in 1925 and served as its president until 1968. A threat to march on Washington with 50,000 African Americans in 1941 resulted in equal rights for African Americans in government and the defense industries. He was a vice-president of the *American Federation of Labor-Congress of Industrial Organizations (AFL-CIO) from 1957 and one of the directors of the 1963 March on Washington for jobs and freedom.

Randolph, Edward Jennings (1753–1813) US statesman. He was a member of the Continental Congress (1779–82) and governor of Virginia (1786–88). As leader of the Virginia delegation to the *Annapolis Convention, he was the author of the *Virginia Plan and wrote the final draft of the US Constitution, but did not sign it. He served as US attorney general (1789–94) and secretary of state (1794–95), retiring after being falsely accused of accepting French bribes. He was defense lawyer for Aaron *Burr in 1807.

Rangoon former name of the capital of Burma. *See* Yangon.

Ranjit Singh, Maharaja (1780–1839) Sikh ruler, known as the Lion of the Punjab. At the age of 20 he took control of Lahore and in 1802 seized Amritsar, the holy city of the Sikhs. With an enormous army based on the European model, he became master of a large part of the Punjab. In spite of uneasy relations with the British, he supported them against Afghanistan in 1838.

Rank, Otto (1884–1939) Austrian psychiatrist, noted for his theory that emotional disorders could stem from psychological trauma experienced during birth. Rank was a colleague of Sigmund *Freud and applied Freudian psychology to an analysis of many literary works, pointing especially to the *Oedipus complex as a commonly recurring theme.

Ranke, Leopold von (1795–1886) German historian. A professor at Berlin University from 1825 to 1871, von Ranke published work on German, French, Spanish, Italian, and English history. His *History of the Latin and Teutonic Nations (1494–1535)* (1824) demonstrated his abilities in source criticism and is generally regarded as the first critical historical work.

Ransom, John Crowe (1888–1974) US poet and critic. At Vanderbilt University he was a founder of the Fugitives, a group of agrarian poets. He founded the *Kenyon Review* (1939), a literary organ for the school of criticism that took its name from his book *The New Criticism* (1941). His formal ironic poetry is included in *Poems About God* (1919), *Chills and Fever* (1924), *Two Gentlemen in Bonds* (1926), *Selected Poems* (1945), and other volumes.

Ranunculaceae A family of herbaceous and woody plants (about 1300 species), found all over the world but most abundant in N temperate and Arctic regions. They are mainly bitter-tasting and sometimes poisonous. The family includes many garden flowers, such as **Anenome, *Aquilegia, *Clematis*, and **Delphinium*, as well as common weeds, e.g. *buttercup.

Rapallo 44 21N 9 13E A port and resort in NW Italy, in Liguria on the Gulf of Genoa. It was the scene of the signing of two treaties after World War I, the first between Italy and Yugoslavia (1920) and the second between the Soviet Union and Germany (1922). Olive oil, wine, and cement are manufactured there. Population (1971): 26,713.

Rapanui. *See* Easter Island.

rape (botany) An annual or biennial herb, **Brassica napus* var. *arvensis*, also called oilseed rape or coleseed, that grows to a height of 40 in (1 m) and has deeply divided lobed leaves and yellow flowers. It is widely cultivated for its seeds, contained in pods, which yield an edible oil; the residue is used as a cattle feed. Family: **Cruciferae.*

rape (law) Sexual intercourse with another person against her or his will or voluntary permission. The accusation must be supported by other evidence; for example, there must be proof of penetration.

Raphael (Raffaello Sanzio; 1483–1520) Italian Renaissance painter and architect, born in Urbino, the son of a painter. He trained under *Perugino, in Perugia, where he painted *The Marriage of the Virgin* before moving to Florence in 1504. There, influenced by *Leonardo and *Michelangelo, he painted numerous Madonnas and also the portraits of Angelo and Maddalena Doni. Settling in Rome in 1508, he decorated the papal apartments in the Vatican with frescoes, which include the *School of Athens* and the *Disputa.* He painted his patron Pope Julius II and the *Sistine Madonna.* In 1514 he succeeded Bramante as architect of St Peter's but only a few of his architectural projects were realized, for example the Chigi chapel in Sta Maria del Popolo. In 1515 he designed tapestries for the Sistine Chapel. His last work, the *Transfiguration,* which was completed by Giulio Romano, anticipates *mannerism.

Rapp, George (Johann Georg R.; 1757–1847) US religious leader, born in Germany. He came to the US in 1803, seeking religious freedom for his sect, the Rappites, and a site upon which to establish a utopian community. They settled Harmony, Penn., in 1805, but, seeking land more suitable for their grape-growing and wine-making businesses, moved W to found Harmonie, Ind. By 1825 they had returned to Pennsylvania and established Economy, on the Ohio River. Rappite members practiced celibacy, which, with lack of new member recruitment, caused the sect to die out by the early 1900s.

Rarotonga 21 15S 159 45W A mountainous island in the SW Pacific Ocean, the administrative center of the *Cook Islands. Copra and citrus fruit are exported. Area: 26 sq mi (67 sq km). Chief town: Avarua.

Rashi (Solomon ben Isaac; 1040–1105) French rabbi. He established a school at Troyes that attracted pupils from many countries. His most celebrated works are his commentaries (in Hebrew) on the Bible and the Babylonian *Talmud, which are remarkable for their simplicity, conciseness, and scholarly accuracy.

Rashid. *See* Rosetta Stone.

rationalism

Rasht (*or* Resht) 37 18N 49 38E A city in N Iran, near the Caspian Sea. It is an agricultural trading center and has a university (1977). Population (1986): 290,897.

Rasmussen, Knud Johan Victor (1879–1933) Danish explorer and ethnologist, who led a series of Arctic expeditions from Thule in Greenland to study Eskimo culture, which he believed to be akin to that of the North American Indians. In the longest recorded dogsled ride (1921–24) he reached the Bering Strait, describing the journey in *Across Arctic America* (1927).

raspberry A prickly woody perennial plant, *Rubus idaeus,* native to woods and heaths of Eurasia and North America. Up to 5 ft (1.5 m) high, it bears five-petaled white flowers, which produce red (or occasionally yellow) sweet fruits. There are many cultivated varieties, fruiting in summer or autumn. Upright canes grow from basal buds and bear fruit in their first autumn or second summer. The old canes, which die after fruiting, should be removed and the young canes pruned. Family: **Rosaceae.*

Rasputin, Grigori Yefimovich (c. 1872–1916) Russian mystic, who was a favorite of Emperor *Nicholas II and *Alexandra. A Siberian peasant, Rasputin's apparent ability to ease the bleeding of the hemophiliac crown prince brought him considerable influence over the royal family and thus over the government: high offices were held by his hangers-on, who were invariably corrupt and incompetent. His unpopularity, aggravated by his debauchery, led to his murder by a group of nobles: his assassins attempted to poison him and when this inexplicably failed he was shot and thrown into the River Neva.

rat A *rodent belonging to the suborder *Myomorpha,* distributed worldwide. Typical rats belong to the Old World genus *Rattus* (137 species) and are among the most successful rodents. The black rat (*R. rattus*), originally Asian, has spread by traveling on ships to most regions of the world, living in human habitations and sewers. The brown rat (*R. norvegicus*), also called Norway rat, is larger, measuring 12–18 in (30–45 cm) including its tail (6–8 in; 15–20 cm), and tends to live outdoors in burrows. It has displaced the black rat in many places. Both species eat a wide variety of plant and animal materials, often causing serious damage to stored food, gnawing through pipes and cables, and transmitting such diseases as typhus and food poisoning. Rats are commonly bred for use as laboratory animals in scientific research. *See also* mouse.

ratel An omnivorous mammal, *Mellivora capensis,* also called honey badger, of Africa and S Asia. About 28 in (70 cm) long, gray above and black underneath, it lives in thick woods, eating almost anything from ants to young antelopes (especially honey). Family: **Mustelidae.*

ratfish. *See* chimaera.

Rathenau, Walther (1867–1922) German industrialist and politician, who organized Germany's economy both during and after World War I. As minister of reconstruction (1921–22), he recommended the prompt payment of German reparations. Becoming foreign minister in 1922, he concluded the Treaty of Rapallo with the Soviet Union shortly before being assassinated. In *The New Economy* (1918) he expressed his belief in industrial self-government with worker participation.

Rathlin Island 55 17N 6 15W An island in Northern Ireland, off the N coast of Antrim in the North Channel. It was the refuge of Robert the Bruce (1306).

rationalism A philosophical movement stemming from 17th-century attempts to study the universe using reason, in the form of deductive and mathematical methods, rather than sense-experience. *Descartes, for example, tried to deduce what God's world is like from the axioms of divine existence and goodness. The scientific interests of the early rationalists made use of their religious views, but conflict between the new sciences and religion developed, and is reflected in the work of *Spinoza, *Arnauld, and *Leibniz. By the 19th century a compromise evolved, allocating science and religion to their separate spheres. Kant was called a rationalist insofar as he believed in the possibility of synthetic *a priori propositions. Recent intuitionists (*see* intuitionism) have been sympathetic to rationalism.

RATEL *This animal uses its long claws to rip open bees' nests for honey. It may be led to a nest by a honeyguide, this bird then sharing the honey that the ratel extracts.*

Ratisbon. *See* Regensburg.

ratite A bird characterized by a smooth breastbone that lacks a keel for the attachment of flight muscles. Ratites are flightless and usually large and swift-running and include the cassowary, emu, kiwi, ostrich, and rhea and the extinct moa.

rat kangaroo A *marsupial belonging to the subfamily *Potoroinae* (9 species), of Australia (including Tasmania). Two species are commonly known as boodies and two others as potoroos. Measuring 9–17 in (23–44 cm) excluding the tail (6–15 in; 15–38 cm), rat kangaroos are related to kangaroos and have a long narrow ratlike face. They have large canine teeth and long claws and forage at night for grubs and tubers. Family: *Macropodidae.*

rattan The stems of climbing *palms of the genus *Calamus* (375 species), native to Old World tropical regions. Up to 425 ft (130 m) long, the stems are stripped of leaves and used in furniture, matting, baskets, brooms, etc.

Rattigan, Sir Terence (1911–77) British dramatist. His highly successful plays include upper-class comedies (*French without Tears,* 1936), more ambitious studies of human relationships (*The Deep Blue Sea,* 1952), and studies of historical characters (*Ross,* 1960). During the late 1950s and 1960s his immaculately constructed plays became unfashionable but in the years immediately preceding his death they were again acclaimed.

rattlesnake A *pit viper belonging to either of two genera, *Sisturus* (2 species) or *Crotalus* (28 species), and characterized by having a rattle composed of loosely connected horny tail segments, which is vibrated to produce a warning sound. Rattlesnakes occur in both North and South America, usually in dry regions, and are 1–8 ft (0.3–2.5 m) long with dark diamond, hexagonal, or spotted markings on a pale background. They feed on rabbits, rodents, lizards, etc., and bear live young. *See also* diamondback; sidewinder.

Rauschenberg, Robert (1925–   ) US artist. A leading exponent of *pop art, he studied under Josef *Albers. In the early 1950s he produced collages and assemblages made from rusty nails, rags, Coca-Cola bottles, etc. His best-known works are probably those produced in the 1960s, when he adopted the silk-screen printing technique for transferring photographic images to canvases.

Rauwolfia A tropical genus of trees and shrubs (50 species). The dried roots of some species, including *R. serpentina* of India and *R. vomitoria* of Africa, contain alkaloids with sedative effects, now used in medicine to treat hypertension. Family: *Apocynaceae.*

Ravel, Maurice (1875–1937) French composer of the impressionist school. A pupil of Fauré, he repeatedly entered compositions for the Prix de Rome, his failures provoking strong critical protest. His works include, for piano, *Pavane pour une infante défunte* (1899), *Valses nobles et sentimentales* (1911), and *Le Tombeau de Couperin* (1914–17), which were all later orchestrated, the suite *Gaspard de la nuit* (1908), and two piano concertos (one for left hand alone); for orchestra, *La Valse* (1920), *Boléro* (1927), and the ballet *Daphnis and Chloe* (1909–12); the opera *L'Enfant et les sortilèges* (1920–25); many songs; and an orchestration (1922) of Mussorgski's *Pictures at an Exhibition.*

raven A large glossy black crow, *Corvus corax,* about 25 in (63 cm) long with bristling feathers at the throat, a massive bill, and a wedge-shaped tail. It feeds on carrion, small animals, seeds, and fruits and often roosts in large colonies. Ravens occur in mountain and moorland regions of the N hemisphere where numbers are increasing again after being almost exterminated.

Ravenna 44 25N 12 12E A city and port in N Italy, in Emilia-Romagna, connected to the Adriatic Sea by canal. Ravenna is said to have been founded by the Sabines. It was the capital of the Western Roman Empire (402–76 AD), of the Ostrogothic kings (476–526), and of the Byzantine exarchate (military governorship) from 584 to 751. It is noted for its ancient mosaics. Today Ravenna is a growing industrial center, based principally on oil and natural-gas refining. Population (1991 est): 136,724.

Ravi River A river in NW India and Pakistan, one of the five rivers of the Punjab. Rising in the Himalayas, it flows W and SW to join the Chenab River. Length: 450 mi (724 km).

Rawalpindi 33 40N 73 08E A city in N Pakistan, 9 mi (14 km) SW of the national capital, Islamabad. From 1959 until 1969 it acted as the interim capital while the new capital at Islamabad was being built. Rawalpindi is an important military, commercial, and trading center with varied industries, including oil refining, chemicals, and railroad engineering. Population (1981): 794,843.

Rawlings, Marjorie (Kinnan) (1896–1953) US author. At first a journalist (1918–28), she became a Florida orange farmer and devoted her spare time to writing. *South Moon Under* (1933) preceded *The Yearling* (1938), which brought her a Pulitzer Prize in 1939 and which became a classic motion picture in 1946. Other works include the novels *Golden Apples* (1935) and *The So-journer* (1953); a short story collection, *When the Whippoorwill* (1940); and an autobiographical work, *Cross Creek Cookery* (1942).

Rawlinson, Sir Henry Creswicke (1810–95) British orientalist. As an army officer and later consul at Baghdad, Rawlinson tried for years (1835–46) to obtain a complete copy of the trilingual *cuneiform text carved (516 BC) by Darius I on the sheer rock face at Behistun (Iran). He eventually deciphered two of its three scripts: Old Persian (1847) and Babylonian (1857).

ray A predominantly marine *cartilaginous fish of the worldwide order *Batoidea* (or *Rajiformes*; about 350 species). Rays have a flattened head and body with greatly enlarged winglike pectoral fins; the tapering tail often bears sharp poison spines. The mouth and gill slits are ventral and a pair of openings (spiracles), located behind the dorsally situated eyes, are used to take in water for respiration. Rays are generally bottom-dwelling and move using their pectoral fins. They feed mainly on fish and invertebrates. Subclass: *Elasmobranchii.* □fish.

Ray, John (1627–1705) English naturalist, who originated basic principles of plant classification. After compiling a survey of English plants, Ray's botanical studies culminated in his *Historia plantarum* (3 vols, 1686–1704). This was followed by works on birds, fishes, quadrupeds, and insects. Ray made the important taxonomic distinction between monocotyledonous and dicotyledonous plants and established the species as the basic taxonomic unit. He emphasized the importance of internal anatomy as a taxonomic criterion.

Ray, Man (1890–1976) The pseudonym of a US artist and photographer, whose real name is unknown. He first achieved prominence as cofounder with *Duchamp of the New York *dada movement (1917) and for his ready-mades, notably his iron armed with nails and ironically called *The Gift* (1921). After moving to Paris (1921), where he was associated with *surrealism, he became highly successful as a portrait and fashion photographer.

Ray, Satyajit (1921–92) Indian film director. He achieved an international reputation with *Pather Panchali* (1955), *The Unvanquished* (1956), and *The World of Apu* (1959), a trilogy of films about social change in modern India. His other films, all characterized by a humanistic understanding of both Eastern and Western values, include *Days and Nights in the Forest* (1970), *The Chess Players* (1977), and *The Home and the World* (1984).

Rayburn, Sam (Samuel Taliaferro R.; 1882–1961) US politician. A member of the US House of Representatives (1913–61) as a Democrat from Texas, he served as Speaker of the House (1940–47, 1949–53, 1955–61), the longest of any Speaker. He was known for his support of *New Deal legislation, knowledge of rules and procedures, and quiet, but effective, vote-mustering.

Rayleigh, John William Strutt, 3rd baron (1842–1919) British physicist. His work on black-body radiation was upset by *Planck's discovery of the quantum theory but he did much valuable work in optics, hydrodynamics, and the theory of electrical units. He was awarded the 1904 Nobel Prize for his discovery of argon, in conjunction with Sir William *Ramsay.

rayon A textile fiber or fabric made from *cellulose. **Viscose rayon** is made by dissolving wood pulp in a mixture of sodium hydroxide and carbon disulfide. The fibers are reconstituted in an acid bath. **Acetate rayon** is made by mixing wood pulp with acetic anhydride, acetic acid, and sulfuric acid to form cellulose acetate, which is then dissolved in a solvent and forced through fine holes to form fibers as the solvent evaporates.

Razi ar- (*or* Rhazes; c. 865–c. 928 AD) Persian physician and philosopher. In his *Comprehensive Book*, he surveyed the medical knowledge of the Greeks, Syrians, and Arabs and he wrote works on alchemy, philosophy, and diseases, such as smallpox and measles.

Razin, Stenka (d. 1671) Cossack leader. From 1667 to 1669 Razin led a group of propertyless Cossacks in raids along the Volga River and the Caspian Sea. In 1670 Razin commanded a revolt against the tsar and was executed after his capture.

RAZORBILL *Formerly killed for its feathers and used for bait by fishermen, this bird is now a protected species. The largest of the auks, it often nests on cliff tops.*

razorbill A black-and-white *auk, *Alca torda*, that breeds around N Atlantic coasts and winters in the Mediterranean; 16 in (40 cm) long, it has a laterally compressed bill. The wings are used as paddles in diving to catch fish, shellfish, and worms.

razor shell A burrowing *bivalve mollusk of the family *Solenidae* (about 40 species), also called a jackknife clam, of Atlantic and Pacific coasts. The common razor (*Ensis siliqua*), about 6 in (15 cm) long, has a narrow □shell with squared ends; its curved foot is used to burrow up to 12 in (30 cm) into sand.

reactance. *See* impedance.

Read, Sir Herbert (1893–1968) British poet and critic. The son of a York-shire farmer, he served as an infantry officer in World War I, and his war poetry constitutes a large proportion of his *Collected Poems* (1966). His art criticism, written from the basis of a personal philosophy of anarchism, promoted the work of Henry *Moore and many other artists of his generation. His literary criticism was chiefly concerned with the romantic poets.

Reade, Charles (1814–84) British novelist. His best-known novel is the historical romance *The Cloister and the Hearth* (1861), set in Europe during the Reformation. His other novels are chiefly concerned with topical social issues.

Reading 51 28N 0 59W A city in S England, the administrative center of Berkshire on the River Thames. It has the remains of a 12th-century Benedictine abbey and a university (1892). An important railroad junction, Reading has light engineering and electronics works and is the headquarters of several international industries. Population (1981): 123,731.

Reading 40 20N 75 55W A city in E Pennsylvania. It grew as an iron and steel center. Industries today include the manufacture of bricks, speciality steels, and textiles. Population (1990): 78,380.

ready-made An everyday manufactured object elevated to artistic status by the personal whim of the artist. The *dada painter Marcel *Duchamp produced the first ready-made, a bicycle wheel on a stool, in 1913; it was followed by his snow shovel (1915), and his notorious urinal (1917). The ready-made is also a feature of *surrealism and *pop art.

Reagan, Ronald (Wilson) (1911–   ) US statesman: 40th president of the United States (1981–89). Beginning his professional career as an actor, Reagan appeared in more than 50 films and twice served as president of one of the most important film labor organizations, The Screen Actors' Guild (1947–52, 1959–60). Reagan became increasingly involved in politics during the early 1960s and although he was formerly a liberal Democrat, he joined the Republican Party in 1962. After serving two terms as governor of California (1966–74), he campaigned unsuccessfully for the Republican presidential nomination in 1976. Four years later, however, he gained the nomination and defeated incumbent Pres. Jimmy *Carter. Reagan began his administration with a series of sweeping economic reforms designed to reduce the growth of federal social programs, but he was also committed to expanding the nation's defense capabilities. The Reagan foreign policy was characterized by a hard line toward the Soviet Union and active military intervention in Central America, the Caribbean, and the Middle East. Early in 1981 he survived an assassination attempt. In 1984 he was reelected in a sweeping victory over Democrat Walter *Mondale. Reagan held summit conferences with Soviet leader Gorbachev in 1986 and 1987, when an agreement to limit nuclear arms was reached. They met again in 1988. Reagan was succeeded as president by George *Bush, his vice president in 1989.

realism 1. The medieval philosophical theory that general terms (called universals) have a real existence, that is that there is some abstract entity that corresponds with the term. For example, blueness is not just one idea of the sum of all blue objects (called particulars), but a really existing entity. *Plato and *Aristotle were realists in believing that the universe contained universals in addition to particulars. The difference between them was that Plato thought universals, which he called Forms, merely could have corresponding particulars and were independent of them, while Aristotle thought that Forms must have particulars and could exist only as instantiated in things. *Aquinas and *Duns Scotus were leading realists. *Compare* nominalism. **2.** In modern philosophy, a stance opposed to *idealism. Realists, such as G. E. *Moore (*see also* common sense, philosophy of), assert that objects exist independently of being perceived. Mathematical realism implies that mathematical entities exist in this way as well and that mathematical truths are independent of our ability to prove them.

real tennis. *See* court tennis.

Réaumur, René-Antoine Ferchault de (1683–1757) French physicist, whose work on thermometers led him to devise the temperature scale that bears his name. On this scale water freezes at 0° and boils at 80°. He also carried out experiments on animals to show that digestion was a chemical process and not, as certain scientists believed, a mechanical one.

RONALD REAGAN *President whose conservative policies helped end a recession and who was overwhelmingly re-elected in 1984.*

Rebellion of 1837 Canadian uprising against British rule and lack of French-Canadian autonomy. Led by Louis *Papineau and William *Mackenzie, the two-year unsuccessful rebellion resulted in the Durham Report (1839) and *Act of Union (1841). *See also* Durham, John George Lambton, 1st earl of.

Reber, Grote (1911–) US astronomer, who, following *Jansky's discovery, built the first radio telescope (1937) and used it to discover a number of radio sources that had no visible counterparts. It was largely as a result of his observations that several large radio telescopes were built after World War II.

recall A political device designed to enable voters dissatisfied with an elected official to replace him before the expiration of his term of office. The recall originated in Switzerland and has been operative in a number of US states since 1903. The usual procedure is the securing of a petition stating the charges against the official, the holding of an election to determine whether the official shall be removed, and the choice of a successor. Usually the official is allowed space on the ballot or petition in which to state his defense.

Recamier, Jeanne Françoise Julie Adelaide (1777–1849) French society hostess. She was married to a wealthy Parisian banker from 1792 to 1830. Her salon was attended by influential statesmen and politicians opposed to Napoleon. Her close friends included Mme de *Staël and *Chateaubriand.

recession A decline in the *trade cycle that, in a serious setback to the economy, becomes a transitory phase between *boom and *depression. In a recession, consumption demand falls off, investment (according to the *accelerator principle) suffers a decline, and business failures become more common.

recessive gene The *allele of a gene the function of which is hidden when the organism concerned is crossed with one carrying a different allele (called the dominant allele) for the same gene. *See* dominance.

Recife (*or* Pernambuco) 8 06S 34 53W A port in NE Brazil, the capital of Pernambuco state, on the Atlantic Ocean. It is a major port; the chief exports are sugar and cotton. Industries include sugar refining and spirit distilling and it has two universities. Population (1980): 1,184,215.

Recklinghausen 51 37N 7 11E A city in NW Germany, in North Rhine-Westphalia in the *Ruhr. Notable buildings include the 13th-century church (founded 1276) and the castle (1702). A port on the Rhine-Herne Canal, its manufactures include iron and steel, machinery, and textiles. Population (1988): 118,000.

Reconstruction (1865–77) The period after the *Civil War during which the defeated *Confederate states were brought back into the Union. Despite the intentions of Pres. Abraham *Lincoln to offer the South a generous peace settlement and an honorable readmission to the Union, the Radical Republicans, led by Secretary of War Edwin *Stanton, insisted on severe measures after Lincoln's assassination in 1865. When Pres. Andrew *Johnson announced his intention to adopt Lincoln's Reconstruction plans, intense opposition arose in Congress. Johnson immediately recognized the governments of Arkansas, Louisiana, Tennessee, and Virginia and had established provisional governments in the other seven Confederate states by early 1866. The Radical Republicans in Congress refused to acknowledge the president's action and overrode Johnson's veto to enact a law establishing five southern military districts subject to martial law. The conflict between the president and Congress led to Johnson's impeachment by the House of Representatives in 1868. However, he was acquitted in a trial before the Senate. Under Johnson's successor as president, Ulysses S. *Grant, the system of military districts was abolished and all of the southern states were readmitted to the Union, after accepting the 14th and 15th Amendments to the US Constitution, which guaranteed full citizenship and voting rights to former slaves. These Reconstruction state governments were controlled by Radical Republicans and their political allies, some of whom were actually transplanted northerners known as "carpetbaggers." The Reconstruction period formally ended with the withdrawal of federal troops from the South in 1877.

recorder (law). *See* judge.

recorder (music) A woodwind instrument of medieval origin, much used in music of the 17th and 18th centuries and revived in the 20th century. In contrast to the side-blown *flute, the recorder is end-blown, through a whistle mouthpiece mounted in a block (*or* fipple). The holes are covered with the fingers; the tone is quieter than that of the flute.

recording of sound A system for storing and reproducing sound. In music recording, the most common methods are tape recording, usually in *cassette form, and compact disks. The phonograph record, long the primary mode for playing, is now rarely manufactured. A record is made by converting the sound into an electrical signal, which is normally temporarily stored on tape. This signal is amplified and used to control a cutter that produces a spiral undulating groove in a master disk. Plastic (vinyl) copies of this are mass-produced for sale. In a record player, the stylus travels along the groove and reproduces the mechanical vibrations of the cutter. The *pick-up then converts these to an electrical signal, which is amplified and fed to a loudspeaker. Many electronic devices are used to ensure that the system will reproduce the original sound with a high fidelity, i.e. that sounds in the frequency range 80–12,000 hertz are reproduced without distortion. In **digital recording** the musical signal itself is not transmitted or recorded. Instead the signal is sampled, up to 30,000 times per second, and the characteristics of the sampled signal are represented by digits (as information is represented in a computer). The digits are then transmitted or recorded and reconstituted in the receiver or player. In this way the actual signal suffers no interference or distortion during transmission or in the recording process. The method is used when very high fidelity is required.

rectifier A device that allows electric current to flow in one direction only; it is generally used to convert alternating current to direct current. *Semiconductor diodes have now replaced thermionic valves (diodes) for lower voltage applications. For power supplies of several megawatts, mercury-arc rectifiers are used.

rectum. *See* intestine.

recycling The repeated use of the same resources. Recycling involves the manufacture of a complex product followed by breakdown of the spent product to release its constituents for reuse. This process—a feature of most natural *ecosystems—is becoming an economic necessity in industry in order to conserve scarce raw materials and reduce the quantities of waste products, which may cause pollution of the environment. Steel scrap, waste paper, and chemical solvents are often recycled.

red admiral A butterfly, *Vanessa atalanta,* found throughout Europe, Asia, and North America. The wings are black with red and white markings. Red admirals migrate to northern regions for the summer but do not survive the cold winters there; in warmer climates they hibernate. The caterpillars feed mainly on stinging nettles. Family: *Nymphalidae.*

red algae *Algae of the division *Rhodophyta* (about 3000 species), which are usually red or blue in color due to the presence of the pigments phycoerythrin (red) or phycocyanin (blue), which mask the green chlorophyll. They range from small unicellular or filamentous forms to branching or sheetlike *seaweeds, found mainly attached to other plants in deep warm seas or sometimes in rock pools. Reproduction is asexual or sexual.

Red Brigades (Italian name: Brigate Rosse) A group of Italian terrorists formed in 1969 and dedicated to the violent overthrow of capitalist society. They were responsible for the murder of the statesman Aldo Moro in 1978. Several of their leading members have been apprehended and sentenced to prison.

Red Cross, International An organization founded by the Geneva Convention of 1864 to provide care for the casualties of war. Inspired by Henri *Dunant, a Swiss philanthropist, its headquarters are in Geneva and its emblem, the red cross, represents the Swiss flag with its colors reversed. Muslim countries, however, have generally adopted the crescent as their emblem. The International Red Cross, which is staffed mainly by volunteers, has twice won the Nobel Peace Prize, in 1917 and 1944. National branches include the **American Red Cross**.

red currant A shrub of the genus *Ribes* (*see* currant), cultivated for its clusters of small acid-tasting red fruits, which may be made into jellies, jams, etc. Cultivated red currants have been derived from *R. rubrum* of Eurasia, *R. sativum* of W Europe, and *R. petraeum* of central and S Europe; they grow up to 7 ft (2 m) high. White currants are varieties that lack red pigment.

red deer A large reddish-brown deer, *Cervus elaphus,* of European and Asian woodlands. Over 48 in (120 cm) high at the shoulder, males have spreading branched antlers up to 50 in (125 cm) long; females are more lightly built. Stags and hinds live apart in spring and summer, coming together in the autumn for the rut, when mature males compete to gather a harem of hinds. As winter comes, stags and pregnant hinds separate. *See also* wapiti.

Redford, Robert (1936–　) US film actor. He costarred with Paul *Newman in *Butch Cassidy and the Sundance Kid* (1969) and *The Sting* (1973). His other films include *The Candidate* (1972) and *All the President's Men* (1976), as well as *Ordinary People* (1991), which he directed and for which he won an Academy Award; *Out of Africa* (1985); and *Havana* (1991). He is a fervent environmentalist.

red fox A *fox, *Vulpes vulpes,* found throughout the N hemisphere. It is about 40 in (100 cm) long, including its bushy tail (20 in; 50 cm). There are a number of local races and the North American red fox and its gray-black variety, the silver fox, were once thought to be a separate species (*V. fulva*).

red giant A greatly distended cool but very luminous star, often variable in nature. It is one of the final evolutionary stages of a normal *star, attained when its central hydrogen has been converted to helium. Hydrogen burning in a shell surrounding the inert helium core causes a rapid expansion and cooling of the outer atmosphere of the star.

Redgrave, Sir Michael (1908–85) British Shakespearean actor, who has also performed in and directed modern plays. His films include *The Browning Version* (1951) and *The Go-Between* (1971). His daughter **Vanessa Redgrave** (1937–　) has acted on stage and in a number of films including *Morgan* (1966), *Blow-Up* (1967), and *Julia* (1977), and is well known for her left-wing political activities. His daughter **Lynn Redgrave** (1944–　) is also an actress.

red grouse A *grouse, *Lagopus lagopus scoticus,* found on moorlands of Great Britain and Ireland, where it is managed as a gamebird; 13–15 in (34–37 cm) long, it feeds chiefly on ling heather. The male is red-brown with red wattles above the eyes and the female is browner and heavily barred: both sexes have white underwing markings and white feathered feet.

Red Guards High-school and university students organized by Mao Tse-tung during the *Cultural Revolution (1966–68) to eliminate revisionism. The Red Guards destroyed property, humiliated foreign diplomats, and attacked those officials who opposed Mao's policies.

red-hot poker A plant of the African genus *Kniphofia,* especially *K. uvaria* and *K. rufa* (and their varieties), cultivated as garden plants; 18–47 in (45–120 cm) tall, they have long reedlike leaves and dense heads of tubular flowers, usually scarlet and/or yellow. Family: *Liliaceae.*

Redmond, John Edward (1856–1918) Irish politician. A member of Parliament from 1881, in 1900 he reunited the pro- and anti-Parnellite factions under his leadership. In 1909 he allied his party with the Liberals to achieve *Home Rule. The rise of *Sinn Féin undermined the appeal of his moderate policies.

red mullet A fish, also called surmullet or goatfish, belonging to the family *Mullidae* (about 50 species), found usually in shallow warm seas. They have an elongated body, up to 10 in (25 cm) long, with two dorsal fins and two long flexible chin barbels. They feed on bottom-dwelling invertebrates and many species are valued food fish. Order: *Perciformes.*

Redon, Odilon (1840–1916) French symbolist painter and lithographer; a forerunner of *surrealism. Working exclusively in black and white in charcoal drawings, lithographs, and etchings until the 1890s, he created a fantasy world of plants with human heads, mythical figures, etc. From the 1890s he turned to oil painting and pastel, producing a number of flower paintings in powdery colors and paintings inspired by literary subjects.

ODILON REDON *One of a set of six lithographs entitled* La Nuit.

Redouté, Pierre Joseph (1759–1841) French flower painter. He worked for all the French courts from Louis XV to Louis Philippe, painting his flowers, notably roses, chiefly in watercolors and after careful scientific study.

redox reactions. *See* oxidation and reduction.

redpoll A tiny finch, *Acanthis flammea,* about 5 in (12 cm) long with a brown streaked plumage, a red crown, and a black chin. The male has a red breast in summer. It breeds in the Arctic tundra and high mountains of Europe, migrating to central Europe and the N US in winter.

Red River (Vietnamese name: Song Hong) The chief river of N Vietnam, rising in S China and flowing SE to enter the Gulf of Tonkin via an extensive delta. Length: 310 mi (500 km).

Red River A river that flows from N Texas E into SW Oklahoma and forms the Texas-Oklahoma and Texas-Arkansas border before flowing S through Arkansas and SW through Louisiana, where it joins the Mississippi River above Baton Rouge. At its beginning it flows through red clay plains that color the water and gave the river its name. Lakes formed by dams, such as Lake Texoma in S Oklahoma, were created for flood control. Length: 1018 mi (1639 km).

Red River of the North (*or* Red River) A river in central North America, rising in W Minnesota and flowing N into Canada to empty into Lake Winnipeg. Although navigable, it is subject to severe floods that damage the farms of its fertile valley. Length: 621 m (1000 km).

Red River Settlement A colony of immigrants led by Thomas Douglas, 5th earl of Selkirk (1771–1820), settled in 1811 on the banks of the Red River in present-day Manitoba. In 1836 it was bought by the Hudson's Bay Company. In 1869 Louis *Riel led an uprising against the proposed transfer of the colony from the Company to Canada. The revolution was unsuccessful, and the transfer took place in 1870.

red salmon. *See* sockeye salmon.

Red Sea A long narrow arm of the Indian Ocean between Africa and Asia, extending some 1490 mi (2400 km) NNW beyond the Gulf of Aden and the Bab el-Mandeb. In the N, it is connected to the Mediterranean Sea by the Suez Canal, which has enormously increased shipping in the Red Sea. It is part of the *Great Rift Valley. Area: 169,076 sq mi (438,000 sq km).

redshank An Old World *sandpiper, *Tringa totanus,* that breeds in cool marshy regions of Eurasia; 12 in (30 cm) long, it has long reddish legs, a black-tipped red bill, and a brown-gray plumage with a white rump. It winters on mud-flats of Africa and Asia, feeding on crustaceans, mollusks, and ragworms.

redshift An overall displacement toward larger wavelengths of the spectral lines of a celestial object. Its astronomical significance was suggested by Edwin *Hubble in 1929, when it was used as the basis of the theory that the universe is expanding (*see* expanding universe). A redshift usually arises from the *Doppler effect, that is from recession of a celestial object. It increases as the object's radial velocity increases and for an extragalactic body can be used as a measure of distance. A **gravitational redshift** occurs whenever radiation is emitted by a body: it is generally negligible except when the gravitational field is very strong.

red squirrel A tree *squirrel, *Sciurus vulgaris,* of Eurasia. About 8 in (20 cm) long with an 8-in (20-cm) tail, red squirrels have dark glossy red fur and tufted ears. They feed mainly on seeds and nuts but will eat buds and dried fungi in winter. They are less aggressive than the immigrant gray squirrels, which have displaced them in many areas.

redstart A small North American wood warbler of the genus *Setophago ruticilla* about 4.5–5.5 in (11–14 cm) long. The male redstart is black with a white belly and orange-patched wings and fanning tail. The female is olive-brown with a white belly and yellow-patched wings and tail. It is found in woodland and thickets from SE Alaska to S US. This species migrates to Central and South America for the winter.

reduction. *See* oxidation and reduction.

reductionism A 20th-century trend in philosophy prompted by skepticism. Reductionists argue that material objects are nothing but collections of sensations; other minds are nothing but the physical manifestations of their owners; statements about the past are nothing but aggregates of statements about the presently available evidence for them. Reduction of the meaning of a statement to statements of the evidence for it was popular among phenomenalists and logical positivists.

redwing A North American bird, *Agelaius phoeniceus,* about 7.5–9.5 in (19–24 cm) long, resembling a blackbird with red patches on the wings. The female is brownish, with heavy striping and a sharply pointed bill. Redwings breed mainly in swamp areas from E Canada to S US, migrating to Central America for the winter.

redwood A coniferous tree, *Sequoia sempervirens,* thought to be the tallest tree in the world and one of the longest lived: a specimen in California is over 364 ft (111 m) tall and some Californian trees are over 2000 years old. Also called coast redwood, it is native to the Pacific coast between Oregon and California and is an important timber tree in North America; in Europe it is planted mainly for ornament. It has brown-red fibrous bark, bladelike leaves, 0.6–0.8 in (1.5–2 cm) long, in two rows along the stems, and woody red-brown globular cones, about 0.8 in (2 cm) long. Family: *Taxodiaceae. See also* dawn redwood; sequoia.

Redwood National Park A national park in NW California, along the Pacific coast. Some of the world's tallest trees, more than 350 ft (110 m) tall, are here. The park was established in 1968 and expanded in 1978 to preserve a coastal species of redwood tree. Included in the park is 30 mi (48 km) of seashore. Area: 166 sq mi (429 sq km).

reed Any of several species of tall aquatic grasses, especially those of the genus *Phragmites* (2–3 species). The common reed (*P. communis*) has a creeping underground stem (rhizome) and grows worldwide along the margins of marshes, lakes, streams, and fens; 5–10 ft (1.5–3 m) tall, it has long flat leaves, 0.4–0.8 in (10–20 mm) wide, a stiff smooth stem, and clusters of purple-brown flowers. Dried reed stems have been used for arrows, basketry, pens, and in musical instruments.

The name is also given to similar but unrelated plants, such as the paper reed, *Cyperus papyrus* (*see* papyrus).

Reed, Sir Carol (1906–76) British film director. His best-known films include *The Fallen Idol* (1948) and *The Third Man* (1949), both with screenplays by Graham *Greene. His later, more commercial, films include *The Agony and the Ecstasy* (1965) and *Oliver!* (1968).

Reed, John (1887–1920) US journalist. He helped found the Communist Labor party in the US and was a personal friend of Lenin. *Ten Days that Shook the World* (1919) is an account of the 1917 Revolution in Russia, where he died.

Reed, Stanley Forman (1884–1980) US jurist; associate justice of the Supreme Court (1938–57). He served as general counsel to the Federal Farm Board (1929–32) and the Reconstruction Finance Corporation (1932–35), and as solicitor general (1935–38) before being appointed to the Supreme Court in 1938. Opposed to censorship and an advocate of civil rights, he was usually a part of the court's liberal faction.

Reed, Walter (1851–1902) US physician. After serving as an army surgeon, Reed was appointed to investigate yellow fever in Cuba, where C. J. *Finlay had suggested that the mosquito was the agent responsible for spreading the disease. Reed and his team subjected themselves to the bites of infected mosquitoes, one of the team dying as a result, but thereby proving that mosquitoes were responsible. Subsequent control of mosquito populations eliminated yellow fever from the region.

reedbuck An African antelope belonging to the genus *Redunca* (3 species). The common reedbuck (*R. arundinium*) grows to 35 in (90 cm) high at the shoulder and has a stiff gray coat and slender ridged horns and inhabits lush grassland. The bohor reedbuck (*R. redunca*) is smaller and lives in swampy regions, while the gregarious mountain reedbuck (*R. fulvorufulda*) lives in hilly areas.

reed instruments Musical instruments in which a column of air is made to vibrate by a reed. The *clarinet family have a single (*or* beating) reed clamped to and vibrating against a slot in the mouthpiece. The *oboe and *bassoon use a double reed, the two halves bound together and forming the mouthpiece. The **reed organ** family contains such instruments as the *harmonium, *concertina, *accordion, and *harmonica, which have free reeds (sometimes made of some other substance, such as brass) that vibrate from side to side of the slot in which they are fixed.

reedling A Eurasian bird, *Panurus biarmicus,* about 6.3 in (16 cm) long, also called bearded tit. It lives in reedbeds, feeding on insects and seeds. The plumage is brown with pale underparts: the male has a gray head with a black moustache of feathers. Reedlings belong to the *babbler family.

reedmace A widely distributed perennial herbaceous plant, *Typha latifolia,* also called bulrush or cat's-tail, growing in reed swamps. It has an erect stem, 5–8.5 ft (1.5–2.5 m) high, bearing a terminal spike of male and female flowers, the latter developing into the cylindrical fruit, which tapers into the stem at its base. There are several other reedmaces of the genus *Typha* (*see* elephant grass). Family: *Typhaceae.*

reed warbler An acrobatic *warbler, *Acrocephalus scirpaeus,* about 5 in (12 cm) long with a reddish-brown plumage, pale underparts, and a pale eye-stripe. It winters in SE Africa and breeds in European reedswamps, building a deep nest around the stems of several reeds and feeding on small marsh insects. It is frequently parasitized by cuckoos.

reef A ridge of rock lying just above or near the surface of the sea, built mainly of the skeletons of *coral or other sedentary marine organisms. **Barrier reefs** lie parallel to the coast with a deep lagoon between; **fringing reefs** are attached to the coast, bioherms are dome-shaped reefs; apron reefs are tabular masses; atolls are circular with a central lagoon. Reef formation was much more widespread in the geological past.

referendum and initiative Votes on specific legislation by the whole electorate. Referendums are votes on particular governmental questions and appear on the ballot during elections of public officials. Initiatives are proposals, drafted by a citizen or group of citizens, that by virtue of attaining a requisite number of signatures on a petition are put to the electorate for acceptance or rejection. Initiatives are used in about half of the states to decide matters of local government. *See also* plebiscite.

reflection The rebounding of a wave of light or other radiation when it strikes a surface. Reflected light obeys two laws: first, the normal (an imaginary line vertical to the surface at the point of impact), the incident ray, and the reflected rays all lie in the same plane; second, the angle of incidence (i.e. the angle between the incident ray and the normal) is equal to the angle of reflection. *See also* mirrors.

reflex An automatic and involuntary response by an organism to a change in the environment. An example is the rapid withdrawal of a finger in response to a pinprick, which occurs before the brain has had time to convey the necessary information to the muscles involved. *See also* conditioned reflex.

Reform Acts The legislation that reformed the British parliamentary system. The Reform Act of 1832 extended the franchise and gave parliamentary representation to new industrial towns, such as Birmingham and Manchester. However, it did not destroy the dominance over the electoral system by the landed classes. The 1867 Reform Act enfranchised many of the working class for the first time. It doubled the existing electorate to 2.4 million. The 1884 Reform Act increased the electorate to about five million. Adult male suffrage was achieved only in 1918 and women had to wait until 1928.

Reformation A religious movement in 16th-century Europe that began as an attempt to reform the *Roman Catholic Church and ended with the establishment of independent Protestant Churches (*see* Protestantism). The Reformation, which was preceded by such reform movements as those led by John *Wycliffe (the *Lollards) and Jan *Hus (the *Hussites), was caused by the inability of the Catholic Church to put its own, increasingly worldly, house in order; the critical examination of the Bible emphasized by the humanists (*see* humanism) and its translation into the vernaculars; the development of printing, which disseminated new ideas more widely and more quickly; and the growth of nationalism, which sought to weaken papal jurisdiction within the states of W Europe.

The Reformation began on Oct 31, 1517, when Martin *Luther nailed his 95 theses on the door of the castle church at Wittenburg. Luther's attack on the sale of *indulgences and, subsequently, on papal authority and the *sacraments (except baptism and the Eucharist) was condemned by the pope and the Holy Roman Emperor but gained the support of several German princes. The consequent conflict (*see* Charles V) was not resolved until 1555 (*see* Augsburg, Peace of).

In Switzerland, the Reformation was initiated by *Zwingli in Zurich in 1520, spreading to Basle, Berne, and also to Geneva, where it was led by John *Calvin. Calvinism was adopted in France, the Low Countries, England, Scotland, and subsequently in North America. In France, where Protestants were called Huguenots, the Reformation became involved in a political struggle for control of the crown, giving rise to the *Wars of Religion, and in the Low Countries it fired the *Revolt of the Netherlands against Spanish rule.

In England, Protestantism finally became the established *Church of England under Elizabeth I. Elsewhere in Europe Lutheranism was adopted by Sweden in 1527, by Denmark in 1546, and also became the established religions of Norway, Finland, and Iceland. *See also* Counter-Reformation.

Reformed Churches. *See* Protestantism.

Reform Judaism A religious movement attempting to adapt traditional Judaism to modern circumstances. It began in Germany in the early 19th century. The Liberal movement (founded 1903) instituted more radical reforms typical of US Reform Judaism. The World Union for Progressive Judaism, founded in London in 1926, is now based in Jerusalem. The reforms include abolition of many of the ritual laws, acceptance of modern biblical criticism, vernacular services, and full equality for women.

refraction The bending of a beam of radiation as it passes from one medium onto another. For a light ray the amount by which it is bent depends on the angle of the incident ray and on the refractive indices of the two media, the exact dependence being given by *Snell's law. Refraction is caused by the difference in the velocity of the radiation in the two media. The ratio of the velocity of light in the two media is known as the **refractive index**. If the first medium is a vacuum, the ratio is known as the absolute refractive index of the second medium. The refractive index of glass lies between 1.5 and 1.7, for diamond it is 2.1, and for water 1.33 (at 77°F [25°C]).

refractories Firebricks or other heat-resisting materials used for lining furnaces to retain the heat and protect the outer shell of the furnace. There are three types, characterized by their chemical interaction with the hot substances in the furnace: acid (e.g. silica); basic (e.g. dolomite); and neutral (e.g. carborundum).

refrigeration The process of lowering the temperature inside a closed insulated container. In the domestic refrigerator the method most commonly used is the vapor-compression cycle in which a liquid refrigerant, such as Freon (a compound of chlorine, fluorine, and carbon), is pumped through cooling coils formed into the ice-making compartment. In these coils the refrigerant evaporates, taking the latent heat required to make it into a gas from the surroundings (i.e. the inside of the ice compartment). It is then passed to an electrically driven compressor; after compression it condenses back to liquid, when the absorbed heat is given out (usually at the back of the refrigerator). This cycle is repeated over and over again until the required temperature (about 34–36°F [1–2°C] in the food chamber and 5°F [−15°C] in the deep-freeze compartment) is achieved. The compressor is then switched on and off by the thermostat. Other cycles (e.g. ammonia absorption) are also used, but in all of them the refrigerator functions as a heat engine in reverse: in order to transfer heat from the cold interior to the warmer surrounding air, work must be done. In the vapor-compression refrigerator this is supplied by the electricity that drives the compressor. *See also* cold storage; freezing.

Regency style An English decorative style fashionable from about 1800 to 1830 and influenced by the French *Empire style. Dark exotic woods and veneers, such as rosewood, were popular and were set off by ormolu mounts and grilles for doors. Leading designers produced rather heavy furniture purporting to derive from antique Greek, Roman, and Egyptian models. Concurrently there was a vogue for oriental motifs (*see* chinoiserie) and some magnificent lacquer was produced. Initially elegant, the style later became somewhat clumsy.

regeneration In biology, the regrowth and development of tissues or organs lost through injury, as a normal process (e.g. during molting), or by any other means. The ability to regenerate is present in all forms of life to some degree: it is particularly well developed in plants and simple animals. Thus, whole plants can regenerate from stem and leaf cuttings and simple animals, such as sponges and planarians, can develop from minute fragments. More complex animals, such as crustaceans, replace lost appendages, while lizards can grow new tails. In mammals regeneration is limited to wound healing and regrowth of peripheral nerve fibers.

Regensburg (English name: Ratisbon) 49 01N 12 07E A city in S Germany, in Bavaria at the confluence of the Danube and Regen rivers. Many medieval buildings survived the bombing of World War II, including the gothic cathedral (1275–1524). Its university was established in 1962. It is a port and commercial and industrial center. *History*: originally a Celtic settlement, it became a Carolingian capital and a prosperous medieval trading center. From 1663 until 1806 the imperial diets (assemblies) were held here. Population (1988): 124,000.

Reger, Max (1873–1916) German composer, organist, and teacher. In Leipzig he was director of music at the university (1907–08) and professor of composition at the conservatory. His vast output includes *Variations and Fugue on a Theme of Mozart* for orchestra and a *Fantasy and Fugue on Bach* for organ.

reggae A style of rock music combining West Indian rhythms and rhythm and blues. It became associated with the Jamaican cult of the Rastafarians and was popular in the US from the mid-1970s.

Reggio di Calabria 38 06N 15 39E A seaport in Italy, in Calabria, on the Strait of Messina. It was founded by Greek colonists in the 8th century BC. Fruit, herbs, and oil are exported. Population (1991 est): 178,496.

Reggio nell'Emilia 44 42N 10 37E A city in Italy, in Emilia-Romagna. Dating from Roman times, it was ruled by the Este family (15th–18th centuries) and has a cathedral (rebuilt in the 13th century). The center of a rich agricultural area, its industries include agricultural engineering and meat canning. Population (1991 est): 131,880.

Regina 50 30N 104 38W A city in W Canada, the capital of Saskatchewan. Founded in 1882, it has expanded rapidly since 1945 as a center of agricultural industries, oil refining, and potash production. It houses the University of Regina (1917). Population (1991): 179,178.

Regiomontanus (Johannes Müller; 1436–76) German astronomer and mathematician, who introduced algebra and trigonometry to Germany. He produced a table of trigonometric functions that was printed by Johann Gutenberg and widely used by navigators. He was an ardent follower of *Ptolemy, producing a new translation of his *Almagest.* He also made observations of the sky and drew a table of planetary motions.

Regnier, Henri François Joseph de (1864–1936) French poet. He published several early collections of symbolist poetry written in *vers libre,* but in his later and better-known volumes, such as *Les Médailles d'argile* (1900), he reverted to classical forms. He also wrote fiction, mostly historical novels set in the 17th and 18th centuries.

Regulus, Marcus Attilus (died c. 251 BC) Roman general of the first *Punic War. In 256 he defeated the Carthaginian navy, invaded Africa, and overwhelmed the Carthaginians. Rejecting his peace terms, in 255 the Carthaginians utterly defeated Regulus, who was captured and sent to Rome to negotiate peace. Urging continued war, he returned to certain death in Carthage.

Rehnquist, William Hubbs (1924–   ) US lawyer and jurist; associate justice of the Supreme Court (1971–86) and chief justice of the US (1986–   ). After private law practice from 1953 he served as assistant attorney general in charge of the Department of Justice's Office of Legal Counsel (1969–71) before being appointed to the Supreme Court by Pres. Richard M. *Nixon. He was an advocate of law and order and gained a reputation for being unsympathetic to issues favoring civil rights and labor. In 1986, President Reagan nominated him to succeed retiring Chief Justice Warren Burger.

Rehoboam King of Judah (c. 922–915 BC); the son of Solomon. His intransigent attitude to the northern tribes resulted in the secession of Israel under Jeroboam and the disintegration of Solomon's empire.

Reich, Robert B. (1946–   ) US Secretary of Labor (1993–   ), who advocated workforce retraining programs and major government investment in industry to promote global competitiveness. A graduate of Dartmouth College and Yale Law School, he studied at Oxford University as a Rhodes scholar. Before becoming Pres. Bill Clinton's labor secretary, Reich held various government positions and was a professor at Harvard University's John F. Kennedy School of Government.

Reich, Wilhelm (1897–1957) US psychiatrist, born in Austria, noted for his controversial notion of a universal energy, which he called orgone, that is released during sexual intercourse. Failure to achieve regular release of this energy resulted, so he claimed, in both personal and social neuroses. Reich's "orgone box" was declared fraudulent and he was jailed for contempt of court in

1956. His works include *The Function of the Orgasm* (1948) and *Character Analysis* (1949).

Reichstag (Imperial Diet) The legislative assembly of the German Empire (1871–1918) and the Weimar Republic (1919–33). Its origins lay in the diet of the Holy Roman Empire. It was divided into an electoral college (*see* electors), a college of princes, and a college of cities. The decline of imperial control over the German states after the Thirty Years' War brought a corresponding decline in the power of the diet until its revival by Bismarck in 1867 as the representative assembly of the *North German Confederation, then of the German Empire, and finally of the Weimar Republic. In 1933 the Reichstag building burned; Nazi allegations of communist responsibility provided an excuse to ban opposition parties, and the Reichstag became a mere puppet under Hitler.

Reid, Thomas (1710–96) Scottish philosopher. He maintained that Hume, in his theory of ideas, had overlooked "common sense," which was to become the cornerstone of his own philosophy. In his *Enquiry into the Human Mind on the Principles of Common Sense* (1764), he discussed "common sense," in linguistic and metaphysical, as well as mundane, contexts.

Reign of Terror (1793–94) The most violent period of the French Revolution. Dominated by *Robespierre, the governing Committee of Public Safety authorized severe measures against the Revolution's opponents. Over 250,000 suspects were arrested and about 1400 were summarily guillotined. Public reaction caused Robespierre's downfall and execution in July 1794, thus ending the Terror.

Reims (*or* Rheims) 49 15N 4 02E A city in NE France, in the Marne department. An important Roman town, it was the scene of the coronations of most of the French kings. The magnificent gothic cathedral was badly damaged in World War I but it has gradually been restored. Its university was established in 1969. A center for the marketing of Champagne wines, it has varied manufacturing industries. Population (1990): 185,164.

reincarnation (*or* metempsychosis) The migration of the soul from one body at death and its reentry into another (human or animal) body. Belief in reincarnation appears in many different cultures, partly because it offers an explanation for the perplexing differences between individuals' characters and destinies, these being ascribable to traces of previous characters and the rewards or punishments for actions in previous lives. The cycle of reincarnation (*samsara*) is fundamental to Hindu, Buddhist, and Jain conceptions of the world, all spiritual effort being directed toward release (*moksa*) from the cycle. *Plato and *Pythagoras also subscribed to reincarnation, but orthodox Christianity rejected it as contrary to belief in the resurrection of the body.

reindeer A large deer, *Rangifer tarandus,* of European and North American tundra (in America it is called a caribou). About 50 in (125 cm) high at the shoulder, reindeer have a gray-brown coat and spreading branched antlers—male antlers are larger with an extra forward point over the face. Reindeer feed mainly on lichens (reindeer moss) but also eat dwarf willow and other shrubs. The small summer groups gather into herds numbering several hundreds for their winter migration southward, at which time their coat fades to a dull white. □mammal.

reindeer moss A gray tufted *lichen, *Cladonia rangiferina,* that is very abundant in Arctic regions, especially Lapland. It has a stalked much-branched body, up to 3 in (8 cm) high, and covers immense areas of tundra, serving as the major food source for reindeer, moose, musk oxen, etc.

Reinhardt, Max (M. Goldmann; 1873–1943) Austrian theater director. His large-scale productions, involving massed crowds and spectacular lighting and scenery, included *Oedipus Rex* in Berlin in 1910 and *The Miracle* in London in 1911. He also directed more conventional theater productions, opera, and a film of *A Midsummer Night's Dream* (1935), and founded the Salzburg Festival in 1920. Fleeing Germany in 1938, he lived in the US.

relative aperture. *See* f-number.

relativistic mass The mass of a body that is moving at a velocity comparable to the *velocity of light. According to the theory of *relativity, if the velocity of the body is v then its mass is $m_0(1-v^2/c^2)^{-1/2}$, where c is the velocity of light and m_0 the rest mass (the mass when stationary). The relativistic mass of an electron traveling at 99% of the velocity of light is seven times its rest mass.

relativity An important theory proposed by Albert *Einstein. The first part of the theory, published in 1905 and known as the special theory, applies only to motion in which there is no acceleration. The problem that Einstein set out to solve was concerned with the speed at which light travels relative to an observer. Up to this time it was thought that light traveled through a stationary medium, called the ether, at a constant speed and that its speed relative to an observer could be calculated in the same way as the relative speed of any two moving objects. For example, if one car (A) traveling at 90 mph (145 kph) on a highway overtakes another (B) traveling at 70 mph (113 kph), the speed of the two cars relative to each other is 20 mph (32 kph). In talking about relative speeds it is necessary to be precise about what a particular speed is relative to. Car A's speed relative to car B is 20 mph (32 kph), but relative to the earth it is 90 mph (145 kph). Relative to the sun it is about 24 million mph (39 million kph). Because two American scientists, Michelson and Morley (*see* Michelson-Morley experiment), had shown that light traveled at the same speed whether measured in the direction of the earth's rotation or at right angles to this direction, Einstein suggested that the restriction about relative motion does not apply to light. It always has the same speed of 2.998×10^8 meters per second (186,000 miles per second), irrespective of the motion of the observer. The velocity of light, Einstein said, is absolute.

This has far-reaching effects. In his special theory Einstein suggested that as bodies increase in speed they become shorter and heavier (*see* Lorentz, Hendrick). This effect is only noticeable as the speed of light is approached. Cars on the highway do get heavier and shorter but the effect is minute. On the other hand, an electron traveling at 99% of the speed of light becomes seven times heavier than its mass at rest. Einstein also showed that no body could actually travel at the speed of light itself. If it did it would be infinitely heavy and have zero length.

The increase in mass and decrease in length that a body undergoes when moving at high speeds led Einstein to the conclusion that mass (m) and energy (E) are two different aspects of the same thing; they are related by the simple equation $E = mc^2$, where c is the speed of light. The atom bomb and *nuclear energy both depend on this equation.

In the general theory of 1915, Einstein considered accelerated relative motion, especially as it is concerned with gravitation. In this theory, the gravitational force experienced by a body is treated as a property of space and time, which Einstein suggested was "curved" by the presence of the mass. The motion of the stars and planets is controlled by this curvature of space in the vicinity of matter. Light, too, is bent by the gravitational field of a massive body. The observed bending of light rays as they pass close to the sun and the shift of certain lines in the solar *spectrum have provided experimental verification of the theory.

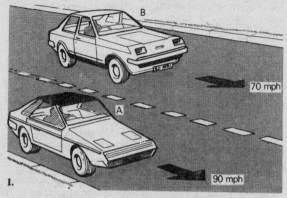

1.

RELATIVITY *1. Two cars, A and B, traveling along a highway. The speed of car A relative to the earth is 90 mph. The speed of car B relative to the earth is 70 mph. The speed of car A relative to car B is 90 − 70 = 20 mph. 2. Car B is now stationary; its headlight beams are turned on as supercar A passes, traveling at 5000 miles per second. The speed of car B's headlight beam relative to car A is 187,000 miles per second (not 187,000 − 5000 miles per second). The velocity of light is absolute.*

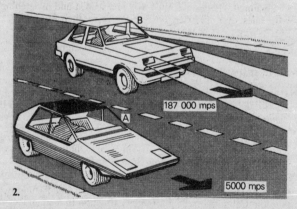

2.

relay, electric An electrical switching device in which one circuit is controlled by a separate circuit, often to avoid the danger of direct contact with high-voltage supplies or to reduce the length of high-current cable needed. Relays may involve mechanical movement and an electromagnetic connection between the two circuits, or may be controlled entirely by *solid-state electronic components.

relief sculpture A form of sculpture in which figures are attached to a background of stone, bronze, or wood, in contrast to free-standing sculpture seen in the round. There are four main types of relief: high relief, in which the figures project almost as much as free-standing sculptures; middle relief; bas-relief, in which the image is only very slightly raised and of which *Donatello developed a variation in the 15th century; and sunken or coelanaglyphic relief, also called *intaglio, particularly associated with ancient Egyptian sculpture.

reluctance (*or* magnetic resistance) The ratio of the *magnetomotive force in a material to the total *magnetic flux induced by it. It is analogous to electrical *resistance.

remanence. *See* ferromagnetism.

Remarque, Erich Maria (1898–1970) German novelist. After being wounded in World War I, he worked as a journalist until the publication of his immediately successful *All Quiet on the Western Front* (1929), describing life in the trenches. His books banned by the Nazis, he lived in the US and Switzerland from 1932.

Rembrandt (Harmenszoon) van Rijn (1606–69) Dutch painter and etcher, born in Leiden, the son of a miller. After studying briefly at Leiden University, he became the pupil of Jacob van Swanenburgh (c. 1571–1638) and later in Amsterdam of Pieter Lastman (1583–1633), who trained him in the Italian *baroque style and had a lasting influence on him, for example in encouraging him to paint historical and religious subjects. Settling permanently in Amsterdam (1631), he made his name as a portrait painter with *The Anatomy Lesson of Dr Tulp* (1632), a group portrait. It was followed by many other portraits, including those of his wife Saskia and culminating in the famous group portrait, *The Nightwatch* (1642). He also treated dramatic mythological and biblical subjects. Rembrandt was a popular teacher of painting and at the height of his success was an avid collector of art. He eventually had financial difficulties and became bankrupt, spending approximately the last 20 years of his life isolated from society. Many of his greatest works belong to this period, when he was no longer popular. He concentrated on depicting the inner life of his sitters and the biblical characters he painted. He also excelled as a landscapist and his etchings, which are among the finest ever produced, are remarkable for their freedom of handling.

Remington, Eliphalet (1793–1863) US inventor and gun manufacturer. His innovations included a method of producing really straight gun barrels and the invention of a lathe for cutting gunstocks. In 1873 the business founded by Remington bought the patent rights of Christopher *Sholes's typewriter.

Remington, Frederic (Sackrider) (1861–1909) US artist and writer. As a young man he lived and worked in the West. His paintings of the frontier West quickly established him as an illustrator for magazines and books in the 1880s and 1890s. He recorded events in words and pictures during the *Spanish American War (1898). After 1895 he also produced many bronze sculptures, including *The Bronco Buster* (1895), and several books, including *Crooked Trails* (1896), *John Ermine of the Yellowstone* (novel and stage play; 1902), and *The Way of an Indian* (1906).

Remonstrants The Dutch adherents of Arminianism (*see* Arminius, Jacobus) who rejected the Calvinist doctrine of *predestination in a statement known as the Remonstrance (1610). Condemned by the Synod of Dort (1618–19), they suffered persecution until 1630. Their liberal theology influenced many subsequent Protestant thinkers, including *Locke and John *Wesley.

remora A dark slender elongated fish, 12–36 in (30–90 cm) long, belonging to a family (*Echeneidae*; 8–10 species) found in warm marine waters. The dorsal fin is modified to form a flat oval sucking disk on its head by which it attaches itself to various marine animals (e.g. sharks and turtles) or ships to feed on scraps of food or the hosts' parasites. Order: *Perciformes*.

REMBRANDT Self-Portrait Aged 63 *(1669), painted when the great artist was no longer popular.*

Remscheid 51 10N 7 11E A city in NW Germany, in North Rhine-Westphalia on the Wupper River. An industrial center, it specializes in tool manufacture. It is the birthplace of Roentgen. Population (1988): 121,000.

Remus. *See* Romulus and Remus.

Renaissance (French: rebirth) An intellectual and cultural movement that began in Italy in the 14th century, spread to N Europe, and flourished until the mid-16th century. Fundamental to the Renaissance were the revival of classical learning, art, and architecture and the concept of the dignity of man, which characterized *humanism. Both were advocated by the 14th-century poet and classical scholar *Petrarch. Other great writers of the Italian Renaissance were *Dante, *Boccaccio, *Machiavelli, and *Ariosto.

The first painter to mirror these new ideals was *Giotto. He was followed in the 15th century by *Masaccio, *Uccello, *Piero della Francesca, *Mantegna, and others, who helped place art on a scientific basis through their concern with the structure and proportions of the human body. They also introduced into painting the use of linear *perspective, the laws of which were developed by the architect *Brunelleschi. Humanism was reflected in the development of portrait painting and the emphasis upon human feelings in religious painting. The High Renaissance denotes the period between about 1500 and about 1520, when the artists

*Leonardo da Vinci, *Raphael, and *Michelangelo were developing the harmony and balance associated with classical art to its highest form.

In sculpture the major figures were Nicola *Pisano, *Donatello, *Ghiberti, *Verrocchio, and Michelangelo. In building Brunelleschi was the first to revive the classical use of the *orders of architecture. Later architects, such as *Bramante, *Alberti, and *Palladio, also revived ancient temples and domed structures. *See also* Italian art.

In the 16th century the Renaissance spread to N Europe, where it manifested itself in the art of *Dürer, the scholarship of *Erasmus, the plays of *Shakespeare, and particularly in the courts of such rulers as Elizabeth I of England, where the ideal of Renaissance civilization was epitomized in the lifestyle of such courtiers as Sir Philip *Sidney.

renin An enzyme, secreted by the kidneys, that breaks down a liver protein to form the peptide angiotensin I. This is converted to angiotensin II, which constricts blood vessels—causing a rise in blood pressure—and increases the secretion of *aldosterone from the adrenal glands.

Rennes 48 06N 1 40W A city in NW France, in the Ille-et-Vilaine department. The capital of the old province of Brittany, it was badly damaged by fire in 1720; most of its notable buildings, including the cathedral and university, were built after that date. The main commercial center of W France, Rennes is an important railroad junction and military headquarters and has textile, electrical, and pharmaceutical industries. Population (1990): 203,533.

rennet An extract, prepared from cows' stomachs, that contain the milk-coagulating enzyme rennin. It is used in the manufacture of cheese and junket.

Reno, Janet (1938–   ) US attorney general (1993–   ), the first woman ever to serve in that post. An advocate of strict laws regarding child abuse and drug-related crimes, she attended Cornell University and Harvard Law School and then practiced law in Florida. She served as Florida's first female state attorney (1978–93) after working as a specialist in juvenile court issues in that office from 1973.

Reno 39 32N 119 49W A city and resort in W Nevada, near the foot of the Sierra Nevada. Founded about 1860, it is known for its easily obtainable divorces and legalized gambling. The University of Nevada (1864) was moved there from Elko in 1886. Population (1990): 133,850.

Renoir, Pierre Auguste (1841–1919) French impressionist painter, born in Limoges. He trained as a decorator of porcelain before entering (1861) the studio of Charles Gleyre (1808–74) and meeting *Monet, with whom he frequently painted on the banks of the Seine. He exhibited at the first three impressionist exhibitions but largely abandoned impressionism after studying Renaissance art in Italy (1881–82). Increasingly crippled by arthritis, he spent his last years in the south of France, painting many sensuous nudes. His best-known works include *Les Parapluies* and *Le Moulin de la Galette*. His son **Jean Renoir** (1894–1978) was a film director whose films, *La Grande Illusion* (1937) and *La Règle du jeu* (1939), are personal and subtle reflections of prewar French society. During World War II he went to Hollywood but returned to Europe to make *The Golden Coach* (1953), *French Can-can* (1955), *Élena et les hommes* (1956), and other films.

Representatives, House of. *See* Congress.

repression In *psychoanalysis, the process of excluding unacceptable ideas from consciousness. Repressed wishes and thoughts continue to exist in the *un-

conscious mind and may give rise to symptoms. One of the goals of psychoana-
lytic treatment is to bring repressed material back into conscious awareness so
that it can be coped with rationally. *See also* defense mechanism.

reproduction In biology, the generation of new individuals of the same
species. In **asexual reproduction** individuals are derived from one parent and
no special reproductive structures are involved. The simplest form is *fission,
occurring mostly in unicellular organisms. Simple multicellular organisms, such
as sponges and coelenterates, reproduce by budding: a new individual arises as
an outgrowth (bud) from the parent. In fragmentation, the individual breaks into
two or more parts, each capable of growth to form a new individual: this is seen
in flatworms and some algae. Most animals and plants, however, reproduce by a
process involving specialized reproductive cells (*see* gamete)—typically male
and female—that fuse to produce a new individual with a different genetic
makeup. This process, **sexual reproduction**, occurs in its simplest form in
*conjugation. In more complex organisms the gametes are produced in special
organs, e.g. the *carpel and *stamen in flowering plants and the *ovary and
*testis in animals. The importance of sexual reproduction in nature is that it al-
lows genetic variation in a population, which is therefore better able to adapt to
the changing environment.

reptile A vertebrate animal belonging to the class *Reptilia* (about 6000
species), which includes *crocodiles, *turtles, *lizards, *snakes, and the *tuatara.
Reptiles occur in terrestrial, freshwater, and marine habitats, chiefly in tropical
regions. They have a covering of horny scales and are cold-blooded, i.e. their
body temperature (and hence their activity) is determined by the environmental
temperature. Fertilization of the egg by sperm takes place within the female, un-
like fish and most amphibians. The egg is large and yolky, has special mem-
branes that nourish the embryo, and a protective leathery or calcareous shell, i.e.
features that enable it to be laid on land. In some lizards and snakes the eggs are
retained inside the female and live young are born. Young reptiles resemble their
parents and—unlike amphibians—do not undergo metamorphosis.

The primitive reptiles evolved from amphibians: their fossils are found in de-
posits of the Upper Carboniferous period, about 300 million years ago. During
the following 240 million years, a variety of forms evolved, including the fish-
like *ichthyosaurs, the flying *pterosaurs, and the mammal-like *therapsids,
culminating in the giant *dinosaurs, which dominated the earth during the Cre-
taceous period (136–65 million years ago).

Republican Party One of the two major political parties in the US (*see also*
Democratic Party). Although the name was used originally by Thomas *Jeffer-
son's Republican-Democratic party, founded in 1792, the modern Republican
party originated in 1854 as a coalition of former Whigs and Independent
Democrats opposed to the extension of slavery to the new western states and ter-
ritories. The first presidential candidate of the Republican party was John C.
*Fremont, who was defeated in the 1856 election. Four years later, with the
nomination and election of Abraham *Lincoln, the Republicans began a long
period of political ascendancy that lasted well into the 20th century. During the
post-Civil War period, the Republican party became increasingly identified with
conservative business interests, and Republican presidents occupied the White
House almost continually until the coming of the *Depression and the defeat of
Herbert *Hoover in 1932. The Republican party came to power again with the
election of Dwight D. *Eisenhower in 1952, and later Republican presidents
Richard *Nixon and Ronald *Reagan actively implemented the conservative
policies of their party.

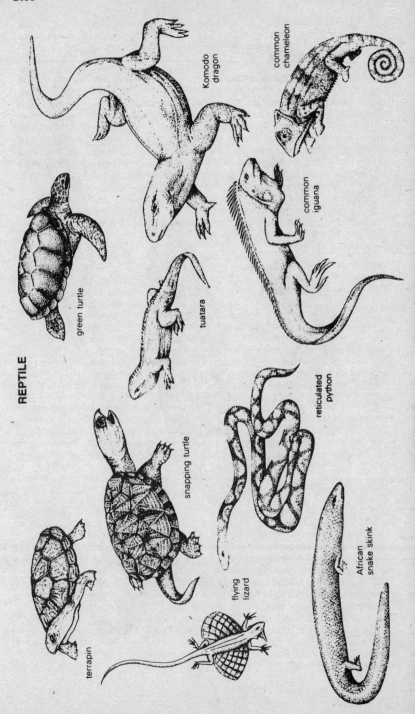

REPTILE

green turtle

Komodo dragon

common chameleon

common iguana

tuatara

terrapin

snapping turtle

reticulated python

flying lizard

African snake skink

REPTILE *Some representative reptiles.*

Republican River A river formed by the junction of the South Fork Republican River and the Arikaree River in SW Nebraska, which flows through S Nebraska and SW through Kansas where it meets the Kansas River at Junction City. Length: 422 mi (680 km).

requiem shark A *shark of the family *Carcharhinidae* (over 60 species), found worldwide mainly in warm and temperate oceans; 5–18 ft (1.5–5.5 m) long, they have two dorsal fins and are carnivorous, feeding on fish and various invertebrates. Some species are dangerous to man, for example the *tiger shark.

reservoirs Natural or artificial lakes in which water is trapped and stored for irrigation, to supply water for municipal needs, for hydroelectric power, or to control water flow. When artificially constructed they are made by placing dams across suitable land formations to create a lake. They may often combine several of the purposes above and are invaluable in areas in which rainfall is low or unpredictable. The water flowing into a reservoir must not contain too much sediment or the capacity of the reservoir will diminish.

Resht. *See* Rasht.

resins Adhesive nonflammable organic polymers, usually insoluble in water but soluble in organic solvents, such as alcohol. **Natural resins**, such as *rosin, *sandarac, and *shellac, are exuded by plants and insects. **Synthetic resins** are made by modifying natural polymers or by polymerization of petrochemicals. Thermosetting resins, those that harden on heating, include *epoxy, *urea-formaldehyde, and some *polyurethane resins. Thermoplastic resins, those that soften on heating, include *polyethylene, *polyvinyl chloride, *polypropylene, and cellulose acetates.

resistance The property of all materials, except superconductors (*see* superconductivity), that reduces the flow of electricity through them. It is defined by *Ohm's law as the ratio of the potential difference between the ends of a conductor to the current flowing through it. The resistance of a conductor depends on its dimensions, the material of which it is made, its temperature, and in some cases the extent to which it is illuminated. The unit of resistance is the *ohm. The reciprocal of the resistance in a direct current circuit is the conductance. Conductance is measured in *siemens (*see also* impedance).

Resnais, Alain (1922–) French film director. His films are characterized by experimental narrative techniques and a concern with the relationship between word and image. The scripts for his films *Hiroshima mon amour* (1959), *Last Year at Marienbad* (1961), and *Providence* (1977) were written by Marguerite Duras, Alain *Robbe-Grillet, and David Mercer respectively.

resolving power The ability of a *microscope to produce separate images of two neighboring points; the closer the two points, the greater the resolving power of the microscope. The resolving power may be increased by using shorter wavelength light (e.g. ultraviolet radiation) or by using very short wavelength electrons (as in the *electron microscope). Alternatively the refractive index of the medium between the specimen being examined and the objective lens may be increased. This is the basis of the *oil-immersion lens.

resonance (chemistry) The existence of a compound with a molecular structure that is intermediate between two or more conventional structures. For example, the polar molecule HCl, in which the hydrogen atom has some positive charge and the chlorine some negative charge, can be regarded as intermediate between two structures. One is the covalent molecule H–Cl and the other the ionic compound H^+Cl^-. The actual molecule is a **resonance hybrid** with contributions from the two forms, written $H–Cl \leftrightarrow H^+Cl^-$.

resonance (physics) The sympathetic oscillation of a system in response to an external excitation. A wire under tension, for example, will not respond to an external vibration unless the vibration is at the natural frequency of oscillation of the wire, which depends on its length, tension, etc. It will then resonate at its natural frequency. Resonance also occurs in electrical, magnetic, and electromagnetic phenomena in which matter or energy is being changed periodically. A **resonant circuit** consists of a capacitance in parallel with an inductance. When the capacitor discharges through the inductor an induced emf is produced, which again charges the capacitor (in the opposite sense). The circuit will then continue to oscillate, provided that energy is supplied from an outside source, at a frequency determined by the values of the capacitor (which is usually a variable device) and the inductor. Such circuits, feeding an aerial, are used in *radio transmitters to generate radio-frequency oscillations and in receivers to detect incoming signals.

resonances Elementary particles with extremely short lifetimes (about 10^{-23} seconds). They are formed when colliding particles react together by the *strong interaction. Resonances are classified as either *mesons or *baryons (*see* particle physics).

Respighi, Ottorino (1879–1936) Italian composer. He became director of the Santa Cecilia in Rome (1923–25). He wrote several operas, the symphonic poems *The Fountains of Rome* (1917) and *The Pines of Rome* (1924), the orchestral suite *The Birds* (1927), based on themes by Rameau and others, and ballets, including *La Boutique fantasque* (1919), based on themes by Rossini.

respiration The process by which an organism takes up oxygen from its environment and discharges carbon dioxide into it. In man and most air-breathing animals the organs through which this takes place are the *lungs (aquatic animals use *gills; insects use *tracheae). Air is transported to and from the lungs by **breathing**, which involves movements of the muscular diaphragm and the rib cage. Oxygen-depleted blood is pumped from the *heart to the air sacs (alveoli) of the lungs, where it receives oxygen (from inhaled air) and releases carbon dioxide (which is exhaled). Oxygen in the blood is carried to the tissues and cells, where it oxidizes foodstuffs to produce energy, used for physiological processes, and carbon dioxide, which is transported in the blood to the lungs. This is called tissue, or cellular, respiration.

respirator A machine used to maintain breathing in patients whose respiratory muscles are paralyzed or not functioning for any other reason. The cabinet respirator (iron lung) encloses the patient in a sealed container from the neck down; by lowering the pressure in the cabinet the chest expands and draws air into the lungs. A positive-pressure respirator pumps air at regular intervals into the lungs through a tube placed in the windpipe; the air is exhaled naturally or removed by suction through the respirator.

Restoration (1660) The reestablishment of the monarchy in England following the fall of the *Protectorate. The Restoration of Charles II, whose father Charles I had been executed (1649) during the English Civil War, was engineered by General *Monck. In April 1660, the Convention Parliament accepted Charles's Declaration of Breda, in which he promised religious toleration and an amnesty to all but 57 of those who had fought against the crown in the Civil War; it also arranged for the restoration of confiscated royalist lands and an income for Charles. The subsequent Cavalier Parliament (1661–79) enacted a religious settlement in the form of the anti-Nonconformist *Clarendon Code.

Restoration literature English literature written during the reigns of Charles II (1660–85) and James II (1685–88), following the Restoration of the monarchy in 1660 and the relaxation of restraints on literature imposed during the Puritan Interregnum. The period was especially distinguished by its drama, notably the witty comedies of manners of *Wycherley, *Etheridge, and *Congreve. In poetry, the period was characterized by the satires of *Dryden and the licentious verse of John Wilmot, earl of *Rochester.

resurrection plant. *See* rose of Jericho.

retina The light-sensitive layer that forms the inner surface of the □eye. Light is focused by the lens onto the retina, which contains numerous interconnecting light-sensitive cells that send signals to the visual center of the brain via the optic nerve. These cells are of two kinds: the rods, which are sensitive to light and dark and are responsible for vision in dim light; and the cones, which are sensitive to color and visual detail. The greatest concentration of cones occurs at a small area at the back of the eye (the fovea), which is therefore the area of greatest visual acuity. *See also* detached retina.

retriever One of several breeds of large strongly built sporting dogs characterized by a "soft" mouth and good swimming ability. All are descended from the *Labrador retriever crossed with other breeds. The flat-coated retriever has a fine dense black or liver-colored coat while the curly-coated retriever has a coat of small tight curls, indicating possible poodle ancestry. The Chesapeake Bay retriever has a short thick coat and has been developed in the US. Height: 22–27 in (56–68 cm). *See also* golden retriever.

Retz, Jean François Paul de Gondi, Cardinal de (1613–79) French churchman, one of the leaders of the rebellion called the *Fronde (1648–53), which he used to further his own political ambitions at the expense of Cardinal *Mazarin. He was made a cardinal in 1652 but arrested soon after. Exiled until 1662 he returned to France to become abbot of Saint-Denis until his death. He is best known for his *Mémoires,* which recall his role in the Fronde.

Reuben, tribe of One of the 12 *tribes of Israel. It claimed descent from Reuben, the eldest son of Jacob and Leah. The territory allocated to Reuben's people was in the Transjordan, E of the Dead Sea.

Réunion A volcanic island and French overseas department in the W Indian Ocean, in the Mascarene Islands. It was settled in about 1642 by the French with their African and Indian slaves; increasing population has caused much emigration. Sugar, rum, and molasses are exported. Area: 970 sq mi (2512 sq km). Population (1978 est): 484,924. Capital: Saint-Denis.

Reuter, Paul Julius, Baron von (Israel Josephat; 1816–99) British founder of the first news agency. Born in Germany, he adopted the name of Reuter in 1844. He went to London in 1851 and opened a telegraph office from which he supplied newspapers with international news. He was made a German baron in 1871.

Reuther, Walter (1907–70) US labor leader. He was an organizer and president of Local 174, *United Automobile Workers (UAW) (1935–46) in Detroit, president of UAW (1946–70), president of the *Congress of Industrial Organizations (1952–55), and head of the AFL-CIO's Industrial Union Department from 1955, after the *American Federation of Labor and the CIO merged. He was known for his plan to produce airplanes in the automobile factories during World War II, for his organization of usually nonviolent strikes, and for union gains achieved through collective bargaining.

Reval. *See* Tallinn.

Revelation, Book of A prophetic book, the last in the New Testament, written perhaps about 90–95 AD by "John the Divine," who is often identified with the apostle John. It consists of seven highly symbolic visions that trace the fortunes of the Christian Church from its inception to the end of the world. The only example of apocalyptic literature in the New Testament, the book may have been written in reaction to the persecutions of the emperor Domitian.

reverberatory furnace A furnace designed for operations in which it is not desirable to mix the material being heated with the fuel. The flame is directed at the roof of the furnace and the heat radiated downward. This type of furnace is used in the smelting of copper and nickel ores.

Revere, Paul (1735–1818) American silversmith and patriot. Prominent in the colonial opposition to Britain, he became famous as the man who, on Apr 18, 1775, rode out to warn the people of Massachusetts that the British troops were on the march. On the following morning the first shots of the American Revolution were fired on the British at Lexington. Revere's ride is celebrated in a poem by Longfellow.

PAUL REVERE *Warning other patriots of the coming of the British at the start of the American Revolution.*

Revolt of the Netherlands The rebellion against Spanish rule in the Netherlands, inspired by political and economic grievances and resentment at the suppression of Protestantism. Revolt broke out in 1568 but only took fire in 1572, when the Dutch cause prospered in the strongly Protestant northern provinces under the leadership of *William the Silent. In 1576 the N was joined by the predominantly Roman Catholic provinces in the S but the union ended with the Spanish victory at Gembloux in 1578, when the S submitted once more to Spain. In the following year the seven northern provinces, by the Union of Utrecht, declared their independence from Spain. War continued, however, until the 12-year truce negotiated in 1609 by William's son and successor *Maurice of Nassau and was renewed in the Thirty Years' War (1618–48). By the Peace of Westphalia (1648) the independence of the United Provinces of the Netherlands was at last acknowledged.

Revolutionary and Napoleonic Wars (1792–1815) A series of European wars precipitated by the *French Revolution and *Napoleon's ambitions for the conquest of Europe. Revolutionary fervor within France and the hostile reaction of Austria and Prussia to the arrest of Louis XVI led to the outbreak of war. Initial French success prompted Britain, the Netherlands, and Spain to close ranks with Austria and Prussia in the first coalition (1793). Hard-pressed, France was transformed into a nation at arms (*see* conscription) and its armies achieved a series of victories. In 1795 Prussia, the Netherlands, and Spain sued for peace and, following Napoleon's first Italian campaign (1796–97), Austria followed suit.

French supremacy was thwarted only by British naval strength and Nelson's great victory of the *Nile (1798) brought Britain control of the Mediterranean. In 1798–99 the second coalition of Britain, the Ottoman Empire, Naples, Portugal, and Austria was formed but collapsed (1801) in the face of Napoleon's victories, especially at *Hohenlinden (1800), and the Revolutionary Wars ended with the uneasy Treaty of Amiens (1802) between Britain and France.

Napoleon's aggression, including his imposition of the *Continental System against Britain, led to the resumption of naval war between Britain and France. In 1805 Pitt the Younger negotiated a third coalition against Napoleon, by now emperor, and Nelson (although mortally wounded) won the naval victory at *Trafalgar. Napoleon now turned on the continental members of the coalition, defeating Austria and Russia at *Ulm and Austerlitz (1805), Prussia at *Jena and Auerstadt (1806), and Russia again at *Friedland (1807). With the failure of the Continental System and Wellington's victories in the *Peninsular War, Napoleon's dominance diminished. Following his disastrous Russian campaign (1812) the allies were able to defeat him at *Leipzig (1813) and then, following his return from exile, at *Waterloo (1815). The post-Napoleonic settlement of Europe was decided at the Congress of *Vienna.

Revolution of 1905 An insurrection in Russia, an expression of the widespread discontent that culminated in the *Russian Revolution of 1917. It began on Jan 22, 1905 (Bloody Sunday), when a group of striking workers marched peacefully on the Winter Palace in St Petersburg and were fired on by troops. The massacre precipitated nationwide strikes, uprisings, and mutinies (including the mutiny on the battleship *Potemkin*). By October, Russia was gripped by a general strike, which with the establishment of the St Petersburg Soviet (workers' council), dominated by the *Mensheviks, including Trotsky, forced Emperor Nicholas II to promise constitutional government (*see* Duma). The Revolution was substantially crushed by the end of December.

Revolutions of 1848 A series of revolutions in continental Europe caused by economic distress and liberal agitation against the conservatism that characterized the post-Napoleonic era. The first revolution broke out in France, where the insurgents overthrew the July Monarchy of Louis Philippe, but a split in their ranks between moderates and socialists led to the suppression of the Left and the election of Louis Napoleon (later *Napoleon III) as president. In the Italian states the revolution had constitutional aims, in which it had some success in Piedmont, but also formed part of the movement against the Austrian presence in Italy (*see* Risorgimento). In the Austrian Empire revolts in Vienna secured the resignation of Metternich and the summoning of a constituent assembly. The revolution spread with short-lived success to Prague and Budapest before being suppressed by Schwarzenberg. In the German states the revolution began in Prussia, where Frederick William IV was forced to convene a constituent assembly. By December, however, the revolutions there and in other German states had been suppressed and in 1849 the Frankfurt Parliament, which had hoped to achieve a united Germany, was dissolved. The revolutions were all quelled but not without some concessions to liberal and nationalist movements, and 1848 is thus generally regarded as ending the post-1815 period of reaction that had been dominated by Metternich.

revolver A short-range *small arm having a revolving cylinder containing the rounds behind the barrel. In single-action types, pressing the trigger cocks the weapon and simultaneously rotates the cylinder; further pressure fires it. Double-action types perform these functions automatically but their stiffer mechanism impairs accuracy. Calibers range from .21–.455 inches (5.3–11.5 millimeters). The first successful revolver was the *Colt, designed in 1835. *See also* pistol.

revue A theatrical entertainment consisting of a succession of songs, dances, and sketches of a topical and often satirical nature. Originating in France, revues attained great popularity in Britain and the US during the early 20th century with such spectacular productions as the *Ziegfeld Follies* (1907). As competition from the movies and television increased, revues became more intimate in form. The success of *Beyond the Fringe* (1961) led to a succession of sophisticated satirical revues during the 1960s.

rex A breed of cat having a curly coat of very short fine hairs. Two breed types are recognized—the Cornish rex and the Devon rex, named for the English counties in which they originated. They have long slender bodies and may be of any color.

Reykjavík 64 10N 21 53W The capital of Iceland, an important fishing port, on Faxa Fjord in the SW. Founded by the Vikings in 874 AD, it became the seat of parliament (the Althing) in 1843 and capital of Iceland in 1918. Its university was founded in 1911. Most of the city's heating comes from natural hot springs. Population (1991 est): 99,600.

Reynaud, Paul (1878–1966) French politician, who was briefly prime minister before the German occupation of France in 1940. He was a forceful opponent of Nazism in the late 1930s and after the collapse of France was arrested by the Germans and held until 1945. After the war he again held ministerial posts and helped draft the constitution of the Fifth Republic (1959).

Reynolds, Sir Joshua (1723–92) British portrait painter. He studied in London (1740–43) under the portraitist Thomas Hudson (1701–79). In 1749 he traveled to Italy, staying for two years in Rome before returning to London. Using the techniques of the Old Masters in such paintings as *Sarah Siddons as the Tragic Muse*, Reynolds aimed to give portraits the prestige of historical paintings. In 1768 he became the first president of the Royal Academy, where he delivered the *Discourses,* which contain his artistic theories. His friends included Dr *Johnson and *Garrick, both of whom he painted.

Reynolds number (*Re*) In fluid dynamics, a dimensionless quantity associated with the flow of a fluid. $Re = \rho v l/\eta$, where ρ and η are the *density and *viscosity of the fluid moving with velocity v through a system characterized by a length l. If the Reynolds number of the fluid is less than about 1500, the flow is streamlined; above this number it becomes turbulent. Named for Osborne Reynolds (1842–1912).

Reza Shah Pahlavi (1878–1944) Shah of Iran (1925–41). After leading an army coup in 1921, he deposed Ahmad Shah Qajar (1898–1930) in 1925. As shah himself, Reza aimed at the modernization of Iran, following the example of *Atatürk in Turkey. In 1941 Britain and the Soviet Union, fearing German influence in Iran, invaded the country and forced Reza Shah to abdicate in favor of his son *Mohammed Reza Pahlavi. He died in exile in South Africa.

rhea A large flightless bird belonging to a family (*Rheidae*; 3 species) occurring in South America; 47 in (120 cm) tall, rheas have a brownish plumage and long legs with three toes. They live in flocks, feeding on leaves, roots, seeds, insects, and small vertebrates. The male builds the nest and incubates the eggs. Order: *Rheiformes.*

Rhea In Greek religion, a Titan, daughter of Uranus and Gaea. Her consort *Cronus swallowed her children, fearing that they would overthrow him. Rhea substituted a stone for one child, *Zeus, who eventually overthrew Cronus and forced him to disgorge the other children.

Rhee, Syngman (1875–1965) Korean statesman; president of South Korea (1948–60). He became leader of South Korea in 1945 during the US occupation and as its first president claimed his government's right to rule over all Korea. Popular unrest forced him to relinquish his post in 1960 and he went into exile.

Rheims. *See* Reims.

rhenium (Re) A dense (relative density 21.02) silvery-white transition metal with a very high melting point. The metal is very ductile and is used to alloy with tungsten. Alloys with molybdenum are superconducting. The metal is obtained as a by-product of molybdenum refining. At no 75; at wt 186.2; mp 5756°F (3180°C); bp 10,158°F (5,620°C).

rhesus factor (Rh factor) A blood protein present on the red cells in 83% of the population: the presence or absence of the Rh factor is the basis of the Rh *blood group system, people with the factor being described as Rh-positive and those without as Rh-negative. If an Rh-negative woman has an Rh-positive baby she may produce anti-Rh antibodies that will react against subsequent Rh-positive pregnancies. The affected baby's blood cells may be destroyed by these antibodies, leading to the severe anemia of hemolytic disease of the newborn. The incidence of this disease has been reduced by taking steps to prevent the formation of maternal anti-Rh antibodies soon after delivery of the first baby.

rhesus monkey A *macaque monkey, *Macaca mulatta,* of S Asia, widely used in medical research. In the wild, rhesus monkeys live in large colonies in forests or on hillsides, sometimes stealing fruit from orchards.

Rheticus (Georg Joachim von Lauchen; 1514–76) German mathematician, who was the first follower of *Copernicus. Rheticus wrote (1540) a summary of Copernicus's ideas and then persuaded him to publish the original book, *De Revolutionibus,* in which they were originally expressed. Rheticus was the first mathematician to regard the trigonometric functions in terms of angles rather than arcs of a circle.

rhetoric The art of using language for communicating information and for intellectual and emotional persuasion. Mastery of rhetoric by orators was considered essential training in ancient Greece and Rome. Influential textbooks were written by *Aristotle, *Quintilian, and *Cicero, and all classical literary criticism was based on rhetorical principles. Aristotle distinguished three modes of persuasion—logical, emotional, and ethical—and codified the rules for rhetorical composition under categories of invention, arrangement, and style. Together with logic and grammar, rhetoric formed the trivium, an essential part of the curriculum in medieval education, and its principles were adapted to medieval forms, such as sermons and legal documents. In the 20th century, the study of rhetoric forms part of the theoretical analysis of techniques of persuasion.

rheumatic fever A disease of children that occurs (rarely) after infection with a streptococcus bacterium. The symptoms develop 10–14 days after the original infection (which is usually of the throat) and include fever, aching joints, chorea (involuntary movements), and inflammation of the heart, which—in a few cases—may lead to chronic heart disease. Treatment is with bed rest, penicillin, aspirin, and sometimes steroids.

rheumatism Any condition involving pain in the joints. This may be caused by a simple strain or by rheumatoid *arthritis, *osteoarthritis, *gout, or *rheumatic fever.

Rhine, Joseph Banks (1895–1980) US psychologist, noted for his experiments in parapsychology, especially extrasensory perception (ESP). Using packs of specially designed cards in scientifically objective tests, Rhine produced statistical evidence to support the occurrence of ESP.

Rhine River (German name: Rhein; Dutch name: Rijn) A river in central and W Europe. Rising in SE Switzerland, it flows N into Lake Constance, continuing W along the Swiss-German border to Basle. It then flows generally N along the Franco-German border and into Germany, turning NW past Bonn, Cologne, Düsseldorf, and Duisburg. It enters the Netherlands below Emmerich and splits into two major distributaries, the Lek and the Waal. The Lek continues W through Rotterdam and enters the North Sea at the Hook of Holland. The Waal joins the Meuse River and enters the North Sea by the Hollandsch Diep. The main tributaries are the Ruhr, Main, Moselle, and Neckar rivers. It is W Europe's main navigable waterway and passes through one of the most highly industrialized regions on the continent. A toxic chemical spill in Switzerland in 1986 caused severe ecological damage on the upper river. Length: 820 mi (1320 km).

Rhineland Palatinate (German name: Rheinland-Pfalz) A *Land* in W Germany, bordering on France, Luxembourg, and Belgium. It includes the historic cities of Mainz, Speyer, Trier, and Worms. Over 75% of Germany's wine is produced in the river valleys of the Rhine, Moselle, and Nahe. Potatoes and grain are grown and livestock is important in the mountainous SW. Industries include chemicals, engineering, and shoe manufacture. Area: 7658 sq mi (19,838 sq km). Population (1991 est): 3,764,000. Capital: Mainz. *See also* Palatinate.

rhinoceros A large hoofed mammal belonging to the family *Rhinocerotidae* (5 species), of Asia and Africa. Rhinos have a massive virtually naked dark-skinned body with short thick legs, a short neck, and a large head. The Indian rhinoceros (*Rhinoceros unicornis*) has a single horn composed of solid fibrous *keratin; all other rhinos have two horns. Rhinos range in size from the large *white rhinoceros to the Sumatran rhinoceros (*Didermocerus sumatrensis*), which is up to 60 in (150 cm) high at the shoulder and weighs 1100–2200 lb (500–1000 kg). Rhinos are generally solitary, grazing or browsing on grass and leaves, and are fond of wallowing in muddy pools. All are now endangered species.

rhinoceros beetle A horned *scarab beetle, of tropical and semitropical regions, up to 6 in (150 mm) long (including the horn), so called because of the resemblance of its horn to that of a rhinoceros. The larvae of most rhinoceros beetles live in rotting wood, although some eat roots or burrow into the stems of palm trees. *Oryctes rhinoceros* is sometimes a serious pest in Oriental coconut groves through its destruction of the leaf bases. *See also* Hercules beetle.

rhizome An underground plant stem producing aerial leaves and shoots. It may extend some distance below ground and can be fleshy (as in the iris) or wiry (as in couch grass). Rhizomes can function both as organs of vegetative reproduction and as overwintering structures. They usually grow horizontally; vertical rhizomes (e.g. of strawberry) are commonly called rootstocks.

Rhode Island A New England state, indented by Narragansett Bay. It is bounded on the N and E by Massachusetts, on the S by the Atlantic Ocean, and on the W by Connecticut. The smallest state, it is also the second most densely populated state. It is highly industrialized, the once important cotton industry having been replaced by modern technological industries, such as electronics and the manufacture of machine tools. It also has important naval installations. Agriculture is limited by the rocky terrain; it is famous for its poultry. *History:* purchasing land from the Narragansett Indians, Puritan Roger Williams established the first settlement at Providence after being banished from the Massachusetts Bay Colony in 1635. The new colony was known for its religious and political liberty. Settlers quickly established a prosperous shipping economy. Rhode Island, strongly opposing British interference in local shipping, was the first of the 13 original colonies to declare its independence. It was also the last to approve the US Constitution and did not become a state until 1790. Shipping declined after the American Revolution, but Rhode Island's plentiful water power resources combined with Samuel Slater's construction of the nation's first successful cotton textile mill (1790) facilitated the rapid growth of manufacturing. The burgeoning manufacturing industry attracted thousands of immigrants to the state. In the 20th century, however, the industry declined as a result of competition from the South. New industries emerged after World War II but unemployment has remained an ongoing problem. The expansion of such new high-technology industries as electronics has aided Rhode Island's economy. Area: 1214 sq mi (3144 sq km). Population (1990): 1,003,464. Capital: Providence.

Rhode Island Red A breed of domestic fowl developed from blackish-red Asiatic breeds kept on Rhode Island farms in the 19th century. It has a deep broad long body with a nearly horizontal back and a slightly curved beak. The plumage is red. It lays brown eggs and is used for both egg and meat production. Weight: 8.4 lb (3.8 kg) (cocks); 6.6 lb (3.0 kg) (hens).

Rhodes (Modern Greek name: Ródhos) A Greek island in the SE Aegean Sea, the largest of the Dodecanese group. It has a mountainous interior with fertile coastal strips, producing cereals, fruit, and wine. Tourism is an important source of revenue. *History*: colonized by Dorians before 1000 BC, Rhodes entered its period of greatest prosperity in the 3rd century BC. It suffered several earthquakes, one of which destroyed the *Colossus of Rhodes in 244 BC. It was occupied by the Knights *Hospitallers from 1282 until 1528, when it became part of the Ottoman Empire. Conquered by Italy in 1912, it was ceded to Greece in 1947. Area: 540 sq mi (1400 sq km). Capital: Rhodes.

Rhodes, Cecil (John) (1853–1902) South African financier and statesman. Born in Britain, he went to Natal in 1870 and then to the Orange Free State to work in the Kimberley diamond mines. In 1888 his company, De Beers Consolidated Mines, bought up the Kimberley mines and in 1889 he gained a charter for the British South Africa Company to develop the territory that in 1895 was named Rhodesia in his honor. He became prime minister of Cape Colony in 1890 but was forced to resign in 1896. Rhodes endowed 170 Rhodes scholarships at Oxford University for students from the British Empire, the US, and Germany.

Rhodesia. *See* Zimbabwe.

Rhodesia and Nyasaland, Federation of (*or* Central African Federation) A former (1953–63) federation of the British colony of Southern Rhodesia (now Zimbabwe) and the British protectorates of Northern Rhodesia (now Zambia) and Nyasaland (now Malawi). It was opposed by Nyasaland nationalists on the grounds that it existed to further the economic interests of Southern Rhodesia, where most of the whites lived. Violent unrest in 1959 led to its dissolution. Zambia and Malawi became independent in 1964; Zimbabwe gained independence in 1980.

Rhodesian ridgeback A breed of hunting □dog originating in South Africa, characterized by a ridge of forward-growing hair along the back. The ridgeback is strongly built with a prominent muzzle and its short glossy coat is yellowish brown to reddish fawn. Height: 25–28 in (63–68 cm) (dogs); 24–26 in (61–66 cm) (bitches).

CECIL RHODES *At the spot called World's View, in the Matopo Hills, Zimbabwe, where he was later buried.*

rhodium (Rh) A metal of the platinum group, discovered in 1803 by W. H. Wollaston (1766–1828). It is alloyed with platinum and palladium to form thermocouples and crucibles and is used in equipment for the production of glass fibers. It is a very hard highly reflective metal and is used to plate jewelry and optical instruments. At no 45; at wt 102.905; mp 3575 ± 5°F (1966 ± 3°C); bp 6747 ± 212°F (3727 ± 100°C).

Rhododendron A genus of small trees and shrubs (about 250 species), mainly of N temperate regions. They have leathery often evergreen leaves, large scaly winter buds, and terminal clusters of colorful fragrant bell- or funnel-shaped flowers. They occur in a variety of habitats and many, including *azaleas, are widely cultivated as ornamentals. Family: *Ericaceae.*

Rhône River A major river in W Europe. Rising in the Rhône Glacier in Switzerland, it flows through Lake Geneva to enter France, flowing generally SW between the Jura and the Alps. It merges with the Saône River at Lyon and flows S to enter the Gulf of Lions via la *Camargue. The Rhône-Saône Valley has historically been an important route and since 1976 the Rhône River has been canalized from Lyon to the Mediterranean Sea. This has provided improved navigation, hydroelectric power, and irrigation for agriculture and has encouraged industrial development along its length. Length 505 mi (812 km).

rhubarb A perennial plant, *Rheum rhaponticum,* possibly of Asian origin, widely cultivated for its juicy red or green leafstalks, up to 40 in (1 m) high, which are cooked in sugar. Later in the season, a central flower stalk may be produced bearing small greenish-white flowers. The leaves are poisonous. Family: *Polygonaceae.*

Rhum. *See* Rum.

rhyme Similarity in sound between two or more words, a device used in poetry to reinforce the metrical pattern of a poem. Usually the rhyme is between words occurring at the ends of lines, but internal rhymes, where the rhyme is between a word within a line and a word at the end of or within another line, are also used. The rhyme scheme of a poem is shown by assigning a single letter to each rhyme; thus the scheme of lines rhyming *house/cat/mouse/rat* would be noted *abab.* Masculine rhyme refers to words having the same vowel sounds in their final syllables (*night/delight*). Feminine rhyme refers to words having similar sounds in the last accented syllable and following syllables (*joviality/morality*). *See also* blank verse.

rhyolite A fine-grained or glassy acid igneous rock, mineralogically the volcanic equivalent of granite. It consists of alkali feldspars and quartz, with some ferromagnesian minerals; many rhyolites are porphyritic and display banding resulting from the flowing lava.

Rhys, Jean (1894–1979) British novelist. Born in Dominica, she wrote five books, including the novels *Voyage in the Dark* (1934) and *Good Morning, Midnight* (1939), about bohemian life in Paris and London. After living in seclusion for many years, she published a novel, *Wide Sargasso Sea* (1966), and two further collections of stories.

rhythm and blues A form of popular music of the 1940s and 1950s, resulting from the fusion of blues and jazz by African-American musicians. Rhythm and blues (often abbreviated to R & B) employed amplified instruments to produce powerful rhythms. One of the earliest rhythm and blues artists was Ray Brown (1926–81), who recorded "Good Rockin' Tonight" (1948). Other rhythm and blues musicians include Little Richard (1935–   ) and Lloyd Price (1932–   ). Rock musicians, such as John Mayall (1933–   ), have been influenced by rhythm and blues.

rhythm method. *See* contraception.

rib A curved bone, 12 pairs of which make up the rib cage, enclosing and protecting the heart and lungs. Each rib forms a joint with the vertebrae of the *spine, permitting movement of the rib cage during breathing. The other ends of the upper seven ribs (the so-called true ribs) are fixed directly to the breastbone by means of a cartilage. Each of the next three pairs (the "false" ribs) is connected by the cartilage to the rib above it, and the two lowest ribs (the floating ribs) end in the muscles of the body wall.

Ribbentrop, Joachim von (1893–1946) German Nazi politician and diplomat. He joined the Nazi party in 1932 and became Hitler's foreign-affairs adviser. From 1936 to 1938 he was ambassador to the UK and then became foreign minister. He secured the Nonaggression Pact with the Soviet Union in 1939 but thereafter his influence declined. He was arrested in 1945, found guilty of war crimes, and hanged.

ribbonfish An offshore marine fish, of the family *Trachipteridae,* that has a long ribbonlike body. Species include the *oarfish. Order: *Lampridiformes.*

ribbonworm A long flat wormlike animal, also called proboscis worm, belonging to the invertebrate phylum *Nemertina* (about 600 species). Ranging in length from 0.04–1200 in (1 mm–30 m), ribbonworms may be black, brown, or white but many are brightly patterned. Most live at the bottom of shallow seas, using a long sticky harpoonlike proboscis to capture annelid worms, mollusks, and crustaceans.

Ribeirão Prêto 21 09S 47 48W A city in S Brazil, in São Paulo state. It is the center of a coffee- and sugar-growing area. Population (1975 est): 258,741.

Ribera, José de (*or* Jusepe R.; 1591–1652) Spanish-born painter and etcher. He settled in Naples (1616), where he was known as Lo Spagnoletto (Little Spaniard). Influenced by the realism and dramatic lighting of *Caravaggio, he painted chiefly religious subjects and some everyday life scenes and portraits, the best examples of which are *The Martyrdom of St Bartholomew* and *Club-footed Boy.* After 1630 he painted in richer colors and chose less gruesome subjects, probably as a result of his study of Venetian art and *Velázquez.

riboflavin. *See* vitamin B complex.

ribonucleic acid. *See* RNA.

ribose A simple sugar ($C_5H_{10}O_5$). Ribose and its derivative deoxyribose are important constitutents of *RNA and *DNA respectively.

ribosome A granular particle present in enormous numbers in the cytoplasm of nearly all *cells, either free or bound to the surface of membranes within the cell. Ribosomes are composed of *RNA and protein and are the site of protein synthesis. During synthesis they often link together in a chain (polyribosome or polysome).

Ricardo, David (1772–1823) British political economist. Ricardo was the first economist to argue systematically from a priori assumptions. His main work, *Principles of Political Economy and Taxation* (1817), argued that exchange value is determined by the labor expended in production and put forward the theory of "comparative costs" as the determining factor in international exchange. As a member of Parliament (1819–23), he contributed greatly to the free-trade movement.

Ricci, Matteo (1552–1610) Italian *Jesuit missionary and scholar. Working in China from 1583 until his death, he proselytized by methods that were later condemned by the Roman Catholic Church. He showed the converts European books, maps, and clocks and allowed them to retain some of their ancient religious traditions.

Ricci, Sebastiano (1659–1734) Venetian painter. Influenced by *Veronese, he worked in Bologna, Rome, Vienna, and London (1712–16), where he painted the *Resurrection* in the apse of Chelsea Hospital chapel. His nephew **Marco Ricci** (1676–1730), a landscape artist, occasionally collaborated with him after about 1707.

Riccio, David (*or* D. Rizzio; c. 1533–66) Italian secretary to *Mary, Queen of Scots. His close relationship with the queen aroused the jealousy of her husband, Lord *Darnley, and other nobles, who had him murdered.

Rice, Elmer (Elmer Leopold Reizenstein; 1892–1967) US dramatist. He became a lawyer in 1913, but did not practice his profession after his first play, *On Trial,* was produced on Broadway in 1914. *The Adding Machine* (1923) and *Street Scene* (1929; Pulitzer Prize) established his reputation as a major playwright. Other works include *Left Bank* (1931), *Counsellor-at-Law* (1931), *We the People* (1933), *Judgment Day* (1934), *Between Two Worlds* (1934), *American Landscape* (1939), and *Dream Girl* (1945).

rice An annual cereal *grass, *Oryza sativa,* or its edible grain, probably native to India but widely cultivated throughout tropical, subtropical, and warm temperate regions. There are many varieties, growing up to 40 in (1m) high and bearing spikes of flower clusters. Seedlings are generally transplanted to flooded paddy fields, although varieties of upland rice do not require flooding. The field is drained to enable mechanical harvesting. Milling the grain removes either the outer husk alone, resulting in brown rice, or both the husk and the bran layer, resulting in vitamin-B-deficient white rice. Apart from being a major staple food, rice is used as a source of starch and for alcohol production.

Rich, Richard, 1st baron (c. 1496–1567) English lawyer, who was the chief prosecutor in the trial of Sir Thomas More. He subsequently assisted in the dissolution of the monasteries, becoming a privy councillor (1540). As Lord Chancellor (1547–51) under Edward VI he helped oust the protector, *Somerset (1549).

Richard (I) the Lionheart (1157–99) King of England (1189–99); a hero of medieval legend, he spent all but six months of his reign abroad. The third son of Henry II and *Eleanor of Aquitaine, he became duke of Aquitaine in 1168 and of Poitiers in 1172. He joined the Third Crusade in 1189 and conquered Messina and Cyprus before arriving in the Holy Land. His victory at Arsuf gained Joppa (1191). On his way home he was captured in Austria and was only released by Emperor Henry VI after payment of an enormous ransom (1194). He returned briefly to England but died campaigning in France.

Richard II (1367–1400) King of England (1377–99). Succeeding his grandfather Edward III, as a minor, government was largely in the hands of his uncle *John of Gaunt. Richard provoked considerable baronial opposition by his autocratic rule, defense of the royal prerogative, and reliance upon favorites. Factional struggles culminated in the banishment in 1398 of Gaunt's son Henry Bolingbroke. He returned in 1399, while Richard was in Ireland, and seized the throne as Henry IV. Richard died shortly afterward in mysterious circumstances.

Richard III (1452–85) King of England (1483–85). He was the youngest brother of Edward IV, on whose death in 1483 he became protector for Edward V, a minor. After destroying the power of the Woodville faction, Richard imprisoned Edward and his brother, declared Edward illegitimate, and seized the throne. It was, and continues to be, alleged that Richard murdered the boys, who disappeared in August 1483. As king, he made important administrative and financial reforms but faced considerable opposition from Henry Tudor (subsequently *Henry VII), by whom Richard was defeated and killed at Bosworth.

Richards, I(vor) A(rmstrong) (1893–1979) English literary critic, linguist, and poet. With C. K. *Ogden, Richards compiled *Basic English and wrote *The Meaning of Meaning* (1923). An emeritus professor of Harvard University, Richards's publications include *Principles of Literary Criticism* (1924), *Goodbye Earth and Other Poems* (1958), and *Tomorrow Morning Faustus!* (1962).

Richardson, Henry Hobson (1838–86) US architect. The first stylistically independent US architect, Richardson graduated from Harvard and studied architecture in Paris. He used a revived romanesque style in different types of buildings, ranging from wholesale stores to railroad stations. Some of his best work was done for Harvard in the 1870s.

Richardson, Sir Ralph (1902–83) British actor. He established his reputation as an actor of Shakespearean and other classical roles while working with the Old Vic Company during the 1930s and 1940s. He also acted in modern plays, such as David Storey's *Home* (1970) and Harold Pinter's *No Man's Land* (1976) and made many films.

Richardson, Samuel (1689–1761) British novelist. His pioneering novel *Pamela* (1740), written in the form of correspondence between the characters, evolved from a publisher's commission for a book of model letters for inexperienced writers. His acute psychological characterization was further developed in *Clarissa* (1748), and in *Sir Charles Grandison* (1753) he attempted to portray the ideal Christian gentleman.

Richelieu, Armand Jean du Plessis, Cardinal de (1585–1642) French statesman, who greatly increased the absolute authority of the crown and France's power in Europe. He rose to prominence as adviser to Louis XIII's mother *Marie de' Medici, entering the king's employ in 1624 and officially becoming his chief minister in 1629. He ruthlessly suppressed the *Huguenots and by means of an extensive secret service thwarted a series of aristocratic conspiracies against himself. He directed France with brilliance in the Thirty Years'

War, although he did not live to see the dominance of Spain over Europe replaced by that of France. A patron of learning, he founded the French Academy and was himself a writer.

RICHARD II *A portrait by an unknown artist of the English king, who ascended the throne at the age of 10.*

Richler, Mordecai (1931–   ) Canadian novelist. He settled in England during the 1950s. He explores the dilemmas of his Jewish protagonists in an exuberant and often bawdy style. His novels include *The Apprenticeship of Duddy Kravitz* (1959), *St Urbain's Horseman* (1971), and *Joshua Then and Now.*

(1981). *Home, Sweet Home* (1984) is a collection of essays about his native Canada.

Richmond 37 34N 77 27W A city and port, the capital of Virginia, on the James River. Richmond was the capital of the Confederate states during the Civil War. It is an important educational center and site of the University of Richmond (1882). The chief manufacture is tobacco. Population (1990): 203,056.

Richter, Hans (1843–1916) Hungarian conductor. In 1866 he became an assistant to Wagner, of whose works he became the leading interpreter. He also conducted the Hallé Orchestra in England and championed the works of Brahms.

Richter, Johann Paul Friedrich. *See* Jean Paul.

Richter, Sviatoslav (Teofilovitch) (1914–   ) Russian pianist. The winner of the Stalin Prize in 1949, he is famous worldwide as a concert and recording artist. He is particularly noted for his performances of Beethoven, Schubert, Schumann, and Prokofiev.

Richter scale A scale of earthquake magnitude devised in 1935 by C. F. Richter in California and now in worldwide use. It is a logarithmic scale from 0 to 9, the largest earthquakes having the highest numbers. It is based on seismic recordings, taking into account distance from the epicenter. The strongest earthquake so far recorded had a Richter scale value of 8.6.

Richthofen, Manfred, Freiherr von (1892–1917) German pilot of World War I, who shot down 80 Allied aircraft before being killed himself in action. His nickname, the Red Baron, referred to the color of his plane.

Rickenbacker, Eddie (Edward Vernon R.; 1890–1973) US aviator. A race car driver, he became a pilot in *World War I, in which he won the Congressional Medal of Honor and was responsible for shooting down 26 German aircraft. After working in the automobile and aircraft industries from 1919, he became president of Eastern Airlines (1938–63), taking leave during *World War II to inspect Pacific air bases. His books include *Fighting the Flying Circus* (1919) about his World War I experiences and *Seven Came Through* (1943) about his 23-day survival on a life raft with seven others after being shot down over the Pacific during World War II.

rickets A disease of children affecting the bones and caused by *vitamin D deficiency. Vitamin D is derived from the diet and can be made in the skin in the presence of sunlight; with a poor diet and/or inadequate sunshine the bones become soft and do not grow properly and the child may be knock-kneed, bowlegged, or pigeon-chested. The disease is readily treated with vitamin D preparations or foods rich in vitamin D.

rickettsia A minute organism belonging to a group of parasites that—like viruses—cannot reproduce outside the bodies of their hosts. They infect arthropods (especially ticks and mites) and can be transmitted to man, in whom they cause such diseases as *typhus and Rocky Mountain spotted fever. All species live within the cytoplasm or nuclei of living cells: they are similar in structure to bacteria and are regarded as intermediate between bacteria and viruses. The name derives from the principal genus (*Rickettsia*), which was named for H. T. Ricketts (1871–1910), a US pathologist who died of typhus while investigating the cause of the disease.

Rickey, Branch (Wesley) (1881–1965) US baseball manager and executive. He held management positions with the St Louis Browns (1913–16), St Louis Cardinals (1917–42; 1962–64), Brooklyn Dodgers (1942–50), and Pittsburgh

Pirates (1950–62). He initiated the farm system (1919) and was instrumental in opening the major leagues to African Americans, signing Jackie *Robinson for the Dodgers (1946). He was elected to the Baseball Hall of Fame (1967).

Rickover, Hyman (George) (1900–86) US naval officer, born in Russia. A graduate of the naval academy (1922) and Columbia University (1929), he headed the Atomic Energy Commission's nuclear propulsion program (1947–82). Called "father of the nuclear navy," he was instrumental in the development of the first nuclear-powered submarine, U.S.S. *Nautilus* (1954). In 1973 he attained the rank of admiral. An outspoken critic of the US education system, he wrote *Education and Freedom* (1959) and *American Education: A National Failure* (1963).

Ridgway, Matthew Bunker (1895–1993) US army officer; chief of staff (1953–55). A graduate of West Point (1917), during World War II he led the 82nd Airborne Division, which played a large part in the invasions of Normandy and Sicily, and later the 18th Airborne Corps in Europe. Commander of the US Eighth Army (1950–51) and then of UN forces in Korea, succeeding Douglas *MacArthur, he was appointed NATO commander in Europe in 1952 before becoming chief of staff.

Riefensthal, Leni (1902–) German film director and photographer. During the 1930s she produced propaganda films for the Nazis, notably *Triumph of the Will* (1936) and *Olympische Spiele* (1936). Her books include two photographic studies of Sudanese tribes, *People of Kau* (1976) and *Last of the Nuba* (1976).

Riel, Louis (1844–85) Canadian rebel. Attempting to resist surveys that he believed would lead to the métis (offspring of Indian-white parents) being robbed of their land, Riel led a rebellion of métis and set up a provisional government at Winnipeg (1869–70). Defeated and outlawed, he later led a similar rebellion (1884–85) that ended in his execution.

Riemann, Georg Friedrich Bernhard (1826–66) German mathematician, who, like *Lobachevski and *Bolyai before him, produced a *non-Euclidean geometry. **Riemannian geometry** involves the development of a generalized space (Riemannian space) of any dimensions in which measurements may vary from point to point. It was used by Einstein in his general theory of *relativity.

Riesman, David (1909–) US social scientist and lawyer. Riesman's published work includes *The Lonely Crowd: A Study of the Changing American Character* (1950), *Individualism Reconsidered* (1954), and *The Perpetual Dream: Experiment and Reform in the American College* (1978). Riesman's insights into US society are as profound and disturbing as those of his friend Erich *Fromm.

Rif A *Berber people of N Morocco. Most of the 19 tribes speak the Rif dialect of the Berber language but a few speak Arabic. Many are light skinned and have blue or gray eyes. The Rif are Muslims and are renowned for their warrior tradition. They are cereal cultivators, herdsmen, and, along the coast, sardine fishers.

rifle A shoulder *small arm with a spiral groove inside its long barrel to make the projectile spin during its trajectory. Invented in the 15th century, rifles were widely used in America in the 18th century. In Europe the rifle superseded the *musket after the invention of the Minié system (by the French officer, Claude-Etienne Minié [1814–79] in 1849) based on an expanding lead bullet. This was made obsolete in 1865 by the introduction of breech-loaded metal cartridges. During the 1880s breech-loading rifles became capable of firing more than one cartridge without reloading. These were the immediate predecessors of the modern repeating rifle. *See also* Mauser rifle; Browning Automatic rifle.

riflebird A large *bird of paradise having a black plumage with iridescent throat patches and small ornamental plumes. The magnificent riflebird (*Craspedophora magnifica*) is about 12 in (30 cm) long with a slender curved bill, a glossy green crown, and a purplish throat. The male performs its courtship display on specially selected and fiercely defended perches.

rifleman A tiny brown passerine bird, *Acanthisitta chloris,* occurring in forested regions of New Zealand. It feeds by creeping up and down tree trunks picking out insects from bark, crevices, and epiphytic plants with its fine pointed bill. Family: *Xenicidae* (New Zealand wrens).

rift valley A steep-sided valley with a flat floor formed as a result of the valley floor subsiding between two roughly parallel faults. Volcanic activity often occurs along these faults. The most notable example of this feature is the vast *Great Rift Valley in Africa; others include the central lowlands of Scotland and the Rhône rift valley.

Riga 56 53N 24 08E A port and the capital of Latvia, on the Gulf of Riga in the Baltic Sea. It is an industrial and cultural center, with ship building, machine-building, and many manufacturing industries. It has many historic buildings, especially in the picturesque old town. *History*: the order of Livonian Knights was founded there in 1201, and in 1282 Riga became a member of the Hanseatic League. A major trading center, after the demise of the Livonian Knights it passed to Poland (1581), to Sweden (1621), and then to Russia (1710). It was the capital of independent Latvia (1918–40) and was occupied by the Germans (1941–44) in World War II. Population (1991 est): 910,000.

Rigel A remote yet very conspicuous blue supergiant, apparent magnitude 0.1 and about 900 light years distant, that is the brightest star in the constellation *Orion.

right ascension An angular distance, analogous to terrestrial longitude, that is used with **declination** to specify the position of an astronomical body on the *celestial sphere. It is measured eastward along the celestial equator from the vernal *equinox. Declination, analogous to terrestrial latitude, is the angular distance of the body N or S of the celestial equator.

Rights of Man and of the Citizen, Declaration of the (1789) The formal expression of the ideals of the *French Revolution. Comprising 17 articles, it was drafted by the National Assembly to preface the constitution of 1791. Incorporating *Enlightenment theories and both English and American precedents (*see* Bill of Rights), the Declaration asserted that "all men are born free and equal in rights," such as equality before the law, freedom of speech, and ownership of property. The Declaration was an inspiration to later revolutionary movements.

right whale A *whale of the family *Balaenidae* (5 species), so called because they were the right whales to catch (by whalers). Up to 60 ft (18 m) long and weighing over 20 tons, they are large-headed slow-moving plankton feeders with very long baleen plates and a double-jetted blowhole.

rigor mortis The stiffening of a body after death caused by chemical changes in the muscle tissue. The time at which rigor mortis appears depends on the external temperature and the circumstances of death. It usually passes away after about 24 hours.

Riis, Jacob August (1849–1914) US journalist and reformer; born in Denmark. After coming to the US in 1870, he was a reporter for the *New York Tribune* (1877–88) and the *New York Evening Sun* (1888–99). Reporting on crime, he exposed conditions in the slums of New York City and crusaded for improvements through his newspaper articles and books. His works include *How the Other Half Lives* (1890), *The Children of the Poor* (1892), and *Children of the Tenements* (1903). He founded (1888) a settlement house, named for him, in New York City.

Rijeka (Italian name: Fiume) 45 20N 14 27E The chief seaport in Croatia, on the Adriatic Sea. Made a free port in 1723, it was annexed by Hungary in 1779. In 1919, following claims by Italian *Irredentists and Yugoslavia, *D'Annunzio led a force to capture it for Italy. It again became a free port in 1920, reverted to Italy in 1924, finally coming to Yugoslavia in 1947 as reparation after World War II, until Croatia's independence in 1991. It has a university (1973) and varied industries, including oil refineries and shipyards. Population (1991): 205,842.

Rijksmuseum A museum and art gallery in Amsterdam, housing the national collection of the Netherlands. It originated in 1808 as the Royal Museum and became the Rijksmuseum in 1817. Its highlights are its paintings of the Dutch school, notably the celebrated *Night Watch* by *Rembrandt.

Rijswijk, Treaty of (1697) The treaty that ended the War of the *Grand Alliance between France and England, Spain, Austria, and the Netherlands. Louis XIV of France surrendered most of the territories he had conquered (retaining Alsace), recognized William III as king of England, and granted trading concessions to the Dutch.

Riley, Bridget Louise (1931–) British painter. In the early 1960s she began her black-and-white all-over patterns of repeated wavy lines, squares, etc., which associate her with *Op art.

Riley, James Whitcomb (1849–1916) US poet. He was born in Indiana and wrote verses for the *Indianapolis Journal* (1877–85) under the name "Benj. F. Johnson, of Boone." Frequently in Hoosier dialect, these verses earned him the title of "Hoosier poet." His poetry collections include *The Old Swimmin' Hole and 'Leven More Poems* (1883), *Afterwhiles* (1887), *Green Fields and Running Brooks* (1892), and *Home Folks* (1900).

Rilke, Rainer Maria (1875–1926) Austrian poet, born in Prague (then in Bohemia). After an unhappy childhood and a brief marriage, he traveled widely in Europe and Russia, becoming in Paris a friend of Rodin, and finally settled in Switzerland. Paris is the setting for the meditative prose of *Die Aufzeichnungen des Malte Laurids Brigge* (1910). In his poetry, the mysticism of his early devotional *Das Stunden-Buch* (1905) develops into a pantheistic celebration of life in the *Duino Elegies* (1923) and the *Sonnets to Orpheus* (1923).

Rimbaud, Arthur (1854–91) French poet. After writing "Le Bateau Ivre" and other early precocious poems he was welcomed to Paris in 1871 by *Verlaine, with whom he formed a tempestuous relationship that eventually ended in a violent quarrel. His visionary theories about poetry were expressed in the prose poems of *Une Saison en enfer* (1873) and *Les Illuminations* (1886). At the age of 20 he renounced poetry and wandered in Europe and the Near East, eventually becoming a gun-runner in Ethiopia. He died in Marseilles.

Rimini (Latin name: Ariminium) 44 03N 12 24E A town and resort in Italy, in Emilia-Romagna on the N Adriatic coast. It has various Roman and medieval remains. There is a textile industry and flour mills; pasta is produced. Population (1980 est): 128,010.

Rimsky-Korsakov, Nikolai (1844–1908) Russian composer. Largely self-taught, he started his career as a naval officer and was appointed professor of composition at the St Petersburg conservatory in 1871. He was a member of the group of nationalist composers known as the Mighty Five, the others being Balakirev, Borodin, César Cui (1835–1918), and Mussorgski. He wrote 15 operas, including *The Snow Maiden* (1880–81) and *The Golden Cockerel* (1906–07), such orchestral works as *Scheherazade* (1888), chamber music, and songs. He also reharmonized Mussorgski's *A Night on Bald Mountain.*

rinderpest A contagious virus disease, also known as cattle plague, affecting cattle and certain wild animals in Asia and Africa. Symptoms arise three to nine days after infection and include loss of appetite, fever, mouth ulcers, dysentery, and emaciation. About 90% of acute cases are fatal; in chronic cases, mortality is lower. Compulsory slaughter and vaccination are used to control outbreaks of the disease.

Rinehart, Mary Roberts (1876–1958) US writer. A prolific writer of mysteries from 1908, she served as a war correspondent during World War I and also wrote plays; the best-known was *Mr. Big* (1920), cowritten with Avery Hopwood. Her novels include *The Circular Staircase* (1908), *The Amazing Adventures of Letitia Carberry* (1911), *Kings, Queens, and Pawns* (1915), *The Altar of Freedom* (1917), *The Amazing Interlude* (1917), *The Breaking Point* (1922), *The Romantics* (1929), *The Wall* (1938), *The Yellow Room* (1945), and *The Frightened Wife* (1953).

ringhals. *See* cobra.

ringlet A *satyrid butterfly characterized by brownish wings marked with small white rings. The larval food plants are mainly grasses. Chief genera: *Aphantopus, Cacnonympha, Erebia.*

ring ouzel A shy songbird, *Turdus torquatus,* related to the blackbird and found in mountainous regions. The male is black with a broad white crescent around the throat; the female is dark brown with less distinct marking. They migrate to S Europe and the Atlas mountains for the winter. Family: *Turdidae* (thrushes).

ringworm A highly infectious disease of the skin, hair, and nails that is caused by various fungi: it is known medically as tinea. Ringworm is usually transmitted by direct contact. The affected area, commonly on the scalp, feet (athletes' foot), armpits, or groin, is usually inflamed, scaly, itchy, and typically ring-shaped (especially on the scalp). Serious infections are treated with the antibiotic griseofulvin.

Río Bravo. *See* Rio Grande.

Rio de Janeiro 22 53S 43 17W The chief port in Brazil, the capital of Rio de Janeiro state situated on the SW shore of Guanabara Bay. Discovered by the Portuguese in 1502, it was the capital of Brazil from 1763 until 1960. Many colonial buildings remain, notably the 17th-century Candelaria church. It is renowned for its spectacular setting backed by mountains, the most famous of which is the conical Sugar Loaf Mountain. Another famous landmark is the giant figure of Christ standing on the highest peak, Corcovado, which is 2264 ft (690 m) high. The city is the site of several universities, the Oswaldo Cruz Institute (specializing in experimental medicine), and the Brazilian Academy of Science. It is an important port and trading center and has a fine natural harbor; exports include coffee, sugar, and iron ore. The chief industries include ship building, sugar refining, and railroad engineering. Population (1991): 5,336,179.

Río de la Plata. *See* Plata, Río de la.

Rio Grande (Spanish names: Río Bravo; Río Bravo del Norte) The fifth longest river of North America. Rising in the Rocky Mountains, in Colorado, it forms the entire border between Texas and Mexico before entering the Gulf of Mexico. Length: 1885 mi (2040 km).

Río Muni. *See* Equatorial Guinea, Republic of.

Ríotinto, Minas de (*or* Minas de Río Tinto) A mining center in SW Spain, in Andalusia near the source of the Río Tinto. Worked since Roman times, its copper mines are among the most valuable in the world.

Ripley, George (1802–80) US reformer, journalist, and critic. A Unitarian minister, he had drifted into transcendentalism by 1841 and resigned from the ministry. He edited *The Dial* (1840–44), a transcendentalist publication he founded, and established *Brook Farm (1841–47), where he served as president and edited the journal *Harbinger* (1945–49). When Brook Farm failed, he moved to New York City and by 1849 became literary critic for the *New York Tribune*, a position he held until his death. *See also* Transcendentalists; New England.

Risorgimento (Italian: resurgence) The nationalist movement in 19th-century Italy that achieved the country's independence and unification. Secret societies, such as the *Carbonari and *Mazzini's Young Italy, encouraged Italian patriotism after 1815, and abortive uprisings occurred in Naples and Sicily (1820) and the papal states, Modena, and Parma (1830–31). Piedmont's attempts in 1848–49 to oust the Austrians from Lombardy ended in defeat at Custozza (1848) and Novara (1849) and afterward *Garibaldi's Roman Republic was suppressed by the French. In 1859, however, the Piedmontese prime minister *Cavour freed Lombardy and in 1860 Garibaldi surrendered to Piedmont the conquests made in the S by his Expedition of the *Thousand. In the same year Tuscany, Modena, Parma, Bologna, and Romagna formed an independent alliance, all accepting entry into the kingdom of Italy under the House of Piedmont, proclaimed in 1861. Unification was completed by Italy's annexation of Venetia in 1866 and of the papal states in 1870.

Rittenhouse, David (1732–96) US astronomer, surveyor, and inventor. He designed and made precision instruments, mainly clocks and optical instruments and is credited with making the first US telescope. Also a surveyor, he helped to establish the *Mason-Dixon line in 1763. By 1769 he had built an observatory at his home and tracked the planets, especially Venus, and refined the transit telescope. He was treasurer of Pennsylvania (1777–89), taught astronomy at the University of Pennsylvania (1779–82), directed the US Mint (1791–96), and was president of the American Philosophical Society (1791–96).

river A large body of water, confined within a channel by banks, that flows into the sea, a lake, or another river. Its source may be a spring, a lake, a number of rivulets, or a glacier. Rivers are sometimes classified according to their development, a youthful river having a narrow V-shaped valley with many rapids and a mature river having a broad flood plain, meanders, and oxbow lakes. Rivers are important in the processes of erosion and the transportation and deposition of material; they are thus responsible for many of the landforms in those parts of the world of which they are a feature. Throughout history rivers have attracted settlement by man; broad river valleys were the site of some of the earliest great civilizations, such as in the Nile valley, and many of the world's major cities are located on rivers. As important communications routes, rivers often provided the point of entry to the surrounding land for explorers, traders, and settlers. Other uses of rivers include irrigation, hydroelectric power generation, and fishing. *See also* flood.

Rivera, Diego (1886–1957) Mexican mural painter. In Mexico in the 1920s, with *Orozco and *Siqueiros, he revived the old techniques of *fresco and *encaustic painting in murals for educational institutions. His social and political subject matter are evident in works for the Ministry of Education in Mexico City (1923–28). His mural for the Rockefeller Center was removed because it included a portrait of Lenin.

Rivers, Larry (1923–   ) US artist. He began painting in the abstract expressionist style in the 1940s and 1950s, but then began incorporating imagery, especially human figures, into his works. His imagery, which sometimes used everyday popular themes, anticipated pop art. He is known for such works as *Washington Crossing the Delaware* (1953), *Double Portrait of Birdie* (1955), and *Dutch Masters Series* (1963).

Riverside 33 59N 117 22W A city in S California, on the Santa Ana River. A long-established citrus town, the state's first navel orange tree was introduced there in 1873. It is the site of the citrus experiment station (1907) of the University of California. Population (1990): 226,505.

Riviera (French name: Rivière) The narrow Mediterranean coastal belt of France and Italy, extending roughly between Toulon (France) and La Spezia (Italy). Its climate, coastal scenery, and beaches have made it a long-standing cosmopolitan resort. Panoramic roads follow the coast; the famous two-tiered Corniche roads extend along the French Riviera (also known as the Côte d'Azur) between Nice and Menton.

Riyadh 24 39N 46 46E A city in Saudi Arabia, in the center of the Arabian Peninsula. Riyadh and Mecca are joint capitals of the kingdom. The discovery of oil in Saudi Arabia in the 1930s has turned Riyadh into a thriving modern city, the commercial and communications center of the country; it has two universities (1950 and 1957). Population (1989 est): 1,500,000.

Rizzio, David *See* Riccio, David.

RNA (*or* ribonucleic acid) A nucleic acid that is important in the synthesis of proteins by living organisms. In some viruses RNA is the genetic material. Structurally, it is similar to *DNA but usually occurs as a single-stranded molecule with the sugar ribose and the base uracil replacing the deoxyribose and thymine of DNA. There are three main types of RNA (most of which occurs in the cell cytoplasm): ribosomal RNA, messenger (m) RNA, and transfer (t) RNA. The *genetic code in DNA contains the information necessary for protein synthesis. This code is transcribed into a strand of mRNA and carried to the ribosomes (small cytoplasmic particles), where it is translated into a particular polypeptide chain. The amino acids making up the protein are brought to their correct positions in the chain by tRNA.

roach One of several freshwater fish related to carp, especially *Rutilus rutilus,* a game fish found in N Europe. It has an elongated body, 6–8 in (15–45 cm) long, olive-green to gray-green above and silvery white below with reddish fins and red eyes. It lives in shoals, feeding on small animals and plants.

Roach, Hal (1892–1993) US film producer. His production company, founded in 1914, produced many of the films of Harold *Lloyd, *Laurel and Hardy, and other comedians of the silent cinema. His single serious film was *Of Mice and Men* (1939). In 1992 he was honored with a special tribute at the Academy Award ceremonies.

roan antelope A large African antelope, *Hippotragus equinus*; 51–59 in (130–150 cm) high at the shoulder, it is roan or reddish gray with a black-and-white face, long tufted ears, and an erect mane. The horns are shorter than those of the related *sable antelope. Roan antelopes live in herds of up to 25 in scrub and woodland.

Roanoke 37 15N 79 58W A city in Virginia, on the Roanoke River. Settled in 1740, it is an industrial center and railroad junction. Manufactures include textiles and chemicals. Population (1990): 96,397.

Robbe-Grillet, Alain (1922–) French novelist. He trained as an agronomist and statistician. He is a leading theorist and practitioner of the *nouveau roman*. *Instantanés* (1961) and *Pour un nouveau roman* (1963) contain a number of influential essays on the subject. As well as his novels, which include *Le Voyeur* (1955) and *La Jalousie* (1957), he has written several film scripts, notably the scenario for *Last Year at Marienbad* (1961).

robber crab (*or* coconut crab) A *crab, *Birgus latro,* found on the shores of the SW Pacific and Indian Oceans. It has an extremely large body (about 40 in [1 m] from head to tail), ranging from violet to deep purple or brown in color. It lives in sand burrows during the day, emerging at night to feed on coconuts broken open by its two large pincers. Tribe: *Anomura.*

robber fly A predatory fly, also called assassin fly, belonging to a worldwide family (*Asilidae*; over 4000 species) of insect eaters. Robber flies have prominent eyes and strong bristly legs. Many species have a humped thorax and a long slender abdomen, but some (e.g. *Asilis crabroniformis*) resemble bees and wasps. Most larvae are herbivorous and live in the soil.

Robbins, Frederick Chapman (1916–) US microbiologist, who, working with John *Enders and Thomas Weller, first cultivated poliomyelitis virus outside living organisms, using cultures of living human tissue in nutrient solution. This technique enabled the development of the polio vaccine and the culture of other viruses. He shared the 1954 Nobel Prize.

Robbins, Jerome (1918–) US ballet dancer and choreographer. He choreographed the dances for many musicals, including *The King and I* (1951), *West Side Story* (1957), and *Fiddler on the Roof* (1964). He was choreographer for the New York City Ballet (1969–83).

Robert (I) the Bruce (1274–1329) King of the Scots (1306–29). After a long career of rebellion against the English crown Robert seized the Scottish throne in 1306. Although immediately forced into exile by Edward I of England, on the accession of Edward II he slowly recovered the kingdom, decisively defeating the English forces at Bannockburn (1314). A period of consolidation of his power followed, culminating in English recognition of Scottish independence in 1328.

Robert (II) the Pious (c. 970–1031) King of France (996–1031), who conquered Burgundy (1015) after years of warfare with a rival claimant. He gained his nickname for his encouragement of monasticism.

Robert II Curthose (c. 1054–1134) Duke of Normandy (1087–1134); the eldest son of William the Conqueror. He twice rebelled against his father (1077, 1083) and came into conflict with his brother William II Rufus. After fighting courageously in the First Crusade, he attempted to usurp the English throne from his youngest brother Henry I and following defeat at Tinchebrai was imprisoned (1106–34).

Robert II (1316–90) The first *Stuart king of the Scots (1371–90). He was three times regent of Scotland (jointly 1334–35; alone 1338–41 and 1346–57) while his father *David II was imprisoned or in exile. His own rule, as an old man, was of little consequence.

Robert the Wise (1278–1343) King of Naples (1309–43), a leader of the Italian *Guelfs (papal party) against the Ghibellines (imperial party). He was an outstanding administrator (hence his nickname) and patron of scientists and writers, including Petrarch and Boccaccio.

PAUL ROBESON

Robeson, Paul (1898–1976) US actor and singer. His best-known stage performances were in the title roles of *Othello* and Eugene O'Neill's *Emperor Jones*. He sang spirituals, made several films, and actively campaigned for African-American civil rights.

Robespierre, Maximilien François Marie Isidore de (1758–94) French revolutionary. A lawyer, Robespierre was elected to the States General in 1789, on the eve of the *French Revolution, and became one of the leaders of the radical *Jacobins. He gained a wide following in Paris and after the execution of Louis XVI was instrumental in the overthrow of the Girondins (1793). He subsequently wielded supreme power on the Committee of *Public Safety, instituting the *Reign of Terror. In 1794 the tide turned against him and his cult of the Supreme Being, and he was denounced in the Legislative Assembly, arrested, and guillotined.

robin A small North American songbird, *Turdus migratorius,* about 8.5–10.5 in (21.5–26.5 cm) long. The male is gray, with a brick-red breast, a blackish tail and head, and a yellow beak. The female's head and tail are not as dark. Common on farmland, in woodland, and in towns and gardens from Canada to S US, a robin defends its territory fiercely, using its warbling song as a signal to warn off intruders. Family: *Turdidae* (thrushes).

Robin Hood An English outlaw, probably legendary, who figures in a series of ballads dating from the 14th century. According to the *Lytell Geste of Robyn Hoode* (c. 1495) he killed the evil sheriff of Nottingham, was visited in his forest home by the king, and was subsequently employed in the royal household. His mistress Maid Marian and his association with Sherwood were later additions to the story.

Robinson, Edward Arlington (1869–1935) US poet. Troubled by poverty and alcoholism throughout his life, he established himself with a novel in verse, *Captain Craig* (1902), and confirmed his reputation with the poems in *The Town Down the River* (1910) and *The Man Against the Sky* (1916). He wrote a large number of dramatic monologues and several long narrative poems, including *Amaranth* and *King Jasper* (1935). Some of his best verse appeared in an early volume, *The Children of Night* (revised 1897). He won three Pulitzer Prizes.

Robinson, Edward G. (Emanuel Goldenberg; 1893–1972) US film actor, born in Romania. He was cast as a gangster in *Little Caesar* (1930) and other films during the 1930s but he played more varied roles in later films, such as *Double Indemnity* (1943) and *The Outrage* (1964).

Robinson, Frank (1935–) US baseball player. An outfielder and first baseman, he played for the Cincinnati Reds (1956–65), the Baltimore Orioles (1966–72), the Los Angeles Dodgers (1972–73), and the California Angels (1973–74). He managed the Cleveland Indians (1974–77), the first African-American manager in major league baseball, and other teams. He was elected to the Baseball Hall of Fame (1982).

Robinson, Jackie (Jack Roosevelt R.; 1919–72) US baseball player. A high school and college star in several sports, he played with the Negro National baseball league in 1945 and was then signed by Branch *Rickey to play with the National League's Brooklyn Dodgers, the first African American ever signed by a major league team. At second base, he began to play for the Dodgers in 1947, winning many honors and compiling a career batting average of .311 before his retirement in 1957. He was elected to the Baseball Hall of Fame (1962).

Robinson, Sir Robert (1886–1975) British chemist, who investigated the structure of the alkaloids *morphine (1925) and *strychnine (1946). The latter work enabled Robert *Woodward to synthesize strychnine eight years later. Robinson received the Nobel Prize in 1947.

Robinson, Sugar Ray (Walker Smith; 1920–89) US boxer, who was world welterweight champion (1946–51) and five times middleweight champion (twice in 1951, 1955, 1957, 1958–60). He fought 202 professional bouts, of which he lost only 19.

Robinson-Patman Act (1936) US law that prohibited price discrimination. Enacted to clarify part of the *Clayton Anti-Trust Act of 1914, this law prevented large chain-type stores from offering merchandise at a low price that could not be matched by small independent retailers.

Rob Roy (Robert Macgregor; 1671–1734) Scottish outlaw, whose violent life was romanticized in Sir Walter Scott's novel *Rob Roy* (1818). He embarked on his career of banditry after losing his family fortunes in 1712. He was eventually arrested and sentenced to transportation but was pardoned in 1727.

Rochester 43 12N 77 37W A city in New York, on Lake Ontario and the Genesee River. Founded in 1789, it is the site of the University of Rochester (1850) and the Rochester Institute of Technology (1829). Its industries include horticulture and the manufacture of photographic and optical equipment. Population (1990): 231,636.

Rochester 44 01N 92 27W A city in Minnesota. It is the site of the Mayo Clinic (1889) and the Mayo Medical Center. Manufactures include electronic and recording equipment. Population (1990): 70,745.

rock (music) A style of popular music dating from the early 1950s, resulting from the fusion of rhythm and blues with country music. The term **rock and roll** was originally applied to such songs as "Rock Around the Clock" (1955) by Bill Haley (1925–81) and the Comets and "Heartbreak Hotel" (1956) by Elvis Presley, whose bands consisted of electric guitars, drums, and amplified vocalists. In the 1960s the term "rock" replaced "rock and roll." Such groups as the Beatles and Chicago expanded the traditional band to include string backing and other instruments, and began to explore the possibilities offered by studio recording techniques, synthesizers, etc. Rock increasingly split into subgroups, such as **acid rock**, based on drug experiences (Jimi Hendrix, the Jefferson Airplane), and **hard rock**, emphasizing a strong rhythmic beat (the Byrds, the Bee Gees), and **progressive rock**, which admitted long instrumental solos and more advanced harmonies. In the late 1970s **punk rock** (*or* new wave) returned to a basic and very aggressive style of performance with such groups as the Sex Pistols. *Compare* pop music.

rock (petrology) A solid mixture of *minerals forming part of the earth's crust. The minerals are usually consolidated to form a hard compact mass, but geologists include unconsolidated material, such as sand, as rock. Rocks are classified according to their formation (*see* igneous rock; metamorphic rock; sedimentary rock), their age (*see* stratigraphy), and their composition. Individual rock types are much more varied in chemical composition than minerals, and most consist of several different minerals. Some minerals in rocks can be seen with the naked eye, such as the quartz, orthoclase, and biotite in granite, whereas the minerals in clay can only be seen under an electron microscope. The principal minerals in rocks are the silicates (including silica), carbonates, and oxides. The essential minerals in a rock are those that determine its classification; accessory minerals are those that do not affect its classification. *Petrology is the study of rocks.

rock crystal. *See* quartz.

rock dove A cliff-nesting dove, *Columba livia,* of S Europe, Asia, and N Africa; 13 in (32 cm) long, it has a gray plumage with a green-and-purple neck patch, two black wing bars, and a white rump. A fast flier with excellent homing ability, it feeds on seeds, grain, shellfish, and seaweed.

Rockefeller, John Davison (1839–1937) US industrialist and financier. Beginning his career as a clerk and bookkeeper, Rockefeller became involved in the early development of the Pennsylvania petroleum industry and organized the Standard Oil Co. in 1867. As president of Standard Oil, Rockefeller methodically eliminated the competition of other firms and by the mid-1870s controlled virtually the entire American oil refining and distribution industry. In 1882 his organization became the Standard Oil Trust, but an adverse ruling by the Ohio Supreme Court forced its dissolution in 1899. Rockefeller subsequently established a holding company for his assets called the Standard Oil Co. of New Jersey, but this too was dissolved by an antitrust ruling of the US Supreme Court in 1911. Having amassed a fortune estimated at more than $1 billion, Rockefeller devoted his later years to philanthropic work. In 1892 he established the endowment of the University of Chicago, and with his son **John Davison Rockefeller, Jr.** (1874–1960), he established the Rockefeller Institute for Medical Research (1901) and the Rockefeller Foundation (1913).

Rockefeller, Nelson Aldrich (1908–79) US politician; vice president of the United States (1974–77). A grandnephew of financier John D. *Rockefeller, he became one of the leaders of the liberal wing of the Republican party, serving four terms as governor of New York (1958–73). Rockefeller unsuccessfully sought the Republican presidential nomination in 1960, 1964, and 1968. In 1974, following the resignation of Richard *Nixon, he finally gained a national office through his appointment as vice president by Gerald *Ford. Rockefeller retired from public life in 1977 to devote himself to philanthropic work.

rocket Any of several annual or biennial herbaceous plants of the genus *Sisymbrium,* having yellow flowers. London rocket (*S. irio*), up to 24 in (60 cm) high, is found on roadsides, walls, and in waste places in Europe, W Asia, North America, and N Africa. Its name results from its abundance after the Great Fire of London in 1666. The name is also given to plants of several other related genera. Family: *Cruciferae.*

rockets Vehicles or missiles powered by jet propulsion that carry their own fuel and oxidizer and can therefore travel both in space and in the atmosphere. Rockets have no lift surfaces (*see* aeronautics), obtaining both lift and thrust from their propulsive jets. Solid-fuel firework rockets were known to the Chinese in the 13th century and have been used sporadically in war ever since. However, the first liquid-fueled rocket to fly was designed by the American R. H. *Goddard in 1926. This achievement attracted little interest, except in Germany, where the *Peenemünde rocket research station was set up. It was here that Werner von *Braun produced the *V-2 rocket in World War II. Intercontinental *ballistic missiles (with nuclear warheads), developed by both the US and Soviet Union from this model, now form part of the armory of all the principal nations. These rockets, in turn, led to the space rockets that carried man to the moon.

Space rockets are built in stages, a high-thrust vehicle providing lift-off and acceleration into the thinner atmosphere, where this first stage is jettisoned and the second stage takes over. The world's biggest space rocket, the US Saturn V, is a three-stage rocket weighing 3000 tons fully laden. The first stage burns kerosene and the second and third stages burn liquid hydrogen. Liquid oxygen (lox) is the oxidizer for all stages. This rocket can carry a load of 45 tons into space. Fuel economy is one of the most important factors in rocket design—the specific impulse of a rocket being its most significant characteristic. The specific impulse is the time in seconds to burn one kilogram of fuel while producing one newton of thrust. Typical values are 3400 s for a solid fuel, 4500 s for liquid hydrogen-lox, and over 10,000 s for an ion engine. In an ion-engine rocket an easily ionized substance, such as cesium, is heated to produce ions, which are accelerated by an electric field to produce thrust. These engines of the future could be powered by nuclear energy or solar energy to produce the necessary 50 kW of electricity for each newton of thrust.

Rockford 42 17N 89 06W A city in N central Illinois, on the W bank of the Rock River, NW of Chicago. Settled in 1834 at a shallow ford, it manufactures machinery, appliances, tools, paints, leather and food products, and furniture. Population (1990): 139,426.

Rockhampton 23 22S 150 32E A city and port in Australia, in central Queensland on the Fitzroy River. It is a commercial center for an extensive hinterland producing meat, gold, copper, and coal. Population (1981): 50,146.

Rockingham, Charles Watson-Wentworth, 2nd marquess of (1730–82) British statesman; prime minister (1765–66, 1782). As leader of the so-called Rockingham Whigs, he supported the American colonies in their conflict with Britain. In 1765 he repealed the *Stamp Act and led the opposition to Lord North's government during the American Revolution.

rockrose A small spreading shrub, *Helianthemum chamaecistus,* up to 11.8 in (30 cm) high with bright-yellow five-petaled flowers; it is found in grassland and scrub of Europe and W Asia. Hybrids of this and similar species are cultivated as garden ornamentals, with many different colored varieties. Family: *Cistaceae.*

rock tripe A leafy *lichen of the genus *Umbilicaria,* found in Arctic and temperate regions. It is rich in carbohydrates and is edible when boiled. In Japan it is considered a delicacy, being eaten in salads or deep fried. Some species are also used as dyes.

Rockwell, Norman (1894–1978) US artist. Best known for his covers for the *Saturday Evening Post,* the first of which appeared on a 1916 issue, he painted pictures of small-town everyday life situations. His *Four Freedoms* mural (1943) is housed in Nassau Tavern in Princeton, N.J., and was used by the Office of War Information during World War II.

Rocky Mountain National Park A national park in N central Colorado, NW of Boulder, that straddles the Continental Divide. Established in 1915, it includes over 100 peaks of the Rockies; the highest point in the park is Long's Peak (14,255 ft; 4345 m). Glaciers and evidences of the glacial age are abundant, as is the wildlife. With the exception of a few roads and camping sites, the park is wilderness. Area: 410 sq mi (1062 sq km).

Rocky Mountains (*or* Rockies) The chief mountain system in North America. It extends roughly N–S for about 3000 mi (4800 km) between New Mexico and the Yukon (Canada), forming the *Continental Divide. It rises to 14,431 ft (4399 m) at Mount Elbert. Some geographers consider the Yukon and Alaska ranges as part of the system, making Mount Logan, at 19,850 ft (6050 m), the highest point.

rococo A style dominant in the fine arts and decorative arts of France between about 1700 and 1750. Developing in reaction to the *baroque pomp of the Louis XIV period, it was characterized by curved forms, slender proportions, asymmetry, pastel colors, and a general effect of intimacy, gaiety, and delicacy. The rococo style was particularly manifest in the interior decoration of Parisian townhouses and furniture, porcelain, and metalwork. Famous rococo artists include the painters *Fragonard, *Boucher, and *Watteau and the sculptor *Clodion. The style spread to Austria and Germany, where the leading exponent was the architect Balthazar *Neumann. England remained largely untouched by it, although some rococo features appear in the work of *Hogarth and *Gainsborough. The rococo was supplanted by *neoclassicism.

rodent A mammal belonging to the order *Rodentia* (over 1700 species). Rodents are distributed worldwide and occupy a wide range of terrestrial and semiaquatic habitats. They range in size from about 2.9 in (7.5 cm) (the smallest mice) to 51 in (130 cm) (the capybara). Rodents have distinctive teeth. The single pairs of chisel-like incisors in each jaw continue to grow throughout life, as they are worn away by gnawing. There are no second incisor or canine teeth, leaving a gap between the front teeth and cheek teeth. When the rodent is gnawing, the cheeks are drawn into the gap and the lower jaw is moved forward so that the upper and lower incisors can meet. This prevents the rodent from swallowing gnawed material and from wearing out its cheek teeth.

Rodents are important to man as agricultural pests, fur animals, and as experimental animals for scientific research. They are divided into three suborders: *Hystricomorpha* (porcupines, cavies, chinchillas, etc.; 180 species); *Sciuromorpha* (squirrels, beavers, marmots, chipmunks, etc.; 366 species); and *Myomorpha* (rats, mice, lemmings, voles, etc.; 1183 species).

rodeo A sport that grew out of ranching skills after the Civil War, now controlled by the Rodeo Cowboys Association, founded in 1945, and the Girl's Rodeo Association, founded in 1948. A rodeo, or contest, includes six main events: bronco riding with and without a saddle, bull riding, calf roping, steer wrestling, and team roping. Professional rodeo riders are not hired to take part, but live on prize money.

Roderic. *See* Rory O'Connor.

Rodgers, Richard Charles (1902–79) US composer of musical comedies. With the lyricist Lorenz Hart (1895–1943) he wrote such works as *The Girl Friend* (1926) and *Pal Joey* (1940). After Hart's death he collaborated with Oscar *Hammerstein II in *Oklahoma* (1943), *The King and I* (1951), and other musicals.

Rodin, Auguste (1840–1917) French sculptor. He produced his first major work, *The Age of Bronze* (1877), after visiting Italy (1875), where he was influenced by the work of *Michelangelo and *Donatello. Its controversial realism was a factor in the vicissitudes of his public commissions: *The Burghers of Calais* (1884–86), his nude monument of Victor Hugo, and his dressing-gowned Balzac were all initially rejected. Nevertheless, by 1900 Rodin had established an international reputation, his bronze portrait busts and his figures in marble, notably *The Kiss* (1886), being particularly admired. His most personal work, *The Gates of Hell,* which was originally a government commission of the 1880s, was left unfinished at his death. Many of its symbolic figures, for example *The Thinker,* became well-known independent sculptures.

Rodney, George Brydges, 1st baron (1719–92) British admiral. He wrecked (1759–60) a French invasion fleet during the Seven Years' War and won victories (1780–82) against the powers that supported the American Revolution. His victory over the French off Dominica (1782) helped Britain to gain favorable terms in the concluding Peace of Versailles (1783).

rods and cones. *See* retina.

Roebling, John Augustus (1806–69) US engineer, who with his son **Washington Augustus Roebling** (1837–1926) designed the Brooklyn Bridge in New York, which was opened in 1883. They also designed major suspension bridges, including those over the Niagara River at the Niagara Falls and over the Ohio River between Cincinnati and Covington. John Roebling died after an accident while supervising the construction of the Brooklyn Bridge.

roe deer A small deer, *Capreolus capreolus,* of temperate Eurasian forests. About 27.5 in (70 cm) high at the shoulder, roe deer have a dark-brown winter coat, a red-brown summer coat, and a large white rump patch; males have small three-pointed antlers. They feed at night on leaves, shoots, and berries and live in pairs or small family groups.

roentgen A unit of dose of ionizing radiation equal to the dose that produces ions of one sign carrying a charge of 2.58×10^{-4} coulomb in air.

Roentgen, Wilhelm Konrad (1845–1923) German physicist, who discovered *X-rays while professor at the University of Würzburg, Bavaria. In 1895 Roentgen was investigating the *luminescence that cathode rays produce in certain substances and discovered that the luminescence persisted when the cathode rays themselves were blocked by cardboard. He correctly concluded that some other type of radiation was coming from the cathode-ray tube. He named the radiation X-rays and his discovery that the rays pass through matter quickly led to their use in medical diagnosis. In 1901, he received the first Nobel Prize in physics. The unit of X-ray dose (*see* roentgen) is named for him.

Roger II (1095–1154) Norman King of Sicily (1130–54). He became count of Sicily in 1105 and created a strong kingdom augmented by the acquisition of Calabria (1122), Apulia (1127), Capua (1136), and Naples (1140) on the Italian mainland. He also attacked the Byzantine Empire, pillaging the coastal cities of

Rolfe, Frederick William

Dalmatia and Epirus. His court was a great intellectual center for both Christian and Muslim scholars.

Rogers, Carl R(ansom) (1902–87) US psychologist who developed client-(or patient-) centered psychotherapy, upon which present-day psychotherapy procedures are based. He believed that only through a personal doctor-patient relationship can a patient realize his potential to solve his own problems. Rogers taught at several universities, including the University of Rochester, the University of Chicago, and the University of Wisconsin. Among his works are *Counseling and Psychotherapy* (1942), *Client-Centered Therapy* (1951), *On Becoming a Person* (1961), *The Therapeutic Relationships with Schizophrenics* (1967), and *Carl Rogers on Personal Power* (1977).

Rogers, Ginger (Virginia McMath; 1911–) US actress and singer. During the 1930s she partnered Fred *Astaire in many popular film musicals, including *Top Hat* (1935), *Swing Time* (1936), and *Follow the Fleet* (1936). She was also a talented comedy actress.

Rogers, Will (William Penn Adair R.; 1879–1935) US entertainer. He had learned the intricacies of lasso roping as a boy in Oklahoma and, from 1904, performed in Wild West and vaudeville shows. His rope-twirling act was combined with casual, but often biting, humorous comments on life and the social scene. He wrote a column for *The New York Times* (1922–35) and several books as well as appearing in movies including *A Connecticut Yankee* (1931), *State Fair* (1933), and *David Harum* (1934). He was killed when a plane, piloted by Wiley Post (1900–35), went down in N Alaska.

Roget, Peter Mark (1779–1869) British physician and philologist. He was secretary of the Royal Society from 1827 to 1849. His well-known *Thesaurus of English Words and Phrases* (1852), a dictionary of synonyms, has been revised in numerous editions.

Röhm, Ernst (1887–1934) German soldier, who organized Hitler's *Brownshirts. Röhm's ambition to increase the power of the Brownshirts led to his execution without trial.

Roh Tae Woo (1932–) South Korean political leader and president (1988–93). An army officer who rose to division commander, he supported the military coup of 1979 and then served in the cabinet of Chun Doo Hwan. In 1985, Roh became the leader of the dominant Democratic Justice party (DJP). When opposition grew to Chun's dictatorial rule and Roh's designation as his successor, Roh unexpectedly embraced the opposition's demands for democratic reform. He won the 1988 presidential election and then embarked on a policy of seeking accord with North Korea, a policy that succeeded from 1991, when the first significant agreements between the long-time enemies were signed.

Rokitansky, Karl, Freiherr von (1804–78) Austrian pathologist, whose detailed anatomical studies of numerous autopsies helped establish the science of pathological anatomy. Rokitansky is noted particularly for describing the different kinds of pneumonia and a liver disease known as Rokitansky's disease.

Roland, Song of. *See* chanson de geste.

Rolfe, Frederick William (1860–1913) British novelist, also known by the pseudonym Baron Corvo. A Roman Catholic convert, who was not accepted as a candidate for the priesthood, his frustration and delusions were expressed in the fantasy *Hadrian the Seventh* (1904), which concerns a convert who becomes pope. His other works include *Stories Toto Told Me* (1898) and *The Desire and Pursuit of the Whole* (1934).

Rolland, Romain (1866–1944) French novelist, dramatist, and essayist. He was also a distinguished musicologist, and his best-known novel, *Jean Christophe* (1904–12), concerns a German composer. His philosophical idealism, much influenced by Tolstoy, was expressed in numerous volumes of essays and biographies. He won the Nobel Prize in 1915.

roller A short-legged bird belonging to a family (*Coraciidae*; 12 species) occurring in warm regions of the Old World; 10–15 in (25–40 cm) long, rollers are blue or violet and have a large head, a strong slightly hooked bill, and a long tail. They feed in flocks on ants, locusts, and lizards. Order: *Coraciiformes* (hornbills, kingfishers, etc.).

Rolling Stones, the A British rock group, formed in 1962. Their early hits included "The Last Time" and "Satisfaction." They became famous for their notorious behavior in public, made successful tours of the US, and recorded a number of albums, including *Beggar's Banquet* (1968). The original members of the group were Mick *Jagger, Keith Richard (1943–   ), Bill Wyman (1941–   ), Charlie Watts (1941–   ), and Brian Jones (1944–69).

Rollo (c. 860–c. 931) Viking leader, who founded the duchy of Normandy. Having invaded NW France, Rollo was given the territory around Rouen by treaty (911) with Charles (III) the Simple (879–929; reigned 898–923), thus becoming the first duke of Normandy.

Rolls, Charles Stewart (1877–1910) British automobile manufacturer and aviator. A car dealer, in 1906 he went into partnership with Henry *Royce to found Rolls-Royce Ltd. Rolls was the first to fly nonstop across the English Channel and back (1910), dying shortly afterward in an airplane crash.

Romains, Jules (Louis Farigoule; 1885–1972) French poet, novelist, and dramatist. He was a leading exponent of the philosophical theory of *unanimisme*, which emphasized collective as opposed to individual emotions and psychology. His best-known works are the satirical play *Knock* (1923) and the novel cycle *Les Hommes de bonne volonté* (1932–46).

Roman art and architecture The styles of art and architecture of the ancient Romans. Deriving principally from their Greek and Etruscan predecessors, Roman styles in the fine and applied arts have profoundly influenced Western traditions. The Romans' main contribution to classical architecture was the formal and structural development of the ☐arch, *dome, and *vault and the introduction of new types of building, such as *thermae, *amphitheaters, and triumphal arches. Their advanced building techniques and use of concrete were unsurpassed until the 19th century. The Pantheon and the Colosseum (both in Rome) remain as fine examples of their monumental building techniques, while the ruins of Pompeii provide an insight into their domestic architecture and their skill in town planning. In the other arts their style was modeled on that of the Greeks, although their sculptures were less idealistic and more inclined to personal portraiture. Little painting has survived, but from the evidence of Pompeii and elsewhere *mosaics and murals seem to have been popular.

Roman Catholic Church The Christian Church of which the pope is the temporal leader (*see* papacy). After the split with the Eastern *Orthodox Churches (1054; *see* Filioque), Roman Catholicism was the unchallenged spiritual authority in W Europe; Church dignitaries possessed great political, as well as spiritual, power and *monasticism flourished. In the early 16th century the rising tide of *Protestantism demonstrated the need for urgent reforms within the Church. The Council of Trent (1545–63), convoked to discuss these reforms, has largely determined the present dogmatic, disciplinary, and liturgical character of Roman Catholicism (*see also* Counter-Reformation), although important reforms were initiated by the second *Vatican Council. In general, a higher reliance is placed by Roman Catholics upon tradition and authority, especially regarding interpretation of the Bible, than is the case in most Protestant Churches. The Church organization is to an advanced degree centralized and hierarchical (*see* cardinals, college of; Roman Curia), and the pope's decisions are reinforced by the doctrine of *infallibility promulgated in 1870. Other accepted doctrines include *transubstantiation and *purgatory. The number of the *sacraments has been fixed at seven since the 12th century. The cult of the Virgin Mary, which flourished in the Middle Ages, underwent a major revival in the 19th century, and the veneration and invocation of *saints are encouraged. Church furnishings, music, and vestments are more elaborate than in Protestant Churches. Until the mid-20th century Latin was the sole language of the Mass. Roman Catholicism has spread worldwide due to strenuous missionary efforts since the 16th century (*see* Jesuits) and is the largest Christian denomination. In a world becoming progressively more disinclined to accept religious authority, the Catholic Church has managed to maintain its strong following, largely as a result of firm direction from Rome. However, some modernization has already taken place (the use of the vernacular in the Mass, changes in monastic dress, etc.), although other controversial issues (abortion, contraception, divorce, married priests, etc.) remain to be resolved.

romance A term loosely applied to a medieval verse or prose narrative that dealt with nonhistorical material and first became popular in 12th-century France. Its central themes were courtly love, chivalry, and adventure, and it was distinguished from the earlier *chanson de geste by being less heroic and more sophisticated in tone. It was intended as entertainment rather than for any religious or political purpose. Romances are conventionally classified into three types according to subject matter: (1) the Matter of Britain—romances based on the *Arthurian legend, which was popular throughout Europe; (2) the Matter of Rome—romances about the Trojan War, Thebes, or Alexander the Great; and (3) the Matter of France—romances about Charlemagne and his knights. Among the most famous medieval romances are the five Arthurian romances of *Chrétien de Troyes; the *Parzival* (c. 1210) of Wolfram von Eschenbach; the *Tristan und Isolde* (c. 1210) of Gottfried von Strassburg; the anonymous Middle English *Gawain and the Green Knight* (c. 1400); and Sir Thomas Malory's *Morte d'Arthur* (c. 1470).

Romance languages Descendants of the *Italic language group, in particular of the spoken form of *Latin, called Vulgar Latin. The group consists of modern *French, *Italian, *Spanish, *Portuguese, *Romanian, *Catalan, the Rhaetian (*see* Romansch) group of dialects, Sardinian, and the now extinct Dalmatian. As this list shows, many Romance languages are in fact regional dialects rather than national languages. They are classified as a group on the basis of a shared section of basic vocabulary, which originated in the influence of the language of the Roman conquerors of the Mediterranean area in which the languages of the group are clustered. Since 1500 their use has spread outside Europe to South America and Africa, with French, Spanish and Portuguese colonization.

Roman comedy A dramatic genre that developed chiefly from Greek sources and flourished in the late 3rd and 2nd centuries BC. The first Latin version of a Greek comedy was written by Livius Andronicus (c. 284–c. 204 BC) in 240 BC. His successors included Naevius (c. 270–c. 201 BC) and *Plautus, whose plays, based on those of Greek *New Comedy writers, especially Menander and Philemon, were enlivened by colloquial language and topical and bawdy humor. The plays of *Terence and Caecilius Statius (c. 219–168 BC) were more sophisti-

Roman Curia

cated in their plots and characterization. At the Renaissance the plays of Plautus and Terence, the only representatives of Roman comedy to survive complete, were revived and became the basis of modern ideas of comedy.

Roman Curia (Latin: *Curia Romana*) The papal court, comprising the chief judicial and administrative bodies of the *Roman Catholic Church. Its powers are delegated by the pope, who takes responsibility for its acts. Extensively reformed in 1967 by Pope Paul VI, it consists of three tribunals, which are mainly concerned with judicial matters; five offices, including the Chancery, which issues papal bulls, and the offices of the Palatinate Secretaries, such as that of the Cardinal Secretary of State, which deals with political affairs; and nine Roman Congregations, which are permanent commissions of cardinals having specific tasks (regarding rites, missions, etc.)

Roman Empire The imperial period of ancient Roman history from 27 BC, when Octavian became emperor as *Augustus, until 476 AD. Under imperial government many of the political institutions of the *Roman Republic, notably the Senate, continued to function, although Augustus and his successors enjoyed supreme power as *princeps* (chief citizen). Augustus, who created an efficient administrative system for the Empire, fostered peace and prosperity, which continued, despite outbreaks of rebellion, under the paternalistic rule of the Flavian (69–96 AD; *see* Vespasian; Titus; Domitian) and Antonine (96–180; *see* Nerva; Trajan; Hadrian; Antoninus Pius; Marcus Aurelius) emperors. Trade and industry flourished throughout the Empire, new cities were founded, and frontiers, although little extended, were strengthened. Civil war, however, followed the death of *Commodus (193), with provincial armies nominating their own imperial candidates. Order was briefly restored by Lucius Septimus *Severus (reigned 193–211), who openly acknowledged his dependence on military might, increasing the powers of the *Praetorian Guard (imperial bodyguard). The 3rd century saw a rapid succession of army-nominated emperors, while Rome's frontiers were threatened by the aggression of the *Sasanians and the Goths. *Diocletian (reigned 284–305) countered these attacks with the reorganization of the Empire between East (*see* Eastern Roman Empire) and West (293). It was reunited (324) under *Constantine the Great, the first Christian emperor, who founded a new imperial capital at Constantinople (*see* Istanbul). His attempts to establish unity were, however, short lived: civil war and economic decline followed his death and the western Empire fell prey to barbarian invasions. The Visigoths sacked Rome in 410; Carthage was captured in 439 by the Vandals, who in 455 also sacked Rome; in 476 the last Roman emperor of the West, *Romulus Augustulus, was deposed by the German king Odoacer. The Eastern Roman, or Byzantine, Empire survived until 1453.

romanesque art and architecture A style of art and architecture that flourished in Europe from the 11th century until the introduction of the *gothic in the mid-12th century. Its origins were mixed, being a combination of Carolingian, Roman, and Byzantine styles, and regional influences produced many variations between areas. Primarily an ecclesiastical art form, it was largely stimulated by the need for more churches, now possible on a large scale because of the arrival of relative peace after centuries of disturbance. The increasing complexity of Church ritual was reflected in the greater number of side chapels. The decline of building techniques since antiquity resulted in very solid buildings with thick walls, windows with semicircular arches, and simple stone vaulting. The other important branch of romanesque art was sculpture. It was primarily used to decorate churches, either with geometrical or plant and animal patterns on the fabric of the building, especially on the capitals, or statues of religious subjects inside the building. Many examples of romanesque art still survive, one of the most notable being Pisa Cathedral. *See also* Norman art and architecture. □arch.

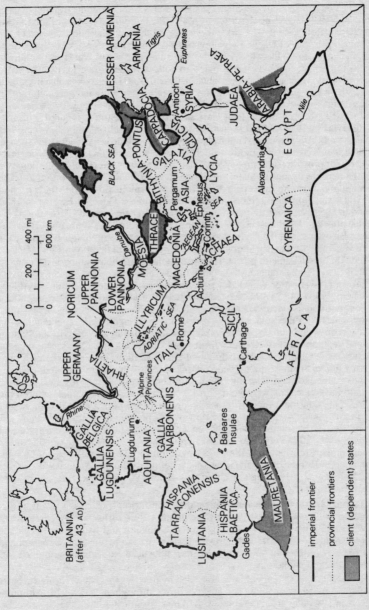

ROMAN EMPIRE *In 14 AD, at the death of Augustus, Roman rule or influence extended all the way around the Mediterranean.*

Romania, Republic of A country in SE Europe, with an E coastline on the Black Sea. The Carpathian Mountains and the Transylvanian Alps in the center of the country separate the plains in the E and S from the Transylvanian plateau in the NW; the Danube River forms most of its S boundary. Most of the inhabitants are Romanians, who trace their ancestry back to the Latin settlers of the Roman province of Dacia. *Economy*: although there has been a pronounced shift in the balance of the economy toward industry since World War II, agriculture is still important, much of it organized in collectives and state farms. The main crops are corn, wheat, potatoes, sugar beet, and fruit. Livestock is also important and there is a growing wine industry. Minerals include oil and gas, salt, lignite, iron, and copper. Hydroelectricity is a valuable source of power, particularly since the opening of the Iron Gate facility on the Danube (shared with Yugoslavia) in 1972. Varied industries, all now nationalized although there has been a relaxation in central controls since 1978, include heavy industries such as mineral and metals, oil, motor vehicles, machinery, and chemicals, the products of which provide the main exports (mainly to communist countries). There is a considerable timber industry and tourism is of increasing importance to the economy. *History*: formed in 1861 from the principalities of *Moldavia and *Walachia, Romania gained independence from the Ottoman Empire in 1880 and in 1881 became a kingdom under Carol I. Romania joined (1916) the Allies in World War I and was occupied by the Germans. In 1918 it obtained Bessarabia, Bukovina, and Transylvania, which it was forced to relinquish to the Axis Powers in 1940. Shortly afterward Carol II abdicated in favor of his son Michael and Antonescu came to power. He gave Romanian military support to Germany until Soviet forces entered the country and Antonescu's government was overthrown (1944). After World War II a communist-dominated coalition was established (1945) and in 1947 Michael abdicated. Elections in 1948 resulted in a clear communist victory. From the early 1960s Romania became increasingly independent of the Soviet Union, especially in foreign affairs, condemning the Soviet invasions of Czechoslovakia and Afghanistan as well as establishing good relations with Western countries and China. Nicolae Ceauşescu, dictator from 1967, suppressed antigovernment demonstrations in 1989. When his own army turned against him, he fled with his wife, but they were captured, tried secretly, and executed. The interim government instituted reforms and, in 1990, multiparty elections were held. Ion Iliescu, a former Communist, entered the presidency during a time of transition and reform and had to deal with violent antigovernment demonstrations, a downward-spiraling economy, and ethnic unrest. Iliescu won reelection in 1992 under a new constitution approved at the end of 1991. In 1993 cooperation agreements were signed with Turkey and other neighbors. President: Ion Iliescu. Prime minister: Theodore Stolojan. Official language: Romanian. Official currency: leu of 100 bani. Area: 91,699 sq mi (237,500 sq km). Population (1990 est): 23,269,000. Capital: Bucharest. Main port: Constanţa.

Romanian A *Romance language, the main form of which is spoken in Romania and is known as Daco-Romanian. Other forms are Aromanian or Macedo-Romanian (Greece, Yugoslavia, Albania, and Bulgaria); Megleno-Romanian (N Greece); and Istro-Romanian (Istrian peninsula). Geographical proximity to the Slavonic languages has influenced Romanian's grammar, vocabulary, and phonology.

Roman law The body of laws compiled by the Romans, which forms the basis of the *civil law of many modern countries throughout the world. Although Roman law dates from the time of the kings (from c. 735 BC), the *Twelve Tables (450 BC) is regarded as the first major codification. Before about 150 BC these laws were elaborated as the *jus civile* (civil law), i.e. the law applicable exclusively to Roman citizens. With increasing territories, commercial interests, and foreign treaties, another system, the *jus gentium* (law of nations), was also applied by Roman courts. This system of international law derived from the philosophical concept of natural law (i.e. a law common to all men and to nature) and was used in cases involving provincial Roman subjects of different states and in suits between a foreigner or provincial and a Roman citizen. It gradually influenced the *jus civile,* and the two systems came to have many identical features. As Roman law developed, by judicial interpretation, by edict, and by legislation, there arose a number of anomalies, until the Byzantine emperor *Justinian I sponsored legal reforms embodied in the definitive codification of Roman law, the *Corpus Juris Civilis* (Body of Civil Law) or Justinian Code, published between 529 and 565 AD. This consisted of four parts: (1) the *Codex Constitutionum,* a chronological collection of the ordinances (*constitutiones*) of the emperors, with all contradictions, anomalies, etc., eliminated; (2) the *Digest,* a collection of statements by jurists on points of law; (3) the *Institutes,* a textbook for law students explaining legal institutions; and (4) the *Novellae* or *Novels,* the new ordinances issued by Justinian after the publication of the *Codex.* Roman law, with local variations, continued in use throughout medieval Europe and after the fall of the Byzantine Empire. The impetus for its spread outside Europe in the 19th century was given by the most influential modern codification based on it, the *Code Napoléon.*

Roman literature. *See* Latin literature.

Romanovs The last ruling dynasty of Russia (1613–1917), noted for their absolutism and for transforming Russia into a large empire. The first Romanov tsar was *Michael, whose election ended the *Time of Troubles. His most famous successors were *Peter the Great, *Catherine the Great, *Alexander I, *Nicholas I, and *Alexander II. In March 1917, during the Russian Revolution, Romanov rule ended with the abdication of *Nicholas II. He and his family were executed.

Roman religion The polytheistic religion of ancient Rome. The earliest cults worshiped local Italian deities of the fields, woods, springs, and hearth. As Rome grew to statehood its religion changed character: the gods of its Sabine and Etruscan neighbors (e.g. Quirinus and *Juno) were absorbed and *Mars, originally an agrarian spirit, became god of war. The state religion with its various priestly colleges (*see also* augury) centered on the temple of *Jupiter on the Capitoline hill (Rome). The influence of *Greek religion caused the identification of many Roman deities with Greek counterparts (Jupiter with *Zeus, *Vesta with *Hestia, etc.), but although their attributes changed their worship remained characteristically Roman. In 204 BC the orgiastic cult of *Cybele reached Rome, followed soon afterward by that of *Dionysus. The eastward expansion of Roman power brought contact with the esoteric cult of *Isis (*see also* mysteries) and *Mithraism. Emperor worship became an important part of official religion and a touchstone of loyalty. In the fringes of the Empire the Roman gods were often assimilated with local deities (e.g. at *Bath, England, Minerva was equated with the resident goddess Sulis and worshiped as Sulis Minerva). Official toleration of Christianity under *Constantine from 313 AD occasioned the gradual extinction of the old religion, despite attempts at revival (360–63) by *Julian the Apostate. *See also* ancestor worship; Feriae.

Roman Republic (510–27 BC) The period of ancient Roman history between the expulsion of *Tarquin the Proud and the proclamation of *Augustus as the first Roman emperor.

Republican government comprised two chief magistrates (later *consuls) elected annually, an increasing number of subordinate magistrates, the *Senate, and popular assemblies (*see* comitia). Power lay in the hands of the *patricians until the *plebeians, after two centuries of struggle, achieved access to all state offices. Roman dominance over the rest of Italy was achieved by the early 3rd century: the tribes of Latium (the Latin League) were reduced by 338, victory against the Samnites of the S Apennines was attained by 290, and the Greek settlements in the S were conquered by 275. By the mid-2nd century Cisalpine *Gaul had been subdued and the *Punic Wars with Carthage brought control of the Mediterranean (146) and Rome's first overseas *provinces (Sicily, Sardinia, Spain, Africa). Concomitantly, dominance over Greece was achieved with the subjection of Illyria, Macedonia (*see* Macedonian Wars), and the Achaean League (*see* Achaea) and, following the acquisition of Pergamum in 133, control of much of Asia Minor. In the mid-1st century *Caesar completed the conquest of Transalpine Gaul.

The conquest of Italy was accompanied by the gradual extension of Roman citizenship (*see* civitas) and the construction of a network of roads, which brought Italy a degree of unity. The emergence, however, of a landowning elite who built up vast estates (*latifundia*) at the expense of small farmers resulted in serious unemployment. The attempts in the second half of the 2nd century of the *Gracchus brothers at agricultural reform, although partially successful, aggravated the conflict between the Optimates (the aristocratic party) and the Populares (the popular party). The Republic was further undermined by provincial unrest, which, together with the military ineptness of the Senate in the late 2nd century, brought a series of ambitious army commanders to the fore.

The first of these, *Marius, emerged as a champion of the people but the popular party lost a bloody power struggle to the aristocrat *Sulla, whose dictatorship (83–79) was marked by legislation to strengthen the Senate. This was revoked in 70 by *Pompey and *Crassus, who 10 years later formed the so-called first *Triumvirate with Caesar. The death of Crassus (53) and Pompey's intrigues with Caesar's senatorial enemies brought civil war. Caesar's victory and subsequent short-lived dictatorship rang the knell of the Roman Republic, which was finally destroyed by Octavian's defeat of *Mark Antony and his assumption of absolute power as Augustus. *See also* Roman Empire.

Romans, Epistle of Paul to the A New Testament book written from Corinth by Paul in about 57 AD to the Christians at Rome. The first 11 chapters are a systematic explanation of Christian doctrine and explain the nature of the salvation provided by Christ. The remaining chapters are practical and explain how believers are expected to live in the Church and in society.

Romansch A *Romance language belonging to the Rhaetian group, spoken in N Italy and in the Rhine Valley in Switzerland. It is one of Switzerland's four national languages.

romanticism A fundamental development in Western art, literature, music, and their related fields of theory in the late 18th and early 19th centuries. Romanticism constituted a reaction against the unquestioned authority of reason and tradition (*see* classicism) and an affirmation of faith in man's innate powers of creativity. Its various manifestations included a passionate concern with the relationship between man and his natural environment and a new interest in the primitive and the irrational. In literature, English romanticism is usually dated from the publication of *Lyrical Ballads* by Wordsworth and Coleridge in 1798 and is associated with the poetry of Keats, Shelley, and Byron and the novels of Walter Scott. Major German romantic writers included the Schlegel brothers, Goethe, and Schiller, and in France, where the theories of Rousseau had anticipated many aspects of the movement, the important writers included Chateaubriand and Victor Hugo. The influence of romanticism is seen in the works of such painters as Turner and Delacroix, and it was the dominant influence on musical composition from the time of Beethoven until the early 20th century.

Romany The language spoken by *gypsies. It is related to *Sanskrit and the *Indo-Aryan languages of N India but diverged from these about 1000 AD, when the gypsies began their nomadic way of life. Romany has been greatly influenced in vocabulary by the languages spoken in regions the gypsies have passed through, resulting in many different dialects. There is little written literature in Romany but a rich oral tradition.

ROME *Piazza Navona, built on the site of the Emperor Domitian's circus. In the center is Bernini's Fountain of the Four Rivers (1648–51). Borromini's imposing façade of S Agnese in Agone (1652) contrasts with the many cafés and restaurants.*

Rome (Italian name: Roma) 41 53N 12 33E The capital of Italy, on the Tiber River. It is mainly an administrative and cultural center and, with the *Vatican City within its boundaries, the focal point of the Roman Catholic Church. Known as the Eternal City, it is one of the world's greatest historical and art centers; tourism is an important source of revenue. The Italian film industry is centered here. Relics of classical times include the Forum, the *Pantheon, and the *Colosseum. There are many ancient churches the origins of which go back to the early Christian era; with the exception of Sta Maria Maggiore, the patriarchal basilicas (St Peter's in the Vatican City, S Giovanni in Laterano, S Lorenzo Fuori le Mura, and S Paolo Fuori le Muri) were built on the sites of martyrs' tombs. The Renaissance produced not only many outstanding buildings, such as St Peter's Basilica, but the paintings and sculpture of such artists as Michelangelo and Raphael. The 17th and 18th centuries brought more fine architecture, with squares, fountains, and façades designed by Borromini, Bernini, and others. The university was founded in 1303. *History*: according to legend Rome was founded on the Palatine Hill in 753 BC by Romulus, its first king, later spreading to six other hills E of the Tiber: the Aventine, Capitoline, Quirinal, Viminal, Esquiline, and Caelian. Seven kings were followed by the *Roman Republic, and the *Roman Empire was founded in the 1st century BC. As the Empire declined in the 5th century AD Rome, no longer its center, was sacked by Germanic tribes. From the time of Pope Gregory in the 6th century it regained importance, this time as an ecclesiastical power. In 800 Charlemagne was crowned emperor here. In succeeding centuries, it was sacked by Arabs and by Normans, and in the Middle Ages there was a continuing struggle between popes and emperors. It remained under papal control until 1871, when it became capital of the newly unified Italy. The popes however refused formally to relinquish their temporal power until the Lateran Treaty of 1929, when their jurisdiction was confined to the Vatican City. Mussolini's March on Rome in 1922 marked the beginning of his fascist rule; the city was occupied by the Allies in World War II. Population (1991 est): 2,791,354.

Rome, Treaties of (1957) Two treaties signed in Rome by the representatives of Belgium, France, Italy, Luxembourg, the Netherlands, and West Germany, which led to the establishment of the *European Economic Community and the *European Atomic Energy Community.

Rommel, Erwin (1891–1944) German general, known as the Desert Fox because of his victories in N Africa in World War II. In 1940 he became commander of the Seventh Panzer Division and, in 1941, of the Afrika Corps. In N Africa he was hailed as a liberator by the Arabs and gained the respect of the enemy but in 1943, after his defeat at Alamein (1942), he was recalled and became commander of the Channel defense. His involvement with the conspirators who attempted to assassinate Hitler in 1944 (see Stauffenberg, Claus, Graf von) led to his suicide, under pressure from Hitler, who wished to avoid a treason trial implicating his most popular general.

Romney, George (1734–1802) British portrait painter. Although his training was limited, he attracted a fashionable clientele and rivaled Reynolds when he moved to London in 1762. He is best known for his numerous portraits of Lady Emma *Hamilton, whom he met in 1781.

Romulus and Remus The legendary founders of Rome, the sons of Mars and Rhea Silvia, daughter of Numitor, king of Alba Longa. Amulius, who had deposed Numitor, threw the twin babies into the Tiber. They were washed ashore and suckled by a she-wolf and later adopted by a shepherd. They eventually founded Rome at the place where they had been rescued. Romulus built the city on the Palatine hill and became the first king.

Romulus Augustulus (b. ?461) The last Roman emperor in the West (475–76 AD). He was deposed by the German ruler *Odoacer.

Roncesvalles (French name: Roncevaux) 43 01N 1 19W A village in N Spain, in the Pyrenees. Nearby is the Pass of Roncesvalles, where Charlemagne's rear guard, under Roland, was ambushed by the Saracens (788 AD) on his retreat to France.

rondeau A short lyrical poem using an intricate verse form developed in 14th- and 15th-century France. Intended for singing, rondeaux were generally 10 or 13 lines long, used only two rhymes, and had an elaborate repetitive pattern of words and lines. Their subjects were the standard themes of the *courtly love tradition. The rondeau's virtuosity reached a peak in *Dufay's compositions.

rondo A musical form in which a recurring theme alternates with contrasting episodes. In its simplest form it consists of the pattern ABACADA, A being the rondo theme and B, C, and D the episodes. In this form it was much used in the 18th century; Mozart, Beethoven, Schubert, and others developed the rondo by combining it with *sonata form.

ronin A samurai (warrior) left masterless by the total defeat of his lord. In the 1860s, however, many patriotic samurai deliberately became *ronin* in order to engage in extremist political activities.

Ronsard, Pierre de (1524–85) French poet. He turned to literature after deafness interrupted his career at court and became a leading member of the *Pléiade. His *Odes* (1550) and *Amours* (1552) gained him the patronage of Charles IX. His later works include *La Françiade* (1572), an unfinished national epic, and *Sonnets pour Hélène* (1578), which contains his best-known love poems.

Roodepoort-Maraisburg 26 10S 27 53E A city in South Africa, in the S Transvaal. A W suburb of Johannesburg, it has developed manufacturing industries and is an important residential area. Population (1986): 141,764.

rood screen (*or* chancel screen) The screen of wood or stone, often elaborately carved, that separated the chancel from the nave in a medieval church. The name derives from the cross (Old English: rood) that surmounted the screen.

rook A large blue-black Eurasian crow, *Corvus frugilegus,* about 18 in (45 cm) long and having a narrow gray bill with pale patches of bare skin at its base. It is highly gregarious, breeding in large colonies and forming well-developed communities. Rooks feed on earthworms, larvae, carrion, and grain, sometimes damaging newly sown crops.

Roon, Albrecht, Graf von (1803–79) Prussian general, who as war minister (1859–73) effected important military reforms. He introduced compulsory three-year service in the face of fierce opposition but his policies, which were supported by Bismarck, were vindicated by Prussian victory in the Austro-Prussian War (1866) and in the Franco-Prussian War (1870–71).

Roosevelt, Franklin Delano (1882–1945) US statesman; 32nd president of the United States (1933–45). Educated as a lawyer, Roosevelt began his political career as New York Democratic state senator (1911–13) and as assistant secretary of the navy during the administration of Woodrow Wilson (1913–20). The unsuccessful Democratic vice-presidential nominee in 1920, he was stricken with poliomyelitis the following year. Despite his handicap, Roosevelt returned to public life and became one of the leaders of the Democratic party with his election as governor of New York in 1928. After reelection in 1930, he received the 1932 Democratic presidential nomination and defeated the incumbent president, Herbert *Hoover.

Roosevelt came to office at a time of economic crisis brought on by the *Depression and immediately after his inauguration began to implement an ambitious program of fiscal and social reform that he called the *New Deal. The New Deal proved to be successful in stimulating employment, industry, and agriculture. Reelected in 1936, Roosevelt unsuccessfully attempted to alter the judicial philosophy of the Supreme Court by adding new justices, but his attempt at "court packing" was unsuccessful.

With the outbreak of war in Europe in 1939, Roosevelt provided considerable military and economic support to Great Britain and the other allies. In 1940 he became the first American president to serve more than two terms, winning reelection against the Republican nominee, Wendell Willkie. After the Japanese bombing of Pearl Harbor in 1941, he led the country into war, being reelected for a fourth term in the White House in 1944. His participation in the *Teheran and *Yalta Conferences with Winston *Churchill and Joseph *Stalin helped to shape the strategic arrangement of the postwar world, but he died before the conclusion of the war. His wife, **(Anna) Eleanor Roosevelt** (1884–1962), was the niece of Theodore *Roosevelt, to whom Franklin himself was distantly related. She was a devoted advocate of human rights and educational causes and served as US ambassador to the United Nations (1945, 1949–52, 1961–62) and as chairperson of the UN Commission on Human Rights (1946–51).

FRANKLIN D. ROOSEVELT

Roosevelt, Theodore (1858–1919) US statesman; 26th president of the United States (1901–09). After spending time as a cattle rancher in North Dakota, Roosevelt entered politics, running unsuccessfully as the Republican candidate for mayor of New York City (1886) and later serving with distinction as US civil service commissioner (1889–95). As assistant secretary of the navy (1897–98) he helped to strengthen the nation's military preparedness and with the outbreak of the *Spanish-American War, he resigned from public office to found the 1st US Volunteer Cavalry, also known as the "Rough Riders." He gained national acclaim for his participation in the *Battle of San Juan Hill and after the war he was elected governor of New York. Roosevelt was elected vice president in 1900, and with the assassination of Pres. William *McKinley the following year, he succeeded to the presidency himself.

As president, Roosevelt introduced the *Square Deal program for social reform and advocated an active foreign policy characterized by his famous dictum, "Talk softly and carry a big stick." He established US control over the construction of the *Panama Canal (1903) and made the US the dominant force in the Western Hemisphere. In 1905 he was awarded the Nobel Peace Prize for his arbitration of the Russo-Japanese War. Roosevelt was elected president in 1904, but chose not to run again in 1908. Becoming increasingly opposed to the policies of his successor, William H. *Taft, Roosevelt contended for the 1912 Republican nomination, and failing to gain it, he campaigned unsuccessfully for president as the candidate of his own Bull Moose party.

root (algebra) **1.** One of the equal factors of a number. The square root is one of two equal factors; for example $\sqrt{9} = \pm 3$; the rth root of a number n is the number that when raised to the *r*th power gives *n*. **2.** The solution of an equation, i.e. the values of the variable that will satisfy the equation. *See* quadratic equation.

root (botany) The part of a □plant that provides anchorage and enables the uptake of water and nutrients from the soil. Roots contain vascular (conducting) tissue and just behind the tip is an area of root hairs, which increase the surface area for absorption. Some plants, such as the dandelion, have one main root with smaller branches—a tap root system; others, such as grasses, have a mass of similar-sized roots—a fibrous root system. Roots can act as food-storage organs, as in the carrot and turnip (tap roots); fibrous roots that become swollen with food are called tuberous roots, such as those of dahlias. Some roots grow in unusual positions, such as the aerial buttress roots of tropical trees, which act as supports.

Root, Elihu (1845–1937) US lawyer and statesman. A lawyer from 1867, he later became secretary of war (1899–1904) and secretary of state (1905–09). His achievements included reforms in the organization of the army, the improvement of relations with Latin America, and the Root-Takahira agreement with Japan (1908), committing the two nations to maintaining the status quo in the Pacific. A member of the Hague Tribunal (the Permanent Court of Arbitration), he received the Nobel Peace Prize in 1912.

root-mean-square value (*or* rms value) The square root of the arithmetic *average of the squares of a set of numbers; for example the rms of 2, 4, 5, 6, is $[(2^2 + 4^2 + 5^2 + 6^2)/4]^{1/2} = 4\frac{1}{2}$. The rms value is useful in continuous quantities, such as alternating electric current, in which the heating effect is proportional to the current squared. The rms value is therefore directly comparable to direct current.

ropes and cables Flexible lengths of material made from strands of natural *fibers (e.g. hemp, jute, sisal, manila), synthetic fibers (e.g. nylon, polypropylene), or wire. In natural-fiber ropes, the material is spun into yarn and then formed into strands, which are twisted around each other in an opposite direction to that of the yarn. For many purposes nylon and polypropylene ropes, made by a similar method, are replacing natural-fiber ropes. A hawser consists of three strands, a cable consists of three hawsers wound together, and a shroud-laid rope has a central strand with three or four strands wound around it. Wire ropes are made by a similar process: high-tensile steel wires are twisted together to form strands, which are then wound around each other to form the rope. In some cases the wires are preformed into helical strands to reduce internal stresses and are wound around a hemp core, which provides lubrication and flexibility.

Roquefort 43 59N 2 58E A village in SE France, in the Aveyron department. Roquefort is famous for the ewes' milk cheese named for it.

Roraima, Mount 5 14N 60 44W A mountain in South America, at the junction of the borders of Brazil, Guyana, and Venezuela. It is the highest peak in the Pacaraima Mountains. Height: 9219 ft (2810 m).

rorqual A small-headed fast-moving baleen *whale of the family *Balaenopteridae* (6 species). The common rorqual (*Balaenoptera physalus*), also called fin whale or razorback, grows up to 80 ft (25 m) long; it has a dark back, shading to white underneath, and a small dorsal fin that shows when it is blowing. Common rorquals are found in all oceans. *See also* blue whale; humpback whale; sei whale.

Rorschach test A psychological test intended to measure aspects of personality. Devised by the Swiss psychiatrist Hermann Rorschach (1884–1922), it consists of 10 inkblots in complex shapes. The way in which the subject describes these pictures gives the tester clues to his character. *See also* projection.

Rory O'Connor (*or* Roderic; ?1116–98) King of Connaught and last High King of Ireland. In 1171 he marched against *Dermot MacMurrough and his English allies but was defeated at Dublin. Later he was forced to recognize the overlordship of Henry II of England.

Rosa, Salvator (1615–73) Italian painter and etcher. Working in Naples, Rome (where he finally settled in 1649), and Florence (1640–49), he was also known as a poet, comic actor, and musician. His lasting reputation, however, rests on his wild and romantic landscapes.

Rosaceae A cosmopolitan family of trees, shrubs, and herbs (about 2000 species). Many are of economic value for their fruits, for example strawberries, raspberries, cherries, apricots, apples, and plums. Others are cultivated as ornamentals, including *Spiraea, Potentilla,* and roses.

Rosario 33 00S 60 40W The second largest city in Argentina, on the Río Paraná. It is an industrial and commercial center and the terminus of the pampas railroads. Industries include sugar refining and food processing. Its university was founded in 1968. Population (1991): 875,664.

rosary In the Roman Catholic Church, a religious devotion consisting of repeated prayers, particularly associated with the cult of the Virgin Mary. The recitation of a rosary is subdivided into 15 decades, each decade comprising an opening Paternoster, 10 Ave Marias, and a concluding Gloria. A subject of meditation, or Mystery, relating to the life of Christ or the Virgin is attached to each decade. By association the string of beads used to count the prayers is also called a rosary. The feast day established in 1716 in honor of the rosary is observed on Oct 7.

Roscelin (died c. 1125) French scholastic philosopher (*see* scholasticism). He was an early proponent of *nominalism, which he may even have originated. His philosophical belief that a being could have no parts led him to the Tritheist heresy, a deviant form of the doctrine of the Trinity. He was opposed by his famous pupil *Abelard.

Roscius, Quintus (d. 62 BC) Roman comic actor. He was praised by Cicero, and his name has been applied as an epithet to many outstanding actors of the modern theater.

Roscommon (Irish name: Ros Comáin) A county in the N Republic of Ireland, in Connacht. Predominantly low lying, it has many lakes and extensive bogs. Agriculture, especially cattle rearing, is the chief occupation. Area: 951 sq mi (2463 sq km). Population (1991): 51,876. County town: Roscommon.

rose A prickly shrub or climber of the genus *Rosa* (200–250 species), native to N temperate regions but widely cultivated.The leaves are compound, with leaflets arranged in pairs and small leafy stipules at the base of the leafstalk. The five-petaled flowers are usually white, yellow, pink, or red and the fruits are red, yellow, or black hips, rich in vitamin C, containing many seeds. Wild species include *dog rose and *sweet briar. Family: *Rosaceae.*

Modern hybrid roses—usually with double flowers—can be divided into several groups, the most important bedding varieties being the hybrid teas and floribundas. The former, derived from the tea rose (*R. odorata*), produce large shapely often fragrant blooms of good color. The floribundas bear clusters of flowers and are usually grown for their color effect rather than for the beauty of individual blooms. The climbers and ramblers are suitable for covering walls, fences, etc. Climbers produce thick basal stems infrequently; they include climbing forms

of hybrid teas and floribundas as well as climbing species (such as *R. banksiae*).
Ramblers, which produce many slender stems from the base each year, include
the wichuraiana group of hybrids.

Rosebery, Archibald Philip Primrose, 5th Earl of (1847–1929) British
statesman; Liberal prime minister (1894–95). He was foreign secretary (1886,
1892–94) under Gladstone, whom he replaced as prime minister. He resigned
the Liberal leadership in 1896.

rosella A brightly colored *parakeet belonging to a genus (*Platycercus*;
7 species) occurring in Australia and New Zealand; 7 in (18 cm) long, rosellas
have a long broad tail, which is usually blue or green edged with white, black
shoulders, and distinctive face and throat markings. They are largely ground-
dwelling.

roselle An annual or perennial fibrous plant, *Hibiscus sabdariffa,* cultivated
in tropical regions for its stem fibers, which are used for sacking and twine, and
for its edible stalks, leaves, and flower parts. It grows up to 16 ft (5 m) high and
bears solitary white or yellow flowers in the leaf axils. Family: *Malvaceae.*

rosemary An evergreen shrub, *Rosmarinus officinalis,* native to the Mediter-
ranean region and W Asia. Up to 7 ft (2 m) high, it has bluish flowers and small
needle-like aromatic leaves, up to 2 in (5 cm) long. It is widely cultivated for its
oil, which is distilled from the flowering tops and used in toiletries; for its
leaves, used as a culinary herb; and for ornament. Family: *Labiatae.*

Rosenberg, Julius (1918–53) US spy, who with his wife **Ethel Rosenberg**
(1915–53) was executed for espionage activities. They were accused of gaining
information about nuclear weapons from Ethel's brother and passing it on via a
courier to the Russian vice consul in New York. Other members of the espi-
onage ring were sentenced to long terms of imprisonment. The Rosenbergs pro-
claimed their innocence. The trial was extremely controversial, and many be-
lieved that the evidence was insufficient, the punishment too severe, and the
verdict was influenced by Cold War hysteria.

rose of Jericho A perennial herb, *Anastatica hierochuntica,* also called res-
urrection plant, native to W Asia. During the dry season the leaves are shed and
the branches curve inward so that the whole plant forms a wickerwork-like ball
that is blown by the wind. When moistened, the plant regains its shape and pro-
duces tiny white flowers. Family: *Cruciferae.*

rose of Sharon. *See* Hibiscus; St John's wort.

Roses, Wars of the (1455–85) The civil wars between the Houses of *Lan-
caster (the red rose) and *York (the white rose) for possession of the English
crown, which both claimed by right of descent from Edward III. The Lancastrian
Henry VI's incompetent rule resulted in factional struggles led by the Lancas-
trian Beauforts and Richard Plantagenet, duke of *York, and the earl of *War-
wick (the Kingmaker). Open warfare broke out in 1455. York was killed in 1460
and his son seized the crown in 1461, becoming Edward IV, and crushed the
Lancastrians. In 1470–71 Henry VI was briefly restored by disaffected Yorkists
but Edward returned after his victory at *Tewkesbury and ruled until 1483. He
was succeeded by his brother Richard III, whose reign ended with his defeat by
Henry (VII) at Bosworth (1485). The remaining Yorkists were finally overcome
at Stoke in 1487.

Rosetta Stone An inscribed stone slab discovered (1799) at Rosetta (Arabic
name: Rashid), near Alexandria (Egypt). It carries a decree (196 BC) of Ptolemy
V Epiphanes (reigned 205–180) in two languages and three scripts: Egyptian
*hieroglyphic and *demotic, and Greek. The repetition of Ptolemy's name in the

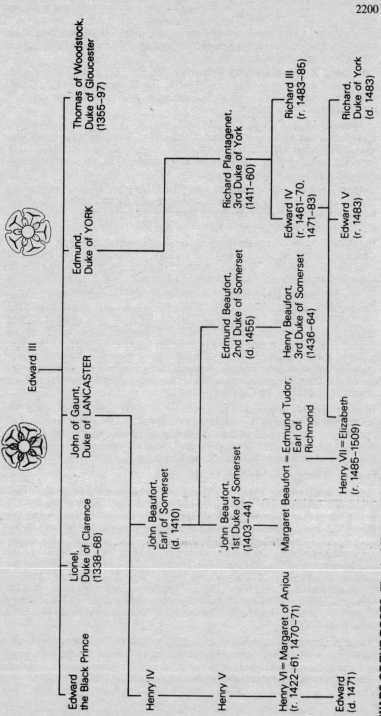

WARS OF THE ROSES *The rival Houses of Lancaster and York in England.*

different scripts gave Thomas *Young the clue to deciphering hieroglyphs; his work was continued by *Champollion.

rose window A decorative circular window in a medieval church. Rose windows, which were probably inspired by Oriental models, had radiating tracery, usually glazed with *stained glass, and reached their apogee in 13th-century French *gothic architecture, although examples are known throughout W Europe.

rosewood An attractive hardwood, usually dark reddish and often rose-scented, derived from several tropical evergreen trees of the genus *Dalbergia* (family *Leguminosae*). These include Brazilian rosewood, or blackwood (*D. nigra*), used for veneers and cabinetwork; Honduras rosewood (*D. stevensoni*), used for musical instruments; and East Indian rosewood (*D. latifolia*), used mostly for small articles. Decreasing supplies have restricted their use.

Rosh Hashana (Hebrew: head of the year) The Jewish New Year festival, celebrated in September or October. Of biblical origin, it is regarded as a time of penitence and preparation for *Yom Kippur. A ram's horn (*shofar*) is blown in the synagogue.

Rosicrucianism An esoteric movement for spiritual renewal that originated in Protestant Germany in the early 17th century and spread across Europe. Its manifesto traces its source to a fictitious brotherhood founded by a certain Christian Rosenkreuz in 1484. The philosophical program propounded by its mainly anonymous adherents was a blend of theosophical and occult traditions, including *alchemy, *Hermeticism, and *Neoplatonism. *See also* freemasonry.

rosin (*or* colophony) A yellowish *resin obtained as a residue from the distillation of *turpentine. It is used in varnishes, soaps, soldering *flux, and to rub on violin bows.

Roskilde 55 39N 12 07E A seaport in Denmark, in Sjaelland. It was the Danish capital until 1443, and most of Denmark's kings are buried in the 13th-century cathedral. A university was established in 1970. Its industries include tanning, meat canning, paper making, and agricultural engineering. Population: 50,690.

Ross, Betsy (Elizabeth Griscom R.; 1752–1836) US patriot. After her husband John Ross's death in 1776, she continued to run his upholstery shop. According to popular legend, a committee headed by George *Washington commissioned her to fashion, from a rough drawing, the "Stars and Stripes," which was then designated the official flag of the US.

Ross, Sir James Clark (1800–62) British explorer. He accompanied (1819–27) Sir William *Parry on his Arctic expeditions and (1829–31) his uncle Sir John Ross (1777–1856), discovering the North Magnetic Pole (1831). He later (1839–43) explored the Antarctic, discovering the sea named for him.

Ross, Sir Ronald (1857–1932) British bacteriologist, who confirmed the theory of Sir Patrick Manson (1844–1922) that mosquitoes transmit malaria. While working in India, Ross discovered malaria parasites in the guts of *Anopheles* mosquitoes. Ross received the 1902 Nobel Prize for his work.

Ross Dependency An area in Antarctica claimed by New Zealand (since 1923), lying between longitudes 160°E and 150°W and including the Ross Sea and islands S of latitude 60°S. Area: about 160,000 sq mi (414,400 sq km).

Rosse, William Parsons, 3rd Earl of (1800–67) Irish astronomer, who constructed a large 72-inch (183 cm) reflecting telescope. In 1848 he used it to study one of the blurred objects listed by *Messier and named it the Crab Nebula, because of its shape. He also discovered the first spiral galaxy in 1845.

Rossellini, Roberto (1906–77) Italian film director. The neorealist style of *Rome, Open City* (1945), which included documentary film shot during the German occupation of Rome, greatly influenced postwar Italian cinema. His other films include *Paisà* (1946), also concerned with wartime Italy, *L'Amore* (1948), and *India* (1958), a documentary film. He subsequently worked mostly in television and the theater.

Rossetti, Dante Gabriel (Gabriel Charles Dante R.; 1828–82) British painter and poet. Rebelling against conventional instruction, in 1848 Rossetti joined with John Everett *Millais, William Holman *Hunt, and other artists to found the *Pre-Raphaelite Brotherhood. He founded the short-lived Pre-Raphaelite journal *The Germ* (1850–51), in which he began publishing his own verse. He later published several volumes of poetry and translations, including *Poems* (1870) and *Ballads and Sonnets* (1881). During his final years he lived virtually as a recluse, suffering from ill health. His sister **Christina Georgina Rossetti** (1830–74), a poet, was deeply influenced by the *Oxford Movement. *Goblin Market and Other Poems* (1862), her first published volume, gave literary expression to Pre-Raphaelite ideals and contains perhaps her best work.

Rossini, Gioacchino Antonio (1792–1868) Italian composer. His father was a trumpeter and his mother an opera singer. He studied at Bologna and wrote 36 highly successful operas, including *Tancredi* (1813), *The Italian Girl in Algiers* (1813), *The Barber of Seville* (1816), *La Cenerentola (Cinderella)* and *The Thieving Magpie* (both 1817), and *William Tell* (1829). At the age of 37 he gave up serious composition, although he did write a light-hearted *Petite Messe solennelle* (1863) and a number of little pieces, collectively entitled "Sins of My Old Age." He invented a number of recipes, including Tournedos Rossini.

Ross Island 77 40S 168 00E A volcanic island in the W Ross Sea, at the edge of the **Ross Ice Shelf**, a vast mass of permanent ice. Mount Erebus is situated here.

Ross Sea A large inlet of the S Pacific Ocean, in the Antarctic continent between Victoria Land and Byrd Land. Its S section is covered by the Ross Ice Shelf.

Rostand, Edmond (1868–1918) French dramatist. He gained international success with *Cyrano de Bergerac* (1897), a romantic comedy about a nobleman with an oversize nose. Sarah Bernhardt acted in many of his plays, notably *L'Aiglon* (1900).

Rostock 54 03N 12 07E A city and Baltic port in N Germany, on the Warnow River. Once an important Hanseatic port, its fine medieval buildings have been restored following damage during World War II. Its university was established in 1419. The main industries are ship building and fisheries. Population (1990 est): 250,000.

Rostov-na-Donu 47 15N 39 45E A port in S Russia, on the Don River near its mouth on the Sea of Azov. It produces agricultural machinery and has ship-repairing, food-processing, and textile industries. Its importance owes much to its position on the route from the W to the Caucasus. Population (1991 est): 1,025,000.

Rostropovich, Mstislav (1927–) Russian cellist. He left the Soviet Union in 1975. He is also a conductor, notably of opera, and as a pianist accompanies his wife, soprano Galina Vishnevskaya. Many composers, including Prokofiev, Britten, and Shostakovich, have written cello works for him.

Roth, Philip (1933–) US novelist. Middle-class Jewish themes predominated in his early works including *Goodbye, Columbus* (1959) and *Portnoy's*

2203 **Rouault, Georges**

Complaint (1969), his most popular success. In later novels, such as *The Great American Novel* (1973), *My Life as a Man* (1974), *The Ghost Writer* (1979), *Zukerman Unbound* (1981), *The Anatomy Lesson* (1983), *Counterlife* (1987), and *Deception* (1990), the targets of his satire are more various. *The Facts* (1988) and *Patrimony* (1991) are autobiographical.

Rotherham 53 26N 1 20W A town in N England, in South Yorkshire on the River Don. Rotherham has iron and steel, brassware, machinery, and glass industries and coal is mined locally. Population (1981): 81,988.

Rothko, Mark (Marcus Rothkovitch; 1903–70) Russian-born painter, who emigrated to the US in 1913. In the late 1940s, with Barnett Newman and Clyfford Still, he pioneered color-field painting (an abstract style using only color) on mural-size canvases covered with horizontal bands of hazy color.

Rothschild, Mayer Amschel (1744–1812) German merchant and banker, whose business in Frankfurt prospered during the Napoleonic Wars, making loans to the various combatants and trading in high-demand goods such as arms, wheat, and cotton. He was succeeded in Frankfurt by his son **Amschel Mayer Rothschild** (1773–1855). Four other sons established branches of the firm abroad. **Salomon Mayer Rothschild** (1774–1855) went to Vienna, **Nathan Mayer Rothschild** (1777–1836), to London, **Karl Mayer Rothschild** (1788–1855), to Naples, and **James Rothschild** (Jakob R.; 1792–1868), to Paris. In London, Nathan's son **Lionel Nathan Rothschild** (1808–79) was a member of Parliament (1858–68, 1869–79) as was (1865–85) his grandson **Nathan Mayer, 1st Baron Rothschild** (1840–1915).

rotifer A tiny invertebrate animal belonging to the phylum *Rotifera* (about 2000 species), also called wheel animalcule, found mainly in fresh water. Rotifers vary in shape from spherical to wormlike and range between 0.004–0.02 in (0.1–0.5 mm) in length. Each has a ring of cilia (corona) around the mouth, beating in a wheel-like manner, for wafting food particles into the mouth and providing a means of locomotion in active species.

Rotterdam 51 55N 4 29E The chief port and second largest city in the Netherlands, in South Holland province on the New Meuse River. It became important during the 19th century, mainly with the opening of the 12 mi (35 km) long Nieuwe Waterweg (New Waterway) in 1872 linking it to the North Sea. During World War II the city center was destroyed; this has since been rebuilt with a subway system. Its notable buildings include the restored Groote Kerk (Great Church). The Erasmus University of Rotterdam was founded in 1973. The largest Atlantic port in Europe, Rotterdam handles considerable export trade from Germany, including Ruhr coal. Its dockyards extend W along the Nieuwe Waterweg and include Europoort, on the North Sea. Begun in 1958, Europoort's huge facilities handle chiefly oil importing and refining. Rotterdam's industries include petroleum refining, ship building, brewing, distilling, and engineering. Population (1991 est): 582,266.

rottweiler A breed of working dog developed originally in Rottweil, Germany, as a guard dog and cattle drovers' dog. It is stockily built, having a broad round body, a strong neck, and a large head with a deep muzzle. The coarse short coat is black with tan markings. Height: 24.8–26.8 in (63–68 cm) (dogs); 22.8–24.8 in (58–63 cm) (bitches).

Rouault, Georges (Henri) (1871–1958) French artist. A major 20th-century religious artist, he was a largely independent figure, except for a brief and loose association with *fauvism. His favorite themes were clowns (sometimes modeled on himself or Christ) and prostitutes, expressing his sympathy with social outcasts. He was influenced by his early training as a stained-glass maker and was the favorite pupil of Gustave *Moreau. Until 1918 he worked chiefly in gouache and watercolor, using rich dark colors and heavy outlines. As a graphic artist his main achievement was his series of etchings (1916–27) entitled *Miserere* and *Guerre*.

Roubaix 50 42N 3 10E A city in N France, in the Nord department on the Roubaix Canal. Famous for its cloth since the 15th century, it is (together with Tourcoing) the center of the country's woolen industry. Population: 109,797.

Roubillac, Louis François (*or* L. F. Roubiliac; 1695–1762) French sculptor. He fled (1727) for religious reasons to England, where his statue of Handel (1738) in London, secured his reputation. His portrait bust of Alexander Pope and full-length statue of Sir Isaac Newton are also outstanding. After a visit to Rome (1752) he executed the Nightingale and Hargreaves monuments in Westminster Abbey, reflecting some of Bernini's dramatic power and skill in composition.

Rouen (Latin name: Rotomagus) 49 26N 1 05E A city and port in NW France, the capital of the Seine-Maritimes department on the Seine River. The ancient capital of Normandy, it was here that Joan of Arc was tried and burned in 1431. Many of its notable buildings, including the cathedral (13th–16th centuries), survived the damage of World War II. Its university was established in 1966. The main industries are textiles, petrochemicals, engineering, paper, and electronics. Population (1990): 105,470.

Rouget de l'Isle, Claude Joseph (1760–1836) French military engineer and composer. He composed the *Marseillaise in 1792 while stationed in Strasbourg at the outbreak of war between France and Austria. He was later imprisoned for a year for refusing to take the oath against the crown; he was reinstated in 1795 and published a volume of 50 *Chants français* in 1825.

Roulers. *See* Roeselare.

roulette A game of chance played in most casinos. Of obscure origins, it was developed in the Monte Carlo casino. The principle of the game is that a small white ball is thrown in a clockwise direction into a horizontal wheel spinning in a counterclockwise direction. The rim of the wheel is divided into numbered compartments. Players bet (against the bank) on the number of the compartment into which they predict the ball will come to rest. There are two main varieties of roulette: French roulette and American roulette. In the French game there are 37 numbered compartments on the wheel (0–36), and the color of the betting chips denotes their denomination. In the American game there are 38 compartments (00, 0–36), and each player has a distinctively colored set of chips. In both games bets are placed on green baize tables on which the numbers of the compartments are laid out in groups of three. In the French game a successful bet on a single number pays 35–1 (and the stake is returned), giving the bank an advantage of 2.7%. In the American game, the bank's advantage is increased to 5.4%. There are also three types of even-money bets that the player can make: red or black, even or odd numbers, and 1–18 or 19–36. The red or black bet arises because alternate numbers on the wheel are colored red and black. Between the extremes of even money odds and 35–1, the player can make virtually any odds he chooses by backing different groups of numbers.

rounders A nine-a-side bat-and-ball field game, which is probably the prototype of *baseball. The two teams take turns at batting and fielding and a match consists of two innings per team. The hard ball is delivered underarm to each batsman in turn until all are out. The batsmen try to score rounders by hitting it and running around the four bases without being caught or run out. The batsman's square and first base, first base and second base, and second base and third base are 39.5 ft (12 m) apart, but third and fourth base are only 28 ft (8.5 m) apart.

Roundheads The parliamentary party during the English *Civil War. The name referred originally to the short haircuts of the apprentices who demonstrated against the king at Westminster in 1640. It was later applied to all parliamentarians and referred to their drab appearance in contrast to the more flamboyant *Cavaliers.

Round Table Conference (1930–32) Three meetings held in London to discuss a form of government acceptable to India. The meetings were attended by representatives of the British Government and of India's major political parties and all its states. Mahatma *Gandhi, representing the *Indian National Congress, boycotted the first meeting. The result of the Conference was the *Government of India Act of 1935.

roundworm. *See* nematode.

Rousseau, Henri (1844–1910) French painter. Although known as Le Douanier (customs official) he was really a toll collector and as a painter was self-taught. From 1886 he exhibited at the Salon des Indépendants but his work, resembling folk art in technique (*see* primitivism), was ridiculed. After 1894, when he exhibited *War* (Louvre), followed by the *Sleeping Gypsy* (1897; New York), he received serious attention, particularly in the 20th century from *Picasso and the poet *Apollinaire. The childlike quality of his vision and the hallucinatory atmosphere in his portraits and jungle landscapes influenced a number of 20th-century painters, particularly several of the surrealists.

Rousseau, Jean Jacques (1712–78) French philosopher and writer. Through his acquaintance with *Diderot, Rousseau joined the *Encyclopedists. In the *Discourse on the Origin and Foundations of Inequality among Men* (1754) he argued that man's perfect nature is spoiled by corrupt society. *Emile* (1762), a novel on education, expanded his views on ideal unfallen human nature. Rousseau's political influence was significant and many of the ideas embodied in such works as *Du contrat social* (1762) were taken up by revolutionaries. His fine style and romantic outlook inspired Shelley, Byron, and Wordsworth. His continued belief in a somewhat emasculated Christianity was an effective counterbalance to the atheism of Voltaire and the rationalists.

Rousseau, (Pierre Étienne) Théodore (1812–67) French romantic landscape painter and leader of the *Barbizon school. His melancholy scenes were influenced by *Constable and *Bonington but his practice of open-air painting anticipated *impressionism. After permanently settling in Barbizon in the 1840s he received official recognition of his work.

Roussel, Albert (1869–1937) French composer. Serving in the French navy until 1894, he sailed to Indochina in 1890. Eastern culture became one of his main sources of inspiration although his later works are predominantly neoclassical. His compositions include the ballet *The Spider's Banquet* (1912), the opera-ballet *Pâdmâvatî* (1914–18), four symphonies, a piano concerto, chamber music, and songs.

Roussel, Raymond (1877–1933) French writer and dramatist. His writings, constructed around elaborately contrived puzzles and linguistic games, include the prose works *Impressions d'Afrique* (1910) and *Locus Solus* (1914) and three plays the first productions of which caused scandals. He is regarded as a precursor of both surrealism and the *nouveau roman*.

Roux, Pierre Paul Emile (1853–1933) French bacteriologist, who, following the discovery of the Klebs-Loeffler (diphtheria) bacillus in 1884, showed that the disease symptoms were caused by a toxin released by the bacilli. Roux helped develop an antitoxin serum for diphtheria and—working with *Pasteur—discovered a vaccine for anthrax using attenuated bacilli. Roux was director of the Pasteur Institute (1904–33).

rove beetle A beetle belonging to the worldwide family *Staphylinidae* (about 27,000 species), having short wing cases covering the folded hindwings. Rove beetles range from 0.03–1.26 in (0.7–32 mm) in length although most are small. They are commonly found near dung and dead animal matter, preying upon the associated insects and mites. Some species, however, live in ant and termite nests. *See also* devil's coach horse.

rowan. *See* mountain ash.

rowing A sport using narrow light boats (*or* shells) propelled by two, four, or eight people and often steered by a coxswain, usually on a river or lake. The oarsmen sit in line in sliding seats, bracing their feet against stretchers. Each controls one oar set in a rowlock, the oars being arranged on alternate sides. **Sculling** is a form of rowing for one, two, or four people per boat, each person controlling two oars. The governing body is the Fédération internationale des Sociétés d'Aviron.

Rowley, Thomas (c. 1585–c. 1642) English dramatist and actor. He collaborated with many other Jacobean dramatists, notably with John Ford and Thomas Dekker on *The Witch of Edmonton* (1621) and with Thomas Middleton on *The Changeling* (1622). His own plays were mostly comedies.

Rowse, A(lfred) L(eslie) (1903–) British historian and literary critic. Rowse is best known for his books on the Tudor period, including *The Elizabethan Renaissance* (1971), and on Shakespeare, whose Dark Lady of the sonnets he controversially identified as Emilia Lanier, daughter of a court musician.

Royal Academy An art society in London, England that holds annual summer exhibitions of contemporary British art, as well as exhibitions of modern artists and the old masters. Founded in 1768, it originally had an important teaching function.

Royal Air Force (RAF) A British armed service formed in 1918 by the amalgamation of the Royal Flying Corps (1912) with the Royal Naval Air Service (1914).

royal antelope The world's smallest antelope, *Neotragus pygmaeus,* of West African forests; 10–12 in (25–30 cm) high at the shoulder, it is red-brown with white underparts; males have short spiky horns. They are nocturnal and usually occur singly or in pairs.

Royal Ballet The leading British ballet company and school. Based at the Royal Opera House since 1946, it was known as the Sadler's Wells Ballet until 1956, when it was granted a royal charter. It was founded by Dame Ninette de Valois in 1931.

Royal Canadian Mounted Police (*or* Mounties) Canadian police force. Founded in 1873 as the North West Mounted Police to keep order in the Canadian west, it has become famous for the efficiency and discipline of its members, dressed in their distinctive scarlet tunics, blue breeches, and wide-brimmed hats.

royal fern. *See* Osmunda.

Royal Greenwich Observatory An observatory founded in 1675 by Charles II at Greenwich, London, in a building designed by Sir Christopher Wren. The meridian through Greenwich (0°) was internationally adopted as the prime meridian in 1884 and became the basis of Greenwich Mean Time.

royal jelly A thick white mixture of proteins, carbohydrates, minerals, and vitamins that is secreted by worker bees and fed to the larvae. Larvae destined to become queens are fed throughout their development on royal jelly. *See also* honeybee.

Royal Society The oldest and most important scientific society in the UK. It originated in 1645 with a group of thinkers, including Robert *Boyle and John Wilkins, who met to discuss the "new or experimental philosophy" popularized by Francis Bacon. It was incorporated by royal charter from Charles II in 1662. With the presidency (1703–27) of Isaac *Newton, the Royal Society achieved great standing and financial security.

Royce, Sir (Frederick) Henry (1863–1933) British automobile manufacturer, who founded (1906), with Charles *Rolls, Rolls-Royce Ltd. In 1884 Royce opened an engineering business in Manchester and in 1904 began to build cars, which much impressed Rolls and led to the merger of their businesses.

Royce, Josiah (1855–1916) US philosopher. As an idealist, influenced by *Hegel, Royce believed that human thought was part of the cosmic order. Governing the natural order was a higher moral order, which it was man's duty to uphold. His numerous books include the *Spirit of Modern Philosophy* (1892).

RR Lyrae stars A class of short-period pulsating *variable stars that are very old giant stars found principally in globular *star clusters, all with about the same mean *luminosity.

Ruapehu, Mount 39 18S 175 36E An active volcano in New Zealand, the highest peak in North Island in Tongariro National Park. The last eruption was in 1945–46. Height: 9175 ft (2797 m).

Rub' al-Khali The S part of the Arabian Desert, mainly in Saudi Arabia. It is low lying and constitutes the largest continuous area of sand in the world. Area: about 308,815 sq mi (800,000 sq km).

rubber A synthetic or natural organic polymer that is elastic and tough. The name comes from its ability to erase pencil marks. **Natural rubber**, which consists mainly of polyisoprene—$(CH_2CH:C.CH_3:CH_2)_n$—is made from latex, a milky fluid collected from the trunk of the *rubber tree, which is specially cultivated for this purpose in Malaysia, Thailand, Indonesia, and other parts of SE Asia. The rubber is coagulated from latex (using acids) and pressed into sheets. *Vulcanization increases its durability.

Synthetic rubbers are made from petrochemicals (*see* oil). Styrene-butadiene rubber (SBR), now the commonest synthetic rubber, was introduced during World War II. It is made by the emulsion process, in which styrene and butadiene are mixed in soapy water containing a catalyst. Different proportions of ingredients and temperatures vary the properties. SBR is used in tires, often mixed with natural rubber to improve its resilience. Butyl rubber is made by *polymerization of isobutylene. It is used for inner tubes. Neoprene (polychloropene) is used for protective clothing and electrical insulation. Nitrile polyisoprene and the newer polyurethane and silicone rubbers are also used for specialist applications.

rubber plant A tree, *Ficus elastica,* native to India and Malaysia, where it grows to a height of 115 ft (35 m) in forests. Its latex is the source of Assam or India rubber. It is also a popular house plant, grown in pots or tubs for its oblong shiny leathery leaves. Family: *Moraceae.*

rubber tree A Brazilian tree, *Hevea brasiliensis,* also called Pará rubber, widely cultivated in humid tropical regions, especially SE Asia. Its milky latex

is the chief source of natural *rubber, which is obtained by making sloping cuts
in the trunk. Trees yield latex from about the sixth year and reach full height,
about 65 ft (20 m), in eight years. *H. guianensis* and *H. pauciflora* are also
sometimes cultivated for rubber. In 1876, some seeds of South American rubber
trees were shipped to England. Seedlings were subsequently exported to Ceylon
and SE Asia to form the basis of the rubber industry. Family: *Euphorbiaceae*.

rubella. *See* German measles.

Rubens, Peter Paul (1577–1640) Flemish painter, who was born in Seigen
(Westphalia) but lived chiefly in Antwerp. The greatest of the *baroque artists
and one of the finest European colorists, Rubens first worked for the Mantuan
court in Italy (1600–08). Returning to Antwerp, he became court painter to the
Archduke Albert and painted his first major works, *The Raising of the Cross* and
Descent from the Cross. Many visits abroad, sometimes as a diplomatic envoy,
and commissions followed, including a cycle for Marie de' Medici commemo-
rating her marriage to Henry IV and the ceiling of the Banqueting House,
Whitehall, for England's Charles I. Aided by a large workshop, he painted
mythological, historical, and religious subjects but his most personal works are
his portraits of his family, notably *Helena Fourment with a Fur Cloak* and such
landscapes as *The Château de Steen*. His Antwerp house, now a museum, con-
tains his fine art collection and furnishings.

Rubicon A stream in N central Italy flowing E into the Adriatic Sea, which
formed the boundary between Italy and Cisalpine Gaul in the time of the Roman
Republic. In 49 BC Julius Caesar, then provincial commander in Gaul, precipi-
tated the civil war with Pompey by leading his army across the Rubicon into
Italy. This action was tantamount to a declaration of war because it was forbid-
den for a general to lead an army outside the province in which he had been
given command. Hence "crossing the Rubicon" has come to mean taking an ir-
revocable step.

rubidium (Rb) A highly electropositive alkali metal, discovered spectroscopi-
cally by R. W. Bunsen and G. R. Kirchhoff in 1861. The element is soft and sil-
very-white. It ignites spontaneously in air and reacts violently with water, liber-
ating hydrogen and then setting fire to it. The isotope ^{87}Rb is radioactive with a
half-life of 5×10^{11} years and is used in *rubidium-strontium dating. Rubidium
forms ionic salts and four oxides (Rb_2O, Rb_2O_2, Rb_2O_3, RbO_2). At no 37; at wt
85.47; mp 102.07°F (38.89°C); bp 1271.64°F (688°C).

rubidium-strontium dating A method of *radiometric dating, used mainly
for rocks, fossils, etc. It utilizes the fact that naturally occurring rubidium con-
tains about 28% of the radioactive isotope rubidium 87, which undergoes *beta
decay to strontium 87 with a *half-life of 5×10^{11} years. Thus by measuring the
ratio of rubidium 87 to strontium 87 in the sample, its age may be estimated.
The method can date items several thousands of millions of years old.

Rubinstein, Anton (1829–94) Russian pianist and composer. He started per-
forming abroad at the age of 12 and founded the St Petersburg conservatory in
1862. His works include 20 operas, 6 symphonies, 5 piano concertos, 2 cello
concertos, and numerous other piano pieces.

Rubinstein, Artur (1888–1982) Polish-born US pianist. He studied in War-
saw and Berlin and soon acquired a worldwide reputation, particularly as a
performer of Chopin. He wrote two autobiographical volumes, *My Young Years*
(1974) and *My Many Years* (1980).

Rublyov, Andrey (*or* A. Rublev; c. 1370–1430) A leading Russian icon
painter. He sometimes collaborated with the Greek painter Theophanes and late
in life became a monk. In his masterpiece *The Old Testament Trinity* (Tretyakov

Gallery, Moscow) the influence of *Byzantine art is modified by a distinctive gracefulness.

RUBENS Le Chapeau de Paille *(c. 1622–25), one of his noted portraits.*

Rubus A genus of prickly perennial herbs and shrubs (225 species), found worldwide, mainly in N temperate regions. Many species, including the *blackberry, *loganberry, and *raspberry, are grown for their juicy edible fruits (each fruit is a cluster of small berries). Family: *Rosaceae.*

ruby A red transparent variety of *corundum, the color being due to traces of chromium. It is used as a gemstone and in lasers, watches, and other precision instruments. Many fine rubies come from Mogok in Myanmar, where they occur in metamorphic limestones with other precious and semiprecious stones. Prior to the 14th century rubies were called carbuncles. Birthstone for July.

Ruda Śląska 51 10N 16 39E A city in SW Poland. The first coal mine in Poland was opened there (1751). Population (1992 est): 171,400.

Rudbeckia. *See* black-eyed Susan.

rudd

2210

rudd A game fish, *Scardinius erythrophthalmus,* found among vegetation in fresh waters of Europe and W Asia. It has a stout body, 14–18 in (35–40 cm) long, colored golden- or olive-brown above and silvery white below, deep-red fins, and golden eyes.

Rudolf, Lake. *See* Turkana, Lake.

Rudolph (1858–89) Archduke of Austria. His liberal views brought him into conflict with his father Emperor Franz Josef. He and his mistress Baroness Marie Vetsera were found dead at his hunting lodge of Mayerling, having apparently committed suicide.

Rudolph I (1218–91) The first *Hapsburg Holy Roman Emperor (1273–91). His conquests in central Europe—Austria, Styria, Carinthia, and Carniola—formed the nucleus of future Hapsburg territorial power.

Rudolph II (1552–1612) Holy Roman Emperor (1576–1612). A dilatory ruler, he was forced to relinquish his powers in Hungary (1608) and Bohemia (1611) to his brother *Matthias.

rue An evergreen shrub, *Ruta graveolens,* also known as herb of grace, native to S Europe. Growing up to 35 in (90 cm) high, it has fleshy blue-green leaves and terminal clusters of yellow flowers. The leaves yield a bitter oil, once used as a spice and in medicines. Family: *Rutaceae.*

ruff An Old World *sandpiper, *Philomachus pugnax,* that breeds in coastal wetlands of N Eurasia and winters on mudflats of South Africa and S Asia. The female (called a reeve) is 10 in (25 cm) long and has a gray-brown plumage; the larger male has a double crest and a multicolored collar in the breeding season.

Ruffin, Edmund (1794–1865) US agriculturalist, publisher, and slavery supporter. He worked with revitalization of soil through fertilization, the addition of calcium carbonate, and crop rotation and promoted his findings through his journal, *The Farmer's Register* (1833–42). At the outbreak of the Civil War he was chosen to fire the first shot on Fort Sumter (1861). He committed suicide after the war.

Rugby 52 23N 1 15W A city in England, in the Midlands, in Warwickshire. According to tradition, the game of rugby football originated there in 1823 at the famous school (1567), which was described in *Tom Brown's Schooldays.* Rugby's industries include engineering and cement. Population (1981): 59,564.

Rügen A German island in the Baltic Sea, 1.5 mi (2.5 km) off Stralsund, to which it is connected by a road and rail causeway. Area: 358 sq mi (926 sq km).

Ruggles, Carl (1876–1971) US composer. His works, although few, had considerable influence; they are generally dissonant and strident and include *Angels* (1939) for brass or strings and the orchestral works *Sun-Treader* (1932) and *Men and Mountains* (1924–36). He devoted the last years of his life to painting.

Ruhr River A river in Germany, rising in the Sauerland and flowing NW and W past Essen to join the Rhine River at Duisburg. The Ruhr Valley (German name: Ruhrgebiet) is the center of the German iron and steel industry. Length: 146 mi (235 km).

Ruisdael, Jacob van (?1628–82) The greatest of Dutch landscape painters. Born in Haarlem, he studied under his father and probably also under his uncle, the landscape painter **Salomon van Ruysdael** (c. 1600–70). His baroque compositions, regularly framed by fantastic trees, are noted for their dramatic contrasts of light and shade. *The Jewish Cemetery* (c. 1660) is a striking evocation of human mortality.

Ruiz, Juan (c. 1283–c. 1350) Spanish poet. Nothing is known of his life apart from the fact that he was archpriest of Hita. His *Libro de buen amor* (1330) consists of a series of love stories interspersed with ironic didactic digressions.

rum A liquor distilled from molasses derived from sugarcane. Rum is colorless and is used in mixed drinks, especially punches, or with soda water, fruit juice, or soft drinks. Better-quality rums are aged in oak casks for several years. It is produced wherever sugarcane is grown, predominantly in the Caribbean region but also in the US.

Rumania. *See* Romania, Republic of.

Rumelia The Balkan possessions of the Ottoman Empire from the 14th to 19th centuries. The Congress of *Berlin (1878) divided Rumelia into the state of Bulgaria under Ottoman suzerainty, the autonomous province of Eastern Rumelia, and the provinces of Edirne, Salonica, and Monastir. Eastern Rumelia was annexed by Bulgaria in 1885 and Monastir and Salonica were ceded to Serbia and Greece respectively in 1913.

Rumford, Benjamin Thompson, Count (1753–1814) American-born scientist, who spied for the British in the American Revolution and was forced to flee to England in 1776. In England he carried out scientific research in ballistics and the theory of heat. Suspected of spying for the French, he left England in 1785 for Paris and then Bavaria, where he worked as an administrator for the elector, Karl Theodor (1724–99), who made him a count of the Holy Roman Empire in 1791. In 1795 he returned to England, where he helped to demolish the caloric theory and found the *Royal Institution (1799).

ruminant A hoofed mammal belonging to the suborder *Ruminantia* (about 175 species), which includes deer, cattle, antelopes, sheep, and goats. Ruminants eat grass, leaves, and other vegetation and are characterized by possession of a four-chambered stomach. The largest chamber (rumen) contains bacteria and protozoa, which ferment the stomach contents and enable the animal to digest and utilize its food efficiently. Ruminants regurgitate their food periodically to "chew the cud," which helps to break up the plant cell walls.

rummy games Various related card games, of which rummy is the basic form. Its object is to form melds (sets or sequences) composed of three or four cards of the same rank (such as four jacks) or sequences of three or more cards of the same suit (such as seven, eight, nine, and 10 of diamonds). In each turn a player takes a card from the pack and discards one. The first player to dispose of his cards wins, scoring points according to the cards left in his opponents' hands. In **gin rummy** (for two players) the object is to reach a certain score before one's opponent. No melds are laid down until a player's unmatched cards make a total of 10 or less, when the player lays his whole hand down. It is a "gin" if he has no unmatched cards. **Canasta** itself has several variants but is usually a partnership game for four players. Two packs are used; the jokers and all the twos are "wild." The winners are the first to score 5000 by making melds and canastas (a meld of seven or more cards of the same value).

Rump Parliament. *See* Long Parliament.

Runcie, Robert Alexander Kennedy (1921–) British churchman; archbishop of Canterbury (1980–91).

Runcorn 53 20N 2 44W A city in NW England, on the Mersey River and Manchester Ship Canal. It has chemical and brewing industries. Population (1981): 64,106.

Rundstedt, (Karl Rudolf) Gerd von (1875–1953) German field marshal, who was recalled from retirement at the outbreak of World War II, becoming

(1942) commander in chief in France. He held command in the battle of the Bulge (1944) and was a competent if uninspired general. He was captured in 1945 but his ill health secured his release.

Runeberg, Johan Ludvig (1804–77) Finnish poet of Swedish origin, who wrote in Swedish and whose style was influenced by his study of Finnish folk poetry. His major works include the epic poem *Kung Fjalar* (*King Fialar*; 1844), in which he attempted a synthesis of Christian and classical pagan ideals, and *Fänrik Ståls sägner* (*Tales of Ensign Stål*; 1848–60), a collection of patriotic ballads, one of which became the Finnish national anthem.

runic alphabet An alphabetical writing system used for Norse and certain other Germanic languages. It originated, probably as a modified version of the Etruscan or the Roman alphabet, in the 2nd or 3rd century AD, and went out of use gradually after the 14th century. The Gothic word *runa* means secret or mystery, and runes were always associated with magical powers. The runic alphabet, called the *futhark* from the names of the first six letters, consisted at first of 24 characters, extended in Old English to 28 and later 31.

runner bean A climbing plant, *Phaseolus coccineus,* also known as scarlet runner, native to South America and widely cultivated as a vegetable crop, especially in Britain. Growing up to 10 ft (3 m) high, it bears usually red five-petaled flowers, which give rise to edible bean pods, 8–24 in (20–60 cm) long, that are eaten cooked. Wild plants are perennial, but cultivated plants are treated as annuals. Family: **Leguminosae.*

Runnymede (*or* Runnimede) 51 26N 0 33W A meadow in SE England, on the S bank of the River Thames. The Magna Carta was granted there by King John (1215).

Runyon, (Alfred) Damon (1884–1946) US humorous writer. For his stories about New York characters, first collected in *Guys and Dolls* (1932) and notable for their lively slang, he drew on his long experience as a journalist and sports reporter. *Guys and Dolls* was made into extremely successful stage and screen productions.

Rupert, Prince (1619–82) Cavalry officer, who fought for the Royalists in the English Civil War; he was the son of Frederick the Winter King of the Palatinate and Elizabeth, daughter of James I of England. After Charles I's surrender he was banished from England. He returned at the Restoration (1660) and served as an admiral in the *Dutch Wars.

Rupert's Land (*or* Prince Rupert's Land) A region in N and W Canada around Hudson Bay. In 1670 it was granted by Charles II to the *Hudson's Bay Company, the first governor of which was Prince *Rupert. It is now an ecclesiastical province of the Anglican Church of Canada.

rupture. *See* hernia.

Rural Electrification Administration (REA) US agency, established in 1935, to expand the availability of electricity in rural areas. Part of Pres. Franklin D. Roosevelt's *New Deal program, it implemented the extension of electric lines, considered unprofitable by privately owned power companies, through government funding and labor.

Rurik (died c. 879) The semilegendary founder of the Rurik dynasty of Russian princes (862–1598). A Varangian chieftain, Rurik was allegedly prince of Novgorod from 862. His descendants were grand princes of Kiev, Vladimir, and Muscovy.

Ruse (Russe *or* Roussé) 43 05N 25 59E A city in central N Bulgaria. It is the site of the Friendship Bridge (1954) over the Danube River into Romania and is Bulgaria's principal river port. Population (1991 est): 192,000.

Rush, Benjamin (1746–1813) US physician, educator, and patriot; signer of the Declaration of Independence. A medical doctor, he practiced in Philadelphia and taught chemistry at (now) the University of Pennsylvania. He was a delegate to the Second Continental Congress (1776) and surgeon general of the Continental Army (1777–78). He was vocal in his campaigns for the abolition of slavery and for prison reform, woman's rights, and opportunities for the poor. He fought a yellow-fever epidemic in Philadelphia in 1793 and was one of the first to link the disease with mosquitoes. A pioneer in the field of mental health, he wrote *Medical Inquiries and Observations upon the Diseases of the Mind* (1812).

rush A grasslike plant of the genus *Juncus* (over 300 species), found worldwide in damp temperate and cold regions. Rushes have tufts of slender rigid stalks, up to about 40 in (1 m) high, bearing long flat leaves and clusters of small green or brown flowers, which produce seed capsules. The leaves are used to make mats, baskets, etc. Family: *Juncaceae*.

The name is also applied to similar plants, including the *bulrush, *flowering rush, and *woodrush.

Rushdie, Salman (1947–   ) British novelist, born in India. His first novel *Grimus* (1975) was followed by the much acclaimed Booker Prize-winner *Midnight's Children* (1981) and *Shame* (1983). *The Satanic Verses* (1988) was declared blasphemous by Muslims and so angered Iran's Ayatollah Khomeini that he called for Rushdie's assassination. Rushdie went into hiding. He also wrote *Haroun and the Sea of Stories* (1990), a children's book.

Rusk, (David) Dean (1909–   ) US statesman. After World War II he held posts in the State Department and in 1950 became assistant secretary of state for Far Eastern affairs, influencing US policy in the Korean War. As secretary of state (1961–69) successively under Presidents Kennedy and Johnson he defended US military involvement in Vietnam. In 1969 he became professor of international law at the University of Georgia.

Ruskin, John (1819–1900) British art and social critic. He began to write his first work of art criticism, *Modern Painters* (1843–60), to defend the paintings of J. M. W. Turner. In *The Stones of Venice* (1851–53) he promoted the gothic style in architecture. In *Unto This Last* (1862) and other volumes of social criticism he denounced materialism and laissez-faire economics from a moral and aesthetic perspective. His sonorous prose style is most fully developed in his unfinished autobiography, *Praeterita* (1885–89). During his last years he suffered recurrent attacks of insanity.

Russell, Bertrand Arthur William, 3rd Earl (1872–1970) British philosopher, grandson of Lord John *Russell. His first major philosophical work, *Principia Mathematica* (1910–13), written with A. N. *Whitehead, presented pure mathematics as a development of *logic. On a smaller logical basis *Our Knowledge of the External World* (1914) attempted a new approach to traditional problems in epistemology. From his pupil *Wittgenstein, he also acquired a lasting interest in language.

His prolific writings on religion, politics, and morals always stimulated interest, often to his own detriment. He was imprisoned (1918) and deprived of a Cambridge University post for his outspoken pacifism. In 1940, a US court disqualified him from holding a professorship at City College of New York because of his moral views. In 1961 he was imprisoned for civil disobedience during the

Campaign for Nuclear Disarmament. He was awarded the Nobel Prize in literature in 1950. He claimed that "longing for love, the search for knowledge, and unbearable pity for mankind" were the governing passions of his life.

BERTRAND RUSSELL

Russell, John, 1st Earl (1792–1878) British statesman; Whig (Liberal) prime minister (1846–52, 1865–66); the grandfather of Bertrand Russell. Elected to Parliament in 1813, he championed parliamentary reform in the 1820s. He was home secretary (1835–39), and secretary for war (1839–41). His first ministry was dominated by his foreign secretary Palmerston. Russell was himself foreign secretary (1852–53) and then colonial secretary (1855). He resigned as prime minister following defeat of a parliamentary reform bill.

Russell, Lillian (Helen Louise Leonard; 1861–1922) US entertainer and singer. She appeared in the light opera *The Great Mogul; or, the Snake Charmer* (1881) and from 1899–1904 with the burlesque team of Weber and Fields. *Barbara's Millions* (1906) and *Wildfire* (1908) were nonmusical comedies. Famous on the stage, she was equally renowned for her marriages and affairs, especially a 40-year relationship with Diamond Jim *Brady.

Russell's viper A common highly venomous viper, *Vipera russelli,* of SE Asia. Up to 5 ft (1.5 m) long, it is patterned with three rows of black-and-white ringed reddish spots. It is the cause of many snakebite deaths.

Russian The main language of Russia, belonging to the East *Slavonic family. It is a highly inflected language with six cases and a notable feature is the frequency of clusters of consonants. It is written in the *Cyrillic alphabet. The standard form is based on the dialect of Moscow.

Russian Federation Independent nation in E Europe and Asia, known as Russia; formerly the Russian Soviet Federal Socialist Republic (RSFSR) of the Soviet Union. It was the largest, most heavily populated, and economically most important of the 15 Soviet republics, occupying some 76% of the total area of the Soviet Union, containing about 54% of its population, and producing 70% of its industrial and agricultural output. Its climate ranges from Arctic to subtropical and its geographical zones include tundra, forest, steppe, and rich agricultural soil. Over 80% of the population are Russians, the remainder consisting of 38 national minorities. Russia contains outstanding mineral resources including iron ore, coal, oil, gold, platinum, copper, zinc, lead, and tin. The major industrial region is around Moscow. It produces ships, trucks, machine tools, electronic equipment, textiles, and chemicals. Because of the extensive forests, timber and related occupations are important. The main agricultural products are wheat, cotton, fruit and vegetables, tobacco, and sugar beet. The RSFSR was formed in 1917 and was joined with the Ukraine, Belorussia, and Transcaucasia in 1922 to constitute the Soviet Union. It consisted of 6 territories, 49 regions, 16 Autonomous Soviet Socialist Republics, 5 autonomous regions, and 10 national areas before independence in 1991. Area: 6,592,658 sq mi (17,074,984 sq km). Population (1992 est): 149,000,000. Capital: Moscow.

Russian literature Until the beginning of the 18th century Russian literature consisted chiefly of chronicles and religious works written in Old Slavonic. The outstanding early work is *The Song of Igor's Campaign* (c. 1187). The development of modern literature owed much to the political reforms of Peter the Great (reigned 1682–1725) and the artistic patronage of Catherine the Great (reigned 1762–96). Major writers of the 18th century included the poet and scholar M. V. Lomonosov (1711–65), the poet G. R. Derzhavin (1743–1816), and the fabulist I. A. Krylov (1768–1844). The first half of the 19th century was dominated by Pushkin and Lermontov and the second half, following the pioneering fiction of Gogol, by the novelists Tolstoy, Dostoievski, and Turgenev. They were followed by the dramatist and short-story writer Chekhov, whose detached compassion contrasted with the strong social commitment of Gorki. The political unrest of the early 20th century stimulated much artistic experimentation, but in the 1930s the Soviet authorities decreed that all literature must adhere to the official doctrine of *socialist realism. Writers whose works were banned in Russia include the poets Akhmatova, Mandelstan, and Tsvetaeva and the novelist Pasternak. The apparent liberalization of culture heralded by the publication of works by Solzhenitsyn, Yevtushenko, and Voznesenskii in the 1960s was short lived and in 1974 Solzhenitsyn joined the growing number of Russian writers living abroad.

Russian Orthodox Church An offshoot of the Greek Orthodox Church, dating from the baptism of the emperor Vladimir (later St Vladimir) in 988. Since 1328 the metropolitan see has been at Moscow. During the 15th century connections with the Greek parent Church were severed. In the 18th century the Church fell increasingly under state control. From the 1917 Revolution until the breakup of the Soviet Union in 1991 it was intermittently persecuted and at best regarded with suspicion and its activities restricted. *See also* Old Believers.

Russian Revolution (1917) The revolution between March and November (Old Style February and October) 1917, that overthrew the Russian monarchy and established the world's first communist state. It began with the February Revolution, when riots over shortage of bread and coal in Petrograd (formerly St Petersburg) led to the establishment of the Petrograd Soviet of Workers' and Soldiers' Deputies, dominated by *Mensheviks and Social Revolutionaries, and of a provisional government of *Duma deputies, which forced *Nicholas II to abdicate. The failure of the provisional government, under Prince *Lvov and then *Kerenski, to end Russia's participation in World War I and to deal with food shortages led to the demand of the *Bolsheviks under *Lenin for "All power to the Soviets." The Bolsheviks, who had gained a majority in the Soviet by September, staged the October (*or* Bolshevik) Revolution, seizing power and establishing the Soviet of People's Commissars. The new government came to terms with Germany in early 1918 but almost immediately faced opposition at home. In the subsequent civil war (1918–21) the Red Army was ultimately victorious against the anticommunist White Russians but with the loss of some 100,000 lives. In addition, some two million Russians emigrated.

Russo-Finnish War (*or* Winter War; 1939–40) The war between the Soviet Union and Finland at the beginning of World War II. It was won by the Soviet Union, the aggressor, which gained part of the Karelian Isthmus.

Russo-Japanese War (1904–05) A confrontation arising from conflicting Japanese and Russian interests in Manchuria, where Russia controlled Port Arthur (now Lüda). In 1904 Japan attacked Port Arthur, which fell in January 1905. In May a Japanese fleet under *Togo Heihachiro destroyed Russia's Baltic Fleet in the Tsushima Straits, forcing Russia's surrender. In the peace conference at Portsmouth, N.H., over which Theodore Roosevelt presided, Japan gained the ascendancy in S Manchuria and Korea.

rust A reddish-brown solid consisting of hydrated iron oxide. Rusting is a special case of corrosion; the mechanism is complicated and still not fully understood but involves the setting up of a cell in which iron is the anode and a metal impurity the cathode. Both water and oxygen must be present for rust to form although the most serious damage, pitting, is always found in an oxygen-free portion of metal. Rust prevention usually involves protective coatings (paint, zinc plating, etc.) or alloying with chromium and other metals to produce stainless steels.

rust fungi Fungi, belonging to the order *Uredinales,* that are parasites of plants, forming spots, blotches, and pustules on the stems and foliage of their hosts. Several are important pests of cereal crops, including black rust (*Puccinia graminis*) of wheat. This forms red pustules on wheat leaves, releasing spores that infect barberry (*Berberis vulgaris*)—the secondary host—in which the life cycle continues. Control therefore involves eradication of barberry in wheat-growing areas as well as developing resistant strains of wheat. Other important wheat rusts include yellow rust (*P. striiformis*) and brown rust (*P. recondita*). Class: *Basidiomycetes.*

rutabaga A biennial herbaceous plant, *Brassica napobrassica* growing to a height of 40 in (1 m), with deeply lobed leaves and yellow flowers. Also known as a swede, and closely related to the turnip, it is cultivated for its fleshy edible taproot, which is yellow or white; this is eaten as a vegetable and also fed to livestock. Family: *Cruciferae.*

Ruth A Gentile from Moab who was an ancestress of David. The Old Testament Book of Ruth, set in the time of the *Judges (c. 1000 BC), records the events by which Ruth came to marry Boaz, a Hebrew.

Ruth, Babe (George Herman R.; 1895–1948) US baseball player. He pitched for the Boston Red Sox (1914–19) and played outfield for the New York Yankees (1920–34) and Boston Braves (1935). Known as the "Sultan of Swat," he held the record for career home runs—714—until 1974. He was elected to the Baseball Hall of Fame in 1938, the year it was founded.

Ruthenia A region comprising the S slopes of the Carpathian Mountains, now part of Ukraine but part of Hungary until it was attached to Czechoslovakia in 1920. Soon after Hitler's seizure of Czechoslovakia in 1939, Ruthenia was annexed by Hungary. After World War II it was ceded to the Soviet Union, becoming part of the independent Ukraine in 1991.

ruthenium (Ru) A hard metal of the platinum group, first separated in 1844 by K. K. Klaus (1796–1864). It is used to harden platinum and palladium for use in electrical contacts and is a versatile catalyst. The tetroxide (RuO_4), like that of osmium, is toxic. The element shows a wide range of *valence states. At no 44; at wt 101.07; mp 4194°F (2310°C); bp 7059°F (3900°C).

Rutherford, Ernest, 1st Baron (1871–1937) English physicist, born in New Zealand, who was a professor at Montreal (1898–1907), Manchester (1907–19), and Cambridge (1919–37). He made fundamental discoveries concerning the nature of *radioactivity, distinguishing between the three types of radiation, which he named alpha, beta, and gamma rays. Working with Hans *Geiger he discovered that alpha radiation consisted of positively charged helium atoms. In 1906, while bombarding gold foil with alpha particles, he deduced the existence of a heavy positively charged core in the atom, which he called the *nucleus. In 1908, Rutherford received the Nobel Prize in chemistry.

Rutherford, Dame Margaret (1892–1972) British actress. She was particularly successful in comedies, such as *Blithe Spirit* (1941). In her films, which included *Murder She Said* (1962) and *The VIPs* (1963), she specialized in the roles of elderly eccentrics.

rutherfordium. *See* kurchatovium.

rutile A brown-to-black form of natural titanium dioxide, TiO_2. It is found as an accessory mineral in igneous and metamorphic rocks, in veins, and as fibers in quartz, known as Venus's hair.

Rutledge, John (1739–1800) US political leader; chief justice of the Supreme Court (1795). He was a delegate to two continental congresses (1774–76; 1782–83), a signer of the US Constitution, and headed South Carolina, first as president (1776–78) and then as governor (1779–82). An associate justice of the US Supreme Court (1789–91), he was appointed chief justice in 1795 by George *Washington. He served for one month, failing to attain Senate confirmation due to his opposition to the recently approved Jay's Treaty. (*See* Jay, John).

Rutledge, Wylie Blount, Jr. (1894–1949) US jurist; associate justice of the Supreme Court (1943–49). After teaching law at several universities, he was appointed to the US Court of Appeals in the District of Columbia (1939–43). A liberal member of the Supreme Court, he was a vigorous supporter of civil rights.

Ruwenzori Mountains A mountain range in East Africa, on the Uganda-Zaïre border between Lakes Albert and Edward, rising to 16,795 ft (5119 m) at Mount Stanley.

Ruyter, Michiel Adriaanszoon de (1607–76) Dutch admiral, who served outstandingly in the *Dutch Wars (1652–54, 1665–67, 1672–78). In the battle of the Medway (1667) he destroyed most of the English fleet and his victories in 1672–73 saved the United Provinces from invasion. He was killed in action.

Rwanda, Republic of A small landlocked country in E central Africa. Lake Kivu forms most of its W boundary and the land is chiefly mountainous and rugged. The majority of the inhabitants are Bantu-speaking Hutu, the Nilotic Tutsi comprising less than 10% of the total. *Economy*: chiefly subsistence agriculture, including livestock. The main food crops are beans, cassava, and corn, and the principal cash crop is coffee, which, along with cassiterite, form the main exports. Methane gas has been found under Lake Kivu. Some small-scale industry is being developed including food processing and textiles. *History*: a Tutsi kingdom from the 16th century, the area (with present-day Burundi) came under German East Africa in 1890. From 1919, after World War I, it was administered by Belgium as the N part of Ruanda-Urundi, which was under League of Nations mandate and then a UN trust territory. In 1959 the Tutsi kingdom was overthrown by the Hutu, who in 1961 declared Rwanda a republic; independence was recognized by Belgium in 1962. There were further massacres of the Tutsi by the Hutu in 1964. In 1973 the government was overthrown in a bloodless coup and Maj. Gen. Juvénal Habyalimana came to power. The first parliament under the new constitution was elected by popular vote in 1981; voting for the one-party list of candidates was mandatory. Rwandan refugees expelled from Uganda and living in border camps exacerbated tensions between the two countries as violence against Rwandans in Uganda escalated. The Tutsi tribe refugees rose up and invaded Rwanda in 1990 and 1991. The attacks were put down by Belgian troops and some from other central African countries; a truce was signed in 1991. A 1991 constitution provided for a multiparty democracy. Civil war erupted in 1992 and 1993, and a peace agreement reached in 1993 disintegrated in 1994 into the decade's worst violence. Official languages: Kinyarwanda and French. Official currency: Rwanda franc of 100 centimes. Area: 10,166 sq mi (26,330 sq km). Population (1990): 7,603,000. Capital: Kigali.

Ryazan 54 37N 39 43E A city in W central Russia. Founded in 1095, it was the capital of a principality until annexed by Russia in 1521. Industries include oil refining, metalworking, and engineering. Population (1991 est): 527,000.

Rybinsk (name from 1946 until 1958: Shcherbakov) 58 01N 38 52E A port in W central Russia, on the Volga River. It is situated below the **Rybinsk Reservoir**, an artificial lake of some 2000 sq mi (5200 sq km) created (1941) through the damming of the Volga at its confluence with the Suda and Sheksna rivers and forming the S stretch of the Volga–Baltic waterway. Rybinsk has a hydroelectric station and ship building, engineering, and food-processing industries. Population (1991 est): 252,500.

Ryder Cup A biennial golf tournament between members of the US and British Professional Golfers' Associations, first played in 1927.

rye A cereal *grass, *Secale cereale,* native to W Asia but widely cultivated in cool temperate and upland regions. 3.5–7 ft (1–2 m) high, it bears a terminal spike, 4–6 in (10–15 cm) long, of numerous two- or three-flowered spikelets. The grain is milled to produce a dark-colored flour, which is used in making black bread or for livestock feed. Rye may be sown in autumn to provide winter grazing or as a green manure crop.

Rye House Plot (1683) A conspiracy to murder Charles II of England and his brother, the duke of York (later James II), near Rye House, Hoddesdon, on their way to London from Newmarket. The plot failed but several conspirators, including Lord William Russell and Algernon Sidney, were tried and executed.

Rykov, Aleksei Ivanovich (1881–1938) Soviet politician. After the *Russian Revolution, Rykov played a prominent part in the Soviet Government until 1930, when he was expelled from the Communist party for opposing the brutality of collectivization. He was forced to recant in 1929 and perished in Stalin's purges.

Ryle, Gilbert (1900–76) British philosopher. He was Waynflete Professor of Metaphysical Philosophy at Oxford (1945–68) and editor of *Mind* (1947–71), exerting considerable influence as a writer and teacher. His philosophy centered around detailed analysis of mental concepts. *The Concept of Mind* (1949) maintained that *Descartes's idea of the human being consisting of mind and body ("the ghost in the machine") was misleading.

Ryle, Sir Martin (1918–84) British astronomer; professor at Cambridge University and astronomer royal (1972–84). A pioneer of radio telescopy, his most important work was the development of a technique for studying distant radio sources by using two radio telescopes placed a distance apart, thus increasing their effective aperture. In 1974 he shared the Nobel Prize in physics with Antony Hewish.

Ryukyu Islands A group of volcanic and coral islands in the W Pacific Ocean, extending almost 400 mi (660 km) from Kyushu to N Taiwan. An independent kingdom until the 14th century, the islands were dominated by the Chinese before becoming a part of Japan (1879). They were under US control (1945–72). The chief industries are agriculture and fishing. Area: 849 sq mi (2196 sq km). Chief city: Naha (on Okinawa).

S

Saale River A river in Germany, rising in NE Bavaria and flowing mainly N past Jena and Halle to join the Rhine River near Magdeburg. Length: 265 mi (426 km).

Saarbrücken (French name: Sarrebruck) 49 15N 6 58E A city in SW Germany, the capital of Saarland on the Saar River near the French border. It was under French administration (1801–15, 1919–35, 1945–57). Some historic buildings, such as the gothic abbey church (1270–1330), survived World War II and it has a university (1948). Its industries include iron and steel and machinery manufacturing. Population (1991): 191,694.

Saarinen, Eero (1910–61) US architect, born in Finland. One of the most innovative of 20th-century architects, Saarinen emigrated (1923) to the US with his father, the architect Eliel Saarinen (1873–1950), and became his partner in 1938. His first independent design was the General Motors Technical Center (1948–56) in Warren, Mich. He designed two buildings for the Massachusetts Institute of Technology. His most famous building is the Trans World Airlines terminal at Kennedy Airport, N.Y. (1956–62), which has reinforced concrete vaults spreading outward to suggest flight. Other works include the St Louis Arch (1964) and Dulles International Airport near Washington, D.C., completed after his death.

Saarland A small *Land* in SW Germany, bordering on France. The area has often passed between French and German control, but plebiscites held in 1935 and 1955 resulted in its union with Germany. Rich in coal, it has a large steel industry. Area: 992 sq mi (2569 sq km). Population (1991 est): 1,075,000. Capital: Saarbrücken.

Saar River (French name: Sarre) A river in W Europe, rising in the Vosges Mountains in NE France and flowing generally N into Germany, then NW through Saarland to join the Moselle River above Trier. The Saar Valley is noted for its wines. Length: 149 mi (240 km).

Sabadell 41 33N 2 07E A city in NE Spain, in Catalonia. It has an important textile industry. Other industries include metallurgy and leather. Population (1991): 184,500.

Sabah (former name: North Borneo) A state in Malaysia, in NE *Borneo on the South China and Sulu Seas. Forested and mountainous, it rises to 13,533 ft (4125 m) at Mount Kinabalu, the highest peak in Malaysia and Borneo. It is largely undeveloped, but on the well-populated western coastal plain rice and rubber are grown. Since 1975 copper and oil resources have been exploited; timber, rubber, copra, and abaca are exported. *History*: until the European colonial period, most contact was with the Philippines. North Borneo was first colonized by the British in 1877, becoming a protectorate in 1882. In 1963 it joined Malaysia under its present name. Area: 29,388 sq mi (76,115 sq km). Population (1990): 1,470,200. Capital: Kota Kinabalu.

Sebatier, Paul (1854–1941) French chemist, who was professor at Toulouse University (1884–1941), where he discovered that nickel catalyzes hydrogenation reactions. Since nickel is relatively cheap, this enabled similar reactions to be performed on an industrial scale, e.g. in the production of margarine. He shared the 1912 Nobel Prize with F. A. V. Grignard, the discoverer of *Grignard reagents.

sabbath In Judaism, the seventh day of the week, ordained by God in the Pentateuch as a day of rest for the benefit of his people. It was reckoned from sunset on Friday to sunset on Saturday. The early Christian Church soon substituted Sunday as the Christian day of rest and worship because the resurrection of Jesus Christ took place on the first day of the (Jewish) week.

saber-toothed tiger An extinct *cat that lived 30 million years ago and became extinct in the Pleistocene epoch (1 million years ago). *Smilodon,* a Pleistocene form, was about the size of a tiger, with very long upper canine teeth used to pierce the thick hide of its prey. □fossil.

Sabin, Albert Bruce (1906–93) US physician, born in Russia. A specialist in virology, he served on the medical school staff at the University of Cincinnati from 1939, where he researched crippling diseases of children and developed a live vaccine (1957) that, given orally, immunized against poliomyelitis (polio).

Sabine River A river that flows from NE Texas SE and then S along the Texas-Louisiana border through Sabine Lake and Sabine Pass into the Gulf of Mexico. Its lower portion is part of the Gulf Intracoastal Waterway. Length: 360 mi (580 km).

Sabines The peoples of the scattered hilltop communities NE of ancient Rome. The legendary abduction of the Sabine women by Roman settlers, a favorite theme in the history of art, indicates the early interbreeding of Sabines with Romans. Sabine influence on Roman religion was especially strong. They became Roman citizens in 268 BC.

Sabin vaccine A vaccine that prevents poliomyelitis, developed by US virologist, A. B. Sabin. It contains a weakened polio virus that stimulates the body's defense against polio without causing the disease. Sabin vaccine is given by mouth (often on a sugar lump) in three consecutive doses. *See also* Salk vaccine.

sable A carnivorous mammal, *Martes zibellina,* native to N Eurasia. It is less than 20 in (50 cm) long and has thicker legs and longer ears than other *martens. Its coat is thick, soft, and glossy and is valued as fur (Siberian sable).

sable antelope A large antelope, *Hippotragus niger,* of S African forests. About 4 ft 3 in (130 cm) high at the shoulder, it has backward-curving ringed horns up to 67 in (170 cm) long. The coat is black in males, lighter in females, with white on the face, rump, and belly.

Sable Island A sandy island in Canada, in the Atlantic Ocean off the coast of Nova Scotia. The scene of many shipwrecks, it is known as "the graveyard of the Atlantic."

Sacagawea (Sacajawea; Sahcargarweah; ?1787–1812?) US Shoshone Indian guide. As a child she was sold by the *Mandan Indians, who had captured her, to Toussaint Charbonneau, a French-Canadian fur trapper. They married (1804) in North Dakota and that next year served as interpreters and guides to the *Lewis and Clark expedition to the Pacific coast. Sacagawea's contacts with the Shoshone ensured the expedition party's safe passage.

saccharin An organic compound ($C_7H_5NO_3S$) used as a sweetening agent in the food industry and as a sugar substitute by diabetics and others. It has about five hundred times the sweetening power of table sugar and passes through the body without being absorbed or changed.

Sacco-Vanzetti case The controversial trial of two US anarchists. Nicola Sacco and Bartolomeo Vanzetti were Italian-born immigrant workers convicted of murder on flimsy evidence. The verdict, which was reached largely because of their political activities and was influenced by current anti-alien and antiradical prejudice, aroused international protests. An investigative committee supported the sentence and Sacco and Vanzetti were executed in 1927, six years after being sentenced.

Sachs, Hans (1494–1576) German poet and folk dramatist, most famous of the *Meistersingers of Nuremberg. He wrote thousands of works, including lively farces still performed at annual festivals throughout Germany, verse tales, religious poetry, and other works in support of *Luther. He is the central character, portrayed as wise and philosophic, of Wagner's opera *The Mastersingers of Nuremberg* (1868).

Sachs, Nelly (Leonie) (1891–1970) German Jewish poet and dramatist. Helped by Selma *Lagerlöf, she escaped from Nazi Germany and settled in Sweden. Her best-known play is *Eli: Ein Mysterienspiel vom Leiden Israels* (1951). In 1966 she shared a Nobel Prize with Shmuel Yosef *Agnon.

sackbut. *See* trombone.

Sackville, Thomas, 1st earl of Dorset (1536–1608) British poet and dramatist. He collaborated with Thomas Norton (1532–83) on *Gorbuduc* (1561), the first English play in blank verse, and planned and introduced *The Mirror for Magistrates* (1563), a collection of narrative poems based on the lives of eminent men.

sacrament In Christian theology, a ritual having a special significance as a visible sign of an inner grace in its participants. The *Roman Catholic Church and *Orthodox Churches accept seven sacraments: baptism, confirmation, penance, the *Eucharist, marriage, ordination, and extreme unction. Baptism and the Eucharist are the only commonly accepted sacraments among the Protestant Churches (*see* Protestantism).

Sacramento 38 32N 121 30W The capital city of California, on the Sacramento River. Founded in 1839, it grew after the discovery of gold at nearby Sutter's Mill in 1848. Linked by canal (1963) to San Francisco Bay, it is a deepwater port and serves an extensive agricultural area. Industries include food processing, aerospace, and printing. Population (1990): 369,365.

Sacramento, Battle of (1847) US-Mexican battle during the *Mexican War. US forces, under Col. Alexander W. Doniphan, defeated Mexican troops N of Chihuahua, Mexico. Mexican casualties were high.

Sacramento River A river that flows from N central California through Shasta Lake to just below Sacramento where it joins the San Joaquin River and flows W through Suisun Bay to San Francisco Bay. The Central Valley Project on the river provides irrigation, hydroelectricity, water, and flood control for the river's valley. Length: 320 mi (515 km).

sacred ibis An African □ibis, *Threskiornis aethiopica*, that was revered in ancient Egypt; 30 in (75 cm) long, it is pure white except for dark ornamental plumes on its back, dark wing tips, and a black head and neck. It has a black bill and feeds in flocks along rivers, taking frogs and small aquatic animals.

Sadat, Anwar (1918–81) Egyptian statesman; president (1970–81). A colleague of *Nasser in the Free Officers movement, Sadat was twice vice president (1964–66, 1969–70) before becoming president on Nasser's death. He moved Egypt away from the Soviet Union and toward the US, under the influence of which he negotiated a peace agreement with Israel in 1979 (□Carter, Jimmy). For this initiative and his courage in visiting Israel in the face of some Arab opposition he was awarded the 1978 Nobel Peace Prize jointly with Menahem Begin. He was assassinated (1981) by Islamic extremists while watching a military display in Egypt.

saddleback A very rare songbird, *Creadion carunculatus,* surviving only on small islands around New Zealand. It has a black plumage with a chestnut patch on its back and orange wattles at the base of the sharp pointed bill. Saddlebacks are weak fliers and feed in the undergrowth on larvae, insects, and fruits. Family: *Callaeidae* (wattlebirds).

Sadducees An ancient Jewish religious and political party. They formed a conservative and aristocratic group centering on the priesthood in Jerusalem. With the destruction of the temple the party ceased to exist, but many of its ideas surfaced later in medieval Jewish sects. *See also* Pharisees.

Sade, Donatien Alphonse François, Marquis de (1740–1814) French novelist. Most of his works of sexual fantasy and perversion, which include *Justine, La Philosophie dans le boudoir,* and *Les 120 Journées de Sodome,* were written in the 1780s and 1790s, during his many years of imprisonment for sexual offenses. During his last years he was confined to the mental asylum of Charenton. His moral nihilism has been seen as a stage in the development of *existentialism. The sexual perversion "sadism," in which sexual pleasure is derived from causing or observing pain, is named for him.

Sa'di (Mosleh al-Din S.; c. 1215–92) Persian poet, born in Shiraz, who studied in Baghdad and subsequently spent much of his life wandering in Asia Minor and Egypt, claiming also to have visited India and central Asia. He returned to Shiraz in 1256. His major works are *Bustan* (*The Orchard*; 1257), a didactic poem illustrating the Islamic virtues of justice, contentedness, and modesty, and *Galestan* (*The Rose Garden*; 1258), a collection of moralistic anecdotes. He also wrote a number of odes and popularized the *ghazal* form later used by *Hafiz.

Sadowa (Czech name: Sadorá) A village in the Czech Republic, in NE Bohemia. It was the scene of a battle in the Austro-Prussian War (1866) in which the Austrians were defeated by the Prussians.

Safavids The ruling dynasty of Persia from 1502 to 1706. It was founded by Esmail I (1486–1524) and named for his ancestor Safi od-Din (1252–1334), a Muslim saint. Esmail established Shiism (*see* Shiites) as the state religion. Among his descendants was *Abbas the Great (reigned 1588–1628). The Safavids were overthrown by *Nader Shah.

safflower An annual herbaceous plant, *Carthamus tinctorius,* native to Asia and Africa; 12–47 in (30–120 cm) tall, it has red, orange, yellow, or white flowers. It is cultivated in India, the Middle East, North America, and Australia for its seeds, which yield safflower oil, used in paints, varnishes, cooking oils, and margarines. A red dye can be obtained from the dried flowers. Family: *Compositae.

saffron The dried orange-yellow stigmas of the saffron crocus (*C. sativa*), used for flavoring and coloring foods and liqueurs and formerly as a dye for fabrics. The crocus, which has purple flowers, is probably native to the Mediterranean region and SW Asia and has been cultivated since ancient times; today the main producing areas are France, Spain, and Italy. About 100,000 flowers are needed to produce 2 lb (1 kg) of saffron.

Safi (ancient name: Asfi) 32 20N 9 17W A port in Morocco, on the Atlantic coast. Its artificial harbor serves Marrakech, and exports include phosphates. Besides its important fishing industry, it manufactures pottery and has a chemical complex. Population (1982): 197,309.

Sagan, Carl (Edward) (1934–   ) US scientist and writer. Professor of astronomy and director of planetary studies at Cornell University (1968–   ), he worked on the Mariner (1962–73) and Viking (1975–76) space probes of Mercury, Venus, and Mars and studied the aftermath of a hypothetical nuclear war (1983). His works include *The Cosmic Connection* (1973), *The Dragons of Eden* (1977; Pulitzer Prize, 1978), *Broca's Brain* (1979), *Cosmos* (1980), and *Contact* (1985).

Sagan, Françoise (Françoise Quoirez; 1935–   ) French novelist. Her best-selling novels include *Bonjour Tristesse* (1954), *Aimez-Vous Brahms?* (1959), and *Silken Eyes* (1977), which concern transitory love affairs between wealthy and cynical characters. She has also written several plays, including *Château en Suède* (1960) and *Zaphorie* (1973).

sagas Heroic prose narratives in Old Norse, the best of which were written down in Iceland in the 12th and 13th centuries (*see* Icelandic literature). Translations of French *romances, Latin histories, and saints' lives were part of the saga tradition but its characteristic subject matter was drawn from ancient Scandinavian oral traditons: fictionalized accounts of the deeds of Norwegian kings (e.g. Snorri *Sturluson's *Heimskringla*), heroic legends of the pagan past (e.g. *Volsungasaga*), and the "family" sagas that mirrored contemporary Icelandic society (e.g. *Egilssaga*, *Gíslasaga*, *Laxdaelasaga*, *Grettissaga*, and *Njálssaga*).

sage A perennial herb or shrub, *Salvia officinalis*, native to the Mediterranean region and widely cultivated for its leaves, which are used for flavoring foods. It grows 18–24 in (45–60 cm) high and has blue, pink, or white flowers. *See also* Salvia.

sage grouse A large □grouse, *Centrocercus urophasianus*, occurring in sagebrush deserts of western US. It is 30 in (75 cm) long and the male has ornamental wattles and a long slender tail, which is fanned out during its courtship display.

Sagittarius (Latin: Archer) A large constellation in the S sky, lying on the *zodiac between Capricornus and Scorpius. The brightest star is the 2nd-magnitude Kaus Australis. The constellation contains several notable *star clusters and emission *nebulae, including the **Lagoon nebula**. The center of the *Galaxy lies in the direction of Sagittarius.

sago A starchy food obtained from the sago *palms (*Metoxylon sagu* and *M. rumphii*), native to Indonesia and cultivated in Malaysia. The palms, up to 30 ft (9 m) high, take 15 years to mature and are harvested just before flowering. Their stems are swollen with a starchy pith, which is extracted, ground, and washed and used to make flour or pearl sago. The pithy stems of a *cycad, *Cycas circinalis*, also called sago palm, are used as a source of sago. The plant is native to tropical Asia and its attractive fernlike leaves are used for ornament.

saguaro A giant cactus, *Cereus* (or *Carnegiea*) *gigantea*, native to the S US and Mexico. It has a ribbed branched stem and is slow-growing, producing its white flowers from the age of 50–75 years; it may live for 200 years and reach a height of 40 ft (12 m).

Saguenay River A river in E Canada, in E Quebec flowing from Lac St Jean ESE into the St Lawrence estuary. Its upper reaches drop steeply, providing hydroelectric power, while the lower course flows between high cliffs, a popular tourist attraction. Length: 105 mi (170 km).

Sagunto (Latin name: Saguntum)   39 40N 0 17W A city in E Spain, in Valencia. It was captured by Hannibal in 219 BC, precipitating the second Punic War. There are many fine Roman remains including a theater and circus. It exports iron ore and citrus fruits. Population (1989 est): 57,500.

Sahara The largest desert in the world, covering most of N Africa. The terrain consists chiefly of a plateau with central mountains rising to 11,204 ft (3415 m) and some areas of sand dunes, such as the *Libyan Desert in the NE. The vegetation is sparse but sufficient in most parts for nomads to keep sheep and goats. Geological evidence shows that the Sahara was once well vegetated and that parts were formerly under the sea. There are large deposits of oil and gas in Algeria and Libya and phosphates in Morocco and Western Sahara. Rainfall is minimal and irregular, but there are numerous scattered oases watered from underground that support small communities and are visited by nomads and travelers. Area: about 3,475,000 sq mi (9,000,000 sq km).

Sahel An area in West Africa, mainly in Mauritania, Mali, Niger, and Chad. It forms a band of savanna between the Sahara desert to the N and tropical vegetation to the S and is used as pasture. The desert is gradually encroaching on the area and from 1973 to 1974 and again in the 1980s it suffered a severe drought.

Saida. *See* Sidon.

saiga A small antelope, of Asian deserts and steppes. About 31 in (80 cm) high at the shoulder, saigas are slightly built with a pale woolly coat and a remarkable swollen snout with convoluted nasal tracts, thought to be an adaptation for warming inhaled air or to be related to their keen sense of smell. Males have straight ridged horns up to 12 in (30 cm) long. Saigas form large herds to migrate southward in winter. □mammal.

Saigon. *See* Ho Chi Minh City.

Saigo Takamori (1828–77) Japanese samurai famous for his tragic role in the Meiji restoration. He played a major part in the overthrow of the *Tokugawa regime (1868) but was opposed to radical modernization and the complete abolition of feudalism. When his supporters clashed with the government in 1877, he was torn between competing loyalties but committed himself to the rebellion and was eventually forced to commit hara-kiri.

sailfish A food and game fish, belonging to a genus (*Istiophorus*) related to marlins, that occurs in warm and temperate seas. Its slender body, deep blue above, silvery below, and up to 11 ft (3.4 m) long, has a long pointed snout, long pelvic fins, and a large sail-like dorsal fin. Sailfish feed mainly on other fish.

sailing Cruising or racing in a boat fitted with one or more sails. Some smaller sailing boats are equipped with an outboard motor; larger boats have one or more inboard auxiliary engines, for use in calm weather and for navigating in and out of harbors. Craft used for recreation and sport range from dinghies of 7.5 ft (2.3 m) to oceangoing yachts of 75 ft (23 m) or more. All classes of boat can be used for racing but boats used primarily for racing have more complex sail plans requiring a relatively large crew, while the emphasis in a cruising boat is more on providing living accommodation. Racing, which became popular in the 19th century, is organized according to class of boat. Races are held either for yachts of the same design or for yachts of different designs competing with appropriate handicaps. Current Olympic classes are: Finn, 470, Flying Dutchman, Star, Soling, Tornado, Europe, and Sailboard.

Until the invention of nylon and Dacron, all sails were made of canvas. Modern sails, made of synthetic fabrics, are more durable, resist mildew (can be stored wet), and retain their shape better than canvas.

Many different types of rigging have been used for sailing vessels throughout history. Square sails, which are of little use except when a vessel is sailing away from the wind, were the type employed on square-riggers, a rig prevalent in Europe from the 14th to the 19th centuries. These were largely replaced by the quadrilateral sails of early schooner-rigged vessels. Called gaffsails because the upper part of the sail was supported by a gaff boom, these were succeeded by triangular sails, which are popular on yachts today. *Sloops, *ketches, *schooners, and *yawls now employ triangular sails. Gaff-rigged vessels have given way to marconi- or Bermuda-rigged sailing boats, i.e. those with triangular sails. Small boats—sailing dinghies, etc.—may have only one sail, usually a gunter-rigged triangular sail supported at the upper leading edge by a boom that fits onto the top of a stubby mast set well forward in the boat. This rig is a modern version of the traditional lateen rig, a native design from the Near East that also uses a triangular sail hung from a very long boom. In the late 19th century, yachtsmen enlarged jibs into foresails called genoas. They also developed lightweight triangular foresails, called spinnakers, which often have a cross section like a part of the surface of a sphere. *See also* ships.

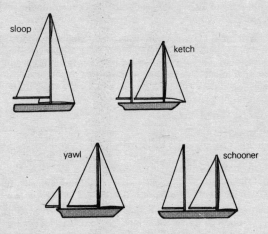

SAILING

Saimaa, Lake A lake in SE Finland. It is the primary lake in a system spread over most of S Finland. Area: about 680 sq mi (1760 sq km).

sainfoin A perennial herb, *Onobrychis viciifolia,* native to temperate regions of Eurasia and found on chalky soils. Up to 20 in (50 cm) tall, it has pale-pink flowers and has been cultivated as a forage plant. Family: *Leguminosae.*

saint In Christian belief, a person characterized by special holiness. In the early Church the term applied to all believers, and certain modern sects follow this practice in calling their adherents saints, for example the *Mormons. In the *Roman Catholic Church saints formally admitted to the calendar of saints by *canonization can be invoked as intercessors, although recently their numbers have been reduced in an effort to cut superstitious practices. *Protestantism rejects the invocation of saints, although the *Church of England's calendar recognizes a number of saints' days.

St Albans 51 46N 0 21W A city in SE England, in Hertfordshire. Across the River Ver stood the important Romano-British town of Verulamium, where the martyrdom of St Alban took place. The Benedictine abbey, founded in honor of the saint in 793 AD, was made a cathedral in 1877. St Albans' industries include printing, electrical equipment, and rubber goods. Population (1981): 50,888.

St Andrews 56 20N 2 48W A resort in E Scotland, on St Andrews Bay. An ancient ecclesiastical center, its university (1412) is the oldest in Scotland. The famous Royal and Ancient Golf Club was founded there in 1754. Population (1981): 11,302.

St Anthony's fire. *See* ergot.

St Augustine 29 54N 81 19W A city in Florida. The oldest city in the US, it was founded by the Spanish in 1565 and for most of the next two and a half centuries remained the most northerly outpost of the Spanish colonial empire. The Castillo de San Marcos (1672) stands as a reminder of Spanish rule. Tourism is the main source of revenue. Population (1990): 11,692.

St Bartholomew's Day Massacre The slaughter of *Huguenots that began on Aug 24, 1572, in Paris. The massacre was ordered by Charles IX of France under the influence of his mother, Catherine de' Medici. Some 3000 Huguenots died in Paris and many more were murdered in the provinces.

St Bernard A breed of large working dog developed in Europe from Asian ancestors and employed as a rescue dog by the hospice of St Bernard in the Swiss Alps since the 17th century. It is massively built, having a large head with drooping ears. The coat may be either short or of medium length and is white marked with red-brown or brindle. Height: 25.5 in (65 cm) minimum.

St Bernard Passes Two mountain passes in the Alps, in central Europe. The **Great St Bernard Pass** on the Swiss-Italian border is one of the highest alpine passes at 8111 ft (2433 m). The hospice at its summit, founded (11th century) by St Bernard of Menthon, is famous for the St Bernard dogs that were formerly used to rescue snowbound travelers. The **Little St Bernard Pass** on the French-Italian border reaches 7177 ft (2187 m) and also has an 11th-century hospice.

St Catherines 43 10N 79 15W A city and port in E Canada, in S Ontario at the entrance to the *Welland Ship Canal. Founded in 1790, it is a fruit-farming and industrial center and houses Brock University (1962). Population (1991): 129,300.

St Clair, Lake A lake in E North America, on the US-Canadian border. It lies near Detroit, between Lakes Huron and Erie. Area: 460 sq mi (1190 sq km).

St Croix (*or* Santa Cruz) A West Indian island, the largest of the US Virgin Islands. The economy is based on tourism and agriculture. Area: 80 sq mi (207 sq km). Chief town: Christiansted.

St Croix River A river that flows from Chiputneticook Lakes in E Maine and W New Brunswick, Canada, S forming the Maine–New Brunswick border to Passamaquoddy Bay on the Atlantic Ocean. Lumbering is important along the river. Length: 129 mi (208 km).

Saint-Cyr, École de French military academy founded in 1803 and established in 1808 at Saint-Cyr-l'École, near Versailles. Its buildings were destroyed in World War II and it is now at Coëtquidan, Brittany.

St Denis, Ruth (Ruth Dennis; 1877–1968) US dancer and choreographer. She began her career in vaudeville but by the early 1900s had become interested in ethnic, especially Oriental, dancing. From 1904 to 1913 she choreographed and performed *Radha, Egypta,* and *O-mika.* With her husband, dancer Ted Shawn (1891–1972), she founded the Denishawn school (1915), out of which came many of the dance innovations of the times.

St-Denis 20 52S 55 27E The capital of Réunion, on the W Indian Ocean. A port on the N of the island, its activities are mainly administrative, with some commerce. Population (1990): 100,926.

St-Denis 48 56N 2 21E A city in France, an industrial suburb of Paris in the Seine-St Denis department on the Seine River. Its gothic abbey contains the tombs of many French kings. Population (1983): 93,000.

Sainte-Beuve, Charles-Augustin (1804–69) French literary historian and critic. He first studied medicine, but abandoned it to write poetry. After writing the novel *Volupté* (1834), based in part on his love affair with Victor Hugo's wife, he devoted himself to criticism. His literary journalism helped to establish many young writers of the romantic movement. His major critical works include *Critiques et portraits littéraires* (1836–39) and *Port-Royal* (1840–59), a study of Jansenism.

St Elias Mountains A mountain range in NW North America, running SE along the Alaska-Yukon (Canada) border. Many summits surpass 16,400 ft (5000 m) and it reaches 19,850 ft (6050 m) at Mount Logan, its highest point. The range also includes the world's largest nonpolar ice cap.

St Elmo's fire A small electrical discharge, with a luminous appearance, that is associated with stormy weather and seen around the extremities of tall objects, such as the tops of trees and mastheads.

St-Étienne 45 27N 4 22E A city in S central France, the capital of the Loire department. It has produced firearms since the 16th century and was the site of France's first steel mill (1815). More recent manufactures include aircraft engines, chemicals, and dyes. It has a famous school of mining engineering (1816) and a university. Population (1990): 201,965.

Saint-Exupéry, Antoine de (1900–44) French novelist and aviator. The themes of his novels, which include *Night Flight* (1931) and *Wind, Sand and Stars* (1939), derive from his experience as a pioneer of air-mail routes in N Africa and South America. He also wrote a fable for children, *The Little Prince* (1943), and an uncompleted philosophical book. He failed to return from a French air force mission.

St Gall (German name: Sankt Gallen) 47 25N 9 23E A city in NE Switzerland, S of Lake Constance. The Celtic missionary St Gall established a hermitage there (612 AD), later to become a Benedictine abbey. Monastic buildings remaining include the cathedral (1755–72) and the library, which contains a fine collection of manuscripts. Population (1987): 126,000.

Saint-Gaudens, Augustus (1848–1907) US sculptor; born in Ireland. He studied cameo cutting and sculpturing in the US, France, and Italy. From his studio in New Hampshire he sculpted bronze statues of American heroes, including Adm. David Farragut (1877), Abraham Lincoln (1887), and Gen. William T. Sherman (1903), and worked with leading architects and artists. His "The Puritan" (Springfield, Mass., 1885), the draped figure on the Adams Memorial (Washington, D.C.; 1891), and Diana (Madison Square Garden, N.Y.C.; 1892), as well as commemorative medals and coins, are among his many other works.

St George's 12 04N 61 44W The capital of Grenada, on the SW coast. Founded by the French in the 17th century, it was capital of the British Windward Islands from 1885 to 1958. It is now a tourist resort as well as an important port. Population (1991): 4,439.

St George's Channel A channel between SE Ireland and Wales, linking the Irish Sea with the Atlantic Ocean. Length: about 100 mi (160 km). Maximum width: 90 mi (145 km).

St Gotthard Pass 46 34N 8 31E A pass in the Alps, in S Switzerland linking central Europe and Italy by road. The St Gotthard railroad tunnel (constructed

St Kitts-Nevis

1872–80) below the pass is 9 mi (15 km) long and the second longest in the Alps. Height: 6935 ft (2114 m).

St Helena 15 58S 5 43W A mountainous island in the S Atlantic Ocean, a British dependent territory. Napoleon I was exiled there (1815–21). The economy declined when sailing ships stopped calling there following the opening of the Suez Canal (1869); it now depends on agriculture and UK subsidies. Area: 47 sq mi (122 sq km). Population (1988 est): 5600. Capital: Jamestown.

Saint John 45 16N 66 03W A city and port in E Canada, in New Brunswick at the mouth of the St John River. Originally a French fort (1631), it developed with the arrival of American Loyalists (1783) into the province's center of heavy industry and commerce. Population (1991): 74,969.

St John River A river in E North America. Rising in Maine, it flows NE to New Brunswick, Canada, and then SE to the Bay of Fundy, where high tides cause the river to reverse its course at the famous Reversing Falls. Length: 418 mi (673 km).

St John's 47 34N 52 41W A city in E Canada, the capital of Newfoundland. Settled in the 16th century, it is Canada's easternmost city, located beside a huge protected harbor. It was here in 1901 that Marconi received the first transatlantic radio message. St John's has two cathedrals (Roman Catholic and Anglican) and is the site of Memorial University (1925). Its industries include fishing, fish and food processing, shipbuilding, timber, and textiles. It is Newfoundland's distribution and commercial center. Population (1991): 95,770.

St John's 17 07N 61 51W The chief port of Antigua, on the NW coast. It handles the island's agricultural produce. Population (1986 est): 36,000.

St John's wort A perennial herb or shrub belonging to the genus *Hypericum* (400 species), found in temperate regions. They have yellow five-petaled flowers with many stamens and many species are cultivated for ornament, including *H. calycinum* (also known as rose of Sharon). The common European St John's wort (*H. perforatum*) reaches a height of 20 in (50 cm). Family: *Guttiferae*.

St Joseph 39 45N 94 51W A city in Missouri, on the Missouri River. Often referred to as St Joe, it is an important grain and livestock center, serving a large agricultural area. It was the home of the outlaw Jesse James. Population (1990): 71,852.

Saint-Just, Louis (Antoine Léon) de (1767–94) French politician, who supported *Robespierre in the French Revolution. His pamphlet, *Esprit de la révolution et de la constitution de France* (1791), calling for a new moral order, brought him to public notice. He was a member of the Committee of *Public Safety, supervising military affairs, and led the attack on the Austrians at Fleurus (1794). He was arrested and guillotined with Robespierre.

St Kitts-Nevis (*or* St Christopher-Nevis) Independent country in the West Indies, member of the Commonwealth of Nations. One of the Leeward Islands, it is located in the E Caribbean Sea. It formerly consisted of three islands, St Kitts, Nevis, and Anguilla, but the latter had its own constitution from 1976 and in 1980 was formally granted the status of a separate British dependency. The economy of St Kitts is primarily agricultural, sugar, molasses, cotton, and coconuts being the main products, but tourism is becoming increasingly important. Formerly a UK associated state, it achieved independence in 1983. A coalition government headed by Monsero Kennedy A. Simmonds was formed to lead the new nation. Area: 101 sq mi (262 sq km). Population (1992): 43,000. Capital: Basseterre, on St Kitts. *See also* Anguilla.

Saint Laurent, Louis Stephen (1882–1973) Canadian statesman; prime minister (1948–57). A French-Canadian, he was a lawyer and law professor (Laval University) from 1914. He served in various national positions from 1941, eventually becoming Liberal party leader and prime minister in 1948. During his administration, Newfoundland was included in the Dominion of Canada (1949) and Canada became stronger internationally and more unified domestically.

Saint-Laurent, Yves (1936–) French fashion designer, who trained with *Dior and took over his fashion house (1957), opening his own in 1962. His creations for women have been predominantly influenced by male fashion and include black leather jackets edged with fur, thigh-length boots, safari jackets, and many trouser designs.

St Lawrence, Gulf of An arm of the Atlantic Ocean in E Canada, at the mouth of the St Lawrence River. Historically the gateway to Canada, it has always been an important fishing ground. Ice closes the gulf to navigation from early December until mid-April.

St Lawrence River A river in North America. Although the river proper is fairly short, it belongs to one of the world's greatest water systems, draining the *Great Lakes into the Atlantic Ocean. From Lake Ontario it flows NE along the Canadian-US border as a broad stream through the Thousand Islands, a major tourist district. Above Montreal it enters Canada and passes through rapids where hydroelectricity is produced. At Quebec it broadens into a long estuary that gradually merges with the Gulf of St Lawrence. The St Lawrence valley is an important agricultural and industrial belt as well as a rail, water, and road corridor. The river served as the original highway into Canada. The upper reaches of the river become unnavigable during winter months. Length: Lake Ontario to Quebec, 298 mi (480 km); St Louis River headwaters to Anticosti Island, 2110 mi (3395 km). *See also* St Lawrence Seaway.

St Lawrence Seaway A navigable waterway in North America through the St Lawrence River and the Great Lakes, completed in 1959. With a season of over eight months, it admits ships of up to 9000 tons, mainly carrying heavy nonperishables.

St Louis 38 40N 90 15W A city and port in Missouri, on the Mississippi River. It was a major center in the colonization of the West, outfitting such exploring parties as that of Lewis and Clark (1804–06), as well as pioneers using the Santa Fe, California, and Oregon Trails. It has four universities, including St Louis University (1818), which maintains a library built to house microfilms of Vatican Library treasures. The state's largest city, it is an important market, trading in livestock, wool, grain, and timber. Industries include aircraft, cars, chemicals, and iron and steel. Population (1990): 396,685.

St Louis 16 00N 16 27W A port in W Senegal, on an island in the Senegal River estuary. It was the capital of Senegal until replaced by Dakar (1958). Population (1992 est): 125,717.

St Lucia An island country in the West Indies, in the Windward Islands in the E Caribbean Sea. It is a mountainous island of volcanic origin. The population is mainly of African descent. *Economy*: mainly agricultural, the chief products are bananas and coconuts. Tourism is a growing industry and attempts are being made to develop the manufacturing sector. An oil-refining and transshipment complex was in the process of being built (S of Castries) at the time of the island's independence (1979). It is a member of CARICOM. *History*: it became internally self-governing in 1967 and attained full independence within the Commonwealth of Nations in February 1979. Prime minister: John Compton. Official language: English. Official currency: East Caribbean dollar of 100 cents. Area: 238 sq mi (616 sq km). Population (1992 est): 135,000. Capital: Castries.

St-Malo 49 39N 2 00W A port and resort in NW France, in the Ille-et-Vilaine department on the English Channel. Many of its old buildings were destroyed during World War II, although its ramparts (12th–18th centuries) remain. A flourishing trading, fishing, and passenger port, it has ship building and electrical industries. Population (1985): 47,500.

St Mark's Cathedral The cathedral church of Venice since 1807. It was built in the 9th century to house the relics of St Mark but rebuilt in the 11th century after a fire. Designed as a Greek cross surmounted by five domes, it is strongly influenced by *Byzantine art and is famous for its opulent mosaic and sculptural decoration both inside and out.

St Martin (Dutch name: Sint Maarten) 18 05N 63 05W A West Indian island in the Lesser Antilles, administratively divided between France and the Netherlands. The N part is a dependency of Guadeloupe, area 20 sq mi (52 sq km) with a population (1974) of 6191; the S is part of the Netherlands Antilles, area 13 sq mi (33 sq km) with a population (1982) of 22,700. Salt is the main export.

St Moritz (German name: Sankt Moritz) 46 30N 9 51E A resort in SE Switzerland, on St Moritz Lake. A renowned winter-sports center at a height of 5978 ft (1822 m), its famous Cresta Run (for bobsleds) dates from 1885. Population (1980): 5900.

St-Nazaire 47 17N 2 12W A major port in W France, in the Loire-Atlantique department on the Loire estuary. An important German submarine base in World War II, it was virtually destroyed by Allied bombing. Its main industries are ship building, aircraft construction, chemicals, and oil refining. Population (1982): 69,000.

St Paul 45 00N 93 10W The capital city of Minnesota, on the Mississippi River. Adjacent to Minneapolis, the Twin Cities comprise the commercial and industrial center of an extensive grain and cattle area. St Paul's industries include oil refining, car assembly, and food processing. Population (1990): 272,235.

St Paul's Cathedral The cathedral of the diocese of London. Originally a Saxon and later a gothic structure, it burned down in the Great Fire of 1666, and Christopher *Wren was appointed to rebuild it. His design (1672–1717), combining *classicism and the *baroque style, features a traditional cruciform plan, a two-tiered portico, a great dome, and flanking towers.

St Peter's Basilica The Catholic basilica in the Vatican City, Rome. The original basilica, a huge gothic building, was pulled down by Pope Julius II in the early 16th century. Its replacement is the largest church in the world. Its general shape was determined by *Bramante, although it was designed together with its enormous dome by *Michelangelo. *Vignola continued the work and the nave and façade were added by *Maderna. *Bernini completed the building in the 17th century, adding the huge baldacchino and the colonnade to the piazza outside.

St Petersburg 27 45N 82 40W A city in Florida, on Tampa Bay. It is primarily a tourist resort. Population (1990): 238,629.

St Petersburg (name from 1703 until 1914: St Petersburg; name from 1914 until 1924: Petrograd; name from 1924 until 1991: Leningrad) 59 55N 30 25E The second largest city in Russia, at the head of the Gulf of Finland on the Neva River. It is a major industrial and commercial center and its port, although frozen between January and April, is one of the largest in the world. Industries include heavy engineering (particularly ship building), metallurgy, electronics, chemicals, car manufacture, and light industries; the city is an important railroad junction. St Petersburg is rich in baroque and neoclassical buildings and is noted for its broad boulevards and many bridges and canals. The most notable buildings include the Peter-Paul Fortress (St Petersburg's oldest building, founded in 1703), the Winter Palace (1754–62, rebuilt 1839), the Gostiny Dvor (1761–85) and Kazan cathedral (1801–11). The city is an important cultural center; it has a university (1918) and many museums, of which the Hermitage Museum, founded by Catherine the Great in 1764, is the most famous with its fine collection of European paintings.

History: the city was founded (1703) by Peter the Great as a "window on Europe" and was the capital of Russia from 1712 until 1918, replacing Archangel as Russia's main seaport. In the late 19th century it developed as an important industrial center and from its labor force emerged several revolutionary parties, later united by Lenin to form the St Petersburg Union for the Struggle for the Liberation of the Working Class. In 1905 a general strike took place and on Bloody Sunday (Jan 9, 1905) more than a thousand people were killed in a march on the Winter Palace. St Petersburg was also prominent in the 1917 revolution (*see* Russian Revolution). During World War II the city withstood a siege by the Germans (Sept 8, 1941–Jan 27, 1944), in which nearly a million people perished. In 1941 a road was constructed across frozen Lake Dadoga over which supplies could be brought. St Petersburg was awarded the status of "Hero City" in recognition of its ordeal. Population (1991 est): 4,466,800.

ST PAUL'S CATHEDRAL *Its dome is considered to be one of the most nearly perfect in the world.*

St Pierre 14 44N 61 11W A small port in Martinique, at the foot of the volcano Mount Pelée. In 1902 an eruption destroyed the town, leaving only one survivor. It is now the center of an area growing sugarcane.

St Pierre et Miquelon A French overseas department, consisting of two neighboring islands in the NW Atlantic Ocean S of Newfoundland. All that remained to France of its Canadian territories after 1763, they have traditionally been bases for fishing and smuggling. More recently tourism has been developed. Area: St Pierre 10 sq mi (26 sq km): Miquelon 83 sq mi (215 sq km).

St-Quentin 49 51N 3 17E A city in NE France, in the Aisne department on the Somme River. It was the scene of French defeats by Spain (1557) and by Prussia (1871) in the Franco-Prussian War and was almost completely destroyed in *World War I. It has textile, electrical, and metallurgical industries. Population (1985): 69,000.

Saint-Saëns, Camille (1835–1921) French composer, conductor, pianist, and organist. He began to perform and compose while still a child. He studied with Halévy and Gounod and held various organ posts, including nearly 20 years at the Madeleine. His piano pupils included Messager and Fauré, and he championed the music of Liszt, Berlioz, and Wagner. He wrote 12 operas, five symphonies (the third with organ; 1886), *The Carnival of the Animals* (published posthumously; 1922) for two pianos and orchestra, five piano, three violin, and two cello concertos, chamber music, and choral works.

Saint-Simon, Claude Henri de Rouvroy, Comte de (1760–1825) The founder of French socialism. Saint-Simon was educated by *D'Alembert. Having witnessed the horror and chaos of the French Revolution, Saint-Simon was concerned to reconstruct society and his writings have a positive and idealistic tone. In *Du système industriel* (1821) he declared his aim of achieving an industrial state in which poverty is eliminated and in which science replaces religion as the spiritual authority.

Saint-Simon, Louis de Rouvroy, Duc de (1675–1755) French memoir writer. He lived at the court of Louis XIV and although he exercised some influence during the regency of Philippe, Duc d'Orléans (1715–23), his ambitions at court were never realized. His *Mémoires,* covering the years 1694–1723, are enlivened by his prejudices, his sharp observation of detail, and his brilliant portraits. The definitive edition was not published until 1879–1923.

St Stephen's Crown The crown of Hungary, which was reputedly first used by Stephen I. It was originally a Byzantine circlet made between 1074 and 1077 and converted into an emperor's crown by Hungarians in the 12th century. It fell into the hands of the US army in 1945 but was returned in 1978.

St Thomas 18 22N 64 57W A West Indian island in the US Virgin Islands, in the Lesser Antilles. After 1680 it became a major Caribbean sugar producer and later, after 1764, the largest slave-trading port. Tourism is now of major importance. Area: 28 sq mi (83 sq km). Capital: Charlotte Amalie.

St Vincent, Cape (Portuguese name: Cabo de São Vicente) 37 01N 8 59W A promontory in the extreme SW of Portugal, in the Algarve on the Atlantic Ocean. A number of naval battles have been fought off the cape; in 1797 the Spanish fleet was defeated by the British under Admiral Jervis during the Napoleonic Wars.

Saint Vincent, Gulf An inlet of the Indian Ocean, in S Australia E of Yorke Peninsula. It has an important salt industry on the E coast. Length: about 90 mi (145 km). Width: about 45 mi (73 km).

St Vincent and the Grenadines A country in the E Caribbean Sea, in the Windward Islands of the Lesser Antilles. It consists of the principal island of St Vincent together with its dependencies of the Grenadine islets. It became a British possession in 1763 and attained internal self-government in 1969. In 1979 it became fully independent. It is predominantly agricultural, the chief crops being arrowroot (of which it is the world's chief producer), sugarcane, and bananas. Prime minister: R. Milton Cato. Area: 150 sq mi (390 sq km). Population (1992 est): 109,000. Capital: Kingstown.

St Vitus's dance The old name for *chorea, so called because of the uncontrolled movements characteristic of the disease and because sufferers in the Middle Ages prayed for a cure at the shrine of St Vitus (the patron saint of dancers).

Salpan 15 12N 145 43E One of the Northern Mariana Islands, in the W Pacific Ocean. It was the administrative center of the UN Trust Territory of the Pacific Islands (1947–75). Area: 70 sq mi (180 sq km). Population (1981): 14,585. Chief town: Susupe.

saithe A food fish, *Pollachius* (or *Gadus*) *virens,* also called coalfish or coley, that is related to cod and lives in shoals in the North Atlantic. Its elongated body, up to about 48 in (120 cm) long, is greenish-brown above and silvery-white below.

Sakai 34 35N 135 28E A city in Japan, in S Honshu on the Yamato delta. Formerly an important port (15th–17th centuries), it is part of the Osaka-Kobe industrial complex. Population (1991): 808,072.

saké (*or* rice wine) An alcoholic drink made in Japan from steamed rice, to which a special yeast is added, and slowly fermented. It resembles a light sherry in taste and is served warm.

Sakhalin (Japanese name: Karafuto) An island in Russia, in the Pacific Ocean between the Sea of Okhotsk and the Sea of Japan. It comprises two parallel mountain ranges on either side of a central valley and is heavily forested. Timber, coal and iron mining, and paper milling are important industrial activities, and there are oil fields in the NE that serve the Russian Far East. Agriculture, principally the cultivation of vegetables and dairy farming, is pursued in the S. *History*: a Russo-Japanese condominium from 1855 until 1875, when it passed to Russia. In 1905 it was again divided between the two countries. In 1945 the Soviet Union acquired the whole island and its Japanese population (some 400,000 people) was expelled. Japan retained its claim on the island. Area: about 29,300 sq mi (76,000 sq km). Population (1981): 650,000.

Sakharov, Andrei Dimitrievich (1921–89) Soviet physicist. After working on the development of the Soviet hydrogen bomb during the 1940s and 1950s he spoke out against nuclear weapons in the 1960s and went on to argue the need for freedom of speech in the Soviet Union. He was awarded the Nobel Peace Prize in 1975. His exile to Gorkii in 1980 aroused international protest.

saki A South American monkey belonging to the genus *Pithecia* (3 species), found in forests. Sakis are 22–50 in (55–125 cm) long including the tail (10–22 in; 25–55 cm) and have a thick shaggy coat and hairy hood. Wholly arboreal, they feed on berries, honey, leaves, and small animals. Family: *Cebidae.*

Saki (H[ector] H[ugh] Munro; 1870–1916) British humorous short-story writer. Born in Burma, he worked as a foreign correspondent before settling in London in 1908. He published several volumes of humorous stories, many of which were based on the outrageous activities of his fastidious and snobbish heroes Clovis and Reginald. He also wrote a novel, *The Unbearable Bassington* (1912). He was killed in action in World War I.

ANDREI SAKHAROV

Sakkara. *See* Saqqarah.

Saladin (Arabic name: Salah ad-Din; ?1137–93) The leader of the Muslims against the Crusaders in Syria. Of Kurdish descent, he obtained control over the Muslim lands in Egypt, of which he became sultan in 1175, and Syria. He then captured the Kingdom of Jerusalem following his great victory over the Crusaders at the battle of Hattin (1187). The last years of his life were spent fighting the Third *Crusade, during which he won his legendary reputation as a chivalrous warrior.

Salado, Río The name of several South American rivers, meaning salty river. **1.** A river in N Argentina, rising in the Andes and flowing SE to join the Río Paraná. Length: 1250 mi (2012 km). **2.** A river in W Argentina, rising near the Chilean border and flowing S to join the Río Colorado. Length: about 850 mi (1365 km).

Salam, Abdus (1926–) Pakistani physicist, who became professor of physics at Imperial College, London, in 1957. He is also director of the International Center for Theoretical Physics in Trieste. In 1979 he shared the Nobel Prize with the US physicists Sheldon Glashow and Steven Weinberg for their work on *weak interactions.

Salamanca 40 58N 5 40W A city in central Spain, in León. During the Peninsular War the battle of Salamanca was fought here on July 22, 1812, in which Wellington secured a decisive victory over the French. An intellectual center of Renaissance Europe, Salamanca remains an important cultural center with a university (founded 1218). Its many notable old buildings include two cathedrals and it has a fine Roman bridge. Population (1991): 162,544.

salamander A tailed *amphibian belonging to a widely distributed order (*Urodela* or *Caudata*; about 225 species). Salamanders have short legs and long bodies and move by bending the body from side to side to give as wide a movement as possible for their feet. They usually hide in damp places when not hunting small worms and insects. Their habits range from the wholly aquatic Japanese giant salamander (*Megalobatrachus japonicus*), 0.6 in (1.5 cm) long, to the American woodland salamanders (genus *Plethodon*) that live entirely on land. *See also* congo eel; hellbender; mudpuppy; olm; newt; siren.

Salamis A Greek island in the Aegean Sea. It was the scene of a Greek naval victory over the Persians in 480 BC. Area: 37 sq mi (95 sq km). Population (1981): 28,600. Chief town: Salamis.

sal ammoniac (*or* ammonium chloride; NH_4Cl) A white crystalline solid, used in batteries and as a pickling agent in zinc coating and tinning.

Salazar, António de Oliveira (1889–1970) Portuguese dictator. Salazar became prime minister in 1932 and ruled until suffering a stroke in 1968. His New State imposed his corporatist ideas on Portugal. It repressed political opposition and fought long colonial wars in Africa, which gravely impeded the country's economic development.

Salé 34 04N 6 50W A port in NW Morocco, on the Atlantic coast opposite Rabat. It was an important medieval port and during the 17th century was the base for the Sallee Rovers, a notorious group of Barbary pirates. Population (1982): 289,400.

Salem 11 38N 78 08E A city in India, in Tamil Nadu. A developing industrial center, it has large-scale textile manufacturing. Population (1991): 363,934.

Salem 42 31N 70 55W A city and port in NE Massachusetts NW of Boston. Settled in 1626, it became considered a center of witchcraft. As fears grew, many people were convicted of witchcraft; ultimately, 19 were hanged. In the early 1700s the witchcraft cases were annulled. Tourism is important to the city; the Salem Maritime National Historic Site and the House of Seven Gables from Nathaniel Hawthorne's novel are there. Industries include leather and chemicals. Population (1990): 38,091.

Salem 42 32N 70 53W The capital city of Oregon on the Willamette River. Founded in 1840, it is a food-processing center for a large agricultural area. Willamette University was established in 1844. Population (1990): 107,786.

Salerno 40 40N 14 46E A port in Italy, in Campania on the Gulf of Salerno. Founded by the Romans in 197 BC, Salerno is best known for its medical school, which flourished here in the Middle Ages. It was the scene of heavy fighting during World War II, following major Allied troop landings in 1943. Notable buildings include the 11th-century cathedral, where Gregory VII is buried. The

Salisbury Plain

chief industries are engineering, flour milling, textiles, and cement. Population (1991 est): 151,374

Salic Law The law of the Salian *Franks issued under Clovis in the early 6th century. Owing little to other contemporary law codes or to Roman law, it is concerned with both criminal and civil law. Its importance for later periods lies in its prohibition against women inheriting land. This canon was invoked in France in 1316 and 1321 to prevent a woman from succeeding to the throne and, in 1328, Edward III's claim to the French crown was rejected on the grounds that his claim was by female descent.

Salicornia. *See* glasswort.

salicylic acid An antiseptic compound ($C_7H_6O_3$) that causes the skin to peel. It is used to treat certain skin conditions, including psoriasis, eczema, warts, and corns. Aspirin (*see* aspirin) is a derivative.

Salieri, Antonio (1750–1825) Italian composer and conductor. He studied and worked in Vienna from 1766. His pupils included Beethoven, Schubert, and Liszt. Because of his rivalry with Mozart, he was fancifully credited with having poisoned him.

Salinas de Gortari, Carlos (1948–) Mexican political leader and president (1988–). An expert in financial planning, educated in Mexico and the United States, he worked in financial posts for the government and directed the 1981 presidential campaign of Manuel de la Madrid. Salinas was then chosen as the 1987 presidential candidate of the ruling Institutional Revolutionary party (PRI) and won the election after a surprisingly strong showing by opposition parties. His first efforts were directed at invigorating Mexico's economy, including increased exports to the United States, an effort capped by the *NAFTA treaty (1993). In 1994 he had to face a peasant rebellion in S Mexico.

Salinger, J(erome) D(avid) (1919–) US novelist. After contributing stories to the *New Yorker* he achieved great popular success with his novel *The Catcher in the Rye* (1951). Later works include *Nine Stories* (1953), *Franny and Zooey* (1961), and *Raise High the Roof Beam, Carpenters,* and *Seymour, An Introduction* (1963).

Salisbury. *See* Harare.

Salisbury 51 05N 1 48W A city in S England, at the confluence of the Avon and Wylye rivers. Its 13th-century cathedral has the highest spire in the country, 403 ft (123 m) high. Nearby is Old Sarum, the site of an Iron Age hill fort with extensive earthworks. Population (1981): 35,355.

Salisbury, Robert Cecil, 1st earl of. *See* Burghley, William Cecil, Lord.

Salisbury, Robert Arthur Talbot Gascoyne-Cecil, 3rd marquess of (1830–1903) British statesman; Conservative prime minister (1886–92, 1895–1900, 1900–02). Elected to Parliament in 1853, he was twice secretary for India (1866–67, 1874–78) before becoming Disraeli's foreign secretary (1878). His policy as prime minister has been characterized as one of "splendid isolation." Although he negotiated the Mediterranean Agreements with Italy and Austria-Hungary in 1887, under Salisbury Britain had no formal ally until alliance was concluded with Japan in 1902.

Salisbury Plain An area of open chalk downs in S England, in Wiltshire. It contains many prehistoric remains, notably *Stonehenge. Extensively used as a military training ground, the first permanent camp was established at Tidworth (1902). Area: about 200 sq mi (518 sq km).

saliva The fluid secreted by three pairs of **salivary glands** around the mouth in response to the sight, smell, taste, or thought of food. Although saliva contains the enzyme *amylase, which aids the digestion of starch, its major role is to bind the food particles and to lubricate the mouth and gullet.

Salk, Jonas (Edward) (1914–   ) US scientist; microbiologist who developed the first poliomyelitis vaccine (1952). An inactive virus vaccine, it was tested (1953–54) and used in the mid- and late 1950s to vaccinate large segments of the population against crippling polio before Albert *Sabin's oral live vaccine was developed.

Sallust (Gaius Sallustius Crispus; c. 86–c. 34 BC) Roman politician and historian. Expelled from the Senate for alleged immorality, he supported Julius Caesar in the war against Pompey and became governor of Numidia. He was accused of corruption and extortion and retired from politics in about 44 BC. His best-known works are the monographs *Bellum Catilinae* and *Bellum Jugurthinum,* noted for their forceful dramatic style.

salmon One of several fish of the genera *Oncorhynchus* or *Salmo,* especially the Atlantic salmon (*S. salar*)—a valuable food and game fish. It has an elongated body, up to 60 in (150 cm) long, and two dorsal fins. Salmon live mainly in the sea, feeding on other fish, especially herrings. However, they migrate into fresh water to spawn, at which time they change from silvery-blue or green to become brownish or greenish with orange markings. The spawned fish (kelts) either die or return to the sea and spawn in successive years. On hatching the young fish are known as alevins, although when they start feeding they are called parr. At about two years the coat becomes silver and the fish (smolt) migrate to the sea to reach maturity. After about two to three years they return to their native spawning waters as grilse, guided upstream by their sense of smell. Salmon is eaten freshly cooked (and canned) or smoked (Scotch salmon being regarded as the best). Family: *Salmonidae*; order: *Salmoniformes.*

Salmonella A genus of rod-shaped bacteria that are parasites of animals and man and cause several diseases: *S. typhi* and *S. paratyphi* cause *typhoid fever in man while *S. typhimurium* is a common cause of *food poisoning. Other species infect other mammals and birds.

Salò, Republic of (1943–45) The fascist government established by *Mussolini after Italy's surrender in World War II. Mussolini, rescued from prison by German parachute troops, set up his government at Salò in German-controlled N Italy. Partisan opposition, Mussolini's death, and Germany's surrender caused its collapse.

Salome The daughter of Herodias by her first husband, Herod Philip. The Jewish historian Josephus identifies her with the unnamed girl in the Gospels who requested the head of *John the Baptist from her stepfather, *Herod Antipas, as a reward for her dancing.

Salon The annual exhibition held by the French Royal Academy, which was founded in 1648. Housed in the Salon d'Apollon, in the Louvre, it became a bulwark of conservative art in the 19th century. The **Salon des Refusés** (1863) was a special exhibition held at the instigation of Napoleon III to exhibit the enormous number of paintings rejected by the Salon jury that year. Its contributors included *Manet, *Pissarro, and *Whistler.

Salon des Indépendants The annual exhibition of the Société des Artistes Indépendants in Paris. The Société was founded in 1884 to enable such avant-garde painters as *Cézanne and *Seurat to exhibit works that had been or would have been rejected by the French Royal Academy's *Salon. Unlike the Salon, the Salon des Indépendants had no jury.

Salonika. *See* Thessaloníki.

salp. *See* tunicate.

salsify A biennial herb, *Tragopogon porrifolius,* native to the Mediterranean region, also called vegetable oyster or oyster plant. It is cultivated in temperate regions for its fleshy white root, supposed to taste like oysters when cooked. The plant has long narrow leaves and a head of purple flowers surrounded by stiff pointed green sepals. The leaves may be eaten in salads. Family: **Compositae.*

salt 1. (sodium chloride; NaCl) The crystalline solid that is used for seasoning and preserving food and is present in sea water and halite, which are its chief sources (naturally occurring sodium chloride is often called rock salt). NaCl forms cubic crystals. It has an important function in the human body and is used in the manufacture of many chemicals, such as soap, fertilizer, and ceramics. **2.** Any similar compound formed, together with water, when an acid reacts with a base, for example the salt potassium sulfate is formed when sulfuric acid reacts with potassium hydroxide: $H_2SO_4 + 2KOH \rightarrow K_2SO_4 + 2H_2O$.

Salta 24 46S 65 28W A city in N Argentina. It is a commercial center on the Trans-Andean Railroad and trades with Bolivia and Chile. Population (1991): 373,856.

SALT Agreements (1968–72) Strategic Arms Limitation Talks agreements reached between the US and the Soviet Union to control the nuclear arms race. Talks begun in 1968 resulted in the signing of agreements in 1972 that limited antiballistic missile and offensive strategic missile systems in both countries. SALT II, signed in 1979, further limited these weapons.

saltbush A salt-tolerant herb or shrub, especially one belonging to either of the genera *Atriplex* or *Chenopodium.* They have inconspicuous flowers and are used as forage plants in dry salty regions of Australia and North America. Family: *Chenopodiaceae.*

Saltillo 25 30N 101 00W A city in NE Mexico. The focal point of road and rail routes, it is the commercial center for an agricultural region. Its university (1867) was refounded in 1957. Population (1980): 321,758.

Salt Lake City 40 45N 111 55W The capital city of Utah near Great Salt Lake. Founded in 1847 by the Mormons under the leadership of Brigham Young, it is the world headquarters of the Mormon Church. The Mormon tabernacle (1867) and the University of Utah (1850) are there. It is a commercial center for nearby mining operations and its industries include food processing, textiles, oil refining, and printing and publishing. Population (1990): 159,936.

Salto 31 27S 57 50W A port in NW Uruguay, on the Uruguay River. It is an important meat-packing center; other products include wine and soft drinks. Population (1985): 80,787.

saltpeter (potassium nitrate *or* niter; KNO_3) A white crystalline solid used as a fertilizer, a food preservative, and in *gunpowder and fireworks.

saltwort An annual or perennial herb belonging to the widely distributed genus *Salsola* (50 species), found on seashores and salt marshes. They have fleshy spiked leaves and small flowers. The European saltwort (*S. kali*) grows up to 24 in (60 cm) tall. Family: *Chenopodiaceae.*

saluki A breed of hunting dog dating back over 8000 years in Egypt and used by Arabs for hunting gazelle. It has a slender streamlined body with long legs, giving speed and agility, and a small head with a long narrow muzzle. The smooth soft coat can be white, brownish, reddish, or black, tan, and white. Height: 20–28 in (50–70 cm).

Salvador (*or* Bahia) 12 58S 38 29W A port in NE Brazil, the capital of Bahia state on the Atlantic Ocean. It has a fine natural harbor; exports include cocoa, sugar, tobacco, and diamonds. The chief industries are food and tobacco processing. It is the seat of two universities. Population (1980): 1,496,276.

Salvador. *See* El Salvador, Republic of.

Salvation Army The international Christian organization founded in 1865 in London by William *Booth. Run on strictly military lines and led by an official called a general, it exacts absolute obedience from its members, who wear a characteristic uniform on public occasions. Morality in practical Christian living is more esteemed than doctrinal niceties and the Army rejects the sacraments. It is famous for its social and missionary work, especially in disaster relief and in poor urban areas, where it runs shelters, soup kitchens, hostels, and counseling, particularly for alcohol and drug abuse.

Salvia A genus of perennial herbs and shrubs (about 700 species), widely distributed in temperate and tropical regions. Many are cultivated for ornament, including the Brazilian scarlet sage (*S. splendens*) and the blue-flowered *S. patens*. Common *sage is the culinary herb. Family: *Labiatae*.

SALVATION ARMY *A band and chorus campaign in a small town in England.*

sal volatile (*or* ammonium carbonate) A mixture of ammonium salts, or their solution in alcohol, that is used in smelling salts. It smells of ammonia and is made by heating ammonium chloride (*or* sal ammoniac) with calcium sulfate.

Salween River (Chinese name: Nu Jiang *or* Nu Chiang) A river in SE China and E Burma, rising in Tibet and flowing E then S to an inlet of the Andaman Sea. Little of its length is navigable but it supplies hydroelectric power. Length: 1500 mi (2400 km).

Salyut A series of manned Soviet space stations first launched into earth orbit in 1971. Salyut 7, launched in 1982, was operational for several years. Cosmonauts from E Europe were conveyed to and from the orbiting laboratory by Soyuz spacecraft. They remained on the space station for long periods, in weightless conditions, conducting a variety of experiments and observations. Their physical and psychological fitness was carefully monitored. Salyut stations were smaller than the US *Skylab space station.

Salzburg 47 54N 13 03E A city in central Austria, the capital of Salzburg. Its many fine buildings include the fortress of Hohensalzburg and the cathedral (1614–28). Salzburg University was refounded in 1962. Mozart was born there and a famous musical event, the Salzburg Festival, is held annually. Industries include textiles and leather. Population (1991): 143,971.

Salzgitter 52 02N 10 22E A city in N Germany, in Lower Saxony, formed in 1942 from 29 separate towns. The area is rich in iron ore, which is used in the manufacture of steel products. Population (1991 est): 114,355.

samadhi The state of perfect concentration attained in deep meditation. In Hinduism it is taken to be union with *Brahman or with a deity. In Buddhism it refers to transcending the distinction between subject and object. Its attainment is a precondition of spiritual liberation.

Samar The third largest island in the Philippines, in the Visayan Islands linked by bridge to Leyte. Its frequent typhoons restrict agriculture; the chief products are rice, coconuts, and hemp. Copper and iron ore are mined. Area: 5181 sq mi (13,415 sq km). Chief town: Catbalogan.

Samara. *See* Kuibyshev.

Samaria 1. The central region of ancient Palestine, which became part of the northern kingdom of Israel in the 10th century BC. *See also* Samaritans. **2.** 32 17N 35 12E The capital from the 9th century until its destruction in about 721 BC of the kingdom of Israel. Occupied from the 4th millennium BC, the site was excavated in 1908–10, 1931–33, and 1935. Among the discoveries unearthed were a collection of 9th-century BC ivory carvings. The city was rebuilt in the 1st century AD under Herod the Great and renamed Sebaste (modern name: Sebastiyah, in Jordan).

Samaritans 1. A people of ancient Samaria (now in N Israel), with a religion closely akin to Judaism. Numerous in Roman and Byzantine times and much disliked by the Jews, they declined under Muslim rule. They now number only a few hundred. They have a conservative religious tradition and many distinctive beliefs and customs. **2.** A telephone service for the suicidal and despairing started in 1953 by the Rev. Chad Varah in London, England. It is now a worldwide organization with several branches in the US, mainly on the east coast (New York, Boston, Providence, etc.).

samarium (Sm) A *lanthanide element discovered spectroscopically by Lecoq de Boisbaudran in 1879. It occurs naturally, with other lanthanides, in monazite ($CePO_4$). The oxide (Sm_2O_3) is used in glasses that absorb infrared radiation and the element is used in lasers as a dopant in calcium fluoride. At no 62; at wt 150.4; mp 1970 ± 9°F (1077 ± 5°C); bp 3256°F (1791°C).

Samarkand 39 40N 66 57E A city in Uzbekistan. The principal industrial activities are cotton and silk manufacturing, wine making, and metalworking but its interest lies chiefly in its past. *History*: it was the chief junction of the ancient *Silk Road between China and the Mediterranean and, conquered by the Arabs in the 8th century, became the Abbasid's capital (9th–10th centuries) and a great Islamic center. In the 14th century it became the capital of Timur's mighty empire, coming later under the rule of the Uzbek people (16th–19th centuries). The city's remarkable historic buildings include Timur's mausoleum. Population (1991 est): 370,000.

samizdat (Russian: self-publication) The underground system of distribution within the Soviet Union of literature, the open publication of which was prohibited by the authorities. Literature circulated in this way, usually in the form of typewritten copies, included work by such writers as *Solzhenitsyn and *Sakharov.

Samoa A chain of volcanic islands in the S central Pacific Ocean. Discovered by the Dutch in the 18th century, the islands were politically divided in 1900 between the US and Germany. **American Samoa**, comprising the E islands of the chain, is an unincorporated US territory consisting of the chief island of Tutuila and several smaller ones. Agriculture is the main occupation; canned tuna is an important export. Area: 76 sq mi (197 sq km). Population (1992): 50,900. Capital: Pago Pago. **Western Samoa** was a German protectorate until World War I and then under New Zealand control, becoming an independent state in 1962. It consists of the main islands of Savai'i and Upolu and several smaller islands and islets. Subsistence agriculture is the main occupation and exports, chiefly to New Zealand, are copra, bananas, and cocoa. Some industrial development has taken place in recent years. Head of state: HH Malietoa Tanumafili II. Official languages: Samoan and English. Official currency: Western Samoa dollar. Area: 1097 sq mi (2842 sq km). Population (1992 est): 190,000.

Sámos A Greek island in the SE Aegean Sea, lying close to the mainland of Turkey. Already one of the principal commercial centers of Greece by the 7th century BC, it achieved its greatest prosperity under the tyrant Polycrates in the 6th century. It is the birthplace of the mathematician and philosopher Pythagoras. Area: 190 sq mi (492 sq km).

Samothrace (Modern Greek name: Samothráki) A Greek island in the N Aegean Sea. The statue of the Winged Victory (now in the Louvre) was discovered there in 1863. Area: 70 sq mi (181 sq km).

Samoyed (dog) A breed of dog developed in Siberia and used by the Samoyed tribesmen as a sledge dog. It is robustly built with husky-like features; the white or cream coat consists of a short soft undercoat and a long coarse outer coat. Height: 20–22 in (51–56 cm) (dogs); 18–20 in (46–51 cm) (bitches).

Samoyed (people) A group of Siberian peoples of the tundra and N forest region of central Russia. They were traditionally nomadic reindeer hunters and fishers, now mainly settled as reindeer breeders. *Shamanism dominates their religious life. Of the five Samoyed languages, which, with the *Finno-Ugric languages, comprise the *Uralic family, only Nenets (or Yurak) has a considerable number of speakers.

samphire A perennial herb, *Crithmum maritimum,* native to rocky coasts of S England. Up to 12 in (30 cm) high, it has small white or yellowish flowers, a succulent stem, and slender fleshy leaves, which may be used in salads or pickles. Family: *Umbelliferae.*

The golden samphire (*Inula crithmoides*), also native to British coasts, grows to 32 in (80 cm) and has broader leaves and larger yellow flowers. Family: *Compositae. See also* glasswort (marsh samphire).

Samsun 41 17N 36 22E A port in central N Turkey, on the Black Sea. It exports cereals, copper, and tobacco and has a university (1975). Population (1990): 303,979.

Samudra Gupta (died c. 380 AD) Emperor of India (c. 330–c. 380) of the *Gupta dynasty and grandson of *Chandra Gupta I. He strove to expand and consolidate his empire, making many conquests, and kings of neighboring dynasties paid him tribute.

Samuel In the Old Testament, the first of the Hebrew prophets and the last of the "judges," who led the Israelites before the establishment of the monarchy in Palestine. The two **Books of Samuel** appear to be compiled from various sources. They are the principal sources for the history of the Israelites in the 11th and 10th centuries BC and contain the biography of Samuel and the history of the reigns of *Saul and *David, both of whom Samuel anointed as the first two kings of Israel.

Samuelson, Paul Anthony (1915–   ) US economist; Nobel Prize in economics (1970). He taught at Massachusetts Institute of Technology where he modified and analyzed the theories of John Maynard *Keynes and used mathematics applied to economic problems in *Foundations of Economic Analysis* (1947). His textbook *Economics* (1st ed., 1948) is widely used.

samurai The provincial warriors (also known as *bushi*; *see* Bushido), who rose to power in Japan in the 11th century. The term originally referred to the armed retainers employed by court nobles from the late 8th century. The samurai mostly became the vassals of *daimyo* and after 1600, when they comprised about 6% of the population, they were generally forced to reside in their lord's castle town. The samurai class was sharply divided from other classes by its superior status and marked distinctions also existed within its own ranks. After the Meiji restoration (1868) the samurai lost their special position but ex-samurai became leaders in various areas of modern Japanese life.

San'a' 15 23N 44 14E The capital of North Yemen, in the center of the country. Until the formation of the state of Israel, there was a large Jewish ghetto in the city. Notable buildings include the Great Mosque, where there is a sacred Muslim shrine, and the Liberty Gate. A university was founded in 1970 with Kuwaiti assistance. Population (1986): 427,187.

San Andreas Fault A notorious fracture in the earth's crust, 750 mi (1200 km) in length, running through California. In 1906 a horizontal displacement of about 20 ft (6 m) and a lateral displacement of only 3 ft (1 m) caused an earthquake that devastated San Francisco. These movements, constantly recorded by seismographs, are now interpreted as resulting from collision of tectonic plates, a rotating Pacific plate and an American plate.

San Antonio 29 25N 98 30W A city in S central Texas. Founded in 1718, it was the scene of the Mexican attack on the *Alamo (1836) during the Texas revolution. San Antonio has several military bases and is a commercial and industrial center for a large agricultural region. The Alamo and other historical places of interest make it a popular tourist center. The mild climate has attracted many retired people. Population (1990): 935,933.

San Bernardino 34 07N 117 18W A city in California. Situated in a fruit-growing area, it is the site of the annual National Orange Show but industrial developments in aerospace and steel are now the main economic activities. Population (1990): 164,164.

San Cristóbal 7 46N 72 15W A city in W Venezuela. It is the commercial center for an area producing maize, cassava, sugarcane, and coffee. Its university was founded in 1962. Population (1990 est): 220,697.

sanctions Penalties imposed for breaking a law, especially international law. First imposed by the *League of Nations on Italy following its invasion of Ethiopia, sanctions have also been imposed by UN countries, such as those against Rhodesia (now *Zimbabwe) following its unilateral declaration of independence in 1965. These sanctions were broken by oil companies and others, which suggests that when there are economic pressures against imposing sanctions, they are difficult to enforce.

sanctuary The holiest part of a church or temple, where the main altar stands. During the Middle Ages criminals could claim right of sanctuary, i.e. they took refuge in a church and were thus immune from prosecution for 40 days, during which time they could opt to accept a safe conduct out of the country.

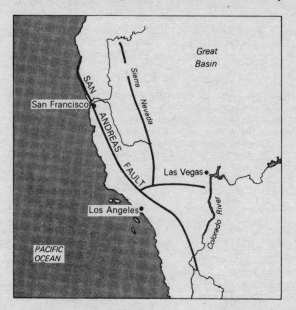

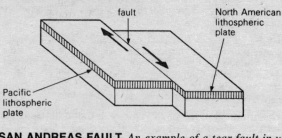

SAN ANDREAS FAULT *An example of a tear fault in which the rocks are being displaced horizontally.*

sand Unconsolidated grains of rock, varying in size from 0.002–0.08 in (0.06–2.00 mm) in diameter. Consolidated sands form *sandstones; grits are coarse sandstones with angular grains. Most sands consist principally of quartz, derived from the weathering of quartz-bearing rocks. Sand is used in glass and cement production, and as an abrasive.

Sand, George (Aurore Dupin, Baronne Dudevant; 1804–76) French novelist. In 1831 she left her husband and went to Paris to write her first novel, *Indiana* (1832), a plea for women's right to independence, the first of an enormous number of successful novels. Among her many lovers were Alfred de Musset and Frédéric Chopin.

sandalwood An evergreen tree belonging to the genus *Santalum* (about 25 species), native to SE Asia and the Pacific Islands. The true sandalwood

(*S. album*) grows to a height of about 33 ft (10 m) and is partially parasitic on the roots of other trees. Its white wood is used to make boxes and furniture and, when distilled, yields sweet-scented sandalwood oil, used in perfumes, incense, candles, etc. Family: *Santalaceae*.

sandarac The *resin of a N African conifer, *Tetraclinis articulata,* used in making varnishes.

Sandburg, Carl (1878–1967) US poet and author. Sandburg first gained a national following with the publication of his *Chicago Poems* (1915). As a historian, he published the first volume of his Lincoln biography, *The Prairie Years*, in 1926 and as a collector of folk songs, he published *The American Songbag* in 1927. Among his later works, *The People, Yes* expressed his hope for an ideal society. In 1940 he won the Pulitzer Prize in history for the second volume of his Lincoln biography, *The War Years*, and in 1951, he won the Pulitzer Prize in poetry for his *Complete Poems*.

sand dollar A marine invertebrate animal, also called cake urchin, belonging to an order (*Clypeastroida*) of *echinoderms. Its round flat rigid body is covered with small spines and saclike organs (tube feet). Sand dollars live on the sea bed and sift minute food particles from the sand in which they burrow. Class: *Echinoidea*.

sand dune The accumulation of wind-blown sand into a mound. Sand dunes are characteristic of desert areas where there is a plentiful sand supply and of coastal areas. They are unvegetated and two main forms occur in desert areas: the barchan, or crescent-shaped dune, and the seif, or longitudinal dune. In coastal areas dunes generally become "fixed" by vegetation.

sanderling A bird, *Calidris alba*, that nests on Arctic coasts and winters on shores worldwide; 8 in (20 cm) long, it has a rust-colored upper plumage, changing to pale-brown in winter, and a long white wing stripe. It feeds on shrimps, sandhoppers, and mollusks with its straight slender bill. Family: *Scolopacidae* (sandpipers).

sand flea. *See* sand hopper.

sandfly A small fly belonging to the widely distributed genus *Phlebotomus*. Sandflies are among the worst pests of the tropics: the bloodsucking females can give a painful bite and several species are carriers of serious human diseases, including infections caused by the parasite *Leishmania* (*see* leishmaniasis).

The name has also been used for many bloodsucking *gnats and *midges of sandy places.

San Francisco Conference on International Organization (1945) Meeting of delegates of 51 nations in San Francisco, Calif., at the end of World War II, to form the United Nations. The UN charter, drafted at this conference in April, was signed in June.

sandgrouse A bird belonging to a family (*Pteroclidae*; 16 species) occurring in warm arid regions of Europe and Africa; 9–16 in (22–40 cm) long, sandgrouse have camouflaging plumage, long pointed wings, short legs, feathered feet, and a very tough skin. They are gregarious and feed on plant material, flying long distances to water at dawn and dusk. Although resembling grouse, they belong to the order *Columbiformes* (pigeons).

sand hopper A small terrestrial jumping *crustacean, also called beach hopper and sand or beach flea, belonging to the family *Talitridae*. Its body, 0.4–1 in (10–25 mm) long, is laterally flattened and lacks a carapace. During the day it is buried in sand but at night it emerges to feed on organic debris under stones or among seaweed. Order: *Amphipoda*.

Sandhurst 51 02N 0 34E A village in SE England. The Royal Military Academy (1799) for training officers is situated there.

San Diego 32 45N 117 10W A city in California, on San Diego Bay. It has a US naval base and large naval air service facilities. Employment is mainly dependent on the aircraft and aerospace industries. San Diego is also an important center of scientific research and is the site of the Scripps Institute of Oceanography (1903). Population (1990): 1,110,549.

sand lizard A slender long-tailed European lizard, *Lacerta agilis*, occurring in sandy regions. Up to 8 in (20 cm) long, it is pale-brown or gray with whitish underparts and three rows of white-centered dark spots along its back. It feeds on insects and spiders. Family: *Lacertidae*.

sandpiper A wading bird belonging to a family (*Scolopacidae*; 82 species) occurring chiefly in the N hemisphere, breeding in N latitudes and migrating S to winter; 5–24 in (12–60 cm) long, sandpipers typically have long legs, long wings, a mottled brown or gray plumage, which commonly changes color seasonally, and a long slender bill. They nest in marshy regions or on mud flats and feed on small invertebrates. Order: *Charadriiformes* (gulls, plovers, etc.)

sandstone A sedimentary rock consisting of consolidated *sand, cemented mainly by calcareous, siliceous, or ferruginous minerals. They may be deposited by wind action in deserts or in shallow seas, estuaries and deltas, and along low-lying coasts by water. Sandstones vary in color from red to yellow to white according to the presence of other minerals (feldspar, mica, glauconite, iron oxides, etc.) in addition to the quartz.

Sandwich Islands. *See* Hawaii.

San Francisco 37 40N 122 25W A city in N California, situated on a peninsula between San Francisco Bay and the Pacific Ocean. A major seaport, San Francisco serves a large agricultural and mining area and is the financial and insurance center of the West Coast. Industries include food processing, ship building, and petroleum refining. Among its many famous landmarks are the San Francisco–Oakland Bay Bridge (1936), the Golden Gate Bridge (1937), Chinatown, and the city's cable cars. A major cultural and educational center, it is the site of several universities and colleges. *History*: founded by the Spanish in 1776, it was still a village when captured by US troops (1846) during the Mexican War. It expanded rapidly following the discovery of gold in California (1848) and it was during this period that the first Chinese settled in the city. In 1906 there was a sudden violent movement in the massive San Andreas Fault, which extends along the Californian coast, and San Francisco was almost completely destroyed by an earthquake and three-day fire. A devastating earthquake severely damaged the city again in 1989. Population (1990): 723,959.

Sanger, Frederick (1918–   ) British biochemist, who determined the order of *amino acids in the insulin molecule. This work, at Cambridge University, started in 1945 and took him eight years to complete. He was awarded Nobel Prizes in 1958 and 1980.

Sanger, Margaret (Higgins) (1883–1966) US reformer. She worked as a nurse in New York City's poorer sections and saw the deaths from self-induced abortions. She went to Europe in 1913 to learn more about contraception methods; upon her return to the US (1914) she published *Woman Rebel*, a magazine about birth control, a term she coined. Her clinic, the first for birth control guidance, opened in 1916 in New York City, and although it was raided and she was jailed many times, she persevered. She founded the National Birth Control League (later Planned Parenthood Federation of America; 1917) and the International Planned Parenthood Federation (1952).

sangha The Buddhist monastic order. Together with the *Buddha and *dharma, it forms the third of the *tri-ratna of Buddhism. An individual may become a monk temporarily or for life.

Sanhedrin The highest court of the Jews, which met in Jerusalem. Its development is unclear; in early New Testament times the Greeks allowed the establishment of a senate and later forms became known as the Sanhedrin. Its composition and its jurisdiction varied with its history. In New Testament times, the high priest was president and its functions were administrative, judicial, and religious.

sanicle A perennial herb belonging to the genus *Sanicula* (37 species), distributed worldwide except for Australia and New Guinea. The common European sanicle (*S. europaea*) grows to a height of 20 in (50 cm) and has several broad lobed leaves and clusters of small pinkish flowers. Family: *Umbelliferae*.

San Jacinto, Battle of (1836) US-Mexican clash that brought independence for Texas. American troops, under Gen. Sam *Houston, defeated forces under Mexican Gen. Antonio *Santa Anna near present-day Houston, Tex. Mexican casualties were high, and Santa Anna was taken prisoner.

San José 37 20N 121 55W A city in N California, on the S arm of San Francisco Bay. Founded in 1777, it was the first city in California and state capital (1849–51). Situated in the fertile Santa Clara Valley, it has many food-processing plants and wineries as well as aerospace and electronics industries. Population (1990): 782,248.

San José 9 50N 84 02W The capital of Costa Rica, situated in the center of the country in a high fertile valley. Founded in 1736, it became a center of the tobacco trade and later of coffee production. The University of Costa Rica was founded in 1843. Population (1991 est): 300,000.

San Juan 18 29N 66 08W The capital and main port of Puerto Rico, in the N. Founded by the Spanish in 1508, it was later attacked by the English and by the Dutch; in 1898 it was captured by the US navy. It has expanded considerably in the 20th century and is now also an industrial and tourist center. The chief exports are coffee, sugar, and tobacco. The Inter-American University of Puerto Rico was founded in 1912 and a campus of the University of Puerto Rico in 1950. Population (1990): 426,832.

San Juan 31 33S 68 31W A city in W Argentina. Severely damaged by an earthquake (1944), it is the commercial center of a wine-producing area. Population (1991 est): 119,400.

San Juan Hill, Battle of (1898) US-Spanish conflict at San Juan, Cuba, during the *Spanish-American War. As part of a land and sea operation, US troops, among them Theodore *Roosevelt and his Rough Rider unit, stormed the hills outside of Santiago, Cuba. Successful, US troops commanded the city and the Spanish admiral, Pascual Cervera, fled the harbor, resulting in the destruction of his fleet.

Sankara (8th century AD) Hindu philosopher. Sankara left his native Kerala to become a wandering holy man. It was popularly believed that he was an incarnation of *Shiva. He wrote commentaries on the *Brahmasutras*, the *Bhagavadgita*, and the *Upanishads* and founded the Smarta Brahmin sect and several monasteries. He made major contributions to the *Vedanta philosophical tradition, believing that the physical world relates to the ultimate reality as a state of ignorance does to knowledge.

San Lorenzo, Treaty of. *See* Pinckney, Charles.

San Luis Potosí 22 10N 101 00W A city in NE Mexico. It is the industrial center for a rich agricultural and silver-mining area and has a fine baroque cathedral and a university (founded 1826). Population (1986): 600,000.

San Marino, Republic of A small independent republic, an enclave in Italian territory, situated on the slopes of the Apennines mountain range, SW of Rimini. *Economy*: farming, tourism, and the sale of postage stamps are the main sources of income. *History*: dating from the 4th century AD, it was an independent commune by the 12th century. In 1862, the newly established kingdom of Italy guaranteed San Marino's independence and a customs union. Executive power lies in the Congress of State and two regents elected by the Great and General Council. In 1992, San Marino became a member of the UN. Official language: Italian. Official currency: both Italian and Vatican City currencies are in use. Area: 24 sq mi (61 sq km). Population (1990 est): 23,000. Capital: San Marino.

SAN MARINO *The first of three fortresses situated on the central limestone mass of Monte Titano.*

San Martin, José de (1778–1850) South American soldier and statesman; the national hero of Argentina. After participating in the struggle of Buenos Aires against the Spanish, he raised and trained an army in Argentina (1814–16), which he led heroically across the Andes and, with Bernardo *O'Higgins, defeated the Spanish at Chacubuco (1817) and Maipo (1818), achieving the liberation of Chile. In 1821, after creating a Chilean navy, he entered Lima, proclaimed the independence of Peru, and became its "protector." He resigned in 1822, after differences with Bolívar, and retired to France.

San Miguel de Tucumán (*or* Tucumán) 26 47S 65 15W A city in NW Argentina, at the foot of the E Andes. It has a cathedral and a university (1914) and is an important sugar-refining center. Population (1991 est): 473,000.

San Pedro Sula 15 26N 88 01W A city in NW Honduras. It serves an agricultural area producing bananas and sugarcane and is the chief industrial center of the country. Population (1989 est): 300,000.

San Salvador 13 59N 89 18W The capital of El Salvador, situated in the center of the country. Founded by the Spanish in 1525, it was the capital of the Central American Federation from 1831 until 1838, becoming the capital of El Salvador in 1839. It has suffered several severe earthquakes. Industries include textiles and food processing. The University of El Salvador was founded in 1841. Population (1987 est): 481,000.

San Salvador Island (former name: Watling Island) 24 00N 74 32W A West Indian island in the central Bahamas. It was Columbus's first sight of land (1492) in the New World. Area: 60 sq mi (156 sq km).

sansculottes (French: without knee breeches) The violent extremists of the French Revolution, so called because they wore trousers rather than the knee breeches of the aristocracy. The original sansculottes were the Paris workers who stormed the Bastille and led the food riots in 1789. Later radical extremists, such as Marat and Danton, who used the Paris mobs to gain control, were also called sansculottes.

San Sebastián 43 19N 1 59W A seaside resort in N Spain, in the Basque Provinces on the Bay of Biscay. It possesses a cathedral and its palace was formerly the summer residence of the Spanish royal family. The La Concha beaches attract many tourists. Population (1986): 180,043.

Sansevieria A genus of herbaceous perennial plants (60 species) native to tropical and S Africa and S Asia. They have a basal rosette of stiff swordlike leaves arising from thick creeping underground stems (rhizomes). *S. trifasciata* var. *laurentii* (mother-in-law's tongue) is a popular houseplant with ornamental leaves, striped green and yellow, up to 35 in (90 cm) long. The leaves of several species (e.g. *S. zeylanica*) yield a fiber (bowstring hemp) used for ropes, mats, etc. Family: *Liliaceae*.

Sanskrit The classical literary language of the Hindu scriptures, belonging to the *Indo-Aryan family. From it the *Prakrits and modern N Indian languages developed. It was spoken in NW India from 1500 BC, became a scholarly language when the grammarian *Panini standardized it (5th century BC), and is still used as a sacred language. It is highly complex and is written in the *Devanagari script.

San Stefano, Treaty of (1878) The treaty that concluded the war between the Ottoman Empire and Russia (1877–78). The defeated Ottomans recognized the independence of Serbia, Romania, and Montenegro and the autonomy of Bosnia-Herzegovina and Bulgaria. At the Congress of *Berlin (1878), the other great powers, fearing that the Balkans would fall under the dominance of Russia, modified the treaty.

Santa Ana 14 00N 79 31W The second largest city in El Salvador. It is a major coffee center and has one of the largest coffee mills in the world. Population (1987 est): 232,000.

Santa Ana 33 43N 117 54W A city in SW California, SE of Los Angeles. Founded in 1869, it produces food goods; rubber, fiberglass, and electronic products; and aircraft. Population (1990): 293,742.

Santa Anna, Antonio López de (1794–1876) Mexican soldier and statesman; president (1833–36) and dictator (1839, 1841–45). After engineering *Iturbide's downfall in 1823, Santa Anna dominated Mexican politics for the next 20 years. He is best known for his defeat of Texan forces at the *Alamo (1836). Subsequently taken prisoner by the Americans, he was forced to retire but twice returned to power before being driven into exile (1845–74).

Santa Barbara 54 25N 119 42W A city on the SW coast of California. The University of California at Santa Barbara (1891) is there. The Santa Barbara Mission, founded in 1786, and the beaches are major tourist attractions. Offshore oil drilling, aerospace research, electronics products, and fishing are important to the economy. Population (1990): 85,571.

Santa Clara 22 25N 79 58W A city in central Cuba. It is the commercial center for an agricultural area producing sugar and tobacco. Population (1989 est): 191,000.

Santa Claus. *See* Nicholas, St.

Santa Cruz 17 45S 63 14W A city in SE Bolivia. It is the commercial center for an area producing chiefly sugarcane, rice, and coffee. Industries include the manufacture of cigarettes and sugar refining. It is the site of a university (1880). Population (1989 est): 529,000.

Santa Cruz de Tenerife 28 28N 16 15W A city in the Canary Islands, in NE Tenerife. An uprising that began the Spanish Civil War took place there (1936). It is a major fueling station with an oil refinery. Population (1986): 211,400.

Santa Fe 35 41N 105 57W A city, resort and the capital of New Mexico, on the Santa Fe River. Following Mexico's attainment of independence from Spain in 1821, Santa Fe developed a commercial route (the **Santa Fe Trail**) with the US. Population (1990): 55,859.

Santa Fé 31 38S 60 43W A port in E Argentina, the furthest point accessible to oceangoing vessels on the Río Paraná. Founded in 1573, it has a cathedral (1685) and a university (1919) and is the center of a grain-growing and stock-rearing area. Population (1991): 442,214.

Santa Fe Trail A trail that began near Independence, Mo., and led W through Raton Pass and along the Arkansas River (later, across the Cimarron Desert) to Santa Fe, N.M. Blazed in 1821 by William Becknell, the trail opened up a southern overland trade route through the central US. Its importance diminished in about 1880 with the coming of the railroad. Length: c. 800 mi (1300 km).

Santa Marta 11 18N 74 10W A port in N Colombia, on the Caribbean Sea. The chief exports are bananas, coffee, and cocoa. Simón *Bolívar, leader of the South American independence movement, died there (1830). Population (1985): 218,200.

Santa Monica 34 01N 118 30W A resort city in SW California, W of Los Angeles, on Santa Monica Bay. Founded in 1875, the city has fine beaches and attracts tourists. Industries include aerospace and plastic components, aircraft, cosmetics, and laser systems. Population (1990): 86,905.

Santander 43 28N 3 48W A city and port in N Spain, in Old Castile on Cape Mayor. Part of the city was rebuilt after being burned in 1941. It possesses a gothic cathedral. Its industries include fishing and ship building. Population (1991): 189,069.

Santayana, George (1863–1952) Spanish-born US philosopher and poet. He taught at Harvard (1889–1911) and eventually settled in Rome (1924). He believed that the mind was largely governed by physical and biological considerations and his philosophy, set out in *Realms of Being* (1927–40), consequently tended toward materialism. He wrote in an unusually witty and urbane style. His works include *The Sense of Beauty* (1896), *The Life of Reason* (1905–06), *Skepticism and Animal Faith* (1923), and *Dominations and Powers* (1951). His novel *The Last Puritan* (1935) was very popular.

Santiago (*or* Santiago de Chile) 33 35S 70 40W The capital of Chile, situated in the center of the country at the foot of the Andes. It was founded by the Spanish in 1541. About half of Chile's industry is centered there, including food processing, textiles, and metallurgy. There are three universities. Population (1991 est): 3,604,056.

São Tomé and Príncipe, Democratic Republic of

Santiago de Compostela 42 52N 8 33W A city in NW Spain, in Galicia. Since the 9th century AD it has been a famous place of pilgrimage reputedly containing the tomb of St James, the patron saint of Spain. Its romanesque cathedral (1078–1211) was built on the site of the tomb. The university was founded in 1532. Population (1986): 104,050.

Santiago de Cuba 20 00N 75 49W A port in Cuba, on the Caribbean Sea. It was the scene of Fidel *Castro's July 26 revolt (1953). Exports include metal ores, sugar, coffee, and tobacco. It is the site of the University of Oriente (1947) and has a large cathedral. Population (1989 est): 397,000.

Santiago del Estero 27 48S 64 15W A city in N Argentina. It is a commercial center serving an agricultural area producing wheat, cotton, maize, and livestock. The chief industry is food processing. Population (1991): 201,709.

Santiago de los Caballeros 19 30N 70 42W A city in the N Dominican Republic. The commercial center for a fertile agricultural region, its industries include the manufacture of cigarettes, pharmaceuticals, and furniture. Population (1986): 308,000.

Santo Domingo 18 32N 69 50W The capital of the Dominican Republic, a port on the S coast. Founded by Bartolomeo Columbus in 1496, it became the capital of the first Spanish colony in the Americas. It was under French rule (1795–1809), and later under that of Haiti, becoming capital of the new Dominican Republic in 1844. During the rule of the dictator *Trujillo, it was known for a time (1936–61) as Ciudad Trujillo. It is the site of the first cathedral (1521) and the first university (1538) in the New World. A second university was established in 1966. Population (1986 est): 1,600,000.

Santoríni. *See* Thera.

Santos 23 56S 46 22W A city in SE Brazil, in São Paulo state on the Atlantic Ocean. It is the leading coffee port of the world. Population (1980): 411,023.

São Luís 2 34S 44 16W A port in N Brazil, the capital of Maranhão state. The chief exports are babaçu palm products, cotton, sugar, and balsam. It is the site of the University of Maranhão (1966). Population (1980): 182,466.

Saône River A river in E France, rising in Lorraine and flowing mainly S to join the Rhône River at Lyons. It is linked by canal to the Moselle, Rhine, Loire, Seine, and Meuse rivers. Length: 298 mi (480 km).

São Paulo 23 33S 46 39W The largest city in Brazil, the capital of São Paulo state. Founded in 1554, it grew rapidly after 1880 with the development of coffee plantations. Coffee remains important but there has been considerable diversification of industry and it is now the fastest-growing city in Brazil, sometimes called the "Chicago of South America." Industries include food processing and the manufacture of textiles, electrical appliances, and chemicals. It has several universities, including the University of São Paulo (1934). It also contains the Butantan Institute, a scientific research establishment with a famous snake farm. Population (1991): 9,480,000.

São Tomé and Príncipe, Democratic Republic of A small island country off the coast of West Africa, in the Gulf of Guinea. An archipelago, it comprises the two main islands with coastal plains rising to volcanic mountains in their interiors, together with the islets of Pedras Tinhosas and Rolas. Most of the population is descended from African slaves and southern Europeans, with comparatively recent influxes from Mozambique and Angola. *Economy*: chiefly agricultural, the main crops being cocoa, copra (which is the main export), palm oil and kernels, and coffee. Rice is being developed and livestock is also important. *History*: discovered by the Portuguese in 1471, the islands came under Portuguese rule in 1522. They became an overseas province in 1951 and gained independence in 1975, forming a democratic republic. The first multiparty elections were held in 1991. President: Mîguel Trovoada. Official language: Portuguese. Official currency: dobra of 100 centavos. Area: 372 sq mi (964 sq km). Population (1990): 125,000. Capital and main port: São Tomé.

sap The fluid found in the vascular (conducting) system of plants. It consists of water and minerals, absorbed from the soil and transported through the plant in the *xylem, and sugars, made in the leaves and distributed in solution in the *phloem.

Sapir, Edward (1884–1939) US linguist and anthropologist, born in Germany. Much of his work was done on American-Indian languages and cultures. His book *Language* (1921) is notably lucid. He was interested in all aspects of communication and in the role played by language in determining the personality of the individual in relation to society. *See also* Whorf, Benjamin Lee.

sapodilla An evergreen tree, *Achras sapota*, native to Central America but cultivated elsewhere in the tropics. Up to 65 ft (20 m) tall, it produces edible brown rounded fruits, up to 4 in (20 cm) across, with a juicy pulp surrounding black seeds. It tastes of pears and brown sugar. Milky latex from the bark is a source of chicle gum, used in chewing gum. Family: *Sapotaceae*.

saponins Plant glycosides (sugar compounds) that form lathery emulsions in water. The saponins are extremely potent in destroying red blood cells. They are used as foam producers in fire extinguishers and as emulsifiers, *detergents, etc.

sappan A tree, *Caesalpinia sappan*, native to SE Asia. The wood (sappanwood) is used in making furniture and yields a red dye. An extract of the bark produces a black dye when mixed with iron salts. Family: *Leguminosae*.

Sapper (H[erman] C[yril] McNeile; 1888–1937) British novelist. After distinguished service in World War I he achieved literary success with his popular thriller *Bulldog Drummond* (1920), about an adventure-seeking ex-officer, and its sequels.

sapphire A transparent variety of *corundum that may be any color except red (see ruby) due to traces of iron and titanium. It is used as a gemstone and in record-player styluses. Sapphires occur in igneous and metamorphic rocks but most are obtained from detrital gravels. Many sapphires come from Sri Lanka, Kashmir, Myanmar, East Africa, the US, and Australia. Artificial sapphires are manufactured from ammonium alum. Birthstone for September.

Sappho (c. 612–c. 580 BC) Greek poet. She and her contemporary *Alcaeus pioneered the form of the brief subjective lyric. Her passionate poetry, which has survived in fragments, was written for her group of female admirers on the island of Lesbos (from which the term "lesbianism" is derived). She appears to have been married and had one child; according to a romantic and unreliable legend, she committed suicide by throwing herself from a rock off the coast of Epirus because of an unhappy love affair.

Sapporo 43 5N 141 21E A city in Japan, in SW Hokkaido. It is the island's main administrative and educational center; Hokkaido University was established there in 1918. It is also a ski resort famed for its annual festival of snow sculpture and was the site of the 1972 Winter Olympics. Industries include flour and timber milling, printing, and machinery manufacture. Population (1991): 1,696,056.

saprophyte An organism that obtains its energy by feeding on dead or decaying tissue. Bacteria and fungi are important saprophytes, using enzymes to break down organic material and release nutrients into the soil, which can be used by plants (*see* decomposition).

Saqqarah A mortuary area near ancient *Memphis. The most famous monument here is the stone-built Step Pyramid, designed (c. 2630 BC) for Pharaoh *Djoser by his architect *Imhotep. It is architecturally the immediate forerunner of the Giza *pyramids. The bulls sacred to *Apis were buried in the Sarapeum.

Saracens Before Islam, the term used by the non-Arab peoples of the Middle East to refer to the Arabs. After the establishment of Islam, Saracen was usually synonymous with Muslim. The origin of the word is unknown.

Saragossa. *See* Zaragoza.

Sarajevo 43 52N 18 26E The capital city of Bosnia and Hercegovina. A center of resistance to Austrian domination, it was there that the heir apparent to the Dual Monarchy of Austria-Hungary, *Francis Ferdinand, was assassinated (June 28, 1914), precipitating World War I. It was the site of the 1984 Winter Olympics. Sarajevo has two cathedrals, several mosques, and a university (1946). A busy industrial center, its manufactures include carpets, pottery, sugar, and beer. In 1992–94, fighting between Bosnians and Serbs destroyed large sections of the city. Population (1991): 525,980.

Saransk 54 12N 45 10E A city in Russia, the capital of the Mordvinian associate republic. It is an industrial center, producing machinery, electrical goods, and food. Population (1991 est): 320,000.

Sarasota 27 20N 82 34W A resort city in W central Florida, S of St Petersburg on the Gulf of Mexico. The winter headquarters of Ringling Brothers Barnum and Bailey Circus is there, as are several circus museums. Tourism is important to the economy. Population (1990): 50,961.

Saratoga, Battles of (Sept 19 and Oct 7, 1777) Two battles fought near Saratoga, N.Y., which formed the turning point of the *American Revolution. The first saw the defeat of the British attempt to open a route to Albany. The second ended with the surrender of General Burgoyne to the Americans. The outcome of the battles helped persuade the French to recognize the US and give it decisive military support.

Saratoga Springs 27 17N 82 28W A resort city in E central New York, N of Albany. Skidmore College (1911) is there. The mineral springs drew visitors from the mid-1800s on, making it the most popular US health resort. Saratoga Race Track has long attracted horse racing enthusiasts and tourists. Population (1990): 25,001.

Saratov 51 30N 45 55E A city in Russia, on the Volga River. Baku oil is transported from there and a natural-gas pipeline supplies Moscow. Other industrial activities include ship repairing and the manufacture of precision instruments. Population (1991 est): 911,000.

Sarawak A state in Malaysia, in NW *Borneo on the South China Sea. It has a mountainous forested interior with a swampy coastal plain, where rubber, pepper, sago, and rice are grown. Oil production is of prime importance; crude oil, petroleum products, timber, and pepper are the chief exports. History: it was given in 1841 by the sultan of Brunei to the Englishman James Brooke, who as "white rajah" tried to suppress piracy and headhunting. Although it became a British protectorate in 1888, it was ruled by the Brooke family until World War II, when it was occupied by the Japanese. Ceded to Britain in 1946, it joined Malaysia in 1963. Area: 48,250 sq mi (124,970 sq km). Population (1990): 1,669,000. Capital: Kuching.

Sarcodina A class of minute single-celled animals (see Protozoa) that form cellular extensions called pseudopodia for locomotion and feeding. Many forms, including *Ameba*, are naked while others, for example the *Foraminifera* and *Radiolaria*, have a shell or skeleton. Sarcodines are chiefly free-living inhabitants of soils, fresh waters, and seas.

sarcoma. See cancer.

sarcophagus A stone or terra-cotta coffin, often elaborately decorated with ritual motifs. Sarcophagi evolved in ancient Egypt to protect mummies, and Minoan, Greek, Roman, and early Christian examples survive.

sardine A young *pilchard or any of several species of food fish of the family *Clupeidae*, especially members of the genera *Sardina*, *Sardinops,* and *Sardinella*. They are canned in oil, an industry centered in Portugal and Spain.

Sardinia (Italian name: Sardegna) The second largest island in the Mediterranean Sea, comprising an autonomous region of Italy. It is largely mountainous. Agriculture is important, especially on the fertile Campidano (a broad alluvial plain in the SW) where cereals, vines, and olives are cultivated. Sheep are raised on the hills. Its major industry is mineral production, especially lead, zinc, coal, fluorspar, and sea salt. Modern industries, especially petrochemicals, chemicals, and food processing, are being developed. Tourism is a growing source of revenue. *History*: first settled by the Phoenicians, it was ceded to Savoy by Austria (1720) in exchange for Sicily and formed the kingdom of Sardinia with Piedmont, which formed the basis of a unified Italy. Area: 9194 sq mi (23,813 sq km). Population (1991): 1,645,192. Capital: Cagliari.

Sardis 38 28N 28 02E The capital of ancient Lydia, 35 mi (56 km) NE of present-day Izmir (Turkey), famous for its coinage and craftwork. After Persia conquered Lydia, overthrowing Croesus about 550 BC, its strategic position made Sardis Asia Minor's political center until Hellenistic times.

sardonyx. See onyx.

Sardou, Victorien (1831–1908) French dramatist. His many successful comedies and historical dramas include *Les Pattes de mouche* (1860) and *Tosca* (1887), a melodrama on which Puccini's opera is based. Sarah Bernhardt acted in many of his plays.

Sargasso Sea An elliptical section of the N Atlantic Ocean, extending between latitudes 20°N and 35°N and longitudes 30°W and 70°W. Contained within a current system, it is still and warm. It takes its name from the floating brown seaweed of the genus *Sargassum*, found abundantly in it.

Sargent, John Singer (1856–1925) US portrait painter, born in Italy. Working in Paris, London, and the US, he achieved considerable success with his elegant portraits of such celebrities as Ellen Terry, R. L. Stevenson, Isabella Stewart Gardner, Madame Gautreau (Mme. X) and John D. Rockefeller. In watercolor, he produced remarkable landscape studies of World War I.

Sargon II (d. 705 BC) King of Assyria (722–705). Perhaps a usurper (Sargon means "legitimate king"), he deliberately named himself after the legendary *Sargon of Akkad. He was constantly occupied in warfare to maintain Assyrian power in Elam, Urartu, Babylonia, Syria, and Palestine, where he captured and depopulated Samaria. He was succeeded by *Sennacherib.

Sargon of Akkad The semilegendary Semitic ruler (c. 2334–c. 2279 BC) of territories extending from the Mediterranean to the Persian Gulf. According to tradition, he was brought up by a gardener, who retrieved his cradle adrift in the Euphrates River. After usurping kingly power, he founded *Akkad and established an empire that lasted more than a century.

Sark (French name: Sercq) 49 26N 2 22W The smallest of the four main Channel Islands, in the English Channel. It consists of Great Sark and Little Sark, connected by a narrow isthmus. It is governed by a hereditary seigneur or dame in a semifeudal system. Area: 2 sq mi (5 sq km).

Sarnia 42 57N 82 24W A city and port in E Canada, in SW Ontario at the S end of Lake Huron. With the discovery of local oil (1858) and the completion of the oil pipeline from Alberta, it grew into a major refining and petrochemical center. Steel and salt are also important. Population (1981): 47,586.

Saronic Gulf (or Gulf of Aegina) An inlet of the W Aegean Sea between the Attic Peninsula (on which lie Athens and its port Piraeus) and the Peloponnese. It contains the island of Salamis.

saros The period of about 18 years (6585.3 days) at which *eclipses of the sun and moon repeat in the same order and with nearly the same time intervals.

Saroyan, William (1908–81) US dramatist and fiction writer. Beginning with *The Daring Young Man on the Flying Trapeze* (1934) he wrote a rapid succession of stories, novels, and autobiographical works. His best-known play is *The Time of Your Life* (1939). His other works include the play *My Heart's in the Highlands* (1939), a novel, *The Human Comedy* (1943), and the autobiographical *My Name Is Aram* (1940) and *Obituarias* (1979).

Sarraute, Nathalie (1902–   ) French novelist, born in Russia. She practiced as a lawyer until 1939. Her work includes *Tropismes* (1939), a collection of sketches analyzing human behavior in great psychological detail, *Le Planétarium* (1959), *Les Fruits d'or* (1963), and the autobiographical *Childhood* (1984). She is a leading exponent of the *nouveau roman, and her essays are collected in *L'Ère du soupçon* (1956).

sarsaparilla An extract of the roots of several perennial climbing or trailing vines of the genus *Smilax, especially *S. aristolochiaefolia*, cultivated in Central and South America. The roots are harvested and dried for use as a tonic and as flavoring for medicines and beverages. Family: *Smilacaceae.*

Sartre, Jean-Paul (1905–80) French philosopher, novelist, dramatist, and critic. After World War II, during which he was an active member of the resistance, he founded the journal *Les Temps modernes* and became a leading public exponent of *existentialism. His major works of philosophy include *Being and Nothingness* (1943) and *Critique de la raison dialectique* (1960). His novels include *Nausea* (1938) and the trilogy *The Roads to Freedom* (1945–49). Among his several plays are *The Flies* (1943), *In Camera* (1944), *The Respectable Prostitute* (1946), and *Lucifer and the Lord* (1951). He also wrote literary criticism and autobiographical works. In 1964 he refused the Nobel Prize. He had a close association with Simone de *Beauvoir, whom he met while a student. He was an adherent of Marxism and frequently supported left-wing political groups.

Sarum. See Salisbury.

Sasanians The dynasty that ruled Persia from 224 AD until overthrown by the Arabs about 636. *Ardashir I (reigned 224–41) founded the dynasty (named for his grandfather Sasan), overthrowing the Parthian empire (*see* Parthia) and seizing its capital *Ctesiphon. His most notable successors were *Shapur II (reigned 309–79), *Khosrau I (reigned 531–79), and *Khosrau II (reigned 590–628). The Sasanian empire, which at its greatest extent stretched from Syria to India, saw the establishment of Zoroastrianism as the state religion and a resurgence of art and architecture (*see* Persian art and architecture).

Sasebo 33 10N 129 42E A port in Japan, in W Kyushu on the East China Sea. It was a village until the late 19th century, when it became a naval base. Its main industries are ship building and engineering. Population (1990): 244,677.

Saskatchewan A province of W Canada, on the Great Plains. The N is covered by forest, mostly noncommercial, with lakes and swamps. The S is open prairie, now chiefly comprising large highly mechanized farms, and is one of the world's most important wheatlands; the province normally produces about two-thirds of Canada's wheat. There are highly developed marketing cooperatives, begun in the early 20th century. Saskatchewan is rich in minerals, including uranium, oil, natural gas, potash, zinc, and copper; associated industries are important. *History*: explored in the 17th and 18th centuries, Saskatchewan was first exploited for furs. Agricultural settlement began slowly (1870s) but sped up in the decade before 1914. The area became a province in 1905 and was the first part of North America to elect a socialist government (1944–64, 1971–82). Area: 220,181 sq mi (570,269 sq km). Population (1991): 988,928. Capital: Regina.

Saskatchewan River A river in W Canada, rising in two separate branches in the Rocky Mountains and flowing generally E through prairie grainlands to unite in central Saskatchewan. The river then continues to Lake Winnipeg. Length: 1205 mi (1940 km).

Saskatoon 52 10N 106 40W A city in W Canada, in central Saskatchewan. Founded in 1883, it is the distribution center of a vast grain area, with numerous agricultural industries. Other industries include potash, metals, clothing, and chemicals. Saskatoon houses the University of Saskatchewan (1907). Population (1991): 186,058.

sassafras A tree, *Sassafras albidum*, native to North America. Up to 65 ft (20 m) high, it bears clusters of yellow flowers and dark-blue berries. The aromatic roots are dried for use in medicines and also yield oil of sassafras, which is used in perfumes and as flavoring for beverages. Family: *Lauraceae*.

Sassari 40 43N 8 34E A city in Italy, near the N coast of Sardinia. It has a cathedral (12th–18th centuries) and a university (1562). It is the agricultural trading center of N Sardinia. Population (1991 est): 120,011.

Sassetta (Stefano di Giovanni; c. 1392–c. 1450) A leading painter of the Sienese school. Some of his work reflects his admiration of Florentine art, for example *Madonna of the Snow*, painted for Siena Cathedral (Contini Bonacossi collection, Florence); his later work, however, typifies the *international gothic style. He painted many altarpieces, for example a now dismembered altarpiece, originally painted for the church of S Francesco in Sansepolcro, notable for its scenes from the life of St Francis of Assisi.

Sassoon, Siegfried (1886–1967) British poet and writer. In 1917 his disgust with World War I led him to make a public refusal to serve. His antiwar poetry appeared in *The Old Huntsman* (1917) and *Counterattack* (1918), and he wrote several volumes of autobiographical war memoirs.

Satan. See Lucifer.

satanism Worship of the forces of evil. Formerly a synonym for atheism or certain heresies, the term now generally applies to beliefs and practices, such as the *black mass, that parody Christian equivalents. Evolving in this form in late-19th-century France, satanism is usually a blend of magic, religion, and bizarre sexual practices. Aleister Crowley (1875–1947) was a notorious modern exponent.

Saturn

satellite 1. A celestial body orbiting a *planet. The planets of the solar system
have 48 known satellites, ranging greatly in size. The small bodies comprising
the rings of Saturn, Uranus, and Jupiter may also be regarded as satellites. Mer-
cury and Venus have no satellites. The earth's satellite is the *moon. The two
small heavily cratered Martian satellites, Phobos and Deimos, have been exten-
sively studied by Mariner and Viking planetary probes. The largest and most
studied of Jupiter's 16 satellites are Io, Europa, and the heavily cratered
Ganymede and Callisto; Io and possibly Europa are volcanically active. Saturn
has 21 satellites, the largest, Titan, having an atmosphere. Uranus has five satel-
lites, four moderately sized, while Neptune has two, Triton and the much
smaller Nereid, both moving in unusual orbits. Pluto, possibly once a satellite of
Neptune, was found in 1978 to possess a satellite. 2. A spacecraft that is
launched into orbit around the earth or enters an orbit around some other solar-
system body. It may be a *communications satellite, retransmitting radio signals
from one location on earth to another. Alternatively, its instruments may gather
information from earth or from other celestial objects and transmit it, by radio
signals, to groundbased receiving stations. This information is used, for exam-
ple, in weather forecasting, navigation, scientific and astronomical research, and
for military purposes. A further function, under investigation, is the conversion
of solar power into microwaves that could be beamed to earth and used as an
energy source.

Satie, Erik (1866–1925) French composer. He studied briefly at the Paris con-
servatory and, aged 39, at the Schola Cantorum with Roussel and d'Indy. Satie
was well known for his eccentricity and for the whimsical titles of his composi-
tions. He influenced such composers as Milhaud and Poulenc by turning away
from impressionism toward a clear-textured style that admitted humor. His
works include the ballet *Parade* (1916), piano pieces, including *Trois Gym-
nopédies* (1888), *Pièces froides* (1897), and *Trois morceaux en forme de poire*
(1903), and many songs.

satinwood A tree, *Chloroxylon swietenia*, native to S India and Sri Lanka. Its
wood is valued in cabinetmaking for its lustrous golden-yellow fine-grained fin-
ish; it was used in particular by Thomas *Sheraton. The wood of certain West
Indian species is also known as satinwood. Family: *Meliaceae*.

satire A literary or dramatic work that ridicules human or social pretensions.
Among the earliest satirists were the Roman poets *Juvenal and *Horace. In Eu-
ropean literature, satire became a dominant literary form during the late 17th
and 18th centuries. Major writers included *Dryden, *Pope, and *Swift in En-
gland and *Voltaire in France. During the 19th century *Byron continued the
tradition of verse satire, but prose fiction became the usual medium, as in the
works of Samuel *Butler. In the 20th century novelists have been the dominant
practitioners, for example Evelyn *Waugh in England and Joseph *Heller in
the US.

Sato Eisaku (1901–75) Japanese conservative statesman, under whose unusu-
ally long prime ministership (1964–72) Japan became an economic superpower.
His most significant personal achievement was the reversion of Okinawa from
US rule (1972). He shared the Nobel Peace Prize in 1974 for his opposition to
nuclear weapons.

satsuma. *See* tangerine.

Saturn (astronomy) The second largest planet, orbiting the sun every 29.5
years at a mean distance of 886,165,000 mi (1427 million km). It is the most
oblate planet (equatorial diameter 74,500 mi [120,000 km], polar diameter
67,000 mi [108,000 km]) and has the lowest mean density (0.7 g cm^{-3}). In a

PLANETARY SATELLITES

Planet & Satellite	diameter (km)	distance from primary (km)	year of discovery	Planet & Satellite	diameter (km)	distance from primary (km)	year of discovery
EARTH				SATURN			
Moon	3476	384 400	—	Janus	200	159 000	1966
MARS				Mimas	400	186 000	1789
Phobos	27	9380	1877	Enceladus	600	238 000	1789
Deimos	15	23 500	1877	Tethys	1000	295 000	1684
JUPITER				Dione	800	377 000	1684
Adrastea	40?	128 000	1979	Rhea	1500	527 000	1672
Metis	40?	128 000	1979	Titan	5800	1 222 000	1655
Amalthea	150	181 000	1892	Hyperion	400	1 483 000	1848
Thebe	80?	221 000	1979	Iapetus	1500	3 560 000	1671
Io	3630	422 000	1610	Phoebe	200	12 950 000	1898
Europa	3140	671 000	1610	URANUS			
Ganymede	5260	1 070 000	1610	Miranda	400	130 000	1948
Callisto	4800	1 880 000	1610	Ariel	1400	192 000	1851
Leda	10?	11 110 000	1974	Umbriel	1000	267 000	1851
Himalia	180?	11 470 000	1904	Titania	1800	438 000	1787
Lysithea	20?	11 710 000	1938	Oberon	1600	586 000	1787
Elara	80?	11 740 000	1905	NEPTUNE			
Ananke	20?	20 700 000	1951	Triton	3800	355 000	1846
Carme	30?	22 350 000	1938	Nereid	300	5 562 000	1949
Pasiphae	40?	23 300 000	1908	PLUTO			
Sinope	30?	23 700 000	1914	1	800?	20 000?	1978

telescope dark and light yellowish cloud bands are visible, running parallel to the equator. The dominant feature, however, is **Saturn's rings**, lying in the equatorial plane and tilted at 27° to the orbital plane. The four rings differ in brightness but are all composed of small icy chunks. The overall diameter is about 169,500 mi (273,000 km) but the thickness is only a few kilometers. The outermost ring, A, and the brightest one, B, are separated by Cassini's division. Saturn also has 21 known *satellites. Saturn is made up primarily of hydrogen and helium, possibly with a central rocky core surrounded by liquid hydrogen. *See also* planetary probe.

Saturn (mythology) The Roman god of agriculture and father of the gods, identified with the Greek *Cronus. His consort was Ops, identified with the Greek *Rhea. Various aspects of the Saturnalia, his annual festival held in December, at which presents were exchanged and normal social rules relaxed, were taken over by the Christian festivals of Christmas and the New Year. His name survives in *Saturday*.

saturniid moth A moth belonging to the widely distributed mainly tropical family *Saturniidae* (about 800 species). They are usually large and characterized by a transparent eyespot near the center of each wing. Their silken cocoons can be a source of silk (*see* silkworm moth) and the larvae are typically green, feeding chiefly on tree foliage. *See also* cecropia moth; emperor moth; hercules moth.

satyagraha The Sanskrit expression referring to *Gandhi's policy of nonviolent resistance to British rule in India.

satyrid butterfly A butterfly of the worldwide family *Satyridae*. The wings are mainly brownish with a few or numerous eyespots. The forelegs are rudimentary and the flight weak and fluttering. Satyrids hide when alarmed, folding the forewings inside the camouflaged hindwings. The striped pale-green or brown caterpillars feed on grasses.

Satyrs and Sileni In Greek mythology, male fertility spirits of the woods and fields, usually portrayed with goats' legs and pointed ears or horns. They were associated with *Dionysus and were typically drunk and lustful. *See also* Silenus.

sauce A thickened savory or sweet liquid accompanying a dish and enhancing its flavor. Many classic dishes are named for the sauce served with them (e.g. *spaghetti bolognese, poulet chasseur, sole bonne femme*). Sauces often require a liaison, which binds together the liquids and other ingredients, the commonest being a *roux* (a paste of melted butter and flour). Other liaisons are egg yolks and butter kneaded with flour (*beurre manié*). Flour-based sauces include béchamel (white sauce), Mornay (cheese sauce), soubise (onion sauce), and parsley sauce. Hollandaise and béarnaise sauces are made with wine vinegar, spices, and egg yolks. Other well-known sauces are mint sauce (with lamb), apple sauce (with pork), cranberry sauce (with turkey), horseradish sauce (with beef), tartar sauce (with fish), and tomato sauce. Among sweet sauces are butterscotch sauce (made with corn syrup and sugar), chocolate sauce, and melba sauce (puréed raspberries and icing sugar).

Saud (1902–69) King of Saudi Arabia (1953–64). He continued the modernization programs begun by his father *Ibn Saud but was unable to deal competently with the financial complexities of Saudi's oil revenues. He was deposed and the throne passed to his brother *Faisal.

Saudi Arabia, Kingdom of A country in the Middle East comprising most of *Arabia, bordering on the Red Sea and the Persian Gulf. In the W a line of mountains runs close to the Red Sea, while the *Najd, the central plateau, slopes downward W–E. In the N and SE are large areas of desert. The population, densest in the SW, is mainly Arab Muslim, the majority being Sunnite with some Shiites in the E. About 27% are nomads. There are also many foreign workers, chiefly unskilled Yemenis and skilled Americans and Europeans. *Economy*: based on oil discovered in 1936 in the Persian Gulf and exploited since 1938; some is refined locally. The country, a member of OPEC, is the world's greatest exporter of oil, the revenues being used to diversify the economy and provide education and health services. Recent industries include petrochemicals, fertilizers, and steel production; considerable mineral resources have also been discovered. Income is also derived from pilgrims visiting Mecca, Medina, and Jidda. Apart from land reclaimed by irrigation, only Asir (the sole part of the country in which there is sufficient rainfall for agriculture) and the oases are cultivated; livestock is kept on the extensive pasture land. Consumer and capital goods and foodstuffs (particularly cereals) are imported, mainly from Japan, the US, Germany, and the UK. *History*: the establishment of Saudi Arabia (1932) under *Ibn Saud followed the 19th-century struggle by the Saud family to dominate the warring tribes of the peninsula and take overall control from Turkey. Asir was incorporated in 1934. Saudi Arabia became a founding member of the Arab League (1945). Under Ibn Saud's son, *Saud, conflict with Egypt developed, especially during the North Yemen civil war, in which Saudi Arabia supported the royalists and Egypt the republicans. Saud's brother, *Faisal Ibn Abdul Aziz, who replaced him (1964), restored relations with Egypt and also used the oil crisis of the early 1970s to increase Saudi holdings in oil operations. On Faisal's apparently motiveless assassination (1975) he was replaced as king by his brother, *Khalid Ibn Abdul Aziz. On Khalid's death (1982) his brother, Fahd Ibn Abdul Aziz, became king. After Iraq invaded Kuwait in 1990, Saudi Arabia asked the UN coalition forces to use the country as a base from which to attack Iraq in the Persian Gulf War in 1991. Saudi Arabia also increased its output of oil to compensate for the loss of oil production from Kuwait. In 1992, Fahd issued a body of laws called "Basic System of Government" that decentralized political power and gave greater autonomy to regional governments, provided for a "bill of rights," and changed the rules for royal succession. He established mechanisms for limited democracy in 1993. Official language: Arabic. Official currency: rial of 100 nilalas. Area: 927,000 sq mi (2,400,000 sq km). Population (1990 est): 16,758,000. Capital: Riyadh. Chief port: Jidda.

Saul In the Old Testament, the first king of Israel, who reigned in the 11th century BC. Son of Kish, he was anointed king by *Samuel. He began his reign with a great victory over the Ammonites, followed by many battles against the Philistines. Following an act of disobedience during the Israelite destruction of the *Amalekites, Saul, according to the Old Testament, lost divine favor; his last years were marked by a growing enmity with *David. He committed suicide after being wounded and defeated by the Philistines.

Sault Ste Marie Canals (also Soo Canals) A series of canals and locks in S Ontario, Canada, and NE Michigan. The canals bypass St Mary's Falls on the St Mary's River, between lakes Superior and Huron. There are two waterways on the US side and one waterway on the Canadian side, and a total of five locks. Begun in 1853, the approximately 1.5 mi (2.7 km) of canals are part of the Great Lakes waterway system.

Sault Ste Marie 46 32N 84 20W A city in E Canada, in NW Ontario on the St Mary's River opposite Sault Ste Marie, Mich. Its canal allows ships to bypass local rapids that provide hydroelectricity for steel and other heavy industry. Population (1991): 81,476.

Sault Ste Marie 46 29N 84 22W A city in Michigan, on the St Mary's River opposite Sault Ste Marie, Canada. It serves the traffic of the St Lawrence Seaway by way of the Soo canals and locks, which attract large numbers of tourists to the city. Population (1990): 14,689.

Saurischia An order of *dinosaurs that were dominant in the Jurassic period (about 195–130 million years ago). They had hip bones arranged like those of modern lizards (the name means "lizard hips") and were mostly bipedal carnivores, although some were large quadrupedal herbivores. *See also* Allosaurus; Apatosaurus; Ornitholestes; Tyrannosaurus.

saury A marine fish, also called skipper, belonging to the family *Scomberesocidae* (about 4 species). It has a long slim body, up to 20 in (50 cm) long, blue or olive above and golden or silvery below, with beaklike jaws and finlets behind the dorsal and anal fins. Sauries occur in large shoals in tropical and temperate surface waters, feeding on crustaceans and small fish. They are often seen leaping or skipping over the surface to escape predators. Order: *Atheriniformes*.

Saussure, Ferdinand de (1857–1913) Swiss linguist. His great influence on 20th-century linguistics is due to the posthumously published *Course in General Linguistics* (1916), compiled by his pupils from lecture notes. It offers an integrated picture of all aspects of language. De Saussure's distinction between *parole* (the utterance of the individual) and *langue* (the common language of the community) was of great importance to both sociolinguistics and structural linguistics (*see* linguistics). He also drew influential distinctions between diachronic (historical) and synchronic linguistics and between syntagmatic (collocational) and paradigmatic (organizational) relations in language.

Savage, Michael Joseph (1872–1940) New Zealand statesman; the first Labour prime minister of New Zealand (1935–40). His ministry, which included (Sir) William Nash, dealt successfully with the economic problems of the Depression.

Savai'i 13 44S 172 18W The largest island of Western Samoa. There was a volcanic eruption in 1905 and lava flows laid waste a large area. Copra, bananas, and cocoa are exported. Area: 662 sq mi (1174 sq km). Population (1986): 44,930. Chief town: Tuasivi.

savanna (*or* savannah) The extensive tropical grasslands, bordering on the equatorial rain forests in both the N and S hemispheres. They cover extensive areas in N Australia, Africa, and South America (where they are known as the *llanos in Venezuela and Colombia and the campos in Brazil). The vegetation of savannas is dominated by tall grasses, such as elephant grass, interspersed with low often flat-topped trees and bushes. Grazed by herds of hooved animals, savannas are ideal cattle-rearing areas.

Savannah 32 04N 81 07W A city in Georgia, on the Savannah River. Established by James Oglethorpe in 1733, it was an important colonial port and settlement. The first Atlantic steamship crossing was from there to Liverpool, England, in 1819. A major tourist center and seaport, its industries include ship building and chemicals. Population (1990): 137,560.

Savery, Thomas (c. 1650–1715) English engineer, who in 1698 constructed the first practical steam engine. Savery's engine, which was dangerous because it utilized high-pressure steam, was superseded by *Newcomen's engine.

savin A low-growing *juniper shrub, *Juniperus sabina*, native to mountainous regions of S and central Europe. It has scalelike leaves and blue-black berrylike cones, 0.16–0.24 in (4–6 mm) long. The shrub has a strong unpleasant smell and yields a poisonous oil used in medicine and veterinary work.

Savona 44 18N 8 28E A port in NW Italy, in Liguria on the Gulf of Genoa. It rivaled Genoa in the Middle Ages but was subjugated by the Genoese in 1528. It has a cathedral dating from the 16th century. Savona is an important center of the Italian iron and steel industry. Population (1990 est): 70,000.

SAVANNA *Flat-topped acacia trees rise above grassland in the Serengeti National Park (Tanzania).*

Savonarola, Girolamo (1452–98) Italian religious reformer. Joining the Dominicans in 1474, he became a lecturer in the Convent of San Marco, Florence, and later its prior (1491). There he began a crusade against religious and political corruption, centering his attacks on the papacy and the Medici. His fervent preaching attracted a large following, and he became the virtual ruler of Florence when the Medici were expelled by the populace in 1494. Excommunicated by Alexander VI in 1497, he was imprisoned, hanged, and burned for heresy by his political rivals.

savory An herb belonging to the genus *Satureja*, of warm and temperate regions. Summer savory (*S. hortensis*) is an annual, native to central Europe and Asia. Both the dried leaves and the oil extract are used for flavoring foods. The perennial winter savory (*S. montana*) grows to a height of 16 in (40 cm), has small white flowers, and is also a culinary herb. Family: *Labiatae*.

Savoy An Alpine frontier region of SE France corresponding to the present-day departments of Savoie and Haute-Savoie. Strategically important for its mountain passes, the county of Savoy was founded in 1034 by Umberto Biancomano (Umberto I). He and his successors extended Savoyard territory, acquiring Piedmont in the 14th century. In 1416 *Amadeus the Peaceful became a duke and was subsequently elected antipope as Felix V. After acquiring Sardinia in 1720, Savoyard dukes took the title king of Sardinia, which in 1748 became the kingdom of Piedmont-Sardinia. Savoy (but not Sardinia) was annexed by France during the Revolutionary Wars but restored in 1815 and Piedmont-Sardinia became the leading spirit in the movement for Italian unification (*see* Risorgimento). Savoy became part of France in 1860 in return for Napoleon III's assistance against Austria but the House of Savoy ruled the newly formed kingdom of Italy (1861–1946).

sawfish A *ray fish of the family *Pristidae* that occurs mainly in salt and brackish waters of tropical and subtropical regions. Its sharklike body, up to 23 ft (7 m) long, bears a long bladelike snout edged with teeth and is used to forage along the bottom or to catch prey.

sawfly An insect belonging to the widely distributed suborder *Symphyta* and so named because the female possesses a needlelike tubular ovipositor, which is used as a saw or drill to insert eggs into foliage and timber. Adults are 0.20–2 in (5–50 mm) long and the larvae, resembling caterpillars, damage trees. Chief families: *Argidae, Siricidae, Cimbicidae, Diprionidae, Tenthredinidae*; order: *Hymenoptera*.

Saxe, Maurice, Comte de (1696–1750) Marshal of France, the illegitimate son of Augustus the Strong of Poland. He fought in the French army, outstandingly in the War of the *Austrian Succession (1740–48), and wrote *Mes Rêveries* (1757) on warfare.

Saxe-Coburg-Gotha The ruling dynasty of a German duchy. The children of Duke Francis Frederick (1750–1806) included Victoria Mary Louisa (1786–1861), who married (1818) Edward, duke of Kent (their daughter was Queen Victoria); and Leopold, who became *Leopold I of Belgium. Francis's son Ernest I (1806–44) was the father of Prince Albert, who married Queen Victoria in 1840. The UK royal house was called Saxe-Coburg-Gotha until 1917, when the name *Windsor was adopted.

saxhorn A valved brass instrument of the bugle type, patented by the Belgian Adolphe Sax (1814–94) in Paris in 1845. It is made in several sizes; the tenor saxhorn (*or* tenor horn) is used in the military and brass bands and occasionally in the orchestra, as in Mahler's seventh symphony.

saxifrage A perennial herb belonging to certain genera of the family *Saxifragaceae*, found in cold and temperate regions. The leaves may either form a basal rosette or occur in pairs along the stem and the flowers are white, yellow, purple, or red. Most are fairly small, although the European meadow saxifrage (*Saxifraga granulata*) may reach a height of 18 in (45 cm). *See also* London pride.

Saxo Grammaticus (c. 1150–c. 1206) Danish chronicler. Little is known of his life, except that he served as secretary to the archbishop of Roskilde. He was the author of *Gesta Danorum*, a Latin history of the Danes, the first part of which is based on mythological and legendary material. It includes the legend of Balder and the story of Amleth, one of the sources for the plot of Shakespeare's *Hamlet*. The latter part of the chronicle contains more definitely historical material.

Saxons A Germanic people who, during the 5th century AD, expanded from their Baltic coastal homelands to other areas of N Germany, the coast of Gaul (France), and (with the *Angles and *Jutes) to Britain. Charlemagne eventually defeated the continental Saxons and converted them to Christianity, incorporating their lands into his empire after a long period of warfare (772–804 AD). *See also* Anglo-Saxons.

Saxony (German name: Sachsen) An ancient NW German duchy. Named for its original inhabitants, the *Saxons (who expanded to Britain in the 5th century), they were conquered by Charlemagne in the 8th century and subsequently became a duchy. In 919 AD Henry, duke of Saxony, became German king and his son *Otto the Great, the first Saxon Holy Roman Emperor. In 1142 Saxony passed to *Henry the Lion but in 1180 the duchy was broken up, to be reformed in various territorial combinations in following centuries. In the 13th century Saxony became an electorate and in the 16th and 17th centuries a leading German Protestant state. In 1697 Elector Frederick Augustus I (1670–1733) became king of Poland and Saxony's subsequent involvement in Polish affairs kept it apart from German power struggles until the 19th century. Conquered by Napoleon in 1806, N Saxony was annexed by Prussia in 1815 and in 1866 joined the Prussian-dominated *North German Confederation. The remainder of Saxony joined the German Empire in 1871.

saxophone A woodwind instrument with a brass body, keys, and a single reed mouthpiece similar to that of a *clarinet. It was invented by the Belgian Adolphe Sax (1814–94) and patented in France in 1846. The most common sizes of saxophone are the soprano, alto, tenor, and baritone. They are most commonly used as solo instruments in jazz; they are sometimes used in classical music.

Sayan Mountains A mountain range in Russia, extending some 500 mi (800 km) E–W and rising to 11,453 ft (3491 m) in Munku Sardyk in the extreme SE. The Yenisei river and many of its tributaries rise here.

Sayers, Dorothy L(eigh) (1893–1957) British writer, educated at Oxford, who is best known for her series of detective novels, beginning with *Whose Body?* (1923), featuring the erudite detective Lord Peter Wimsey. She also wrote plays on Christian themes and a translation of Dante's *Divine Comedy*.

scabies A contagious skin infection caused by the *itch mite, which tunnels and breeds in the skin, causing intense itching. The burrows of the mites are seen between the fingers, on the side of the hands, in the armpits, and on the groin, nipples, and buttocks. Treatment is by application of benzylbenzoate cream, and clothing and bedding should be disinfested.

scabious An annual or perennial herb belonging to the genus *Scabiosa* (80–100 species), native to the Mediterranean region and temperate parts of Eurasia and Africa. The small scabious (*S. columbaria*) is widely distributed on chalky soils; 6–27.5 in (15–70 cm) high, it has a cluster of small bluish-lilac flowers borne on a long stalk. The field scabious, *S.* (or *Knautia*) *arvensis*, is very similar and may reach a height of 40 in (1 m). Family: *Dipsacaceae*.

Scafell Pike 54 28N 3 12W The highest peak in England, in Cumbria, in the Lake District. It is popular for walking and rock climbing. Height: 3210 ft (978 m).

scalar quantity A quantity that is represented by magnitude only. Unlike a *vector quantity, a scalar quantity has no direction. Examples include mass, time, and speed.

scale (music) An ascending or descending succession of notes, characterized by a fixed succession of intervals between the notes that constitute it. Many thousands of different scales exist; all the major musical traditions of the world are based upon them.

In Western music there are three **diatonic scales**, which derive from the ancient Greek *modes: the major scale, the harmonic minor scale, and the melodic minor scale. The octave is divided into 12 notes (*see* temperament) and any of these scales may be constructed on any of these notes. The version of the scale produced is associated with a particular *tonality. The **chromatic scale** includes all 12 semitones of the octave. The **pentatonic scale**, consisting of only 5 notes, is common in Chinese and Scottish music.

scale (zoology) A platelike structure that generally forms part of a protective body covering in many vertebrate animals. Fish and certain reptiles have an overlapping series of bony scales, derived from the deep layers of the skin (dermis). The periodic growth of fish scales gives rise to annual rings, by which the age of the fish may be estimated. In reptiles the scales are periodically renewed and may be modified and enlarged as spines.

scale insect An insect belonging to the superfamily *Coccoidea* (about 4000 species), abundant in warm and tropical regions. Scale insects are usually small (on average 0.04–0.59 in [1–15 mm] long) and the females are often legless, wingless, and eyeless and covered by a waxy scale or mass of threads. They become encrusted on plants and suck the juices, often becoming serious pests. Other species are of value by producing *shellac, *cochineal, and various waxes. Suborder: *Homoptera*; order: **Hemiptera*.

Scalia, Antonin (1936–   ) Associate justice of the US Supreme Court. A Harvard Law School graduate and then a law school professor, he served in the Justice Department (1974–77) and was appointed to the U.S. Court of Appeals by President Reagan in 1982. Before his appointment to the Court, he was noted for his articulate support of conservative legal positions.

Scaliger, Julius Caesar (1484–1558) Italian humanist scholar. He engaged in controversy with *Erasmus and wrote several commentaries on classical writers.

scallion Any *onion or related plant that produces small white-skinned mild-flavored bulbs, with a long neck and stiff leaves.

scallop A *bivalve mollusk belonging to the family *Pectinidae* (about 400 species), of warm and temperate seas; 0.8–8 in (2–20 cm) across, the valves of the shell are broad, flattened, and deeply fluted, and the animal swims by flapping them with a single powerful muscle. Scallops are important as seafood.

scaly-tailed squirrel An African arboreal *rodent belonging to the family *Anomaluridae* (9 species). They range in size from 3–18 in (8–45 cm) and most species have a gliding membrane like that of the *flying squirrel. Their name refers to the backward-pointing scales under the tail that grip the tree trunk when the squirrel is clinging to it.

Scandinavia Geographically, a peninsula in NW Europe, comprising Norway and Sweden. Culturally and historically, it also includes Denmark, Iceland, and the Faeroe Islands, and Finland, too, is often considered part of the region.

Scandinavian languages A subgroup of the *Germanic group of languages consisting of *Swedish, *Norwegian, *Danish, *Icelandic, and Faeroese. The first three are similar enough to be mutually intelligible, their separateness being imposed by their history and political boundaries. They all developed from a common Scandinavian ancestor, which originally used the *runic alphabet (*see also* Old Norse). This language spread with the Vikings to Iceland, the Faeroes, and to other Baltic and Atlantic islands.

scandium (Sc) The first transition metal, predicted by Mendeleyev and discovered in 1879 by L. F. Nilson (1840–99). It is trivalent, forming an oxide (Sc_2O_3), halides (for example ScF_3), and other compounds. It is light (relative density 2.989) and has a much higher melting point than aluminum, making it of interest as a possible spacecraft material. At no 21; at wt 44.956; mp 2809°F (1541°C); bp 5133°F (2831°C).

Scapa Flow A section of the Atlantic Ocean off the N coast of Scotland, in the Orkney Islands. Of naval importance during both world wars, it was the main base of the British Grand Fleet during World War I. Following its surrender, the German fleet scuttled itself there (1919). Length: about 15 mi (24 km). Width: 8 mi (13 km).

scapegoat An animal, person, or object chosen as the symbolic bearer of the sins or misfortunes of an individual or group. At the ancient Jewish ritual of the Day of Atonement, a goat was chosen to bear the sins of the people and then driven off or thrown from a cliff. Similar rituals were practiced in ancient Greece and Rome and among many primitive peoples.

scapula. *See* shoulder.

scarab An ancient Egyptian seal or amulet made of stone or faience in the shape of a dung beetle. Associated with the sun's regenerative powers, scarabs were often buried with the dead.

scarab beetle A beetle belonging to the worldwide family *Scarabaeidae* (over 19,000 species). Scarabs show a great variety in size and form: the largest beetles—the *goliath and *hercules beetles—are scarabs, while other species have developed extraordinary horns (*see* rhinoceros beetle). In general the family can be divided into two main groups—the *dung beetles and *chafers. Certain dungrolling beetles, especially *Scarabaeus sacer*, were the sacred scarabs of the ancient Egyptians.

Scarlatti, Domenico (1685–1757) Italian composer and noted harpsichordist and organist. After studying in Venice and holding court posts in Rome and Naples, he was engaged by Princess Maria Barbara of Portugal in Lisbon in 1720. When she married into the Spanish royal family in 1729 he moved with her to Madrid, where he stayed until his death. Besides some operas and church music, he wrote over 600 harpsichord sonatas, many of which were highly innovative and contributed to subsequent piano technique. His father **Alessandro Scarlatti** (1660–1725) was also a composer. He worked chiefly in Rome and Naples. He was maestro successively to Queen Christina of Sweden, to the Spanish viceroy, at Sta Maria Maggiore in Rome, and at the royal chapel in Napels. His works include over a hundred operas, 600 chamber cantatas, 200 masses, 12 chamber symphonies, and 14 oratorios.

scarlet fever A highly infectious disease of children caused by streptococcus bacteria. Since these bacteria are much less virulent now than formerly, the disease is much milder now than it was at the beginning of the century. After an incubation period of 2 to 4 days the child develops a sore throat, fever, and headache; 24 to 48 hours later a red rash spreads from the chest over the whole body. Before antibiotics, scarlet fever killed many children or left them disabled with *rheumatic fever, kidney disease, or ear infections; it can now be rapidly cured with penicillin.

Scarron, Paul (1610–60) French poet, dramatist, and satirist. His writings are enlivened by a burlesque irreverent style. His best-known work is the picaresque novel *Le Roman comique* (1651–57). From the age of 30 he suffered from paralysis. Despite this handicap, in 1652 he married Françoise d'Aubigné, who later became, as Madame de Maintenon, the wife of Louis XIV.

scattering The deflection of waves or particles by the atoms or molecules of the medium through which they are passing or by other particles. The scattering of waves is due to either *reflection or *diffraction. For particles, the scattering is described as inelastic if the scattered particles gain or lose energy during the process. Otherwise it is elastic. An example of inelastic scattering is the *Raman effect.

scaup A *diving duck, *Aythya marila*, that breeds in northern latitudes and winters on more southerly coasts; 16–18 in (40–45 cm) long, it dives deeply to feed on mussels and small crabs. The male has green-black fore parts, a gray back, white flanks, and a brown rump and tail; females are dark brown with a white patch around the bill.

Schacht, Hjalmar (1877–1970) German financier and politician. As president of the Reichsbank (1923–30), he checked Germany's rampant inflation. He was reappointed by Hitler in 1933 but was dismissed in 1939. From 1934 to 1937 he served as minister of economics. He was acquitted at Nuremberg of war crimes.

Schechter Poultry Corporation v. United States (1935) US Supreme Court decision that declared the *New Deal's National Recovery Act invalid.

Violations, by the Schechter Corp., of fair competition codes established in the act were at issue, and the Court ruled that those not involved in interstate commerce were not liable under the act.

SCAUP *A female on its nest. Scaups breed in groups on lake islands.*

Scheel, Walter (1919–) West German statesman; president (1974–79). He served in the Luftwaffe during World War II and was minister for economic co-operation (1961–66) and foreign minister (1969–74) before becoming president. In 1967 he became chairman of the Free Democrats.

Scheele, Carl Wilhelm (1742–86) Swedish chemist, who discovered a number of compounds and elements. His greatest work in this field was the discovery of oxygen (c. 1771), but as his results were not published until 1777 *Priestley is usually credited with the discovery. Scheele was also the first to isolate and prepare the gases hydrogen sulfide, hydrogen cyanide, and hydrogen fluoride.

scheelite A tungsten ore mineral, $CaWO_4$, occurring in veins and contact-metamorphic rocks. It is yellowish white or brown. *See also* wolframite.

Scheldt River (French name: Escaut; Flemish and Dutch name: Schelde) A river in W Europe. Rising in NE France, it flows generally NNE through W Belgium to Antwerp, then NW to the North Sea in the SW Netherlands. Canals connect it to the Somme, Seine, Sambre, Meuse, and Rhine rivers. Length: 270 mi (435 km).

Schelling, Friedrich (1775–1854) German philosopher. Schelling was first influenced by the writings of *Fichte and *Kant. Later, he became convinced that knowledge could not be confined to phenomena and argued that there was "a secret wonderful faculty which dwells in us all." His *System of Transcendental Idealism* (1800) contains his metaphysical philosophy, which, with his insistence that human consciousness is fulfilled by art, made him an important influence upon *romanticism and in particular upon *Coleridge.

Schenectady 42 48N 73 57W A city in New York, on the Mohawk River. In 1886 the Thomas Edison Machine Works was moved there, later becoming the General Electric Company, which dominates the city today. Population (1990): 65,566.

Schenck v. United States (1919) US Supreme Court decision that introduced the *clear and present danger interpretation regarding the First Amendment. The Court ruled that Congress can prevent speech that presents a "clear and present danger that . . . will bring about . . . substantive evils." The case was brought against Charles Schenck of the Socialist party for attempts to encourage military insubordination and to discourage military service.

Schiaparelli, Elsa (1896–1973) Italian-born fashion designer, who opened fashion houses in Paris (late 1920s) and New York (1949). Her designs and use of color were flamboyant and daring; she is particularly associated with the padded shoulder and "shocking pink."

Schick test A skin test for the presence of antibodies to *diphtheria. Injection of small amounts of diphtheria toxin causes a localized inflammation of the skin in those who have not been vaccinated or have not had diphtheria. The test was devised in 1913 by an Austrian pediatrician, Bela Schick (1877–1967).

Schiedam 51 55N 4 25E A city in the W Netherlands, in South Holland province. It has famous gin distilleries. Population (1981 est): 74,233.

Schiele, Egon (1890–1918) Austrian expressionist painter. Influenced first by the French impressionists and by *Klimt, Schiele often painted portraits and nudes and was able to express both a disturbing anguished quality and eroticism through a distorted use of line. With *Kokoschka he was a leader of Austrian expressionism until his untimely death from influenza.

Schiller, (Johann Christoph) Friedrich (von) (1759–1805) German dramatist, poet, and writer. His first, anonymously published, play, *Die Räuber* (1781), typifies the *Sturm und Drang call for political freedom. His next important play and his first in blank verse was the tragedy *Don Carlos* (1787), set in the time of Philip II of Spain. With Goethe's friendly encouragement from 1794, Schiller turned from the historical and academic studies with which he had been involved and produced the brilliant dramas of the last decade of his life: the trilogy *Wallenstein* (1798–99), *Maria Stuart* (1800), based on the life of Mary, Queen of Scots, *Die Jungfrau von Orleans* (1801), concerned with Joan of Arc, and *Wilhelm Tell* (1804). His nondramatic works include poems, the important essay on aesthetics, *Über naïve und sentimentalische Dichtung* (1795–96), and a history of the Thirty Years' War (1793).

schipperke A breed of □dog originating in Flanders and used as a guard dog on barges. It has a stocky tailless body with short legs and a foxlike head with erect ears. The dense coat is usually black and thick around the neck, forming a mane. Height: 12–13 in (30.5–33 cm).

schist A coarse-grained *metamorphic rock with a pronounced banded structure, in which the minerals show parallel alignment at right angles to the direction of stress, leaving no trace of the original bedding. The minerals are segregated into alternate thin layers rich in mica and quartz/feldspar, and the rock readily splits along these schistosity planes. Schists are named according to the dominant minerals, e.g. mica-schist.

schistosomiasis (*or* bilharziasis) A widespread disease of the tropics caused by blood flukes of the genus *Schistosoma* (or *Bilharzia*). The disease is contracted by bathing in water contaminated by snails, which harbor the larvae of the parasite. The larvae penetrate the skin and—when mature—settle in the blood vessels of the intestine or bladder. Symptoms, caused by the release of eggs by adult flukes, include anemia, inflammation, and diarrhea and dysentery (from an intestinal infection), or cystitis and blood in the urine (from a bladder infection). The disease is treated by drugs that destroy the parasite.